THE EVOLUTION OF SOCIETY

Selections from Herbert Spencer's *Principles of Sociology*
Edited and with an Introduction by Robert L. Carneiro

THE UNIVERSITY OF CHICAGO PRESS / CHICAGO & LONDON

The three volumes of *Principles of Sociology* were published simultaneously by Williams & Norgate, Ltd. in London and D. Appleton and Company in New York, Volume I first appeared in 1876; Volume II, 1882; Volume III, 1896. The text of the present volume was taken from the revised edition of Volume I (1885) and from the corrected reissue of Volume II (1886).

The University of Chicago Press, Chicago 60637
The University of Chicago Press, Ltd., London

Published 1967. Midway Reprint 1974
Printed in the United States of America

International Standard Book Number: 0-226-76895-3
Library of Congress Catalog Card Number: 67-20581

THE EVOLUTION OF SOCIETY

CLASSICS IN ANTHROPOLOGY

Paul Bohannan, Editor

CONTENTS

EDITOR'S PREFACE

Herbert Spencer's *Principles of Sociology* is unquestionably one of the great works of nineteenth-century anthropology, and as such deserves to be included in this series of Classics in Anthropology. However, the original text is so long—more than two thousand pages in three volumes—that reprinting it in its entirety was out of the question. An abridgment had to be made.

Two courses are open in abridging a scholarly work from a previous era. One is to make representative selections and thus inevitably include some chaff with the wheat. The other is to select only those portions of the work which remain sound and illuminating. I have chosen the latter course. It was my feeling that since there is much more of lasting value in *Principles of Sociology* than can be included in a volume of moderate size, it would be a waste to select anything not of the highest order.

The sections I finally chose to include in this edition were the two that seemed to me best of all. One deals with the structure and function of society in general, the other with the evolution of the regulative institutions of society. Specifically, from Volume 1, Part II, "The Inductions of Sociology," I have taken chapters 1–6, 9–10, and 12, and from Volume 2, Part V, "Political Institutions," I have included chapters 2–7 and 11–16. Despite the fact that these selections do not run consecutively in the original, they strike me as having a good deal of continuity, cohesion, and unity. The relative order of the chapters has not been changed except that chapter 12 of Volume 1 has been placed at the very end. The original chapter headings have been retained save for two minor changes. Spencer revised some parts of *Principles of Sociology*, and I have used the last published version of each chapter.

In editing the chapters selected for inclusion in this volume I have deleted sentences and paragraphs which seemed to me either to blur the argument or to belabor the point. I have also left out a number of biological analogies when it seemed that other examples already cited by Spencer had made the parallel sufficiently clear. When Spencer went beyond the bounds of science and introduced considerations of ethics or values, such passages have generally been deleted. Occasional passages in which Spencer proposed racial explanations for certain cultural features have also been omitted. Their omission is not intended to conceal the fact that Spencer held such views; it was made in order to exclude from the volume interpretations that are no longer tenable.

Paragraphs which I felt were excessively long have been broken up into shorter ones. By modern standards Spencer overpunctuated, and in this edition I have tried to simplify his punctuation and thus make it accord with present-day usage. Whenever any part of the text has been omitted this fact has been indicated with ellipses. Section numbers, which Spencer used in all the volumes of his "Synthetic Philosophy," have been left out. The spelling of tribal names has been modernized where it seemed warranted: "Esquimaux" has been changed to "Eskimos," "Yncas" to "Incas," "Sandwich Islanders" to "Hawaiian Islanders," and so on. British spellings have been Americanized. In one place Spencer referred to "Polynesia" when "Indonesia" was intended, and elsewhere he used the word "compound" when it is clear from the context that he meant "doubly compound." These and one or two other minor errors have been corrected.

The system of bibliographic references employed by Spencer in *Principles of Sociology* made it something of a chore to track down the source of any quoted passage. Since it is often asserted that Spencer drew his data from naïve and prejudiced authors, and that he used their statements uncritically, it has seemed to me highly desirable for the reader of this edition to be able to locate Spencer's sources as easily as possible, so that he can check their reliability for himself. Accordingly, I have employed an up-to-date system of bibliographic citations. For assistance in the arduous task of changing the references from the old system to the new, I am indebted to Frank Murphy.

Except in a few cases, the accuracy of page references to other works has not been verified. Spencer himself had lost the references to some of the passages he quoted, and in some instances it has been possible to supply these. Where this was not possible and a passage stands without attribution, I have added the notation "[ref. lost]."

EDITOR'S INTRODUCTION

"Who now reads Spencer?" inquired Crane Brinton more than thirty years ago,[1] and Talcott Parsons, echoing Brinton, agreed that "Spencer is dead."[2] More recently, another sociologist, Robert E. L. Faris, has written that "the evolutionary conceptions of Spencer and his followers have all but disappeared from modern sociology,"[3] and the political scientist, Edward S. Corwin, has asserted that "Spencer's influence is today extinct."[4] The neglect into which Herbert Spencer has fallen is perhaps best exemplified by the fact that in Robert H. Lowie's *History of Ethnological Theory* his work is completely passed over,[5] while in Bertrand Russell's *History of Western Philosophy* there is not even a mention of his name.[6]

But if Spencer is no longer studied or esteemed, it was not always so. During his lifetime he was widely read, greatly admired, and enormously influential. He enjoyed the high regard of the leading men of science of his day, especially those closely associated with evolution. Alfred Russel Wallace considered Spencer "the greatest all-round thinker and most illuminating reasoner of the Nineteenth Century,"[7] and Charles Darwin was once moved to call Spencer "about a dozen times my superior."[8] In discussing Spencer again some years later, Darwin said of him, "I suspect that hereafter he will be looked at as by far the greatest living philosopher in England; perhaps equal to any that have lived."[9]

I would like to express my appreciation to the following persons for reading an earlier version of this Introduction and offering many comments and suggestions which proved helpful in revising it: Lewis S. Brown, Napoleon Chagnon, Marvin Harris, Daisy F. Hilse, Edward Norbeck, Irving Rouse, Elman R. Service, George H. Stocking, Jr., Stephen F. Tobias, Gerald Weiss, and Leslie A. White.

[1] *English Political Thought in the Nineteenth Century* (London: Ernest Benn, 1933), p. 226.

[2] *The Structure of Social Action* (New York: McGraw-Hill Book Co., 1937), p. 3.

[3] "Evolution and American Sociology," in *Evolutionary Thought in America*, ed. Stow Persons (New York: George Braziller, 1956), pp. 160–80, p. 176.

[4] "The Impact of the Idea of Evolution on American Political and Constitutional Tradition," in *Evolutionary Thought in America*, pp. 182–99, p. 187.

[5] New York: Rinehart & Co., 1937. Spencer's name does appear twice in this book (on pages 19 and 66) but the references to him are only in passing.

[6] New York: Simon and Schuster, 1945.

[7] Alfred Russel Wallace to Raphael Meldola, June 23, 1910, quoted in Raphael Meldola, *Evolution: Darwinian and Spencerian*, The Herbert Spencer Lecture for 1910, (Oxford: Clarendon Press, 1910), p. 44.

[8] Letter to Joseph Hooker, December 10, 1866, in *The Life and Letters of Charles Darwin*, edited by his son, Francis Darwin, 2 vols., (New York: Basic Books, 1959), 2:239.

[9] Letter to E. Ray Lankester, March 15, 1870, in *The Life and Letters of Charles Darwin*, 2:301.

The primary significance of Spencer for the history of science lies in the fact that it was he who first expounded the idea of evolution as a cosmic process. As one contemporary reviewer expressed it, "The doctrine of evolution when taken up by Mr. Spencer was little more than a crotchet. He has made it the idea of the age."[10]

Darwin is popularly regarded as the father of evolution, but in 1857, two years before the publication of *The Origin of Species*, Spencer had already recognized the universal nature of the evolutionary process. In *First Principles*, written in 1862, he elaborated the concept of evolution and exhibited instances of its operation among all orders of phenomena. "Such of us as ventured to read the *First Principles*," wrote Raphael Meldola, a British biologist trained during this period, "learnt that the theory of organic evolution propounded in the *Origin of Species* was the application to one domain of Nature of a broader principle which Spencer has shown held good throughout every domain of Nature. . . ."[11]

Similarly, Spencer's major contribution to anthropology centered in his application of the principle of evolution to the phenomena of human society. Along with E. B. Tylor and Lewis H. Morgan, Spencer stands as one of the three outstanding cultural evolutionists of the nineteenth century.

Although Spencer achieved great renown in his native England and on the Continent, it was in the United States that his writings had the greatest impact.[12] According to Vernon Parrington, "Spencer laid out the broad highway over which American thought traveled in the later years of the [nineteenth] century."[13] Most important of all was the fact that Spencer's writings proved to be the most effective single force leading to the establishment of social science in America. "I imagine that nearly all of us who took up sociology between 1870, say, and 1890," wrote Charles Horton Cooley, "did so at the instigation of Spencer."[14]

Spencer's influence was far from being confined to the academic world,

[10] Douglas A. Spalding, "Herbert Spencer's Psychology," *Nature* 7 (1873): 298–300, p. 298.

[11] Meldola, *Evolution: Darwinian and Spencerian*, p. 13.

[12] Between 1860 and 1903 Spencer's books sold a total of 368,755 copies in authorized editions in the United States and a good many more in unauthorized editions. (Malcolm Cowley, "Naturalism in American Literature," in *Evolutionary Thought in America*, pp. 300–33, p. 302).

[13] *Main Currents in American Thought*, vol. 3: *The Beginnings of Critical Realism in America* (New York: Harcourt, Brace & Co., 1930), p. 198. Among American subscribers to Spencer's "Synthetic Philosophy," and therefore also presumably influenced by his writings, were Charles Sumner, Wendell Phillips, Edward Everett, Horace Greeley, Jared Sparks, George Bancroft, Charles A. Dana, Henry C. Carey, Joseph Henry, Asa Gray, Benjamin Silliman, Joseph Le Conte, and Rev. Henry Ward Beecher (Herbert Spencer, *Education: Intellectual, Moral, and Physical* [New York: D. Appleton and Co., 1862], pp. viii–x).

[14] "Reflections upon the Sociology of Herbert Spencer," *American Journal of Sociology* 26 (1920): 129–45, p. 129.

however. The effect of his ideas was felt by intellectuals of every kind, and they left ample testimony of this fact. Beatrice Webb, who knew Spencer personally, wrote that "he taught me to look on all social institutions as if they were plants or animals — things that could be observed, classified and explained."[15] Of *First Principles*, Spencer's evolutionary manifesto, Mrs. Webb tells us that it had "a very great influence on my feelings and thoughts."[16] The English novelist Arnold Bennett, speaking of the same work, wrote in his *Journal*: "By filling me with the sense of causation everywhere, [it] has altered my whole view of life. . . . You can see *First Principles* in nearly every line I write."[17]

This same work of Spencer's had a galvanizing effect on American writers too. Henry Holt declared that when he first read it, "my eyes opened to a new heaven and a new earth."[18] Theodore Dreiser remarked that in *First Principles* Spencer marshaled "the whole universe in review before you . . . showing you how certain beautiful laws exist, and how, by these laws, all animate things have developed and arranged themselves."[19] And Jack London, in his largely autobiographical novel *Martin Eden*, described the effect that *First Principles* had on his hero in the following words: ". . . here was the man Spencer, organizing all knowledge for him, reducing everything to unity, elaborating ultimate realities, and presenting to his startled gaze a universe so concrete of realization that it was like the model of a ship such as sailors make and put into glass bottles. There was no caprice, no chance. All was law."[20]

Unquestionably, then, at its height Spencer's influence was not only widespread but profound.[21] This influence, however, did not long survive Spencer's death. The rise, brilliant glow, and eventual eclipse of Spencer's system of thought make up one of the most interesting chapters of modern intellectual history, yet one that has seldom been presented fully and accurately.

Spencer was born on April 27, 1820, in Derby in the English Midlands, the eldest of nine children, and the only one who survived infancy. The family were staunch Dissenters, in whom religious liberty, political indi-

---

[15] Beatrice Webb, *My Apprenticeship* (London: Longmans, Green & Co., 1926), p. 37.

[16] *My Apprenticeship*, p. 37.

[17] *The Journal of Arnold Bennett, 1896–1910* (New York: Book League of America, 1932), p. 392.

[18] *Garrulities of an Octogenarian Editor* (Boston: Houghton Mifflin Co., 1923), p. 47.

[19] Quoted in F. O. Matthiessen, *Theodore Dreiser* (New York: William Sloane Associates, 1951), pp. 40–41.

[20] *Martin Eden* (New York: Macmillan Co., 1957), p. 99.

[21] "Probably no other philosopher ever had such a vogue as Spencer had from about 1870 to 1890" (Henry Holt, *Garrulities of an Octogenarian Editor*, p. 298).

vidualism, and social egalitarianism were strongly rooted. This background was to have a considerable effect on Spencer's writings, particularly on those dealing with ethics and political theory.

Except for a period of three months, Spencer never went to school. His father, a schoolmaster, and later an uncle who was a minister and social reformer educated him at home. As Spencer's father disliked the use of discipline in education, the boy's training in academic subjects was uneven. At thirteen he knew almost "nothing worth mentioning of Latin or Greek." He had received no formal instruction in English, knew only a little arithmetic, and was altogether ignorant of English history.

Although he resisted studying subjects which were traditionally learned by rote, Spencer was eager to pursue those based on general principles and logic. Thus from the age of thirteen to sixteen, when he lived with and was taught by his uncle Thomas, Spencer studied geometry, algebra, trigonometry, and mechanics, including the first part of Newton's *Principia*.[22] The elder Spencer wanted his nephew to attend Cambridge, as he had done, but Herbert declined, feeling that he was "unfit" for a university career.[23]

The fact that he never received a university education was reflected in the nature of Spencer's contributions to philosophy and science. Once, in assessing the pros and cons of formal academic training, Spencer concluded that in his own case "the advantages which intellectual freedom confers seem to have outweighed the disadvantages."[24]

From an early age Spencer demonstrated a marked inclination toward science, and in this he was strongly encouraged by his father. Writing of his father's influence on him during the period immediately preceding his teens, Spencer said:

"Always the tendency in himself, and the tendency strengthened in me, was to regard everything as naturally caused; and I doubt not that while the notion of causation was thus rendered much more definite in me than in most of my age, there was established a habit of seeking for causes, as well as a tacit belief in the universality of causation. Along with this there went absence of all suggestion of the miraculous."[25]

Spencer apparently never held any fixed religious beliefs. He relates that at twenty he received a letter from his father which "called my attention

[22] David Duncan, *The Life and Letters of Herbert Spencer* (London: Methuen & Co., 1908), p. 417. (All subsequent references to this work are to the Methuen edition.)
[23] Hector Macpherson, *Spencer and Spencerism* (New York: Doubleday, Page & Co., 1900), p. 12.
[24] Herbert Spencer, *An Autobiography*, 2 vols. (London: Watts & Co., 1926), 1:337. (All subsequent references to this work are to the Watts edition.) In his *Autobiography* Spencer accomplished just what he set out to do, namely, to write a natural history of himself (1:vii).
[25] *An Autobiography*, 1:89.

to religious questions and appealed to religious feelings — seeking for some response."[26] But no such response was forthcoming. As Spencer wrote,

"The acquisition of scientific knowledge, especially physical, had cooperated with the natural tendency thus shown [a dislike for authority and ritual]; and had practically excluded the ordinary idea of the supernatural. A breach in the course of causation had come to be, if not an impossible thought, yet a thought never entertained. Necessarily, therefore, the current creed became more and more alien to the set of convictions gradually formed in me, and slowly dropped away unawares."[27]

An interest in broad generalizations was at this time also beginning to emerge as an important part of Spencer's intellectual makeup. As he wrote of himself in his *Autobiography*, "there was commonly shown a faculty of seizing cardinal truths rather than accumulating detailed information. The implications of the phenomena were then, as always, more interesting than the phenomena themselves."[28] This attitude made "fundamental principles objects of greater attention than the various concrete illustrations of them."[29]

Spencer's great aptitude for mathematics is revealed by his discovery at sixteen or seventeen of a property of the circle then unknown to descriptive geometry.[30]

At the age of seventeen Spencer was employed by the London and Birmingham Railway, and acquired during the course of his railroad work knowledge equivalent to that of a civil engineer. Although his dramatic ten-mile ride on a runaway train, vividly described in his *Autobiography*,[31] is perhaps the event of Spencer's engineering career most often noted, the influence of an engineering background on his later scientific work — an influence often overlooked[32] — was of much greater significance.

Largely because of his training in engineering, Spencer was able to perceive and formulate certain relationships between growth and structure that hold among all living organisms. He noted that for regularly shaped bodies, such as cells, the surface area increases as the *square* of the linear dimensions, while the volume increases as the *cube* of these dimen-

[26] *Ibid.*, p. 150.
[27] *Ibid.*, pp. 152–53.
[28] *Ibid.*, p. 335.
[29] *Ibid.*, p. 336.
[30] This theorem and its demonstration were subsequently published in *The Civil Engineer and Architect's Journal* in 1840 (ibid., pp. 119, 164, 520–21).
[31] *Ibid.*, pp. 134–38.
[32] Not by Joseph Needham, however, who characterized Spencer's system of ideas as "a philosophy which, well-articulated and riveted firmly together in every part, seemed to issue fully armed from the brain of a master engineer" (*The Sceptical Biologist* [London: Chatto & Windus, 1929], p. 50).

sions.[33] Thus, as cells grow, volume quickly outruns surface area, and since it is through their surface membrane that cells are nourished, a limit is set to the size that a cell can attain. It is this fact that explains why animals as different in size as a gnat and an elephant are made up of cells of essentially the same size.

Although he originally formulated this principle in connection with biology, Spencer later introduced it into sociology in order to explain why larger societies are less cohesive than smaller ones.[34]

Engineers have long known what to the layman seems incomprehensible, namely, that of two bridges built to the same proportions the larger one is the weaker. Taking this principle from engineering, Spencer applied it to the realm of biology. He pointed out that while the mass of a living body increases as the cube of its dimensions, the strength of its bones and muscles, being proportional to their cross-section areas, increases only as the square of their dimensions. Thus of two animals of different size but geometrically similar, the larger one would be less well able to support its own weight. This is why the supporting limbs of larger animals tend to be proportionately, as well as absolutely, larger than those of smaller animals.[35]

Today these relationships are common knowledge in biology and are recognized as being of fundamental importance, yet probably not one biologist in a hundred is aware that it was Herbert Spencer who formulated them.

In writing about other fields of knowledge, Spencer often used modes of expression having the form and precision of the language of physics or engineering. Thus, for example, in discussing the evolutionary process he speaks of "the law that motion is along the line of least resistance or the line of greatest traction or the resultant of the two."[36]

Spencer's interest in evolution began during his early twenties. While employed by the Birmingham and Gloucester Railway he had occasion to see a number of fossils that had been removed from railroad cuts. Thereafter, he himself began to look for fossils during frequent walks along these cuts, and his discoveries included the fossil of a plesiosaur. His

[33] Herbert Spencer, *The Principles of Biology* (New York: D. Appleton & Co., 1866), 1:122–23.

[34] Herbert Spencer, *The Principles of Sociology*, vol. 2 (New York: D. Appleton & Co. 1899), p. 281.

[35] *Principles of Biology*, 1:122–23. See aso J. Arthur Thomson, *Herbert Spencer* (London: J. M. Dent & Co., 1906), pp. 112–13; and D'Arcy W. Thompson, *On Growth and Form* (Cambridge: Cambridge University Press, 1917), p. 18. In his discussion of the principles involved in this relationship Spencer had been anticipated by Galileo (*Dialogues Concerning Two New Sciences* [New York: McGraw-Hill Book Co., 1963], pp. 125–26).

[36] *Principles of Sociology*, vol. 3 (New York: D. Appleton & Co., 1900), p. 359.

interest in geology and paleontology thus aroused, Spencer sought to extend his knowledge by purchasing a copy of Charles Lyell's *Principles of Geology*, which had recently appeared.

Spencer wrote: "I name this purchase chiefly as serving to introduce a fact of considerable significance. I had during previous years been cognizant of the hypothesis that the human race had been developed from some lower race; though what degree of acceptance it had from me memory does not say. But my reading of Lyell, one of whose chapters was devoted to a refutation of Lamarck's views concerning the origin of species, had the effect of giving me a decided leaning to them. Why Lyell's arguments produced the opposite effect to that intended, I cannot say. Probably it was that the discussion presented, more clearly than had been done previously, the conception of the natural genesis of organic forms. . . . My inclination to accept it as true, in spite of Lyell's adverse criticisms, was, doubtless, chiefly due to its harmony with that general idea of the order of Nature toward which I had, throughout life, been growing."[37]

In the spring of 1843, nearly two years after leaving the employ of the railroads, Spencer moved to London and began his literary career. After several false starts, which caused him to return to railroad work for a time, he eventually obtained a position as sub-editor of the *Economist*, a post which allowed him enough free time to proceed with serious writing.

In 1842 Spencer had written a series of twelve letters on "The Proper Sphere of Government," which had been published in *The Nonconformist*, a recently established publication of radical Dissenters. These letters he later expanded into his first book, *Social Statics*, published in 1850. This work was primarily a statement of his political philosophy, but in parts of it Spencer foreshadowed some of his later ideas on evolution.[38]

In 1851 Spencer attended a series of lectures by the celebrated anatomist Richard Owen on comparative osteology, a subject which had considerable bearing on the problem of the origin of animal forms.[39] During the summer of the same year Spencer traveled to Kent with George H. Lewes (later the consort of George Eliot). As Spencer wrote in his *Autobiography*, "[Lewes] had brought with him a volume of Milne Edwards, and in it for the first time I met with the expression — 'the physiological division of labour.' Though the conception was not new to me, . . . yet the mode of formulating it was; and the phrase thereafter played a part in my course of thought."[40]

The same year, Spencer was asked to review W. B. Carpenter's *Principles of Physiology* for *The Westminster Review*.

[37] *An Autobiography*, 1:176.
[38] *Ibid.*, 2:7–8.
[39] *Ibid.*, 1:368.
[40] *Ibid.*, 1:37.

"In the course of such perusal as was needed to give an account of its contents [Spencer later wrote], I came across von Baer's formula expressing the course of development through which every plant and animal passes — the change from homogeneity to heterogeneity. . . . this phrase of von Baer expressing the law of individual development, awakened my attention to the fact that the law which holds of the ascending stages of each individual organism is also the law which holds of the ascending grades of organisms of all kinds. And it had the further advantage that it presented in brief form, a more graphic image of the transformation, and thus facilitated further thought."[41]

The following year, 1852, Spencer published in *The Leader* his now famous article "The Development Hypothesis." Writing with what Darwin was to call "remarkable skill and force,"[42] Spencer openly rejected special creation as an explanation of the diversity of animal species and espoused instead the process of organic evolution through successive modifications.

Shortly after reading this essay in 1858 Darwin wrote to Spencer:

"Your remarks on the general argument of the so-called development theory seem to me admirable. I am at present preparing an Abstract of a larger work on the changes of species [*The Origin of Species*]; but I treat the subject simply as a naturalist, and not from a general point of view, otherwise, in my opinion, your argument could not have been improved on, and might have been quoted by me with great advantage. . . ."[43]

The writings that followed show Spencer's notion of evolution undergoing further elaboration. At the same time that he saw evolution being manifested by more kinds of phenomena, he discerned more aspects of the process itself. In "The Genesis of Science" and "The Art of Education," both published in 1854, an "increase of definiteness had been recognized as a characteristic of advancing development," and "there had also been recognized as characterizing one or other kind of development, a growing integration."[44]

"Doubtless it was during the preceding autumn [that of 1854] that the change from homogeneity to heterogeneity, which we have already seen was in course of being recognized as characterising the change from lower

[41] *Ibid.*, pp. 384–85. Spencer considered this chance acquaintance with von Baer's principle to have been the turning point of his life. In 1864, after he had launched his "Synthetic Philosophy," he wrote in a letter to Lewes: "If anyone says that had von Baer never written I should not be doing that which I now am, I have nothing to say to the contrary — I should reply it is highly probable" (*ibid.*, 2:486).

[42] *The Origin of Species*, 6th ed. (London: John Murray, 1890), p. xix.

[43] Charles Darwin to Herbert Spencer, November 25, 1858, in *Life and Letters of Charles Darwin*, 1:497.

[44] *An Autobiography*, 1:501.

to higher in several diverse groups of phenomena, was recognized as characterizing this change in all groups of phenomena. And doubtless this development of the conception took place while writing the "General Synthesis" [in *Principles of Psychology*]; two chapters of which trace, among mental phenomena, the progress from the homogeneous to the heterogeneous, and two other chapters of which exhibit the progress in specialty and in complexity, both involving the same trait."[45]

Thus, brick by brick, Spencer was building up the concept of evolution. The term "evolution" itself was made current by Spencer, whose first use of it was in "The Ultimate Laws of Physiology," an article published in October, 1857.[46] Years later, in discussing his adoption of the term, Spencer wrote, "I did not, however, introduce it in the place of 'epigenesis,' or any word of specially biological application, but as a word fit for expressing the process of evolution throughout its entire range, inorganic and organic." In explaining why he had replaced the term "progress," which he had used as late as April, 1857, in his article "Progress: Its Law and Cause," Spencer noted that " 'progress' has an anthropocentric meaning, and . . . there needed a word free from that."[47]

Although in *First Principles* Spencer presented a rather elaborate formulation of the general process of evolution,[48] in his later writings he inclined toward a simplified version: *Evolution is a change from a state of relatively indefinite, incoherent, homogeneity to a state of relatively definite, coherent, heterogeneity.*[49]

Much of the rest of Spencer's life was devoted to discovering, exhibiting, and explaining manifestations of evolution throughout the cosmos. "Once having become possessed by the conception of Evolution in its comprehensive form," he wrote, "the desire to elaborate and set it forth was so strong

[45] *Ibid.*, p. 462.

[46] *Ibid.*, pp. 503, 504. The earliest use of the word "evolution" in biology was apparently by the Swiss naturalist Charles Bonnet in 1762. A believer in the doctrine of preformation, Bonnet applied the term to the supposed "unfolding" of the completely formed parts of a tiny "homunculus" during the course of embryological development (Henry Fairfield Osborn, *From the Greeks to Darwin* [New York: Charles Scribner's Sons, 1927], pp. 118–21; Philip G. Fothergill, *Historical Aspects of Organic Evolution* [London: Hollis & Carter, 1952], pp. 45–46). It is a curious fact — and one not generally known — that Darwin did not use the term "evolution" in the earlier editions of *The Origin of Species.*

[47] In a letter to the American entomologist A. S. Packard, August 15, 1902, quoted in David Duncan, *The Life and Letters of Herbert Spencer*, p. 551 n.

[48] "Evolution is an integration of matter and concomitant dissipation of motion; during which the matter passes from an indefinite incoherent homogeneity to a definite coherent heterogeneity; and during which the retained motion undergoes a parallel transformation" (*First Principles*, 6th ed. [New York: D. Appleton & Co., 1912], p. 367).

[49] "What Is Social Evolution?" *Nineteenth Century* 44 (1898): 348–58, p. 353; *First Principles*, 6th ed., p. 367.

that to have passed life in doing something else would, I think, have been almost intolerable." [50]

Although he had discussed the evolution of such things as manners, fashions, mind, and science itself in several previous articles, it was in "Progress: Its Law and Cause," published originally in *The Westminster Review* in 1857, that Spencer first applied the concept of evolution systematically to the universe at large, and especially to human society:

"The advance from the simple to the complex, through a process of successive differentiations, is seen alike in the earliest changes of the Universe to which we can reason our way back; and in the earliest changes which we can inductively establish; it is seen in the geologic and climatic evolution of the Earth, and of every single organism on its surface; it is seen in the evolution of Humanity, whether contemplated in the civilized individual, or in the aggregation of races; it is seen in the evolution of Society in respect alike of its political, its religious, and its economical organisation; and it is seen in the evolution of all . . . [the] endless concrete and abstract products of human activity. . . ." [51]

Spencer was not only the first expositor of general evolution, he also contributed in a significant way to the growth of the idea of organic evolution. Let us examine this contribution in some detail. We have seen that as early as 1852, seven years before the publication of *The Origin of Species*, Spencer had publicly disavowed special creation and come out in favor of a theory of biological evolution. In 1855, in the first edition of *Principles of Psychology*, he wrote: "Life under all its forms has arisen by a progressive, unbroken evolution. . . . out of the lowest and simplest beginnings. . . . and through the immediate instrumentality of . . . natural causes." [52]

Thus Spencer's acceptance of organic evolution preceded that of most of the men who were to become the theory's leading supporters, including Thomas Henry Huxley, who later gained renown as Darwin's most forceful champion. Spencer and Huxley, who were close friends almost from their first meeting in 1852, had frequent conversations on the subject during long walks together in London. Writing in his *Autobiography* for the year 1857 or thereabouts, Spencer said:

"Involved as the hypothesis of organic evolution was in most of my thinking, it not unfrequently cropped up in our talk, and led to animated discussions in which, having a knowledge of the facts immensely greater than mine, he habitually demolished now this and now that argument which I used. But though continually knocked down, I continually got up

[50] *An Autobiography*, 2:460.
[51] "Progress: Its Law and Cause," *The Westminster Review* n.s., 11 (1857): 445–85, p. 465.
[52] (New York: D. Appleton & Co., 1896), 1:465 n.

again. The principle which he acted upon was that of keeping judgment in suspense in the absence of adequate evidence. But acknowledging, though I did, the propriety of his course, I found myself in this case unable to adopt it. There were, as it seemed to me, but two imaginable possibilities — special creation and progressive development; and since the doctrine of special creation, unsupported by evidence, was also intrinsically incredible, because incongruous with all we know of the order of Nature, the doctrine of development was accepted by me as the only alternative. Hence, fallacious as proved this or the other special reason assigned in support of it, my belief in it perpetually revived." [53]

When Darwin's *The Origin of Species* appeared in 1859, Spencer welcomed it warmly, finding in it massive support for the general theory he himself had long upheld. What Darwin supplied that Spencer had not was a satisfactory mechanism — natural selection — to explain organic evolution. Somewhat chagrined at failing to hit upon the principle of natural selection himself, Spencer attempted to account for this failure as follows:

"One [reason] was my espousal of the belief that the inheritance of functionally-produced modifications suffices to explain the facts. Recognizing this as a sufficient cause for many orders of changes in organisms, I concluded that it was a sufficient cause for all orders of changes. There are, it is true, various phenomena which did not seem reconcilable with this conclusion; but I lived in the faith that some way of accounting for them would eventually be found. Had I looked more carefully into the evidence, and observed how multitudinous these inexplicable facts are — had I not slurred over the difficulties, but deliberately contemplated them; I might perhaps have seen that here was the additional factor wanted." [54]

As it was, in an essay entitled "A Theory of Population Deduced from the General Law of Animal Fertility," published in *The Westminster Review* in 1852, Spencer "came within an ace of recognising that the struggle for existence was a factor in organic evolution." [55]

Discussing differential survival among members of human populations Spencer noted:

[53] 1:505. In his own writings Huxley has left us an account of the same discussions which is substantially the same as Spencer's: "Many and prolonged were the battles we fought on this topic. But even my friend's rare dialectic skill and copiousness of apt illustration could not drive me from my agnostic position. I took the stand upon two grounds: — Firstly, that up to that time, the evidence in favour of transmutation [of species] was wholly insufficient; and secondly, that no suggestion respecting the causes of transmutation assumed, which had been made, was in any way adequate to explain the phenomena. Looking back at the state of knowledge at that time, I really do not see that any other conclusion was justifiable." (Leonard Huxley, *Life and Letters of Thomas Henry Huxley*, 2 vols. [New York: D. Appleton & Co., 1900], 1:180).

[54] *An Autobiography*, 1:390.

[55] J. Arthur Thomson, "Darwin's Predecessors," in *Evolution in Modern Thought*, pp. 1–22 (New York: Boni & Liveright, n.d.), p. 17.

"For as those prematurely carried off must, in the average of cases, be those in whom the power of self-preservation is the least, it unavoidably follows, that those left behind to continue the race are those in whom the power of self-preservation is the greatest — are the select of their generation. So that, whether the dangers to existence be of the kind produced by excess of fertility, or of any other kind, it is clear, that by the ceaseless exercise of the faculties needed to contend with them successfully, there is ensured a constant progress toward a higher degree of skill, intelligence, and self-regulation. . . ."[56]

In *Principles of Biology*, published in 1864, Spencer proposed the phrase "the survival of the fittest" as equivalent to Darwin's "natural selection."[57] Alfred Russel Wallace found it preferable to the latter, and in correspondence with Darwin urged him to adopt it.

Wallace argued that, as several of Darwin's critics had already pointed out, "natural selection" implied an intelligent agent doing the selecting, and that in fact in *The Origin of Species* Darwin himself had frequently fallen into the practice of personifying nature as "selecting," "preferring," "seeking only the good of the species," etc. This Wallace decried, and suggested to Darwin

"the possibility of entirely avoiding this source of misconception in your great work . . . by adopting Spencer's term . . . 'Survival of the Fittest.' This term is the plain expression of the *fact*; 'Natural Selection' is a metaphorical expression of it, and to a certain degree *indirect* and *incorrect*, since even personifying Nature she does not so much select special variations as exterminate the most unfavourable ones."[58]

Darwin's reply was positive:

"I fully agree with all that you say on the advantages of H. Spencer's excellent expression of 'the survival of the fittest'. . . . I wish I had received your letter two months ago, for I would have worked in 'the survival,' etc., often in the new edition of the 'Origin,' which is now almost printed off. . . ."

Nevertheless, he added, "the term Natural Selection has now been so largely used . . . that I doubt whether it could be given up. . . . Whether it will be rejected must now depend on the 'survival of the fittest.'"[59]

Although it was Huxley who received the epithet of "Darwin's Bulldog," Spencer also came to Darwin's defense when the latter, never a polemicist,

[56] *The Westminster Review* 57 (1852): 468–501, p. 500.
[57] *Principles of Biology*, 1:444–45.
[58] Alfred Russel Wallace to Charles Darwin, July 2, 1866, in *Alfred Russel Wallace: Letters and Reminiscences*, ed. James Marchant, 2 vols. (London: Cassell & Co., 1916), 1:170, 171.
[59] Charles Darwin to Alfred Russel Wallace, July 5, 1866, *ibid.*, pp. 174–75.

chose to ignore attacks made on his theory.[60] Years later, with Darwin dead and Huxley in failing health, an article written by Lord Salisbury appeared which attacked evolution by distorting the principle of natural selection. Unable to persuade Wallace to reply to the article, Spencer did so himself.[61] Later, Wallace remarked that Spencer's rebuttal "was thoroughly well done, so that I had no reason to regret not having undertaken it myself."[62] Summarizing Spencer's contribution to the struggle that resulted in the general acceptance of organic evolution, the noted biologist H. H. Newman, wrote: "It was largely due to his forceful writings that Darwinism won the battle against dogmatism."[63]

In 1858, while preparing an article on "The Nebular Hypothesis," Spencer conceived the grand scheme of surveying the fields of biology, psychology, sociology, and morals from an evolutionary perspective. The original draft of this plan included one volume to be called *The Principles of Sociology*.[64] By 1860 Spencer's ideas for this scheme had crystalized, and he issued a prospectus announcing its future publication in successive parts. In this prospectus *The Principles of Sociology* occupied an enlarged place, having been expanded from one volume to three. As Spencer envisioned it then, *Principles of Sociology* was to deal with "General facts, structural and functional, as gathered from a survey of Societies and their changes: in other words, the empirical generalizations that are arrived at by comparing the different societies, and successive phases of the same society."[65]

Thus, before any of the classical evolutionists had published their theoretical works, Spencer already had a clear notion of a comparative science of society based on evolutionary principles.

In propounding a science of sociology Spencer was preceded by Auguste Comte, and during Spencer's lifetime as well as afterward a number of writers alleged Spencer's indebtedness to Comte.[66] To such allegations Spencer took strong exception. In the first place, he affirmed, he had not

[60] For example, when Darwin declined to reply to the criticisms in Sir Alexander Grant's article, "Philosophy and Mr. Darwin" (*Contemporary Review* 17 [1871]: 274–81). See Duncan, *Life and Letters of Herbert Spencer*, p. 149.

[61] Marchant, ed., *Alfred Russel Wallace: Letters and Reminiscences*, 2:59–60, p. 65; Herbert Spencer, "Lord Salisbury on Evolution," *Nineteenth Century* 38 (1895): 740–57.

[62] Alfred Russel Wallace, *My Life*, 2 vols. (New York: Dodd, Mead & Co., 1905), 2:32.

[63] "Historical Account of the Development of the Evolution Theory," in *Readings in Evolution, Genetics, and Eugenics*, ed. H. H. Newman, pp. 10–45 (Chicago: University of Chicago Press, 1921), p. 28.

[64] *An Autobiography*, 2:15–16.

[65] *Ibid.*, p. 481.

[66] For example, René Hubert in his article on Comte in the *Encyclopedia of the Social Sciences*, 4:151–53 (New York: Macmillan Co., 1930), p. 152.

read Comte when, in 1850 in his *Social Statics*, he first began to deal with concepts such as the social organism and to see that in individual and social organisms "progress from low types to high types is progress from uniformity of structure to multiformity of structure."[67] Thus Comte's ideas could not have entered into his thinking on comparative sociology. In the second place, Spencer pointed out, his approach to society and to phenomena in general was radically different from Comte's.

In a letter to George H. Lewes, an admirer and supporter of Comte, Spencer wrote:

"What is Comte's professed aim? To give a coherent account of the progress of *human conceptions*. What is my aim? To give a coherent account of the progress of the *external world*. Comte proposes to describe the necessary, and the actual, filiation of *ideas*. I propose to describe the necessary, and the actual, filiation of *things*. Comte professes to interpret the genesis of our *knowledge of nature*. My aim is to interpret, as far as it is possible, the genesis of the phenomena *which constitute nature*. The one end is *subjective*. The other is *objective*. How then can the one be the originator of the other?"[68]

In writing the first five volumes of his "Synthetic Philosophy" — *First Principles* (1862), the two volumes of *Principles of Biology* (1864–67), and the two volumes recasting *Principles of Psychology* (1870–72) — Spencer had drawn on his own store of knowledge and ideas, supplementing them only to a very limited extent by additional reading. "But I had long been conscious," he wrote, "that when I came to treat of Sociology, the case would be widely different. There would be required an immense accumulation of facts so classified and arranged as to facilitate generalization."[69] Accordingly, in 1867, several years before he expected to begin work on *Principles of Sociology*, he enlisted the services of a young university graduate, David Duncan (later to become his official biographer), to serve in the capacity of researcher. When Duncan left his employ in 1870, Spencer hired James Collier and Richard Scheppig to continue reading and extracting ethnographic and historical data. Material was taken from original sources and organized according to a system of headings and subheadings devised by Spencer which was much like the divisions of a modern ethnographic monograph.

Spencer was convinced that "exhibiting sociological phenomena in such wise that comparisons of them in their coexistences and sequences, as occurring among various peoples in different stages, were made easy, would immensely facilitate the discovery of sociological truths."[70] The

[67] *An Autobiography*, 2:488; see also ibid., p. 9.
[68] *Ibid.*, p. 488.
[69] *Ibid.*, p. 171.
[70] *Ibid.*, pp. 264–65.

result of this undertaking was the publication of separate volumes of ethnographic materials under the general title of *Descriptive Sociology*. This series of publications, a treasure trove of carefully organized ethnographic facts, sits today in but a few libraries, gathering dust, untapped and all but unknown, even to professional anthropologists. Yet its compilation indisputably marks Spencer as the founder of systematic, inductive, comparative sociology.[71]

Eight large folio volumes of *Descriptive Sociology* appeared between 1873 and 1881. In reviewing the first volume of the series, devoted to the English, E. B. Tylor wrote that it provided "a sufficient answer to all disbelievers in the possibility of a science of history. Where the chronicle of individual lives often perplexes and mystifies the scholar, the generalization of social principles from the chronicler's materials shows an order of human affairs where cause and effect take their inevitable course, as in Physics or Biology."[72]

The same volume was also favorably reviewed in the United States by William Graham Sumner, who wrote: "It presents history as a social evolution, in which no factor is contemptible, because the social outcome of a nation's life is the resultant of a vast number of forces. . . ."[73]

Spencer expected these compilations of the culture of ancient and exotic peoples to be popular, but in this he was completely mistaken and bitterly disappointed. The volumes had very little sale, and, until the discontinuance of the series in 1881, *Descriptive Sociology* represented a net financial loss to Spencer of £3,250.

But Spencer never gave up on the idea of this series. In his will he provided for the setting up of a trust to continue the compilation and publication of the remainder of the projected volumes of *Descriptive Sociology*, and stipulated that the interest from his investments and the income from the sale of his works be allocated to this end.[74] Nine volumes of the series were published after Spencer's death.[75]

[71] The existence of *Descriptive Sociology* refutes such notions as that of A. C. Haddon that Spencer was a "speculative" social philosopher and did not contribute to "the solid foundations of inductive sociology" (*History of Anthropology*, The Thinker's Library [London: Watts & Co., 1934], p. 126).

[72] "Spencer's Descriptive Sociology," *Nature* 8 (1873): 544–47, p. 546.

[73] *The Independent* (New York), 26 (May 14, 1874): 9.

[74] Sir Arthur Keith, *An Autobiography* (London: Watts & Co., 1950), pp. 427–28.

[75] The full list of volumes of *Descriptive Sociology* is as follows: 1. *English* (1873); 2. *Ancient Mexicans, Central Americans, Chibchans, Ancient Peruvians* (1874); 3. *Types of Lowest Races, Negritto, and Malayo-Polynesian Races* (1874); 4. *African Races* (1875); 5. *Asiatic Races* (1876); 6. *North and South American Races* (1878); 7. *Hebrews and Phoenicians* (1880); 8. *French* (1881); 9. *Chinese* (1910); 10. *Hellenic Greeks* (1910); 11. *Ancient Egyptians* (1925); 12. *Hellenistic Greeks* (1928); 13. *Mesopotamia* (1929); 14. *African Races* (1930); and 15. *Ancient Romans* (1934). A revised edition of No. 3, edited by D. Duncan and H. Tedder, was published in 1925; a second edition of No. 6 appeared in 1885; No. 14 is a redoing by Emil Torday of No. 4.

In 1936, considering their work to be at an end, the members of the Herbert Spencer Trust declared the trust dissolved, and, following the provisions of Spencer's will, distributed the principal of the bequest among several scientific societies — primarily the British Association for the Advancement of Science and the Royal Anthropological Institute.[76]

In 1872, at the urging of Professor Edward L. Youmans, an American disciple and close friend, Spencer temporarily discontinued work on his "Synthetic Philosophy" to write a volume for the "International Scientific Series," of which Youmans was originator and editor.[77] His contribution to this series was *The Study of Sociology.* Although it was regarded by its author as "popular both in manner and matter,"[78] *The Study of Sociology* was not unrelated to Spencer's projected major treatise on the same subject. He explained that "various considerations which seemed needful by way of introduction to the *Principles of Sociology*, presently to be written, and which yet could not be conveniently included in it, have found, in this preliminary volume, a fit place."[79]

The Study of Sociology was written in part to demonstrate that a science of sociology was indeed possible, a proposition which at the time was more often denied than affirmed. "There can be no complete acceptance of Sociology as a science," wrote Spencer, "so long as the belief in a social order not conforming to natural law, survives."[80] Such a view was especially prevalent among historians for whom the issue revolved around the question of free will. As James Anthony Froude expressed it in a passage quoted by Spencer, "When natural causes are liable to be set aside and neutralized by what is called volition, the word Science is out of place. If it is free to a man to choose what he will do or not do, there is no adequate science of him. If there is a science of him, there is no free choice. . . ."[81] On this

---

In addition to these volumes, which are in folio size, two unnumbered works appeared in octavo: Ruben Long, *The Sociology of Islam*, 2 vols. (1931–33), and John Garstang, *The Heritage of Solomon: an Historical Introduction to the Sociology of Ancient Palestine* (1934).

[76] Keith, *An Autobiography*, pp. 633–34.

[77] Other volumes of anthropological interest written for and published in this series include E. B. Tylor, *Anthropology* (No. 62); C. N. Starcke, *The Primitive Family* (No. 65); Alphonse de Candolle, *Origin of Cultivated Plants* (No. 48); and A. de Quatrefages, *The Human Species* (No. 27).

[78] *An Autobiography*, 2:244. Arrangements were made to have *The Study of Sociology* appear in installments in the *Contemporary Review* in England, and the plan was to do the same in a comparable journal in the United States. But when Youmans found no journal willing to undertake publication of the work in this form, he decided to start a new periodical which would serve as a vehicle for installments of *The Study of Sociology* as well as for other scientific articles of general interest. Thus was born *The Popular Science Monthly.*

[79] *The Study of Sociology* (New York: D. Appleton & Co., 1873), p. x.

[80] *Ibid.*, p. 360.

[81] *Ibid.*, p. 33.

issue Spencer's stand was unequivocal. A thoroughgoing determinist, he saw the principle of causation as operating in the sphere of human behavior no less strictly than throughout the rest of nature. Free will he regarded as merely an illusion.[82]

Spencer not only assailed the anti-scientific attitude of conventional historians, he was also disdainful of their published works. "I take but little interest in what are called histories," he wrote, "but am interested only in Sociology, which stands related to these so-called histories much as a vast building stands related to the heaps of stones and bricks around it."[83]

Spencer's charge against historians was not merely that they did little more than compile facts but that they compiled the wrong kinds of facts. As early as 1859, in an article entitled "What Knowledge Is of Most Worth?" Spencer had taken historians to task for presenting trivial rather than essential facts of human history:

"That which constitutes History, properly so called, is in great part omitted from works on the subject. Only of late years have historians commenced giving us, in any considerable quantity, the truly valuable information. As in past ages the king was everything and the people nothing; so, in past histories the doings of the king fill the entire picture, to which the national life forms an obscure background. . . . The thing it really concerns us to know, is the natural history of society."[84]

Later in the same article he added:

"The only history that is of practical value, is what may be called Descriptive Sociology. And the highest office which the historian can discharge, is that of narrating the lives of nations, as to furnish materials for a Comparative Sociology; and for the subsequent determination of the ultimate laws to which social phenomena conform."[85]

Spencer felt a similar disdain for classical scholars, whom he disparaged as "men who would blush if caught saying Iphigénia instead of Iphigenía, or would resent as an insult any imputation of ignorance respecting the fabled labours of a fabled demi-god, [but who] show not the slightest shame in confessing that they do not know where the Eustachian tubes are, what are the actions of the spinal cord, what is the normal rate of pulsation, or how the lungs are inflated."[86]

[82] *The Principles of Psychology*, 2 vols., 3rd ed. (New York: D. Appleton & Co., 1896), 1:500–504.

[83] *An Autobiography*, 2:185.

[84] Reprinted in *Education: Intellectual, Moral, and Physical*, pp. 21–96 (New York: D. Appleton & Co., 1862), p. 67. Harry Elmer Barnes seems to regard this essay as the opening gun in the intellectual movement that culminated in the "New History" of James Harvey Robinson, James T. Shotwell, Frederick Jackson Turner, and Charles A. Beard (*The New History and the Social Studies* [New York: Century Co., 1925], p. 3).

[85] *Education: Intellectual, Moral, and Physical*, pp. 69–70.

[86] *Ibid.*, p. 43.

When *The Study of Sociology* appeared, it found a surprisingly large and receptive audience. The book had a particularly strong impact in the United States, where, according to Charles Horton Cooley, it "probably did more to arouse interest in the subject than any other publication before or since."[87] William Graham Sumner was very much struck by the work and wrote of it: "The conception of society, of social forces, and of the science of society there offered, was just the one which I had been groping after, but had not been able to reduce for myself. It solved the old difficulty about the relation of social science to history, rescued social science from the dominion of the cranks, and offered a definite and magnificent field for work. . . ."[88]

Not long after the appearance of *The Study of Sociology*, Sumner established a new course at Yale for reading and discussing the book, apparently the first course in sociology ever given in an American university.[89] However, when the content of the book became known to the Rev. Noah Porter, president of Yale, he strongly objected to its use in a college "intimately associated in its history and constitution with the Christian religion."[90] In a letter to Sumner, Porter complained:

". . . the freedom and unfairness with which it attacks every Theistic Philosophy of society and of history, and the cool yet sarcastic effrontery with which he [Spencer] assumes that material elements and laws are the only forces which any scientific man can recognize, seem to me to condemn the book as a textbook for a miscellaneous class in an undergraduate course. . . . the use of it will inevitably and reasonably work serious havoc to the reputation of the college."[91]

Sumner threatened to resign if he was not allowed to use the book in class, but was persuaded to remain. However, he thereafter voluntarily refrained from using it "on the ground that the controversy had undermined its value as a textbook."[92] Sumner nevertheless continued to teach

[87] "Reflections upon the Sociology of Herbert Spencer," *American Journal of Sociology*, 26 (1920): 129–45, p. 129.

[88] "Sketch of William Graham Sumner," *Popular Science Monthly* 35 (1889): 261–68, p. 266.

[89] Harris E. Starr, *William Graham Sumner* (New York: Henry Holt & Co., 1925), p. 387.

[90] Duncan, *The Life and Letters of Herbert Spencer*, p. 208.

[91] Quoted by Harris E. Starr in *William Graham Sumner*, pp. 346, 347. Porter had had trouble with Spencer before: "Dear old Noah Porter, who of course was a Platonist, took a class thru Spencer's *First Principles*, for the sake of guarding them against its dangerous influences; and every man-jack of them came out a confirmed Spencerian" (Henry Holt, *Garrulities of an Octogenarian Editor* [Boston: Houghton Mifflin Co., 1923], pp. 306–7.

[92] Richard Hofstadter, *Social Darwinism in American Thought*, rev. ed. (Boston: Beacon Press, 1955), p. 20.

sociology at Yale, and during the years that followed succeeded in gaining greater general acceptance for the idea of a science of society.

Spencer began the actual writing of Volume I of *Principles of Sociology* early in 1874, with the first installment being distributed to subscribers in June of the same year.[93] The first volume of the work was published in book form in 1876. Because of Spencer's poor health, the second and third volumes were long delayed, the former appearing only in 1882, and the latter not until 1896.

Principles of Sociology represented the culmination of a long and extraordinarily productive life of thought and scholarship. When the last volume finally appeared, marking the end of the monumental "Synthetic Philosophy" he had first envisioned some forty years before, Spencer was already broken in health. In the Preface to this work he wrote:

"Doubtless in earlier days some exultation would have resulted; but as age creeps on feelings weaken, and now my chief pleasure is in my emancipation. Still there is satisfaction in the consciousness that losses, discouragements, and shattered health, have not prevented me from fulfilling the purpose of my life."[94]

Considering the many years of study and effort he had devoted to writing *Principles of Sociology*, Spencer was understandably disappointed at the meager reception it was accorded. Concerning the relative lack of interest shown in one volume in particular, he noted: "Beliefs, like creatures, must have fit environments before they can live and grow; and the environment furnished by the ideas and sentiments now current, is an unfit environment for the beliefs which the volume sets forth."[95] Recalling that his first book, *Social Statics*, a work he regarded as immature, "was more extensively, as well as more favourably, noticed, than any one of my

---

[93] As a means of defraying publishing expenses which he could not otherwise meet, Spencer had earlier hit upon the plan of issuing his "Synthetic Philosophy" in sections, as they were completed, to subscribers. At one time he had as many as 600 subscribers, 400 in England and 200 in the United States (*An Autobiography*, 2:54).

[94] *Principles of Sociology*, 3:vi. Of this preface Howard Becker and Harry Elmer Barnes have written: "To an understanding reader there are few more inspiring pages in literature than these few paragraphs" (*Social Thought from Lore to Science*, 2 vols., 2d ed. [Washington, D.C.: Harren Press, 1952], 1:lxxv). Spencer's secretary, Walter Troughton, has left us a description of the moment when Spencer finished dictating the last words of *Principles of Sociology*: "Rising slowly from his seat in the study . . . , his face beaming with joy, he extended his hand across the table and we shook hands on the auspicious event. 'I have finished the task I have lived for' was all he said, and then resumed his seat. The elation was only momentary and his features quickly resumed their customary composure" (quoted in Duncan, *The Life and Letters of Herbert Spencer*, p. 380).

[95] *An Autobiography*, 2:374.

later books," Spencer added sadly that this was "a fact well illustrating the worth of current criticism."[96]

Well before the publication of the final volume of *Principles of Sociology*, Spencer was already a philosopher-scientist of distinction and acclaim. His books were widely read, and his views commanded attention if not complete acceptance. His *Principles of Biology* was, to Spencer's considerable surprise, adopted as a textbook at Oxford. His *Principles of Psychology* was used by William James at Harvard as the text for a course entitled "Physiological Psychology," and his *First Principles* was used by James in another of his courses, "The Philosophy of Evolution."[97] Spencer had, in short, become a towering figure in the world of learning. Yet no one could have been less academic. His formal schooling lasted only three months. He never took an examination, never taught a course, and rarely lectured. In 1867 when asked to become a candidate for the professorship of Mental Philosophy and Logic at University College, London, Spencer declined. Between 1871 and 1903 he was offered no fewer than thirty-two academic honors — memberships, fellowships, honorary degrees, professorships, presidencies — but with one or two exceptions he refused them all.[98]

Spencer never married, and in his later years, mostly because of ill health, he became something of a recluse. He had very few close friends and seldom ventured out except to meetings of the X Club (which included such other distinguished members as Huxley, Tyndall, Hooker, and Lubbock) and to the Athenaeum Club, where he read the current periodicals and played billiards,[99] almost his only recreation.

Spencer lived for seven years beyond the publication of the third volume of *Principles of Sociology*. During these years he spent what little time he was able to work writing on a wide variety of controversial issues ranging from the Boer War to the proposed adoption of the metric system in England. He died on December 8, 1903, at the age of eighty-three, and, following the provisions of his will, he was cremated. At the interment of his ashes an admirer, Shyamaji Krishnavarma, announced that he was donating the sum of £1,000 to Oxford University for the establishment of a Herbert Spencer Lectureship in his memory. The first lecture was

---

[96] *Ibid.*, 1:365.

[97] Ralph Barton Perry, *The Thought and Character of William James*, 2 vols. (Boston: Little, Brown, & Co., 1935), 1:475, 482. James was, however, an antagonist of Spencer, especially on the issues of free will vs. determinism and the Great Man vs. the culture process.

[98] *An Autobiography*, 2:146–47; Duncan, *The Life and Letters of Herbert Spencer*, pp. 588–89.

[99] Spencer is often credited — erroneously — with originating the remark that excelling at billiards is a sure sign of a misspent youth (see Duncan, *The Life and Letters of Herbert Spencer*, pp. 298–99).

delivered in 1905 by Frederic Harrison, and a lecture has been given annually since.[100]

Before examining some of the theories set forth in *Principles of Sociology* something should be said of Spencer's intellectual attributes. There is no question that he possessed one of the great minds of the nineteenth century. Indeed, Frederick Barnard, president of Columbia University at the time that Spencer's influence was at its height, wrote of him: "As it seems to me, we have in Herbert Spencer not only the profoundest thinker of our time, but the most capacious and most powerful intellect of all time."[101]

Spencer's ability to penetrate, to analyze, to clarify, and to summarize seldom failed to impress. Once, after reading proofs of *First Principles*, Huxley wrote to Spencer: "It seems as if all the thoughts in what you have written were my own, and yet I am conscious of the enormous difference your presentation of them makes in my intellectual state. One is thought in the state of hemp yarn, and the other in the state of rope."[102]

Undoubtedly Spencer's most striking intellectual characteristic was his capacity for generalization and synthesis. Francis Galton, for example, wrote that "the power of Spencer's mind that I most admired, was that of widely founded generalizations."[103] C. Lloyd Morgan, echoing Galton's thought, referred to Spencer as "a thinker whose powers of generalization have seldom been equalled and perhaps never surpassed."[104]

On occasion, though, Spencer's theorizing went beyond what the evidence would allow, and an amusing account of such an instance has been left to us by Galton.

At Spencer's request, Galton once showed him through his laboratory, and described the pioneer work he was doing on finger prints as a means of identification.

"Then I spoke of the failure to discover the origin of these patterns [whorls, loops, etc.], and how the fingers of unborn children had been dissected to ascertain their earliest stages, and so forth. Spencer remarked that this was beginning in the wrong way; that I ought to consider the purpose the ridges had to fulfil, and to work backwards. Here, he said, it was obvious that the delicate mouths of the sudorific glands required the pro-

[100] *Ibid.*, p. 483.

[101] Quoted in Hofstadter, *Social Darwinism in American Thought*, p. 31. When a later president of Columbia University, Nicholas Murray Butler, remarked that "Philosophy begins where Spencer stops," Henry Holt, an admirer of Spencer, replied, "If so, God help Philosophy!" (Holt, *Garrulities of an Octogenarian Editor*, p. 317).

[102] Letter, September 3, 1860, in Leonard Huxley, *Life and Letters of Thomas Henry Huxley*, 1:229.

[103] Quoted in Duncan, *The Life and Letters of Herbert Spencer*, p. 502.

[104] "Mr Herbert Spencer's Biology," *Natural Science*, 13 (1898): 377–83, p. 377.

tection given to them by the ridges on either side of them, and therefrom he elaborated a consistent and ingenious hypothesis at great length.

"I replied that his arguments were beautiful and deserved to be true, but it happened that the mouths of the ducts did not run in the valleys between the crests, but along the crests of the ridges themselves. He burst into a good-humoured and uproarious laugh, and told me the famous story which I have heard from each of the other two who were present on the occurrence. Huxley was one of them. Spencer, during a pause in conversation at dinner at the Athenaeum, said, 'You would little think it, but I once wrote a tragedy.' Huxley answered promptly, 'I know the catastrophe.' Spencer declared it was impossible, for he had never spoken about it before then. Huxley insisted. Spencer asked what it was. Huxley replied, 'A beautiful theory, killed by a nasty, ugly little fact.' "[105]

Another of Spencer's prominent characteristics of mind was his originality and independence.[106] With few exceptions, the theories he elaborated he had also originated. In his sociological and anthropological writings Spencer cites the works of many authors, but, except for a few cases, what he derives from them are facts rather than ideas. His arguments were habitually supported with ethnographic and historical evidence rather than with scholarly opinion.

While Spencer was familiar with at least the major theoretical works of most of the other classical evolutionists — Tylor, Morgan,[107] Maine, McLennan, and Lubbock, for example — he rarely alludes to them, and when he does so, it is generally to disagree with their views. Intellectual independence of other proponents of evolutionary theory was indeed asserted by most of the nineteenth-century evolutionists. Tylor, for instance, specifically proclaimed the independence of his views on cultural evolution from those of Darwin and Spencer.[108]

The question of priority in enunciating a theory once led Tylor and Spencer to engage in a protracted debate. In reviewing the first volume of

[105] Francis Galton, *Memories of My Life* (New York: E. P. Dutton & Co., 1909), pp. 257–58. See also Spencer, *An Autobiography*, 1:403.

[106] ". . . there can be little doubt that for original productivity of mind Spencer is quite unequaled" (Becker and Barnes, *Social Thought from Lore to Science,* 1:665).

[107] In acknowledging receipt of a copy of *Ancient Society,* Spencer wrote to Morgan: "It would have been useful to me had I had it earlier, when I was treating of the social composition and of family arrangements. I doubt not that hereafter when I come to deal with political organization, I shall find much matter in it of value to me" (letter, July 19, 1877, quoted in Bernhard J. Stern, *Lewis Henry Morgan: Social Evolutionist,* [Chicago: University of Chicago Press, 1931], p. 108). However, Spencer never did cite this work in the two subsequent volumes of *Principles of Sociology,* nor can it be said that he adopted or elaborated any of the theories that Morgan set forth in it.

[108] *Primitive Culture,* 2 vols., 3d American ed. from the 2d English ed. (New York: Henry Holt & Co., 1889), pp. vii–viii.

Principles of Sociology, Tylor asserted that Spencer's discussion of animism "followed lines already traced" by Tylor himself in *Primitive Culture* and in earlier papers.[109] An exchange of letters between Spencer and Tylor followed in the pages of *Mind*[110] and *The Academy*[111] in which each writer attempted to substantiate his claim to priority and independence.[112]

In the end, replying to allegations of plagiarism, Spencer turned Tylor's own words against him, and the latter found no effective reply. Tylor had said:

". . . in its main principles, the theory [of animism] requires no great stretch of scientific imagination to arrive at it, inasmuch as it is plainly suggested by the savages themselves in their own accounts of their own religious beliefs. It is not too much to say that, given an unprejudiced student with the means (only of late years available) of making a thorough survey of the evidence, it is three to one that the scheme of the development of religious doctrine and worship he draws up will be an Animistic scheme."[113]

To this Spencer remarked wryly that "Mr. Tylor takes the one chance against three, and prefers to think that I did not draw the inferences myself, but plagiarized upon him."[114]

Let us now attempt a brief survey of some of Spencer's contributions to social science, especially those embodied in *Principles of Sociology*. One of the striking features of this work is the extensive documentation that underlies its generalizations. Volume I alone, in its revised edition, contains some 2,500 references to 455 works.[115]

The empirical evidence cited in *Principles of Sociology* is impressive not only in amount but also in scope. Spencer was a comparative sociologist in the fullest sense. He drew his facts from societies of all kinds — from hunting bands and horticultural tribes, from the chiefdoms of Polynesia and the kingdoms of Africa, from the civilizations of the classical world, of ancient America, and of western Europe. His extensive use of data from European history, for example, is particularly enlightening

[109] "Mr. Spencer's *Principles of Sociology*," *Mind*, 2 (1877): 141–56, p. 141.
[110] *Ibid.*, 415–19, 419–23, 423–29, 429.
[111] 2 (1877): 344, 367–68, 392, 416, 462.
[112] Spencer's position was that the idea of a human soul was the earliest supernatural belief entertained by man ("the ghost theory"), and that the notion of spirit was later extended beyond human beings to animals, plants, and inanimate objects. On the other hand, Spencer argued, Tylor's original theory was that of a primary "animism," that is, the attribution of spirits to animals, plants, and inanimate objects prior to — or at least no later than — their attribution to human beings.
[113] "Mr. Spencer's *Principles of Sociology*," p. 143.
[114] *Mind*, 2 (1877): 426.
[115] *An Autobiography*, 2:299.

and convincing, since by means of it he is able to illustrate evolutionary processes which, on the basis of ethnographic evidence alone, might appear purely conjectural.

It is well known that Spencer was first and foremost an evolutionist. What is not so generally recognized is that he was also a thoroughgoing functionalist. He saw social structures arising out of social functions. "There can be no true conception of a structure without a true conception of its function. To understand how an organization originated and developed, it is requisite to understand the need subserved at the outset and afterwards."[116] Elsewhere Spencer spoke of "the general law of organization that difference of functions entails differentiation and division of the parts performing them. . . ."[117] This principle he illustrated repeatedly, showing, for example, how military functions gave rise to elaborate military organizations among the Incas and the Spartans.[118] Indeed, much of *Principles of Sociology* is devoted to tracing the increased specialization of functions and the accompanying differentiation of structures, continually illustrating in this manner the close interrelationship between function, structure, and evolution.

More than any other writer of his time, Spencer made the English-speaking public familiar with the term "sociology,"[119] a word that he borrowed from Comte.[120]

Spencer himself coined the term "superorganic," which, following its use by Kroeber in his famous article "The Superorganic,"[121] came to be regarded as designating the unique and distinct elements in human behavior and therefore as synonymous with "culture." But by "superorganic" Spencer meant no more than what the term means literally: "super-organic"[122]—that is, something beyond the purely biological. To him the term was essentially equivalent to "social," and he included within its compass the behavior of bees, wasps, ants, rooks, beavers, and bison, as well as that of man.[123]

It has been argued that Spencer's notion of the superorganic not only failed to distinguish the cultural from the social but also that it hardly went beyond the organic itself. Durkheim maintained that Spencer "pre-

---

[116] *Principles of Sociology*, 3:3.

[117] *Ibid.*, 2:441.

[118] *Ibid.*, pp. 580–84.

[119] Speaking for his contemporaries among American sociologists, Charles Horton Cooley said, "most of us had never heard it before" ("Reflections upon the Sociology of Herbert Spencer," *American Journal of Sociology*, 26 [1920]: 129–45, p. 129).

[120] The word "sociology" was virtually the only thing Spencer ever acknowledged borrowing from Comte (*An Autobiography*, 1:445–46).

[121] *American Anthropologist*, 19 (1917): 163–213.

[122] Spencer always wrote the word with a hyphen.

[123] *Principles of Sociology*, 3d ed., 1:4–7.

sent[s] social life as a simple resultant of individual natures," and that he "does not see a reality *sui generis* in society, which exists by itself and by virtue of specific and necessary causes, . . . but he sees it as an arrangement instituted by individuals to extend individual life in length and breadth."[124] In "The Superorganic," Kroeber went further, arguing that "in spite of . . . [Spencer's] happy coinage of the term which has been prefixed as a title to the present essay, he did not adequately conceive of human society as holding a specific content that is non-organic."[125]

Here both Durkheim and Kroeber appear to overstate the case. Spencer never conceived of human society as simply an automatic response of human beings to a "social instinct." He consistently held that "social phenomena depend in part on the natures of the individuals and in part on the forces the individuals are subject to. . . ."[126] In fact he expressed the view that practical considerations involving enhanced survival lay at the root of human sociality. "Living together arose because, on the average, it proved more advantageous to each than living apart. . . ." And once in existence, social life was perpetuated because "maintenance of combination [of individuals in society] is maintenance of . . . conditions . . . more satisfactory [to] living than the combined persons would otherwise have."[127]

But if Spencer saw societies as something more than mere aggregations of individuals behaving instinctually, he nevertheless did not regard the behavior of social animals and that of man as sufficiently different to warrant making a categorical distinction between them. In the 2,100 pages of *Principles of Sociology* he almost never used the word "culture" to label "that complex whole which includes knowledge, belief, art, morals, laws [and] customs," although the term had already been given this definition by Tylor in his *Primitive Culture* in 1871.[128] Clearly, if human behavior was not conceived of as categorically distinct from subhuman behavior, then it was unnecessary to denote it with a special term.[129]

[124] *The Division of Labor in Society*, trans. George Simpson (Glencoe: Free Press, 1933), pp. 349, 342–43.

[125] *American Anthropologist*, 19 (1917): 188.

[126] *Principles of Sociology*, 3d ed. 1:14.

[127] *The Principles of Ethics*, vol. 1 (New York: D. Appleton & Co., 1904), p. 134.

[128] Exceptions occur in 2:568, and in 3:7.

[129] Spencer's failure to do so is partially to be explained by the fact that his evolutionism led him to emphasize continuity in nature rather than discontinuity. The idea of emergence, of qualitatively new and distinct levels of phenomena arising during the course of evolution, did not play a major role in Spencer's thinking. As a matter of fact, Spencer was, to a considerable extent, a reductionist, especially during his earlier years. Where possible, he sought to explain phenomena of higher levels in terms of the laws and principles of lower levels. For example, in an early work he wrote that "the actions of individuals depend on the laws of their natures; and their actions cannot be understood until these laws are understood. These laws, however,

While Spencer perceived this difference as one of degree rather than of kind, he nevertheless did not fail to be impressed by its enormous magnitude. He remarked that the "various orders of super-organic products [of human societies] . . . constitute an immensely-voluminous, immensely-complicated, and immensely-powerful set of influences,"[130] and maintained that these orders so transcend all others "in extent, in complication, in importance, as to make them relatively insignificant. . . ."[131]

It is possible that during his later years Spencer came closer to recognizing in culture a distinct order of reality. Thus, in the final edition of *First Principles*, which he revised three years before his death, he wrote: ". . . as fast as societies become large and highly organized they acquire such separateness from individual efforts as to give them a character of their own." As an example of this he noted: ". . . the prices of stocks, the rates of discount, the reported demand for this or that commodity . . . show us large movements and changes scarcely at all affected by the lives and deaths and deeds of persons."[132]

Spencer appears to have been the first writer to distinguish explicitly between growth and development.[133] But while this distinction was quickly recognized as of fundamental importance in biology and soon became well established in that science, it has been overlooked or ignored in cultural anthropology. His distinction between operative and regulative institutions has likewise failed to be adopted in social science despite the basic significance of the dichotomy it makes.

Spencer also proposed an objective classification of societies into simple, compound, doubly-compound, and trebly-compound, depending upon the number of levels of political integration.[134] Yet, as concerned as anthropologists have been with classifying societies, they have failed to take account of this scheme.

Spencer never thought of himself as a materialist; in fact he considered the section of *First Principles*, entitled "The Unknowable," to be a "repudia-

---

when reduced to their simplest expressions, prove to be corollaries from the laws of body and mind in general. Hence it follows, that biology and psychology are indispensable as interpreters of sociology" (*Education: Intellectual, Moral, and Physical*, pp. 70–71; see also *The Study of Sociology*, pp. 348, 349, 365).

[130] *Principles of Sociology*, 3d ed., 1:13–14.

[131] *Ibid.*, p. 7.

[132] *First Principles*, 6th ed., The Thinker's Library, No. 62 (London: Watts & Co., 1937), p. 197.

[133] "In ordinary speech, Development is often used as synonymous with Growth. It hence seems needful to say, that Development as here and hereafter used, means *increase of structure*, and not *increase of bulk*. It may be added, that the word Evolution, comprehending Growth as well as Development, is to be reserved for occasions when both are implied" (*The Principles of Biology*, 1:133 n.).

[134] *Principles of Sociology*, 3d ed., 1:551, 552, 554.

tion of materialism."[135] Moreover, in some of his other writings one can find passages which express an antimaterialistic position. For example, in *Principles of Psychology* he wrote: ". . . were we compelled to choose between the alternatives of translating mental phenomena into physical phenomena, or of translating physical phenomena into mental phenomena, the latter alternative would seem the more acceptable of the two."[136]

Nevertheless, despite repeated disclaimers, materialistic and mechanistic interpretations permeate much of Spencer's writings. For him the universe consists basically of matter and energy, and is to be explained in these terms. In the concluding paragraph of *First Principles*, for example, Spencer wrote: ". . . the deepest truths we can reach, are simply statements of the widest uniformities in our experiences of the relations of Matter, Motion, and Force. . . ."[137] Indeed, most of the chapters of this book are devoted to an explanation of phenomena of every kind in terms of laws which are, at bottom, expressions of physical principles. The entire process of evolution, in fact, Spencer saw as deducible from the principle he called the Persistence of Force,[138] which is essentially equivalent to the conservation of energy.

In view of this mechanistic attitude on Spencer's part it is not surprising that he should have perceived the fundamental importance of the harnessing of energy for the evolution of culture. He was, indeed, one of the first writers to recognize this relationship explicitly.

"Based as the life of a society is on animal and vegetal products, and dependent as these are on the light and heat of the Sun, it follows that the changes wrought by men as socially organized, are effects of forces having a common origin with those which produce all . . . other orders of changes. . . . Not only is the energy expended by the horse harnessed to the plough, and by the labourer guiding it, derived from the same reservoir as is the energy of the cataract and the hurricane; but to this same reservoir are traceable those subtler and more complex manifestations of energy which humanity, as socially embodied, evolves. . . . Whatever takes place in a society results either from the undirected physical energies around, from these energies as directed by men, or from the energies of the men themselves."[139]

So novel must this interpretation have seemed at the time that Spencer

[135] *An Autobiography,* 2:75.
[136] *The Principles of Psychology,* 2 vols., 3d ed. (New York: D. Appleton & Co., 1896), 1:159.
[137] *First Principles,* p. 497.
[138] *Ibid.,* p. 361.
[139] *Ibid.,* pp. 198, 197.

felt compelled to add: "The assertion is startling but it is an unavoidable deduction."[140]

Spencer was one of the earliest social scientists to argue that culture change can be better explained in terms of the operation of socio-cultural forces than as the result of the actions of important men.[141] He first questioned the Great Man Theory of history in "The Social Organism" in 1860,[142] and attacked it outright in *The Study of Sociology*,[143] where he challenged Carlyle's dictum that "universal history . . . is at bottom the history of the great men who have worked here." In *Principles of Sociology* he returned to the issue again, showing, for example, how unrealistic it was to think of Lycurgus as having originated the Spartan constitution.[144] He also argued that it was not the personal initiative of Cleisthenes that brought about democratic organization in Athens, but rather that his political reorganization was prompted by, and was successful only because of, the large numbers of non-clan-organized persons living in that city at the time.[145] Later, in a very perceptive and original passage, Spencer showed that a militant society fosters the notion of personal causation in social affairs and thus prevents or retards the rise of the scientific notion of impersonal causation.[146]

Spencer went beyond stating that great men did not create social and political institutions. He held that their rise was not a matter of the exercise of deliberate choice at all: "Society is a growth and not a manufacture."[147] He denied that recognition of "advantages or disadvantages of this or that arrangement furnished motives for establishing or maintaining" a form of government, and argued instead that "conditions and not intentions determine."[148] Correspondingly, he saw the values and attitudes of a society, not as shaping but as reflecting the society: ". . . for every society, and for each stage in its evolution, there is an appropriate mode of feeling and thinking. . . . [which] is a function of the social structure. . . ."[149]

If there is one theme that stands out above all others in *Principles of*

[140] *Ibid.*, p. 198.

[141] He was also one of the writers to do so most effectively. According to Sidney Hook, "the extent to which Spencer's views have influenced modern social thought on the subject of the great man and his environment can hardly be exaggerated" (*The Hero in History* [New York: Humanities Press, 1950], p. 67 n.).

[142] *The Westminster Review*, 73 (1860): 90–121.

[143] Pp. 26–33.

[144] 2:376 n.

[145] 2:424–25.

[146] 2:599–600.

[147] *Principles of Sociology*, 3:321; also in "The Social Organism," *The Westminster Review* 73 (1860): 93.

[148] *Principles of Sociology*, 2:395.

[149] *The Study of Sociology*, p. 356.

Sociology, it is the importance of war in the development of complex society.[150] Spencer wrote:

"We must recognize the truth that the struggles for existence between societies have been instrumental to their evolution. Neither the consolidation and re-consolidation of small groups into large ones; nor the organization of such compound and doubly-compound groups; nor the concomitant developments of those aids to a higher life which civilization has brought; would have been possible without inter-tribal and inter-national conflicts."[151]

Spencer's recognition of the contribution of warfare to political evolution is particularly noteworthy since he found war "everywhere and always hateful."[152] His sympathies lay with the peacefulness and personal freedom he thought characteristic of industrially organized societies, and he detested the belligerence and regimentation typical of the militant state.

Although he assigned first place to war among the factors molding social organization, Spencer did not fail to appreciate the effect of environment on institutions. He demonstrated, for example, that rugged, mountainous terrain, like that of Greece, fostered the development of confederacies rather than of strongly centralized monarchies.[153] Elsewhere he showed how the relative abundance and distribution of pasture affected the size and mobility of pastoral nomad groups.[154]

The importance of economic factors in the origin and development of customs and institutions likewise did not go unperceived by Spencer. His analysis of the role of commerce and industry in widening the base of Anthenian oligarchy and thus paving the way for Greek democracy is brilliant and convincing.[155] His thesis that representative government and the democratic state result from an increased concentration of people in towns, from the rise of artisan and merchant classes, and from expanding production and commerce is also illuminating and persuasive.[156]

Like other evolutionists of the period, Spencer gave considerable attention to the problem of primal human social organization. Many pages of *Principles of Sociology* are devoted to the development of marriage and forms of the family, early concepts of property, and the like. With regard

---

[150] One of the few social scientists who gives evidence of having carefully read Spencer's discussion of the subject and of having recognized the correctness and importance of his analysis, is Pitirim Sorokin. See his *Contemporary Sociological Theories* (New York: Harper & Bros., 1928), pp. 344–46.

[151] *Principles of Sociology,* 2:241.

[152] "The Filiation of Ideas," in Duncan, *The Life and Letters of Herbert Spencer,* pp. 533–76, p. 569.

[153] *Principles of Sociology,* 2:373, 395.

[154] *Ibid.,* 1st ed. 1:724–25.

[155] *Ibid.,* 2:391–93, 424–25.

[156] *Ibid.,* pp. 421–23.

to most of these issues, Spencer's thinking was sound and surprisingly modern. For example, he did not believe that the incest taboo was innate.[157] Nor did he believe that promiscuity was the earliest stage of human marriage. "I do not think the evidence warrants us in concluding that promiscuity ever existed in an unqualified form. . . ."[158] He did, however, think that promiscuity was at one time common and that the resulting difficulty in establishing paternity led to the early reckoning of kinship in the female line.[159] Nevertheless, Spencer had reservations on this point, and stressed the fact that even in primitive matrilineal societies a term for "father" always existed, implying a consciousness of male kinship.[160]

Spencer likewise did not believe that polygyny had preceded monogamy, but that monogamy went back as far as any form of marriage.[161] "Always the state of having two wives," he wrote, "must be preceded by the state of having one. And the state of having one must in many cases continue because of the difficulty of getting two where the surplus of women is not great."[162]

Similarly, Spencer rejected the notion of an early stage of "primitive communism" applying to all forms of property. While recognizing that everywhere "land is jointly held by hunters because it cannot be otherwise held,"[163] he noted that among contemporary primitive peoples, tools, utensils, weapons, and ornaments are habitually owned individually, and concluded that a similar situation probably prevailed in very early times.

Although it is acknowledged to be one of the classics of nineteenth-century anthropology, Spencer's *Principles of Sociology*, unlike some of his other writings, went almost unread. It never became as well known as either Tylor's *Primitive Culture* or Morgan's *Ancient Society*, the other two great classics of cultural evolutionism. Undoubtedly its bulk — more than two thousand pages — its precise and somewhat monotonous style,[164] and its superabundance of illustrations all contributed to its failure to gain a large audience.

Lack of firsthand familiarity with this and other of Spencer's works did not, however, prevent anthropologists and sociologists from expressing decided opinions about what they took to be his theories and ideas. When the reaction against cultural evolutionism began, certain errors and in-

[157] *Ibid.*, 3d ed., 1:619.
[158] *Ibid.*, 1st ed., 1:662.
[159] *Ibid.*, 3d ed., 1:647.
[160] *Ibid.*, p. 648.
[161] *Ibid.*, p. 679.
[162] *Ibid.*, p. 680.
[163] *Ibid.*, p. 645.
[164] Spencer once remarked: "Though my style is lucid, it has, as compared with some styles, a monotony that displeases me. There is a lack of variety in its verbal forms . . ., and there is a lack of vigour in its phrases" (*An Autobiography*, 2:451).

adequacies attributed to nineteenth-century evolutionists generally were ascribed to Spencer in particular. Let us examine some of these criticisms and see to what extent they are justified.

One objection frequently leveled at Spencer, during his lifetime as well as afterward, was that he was too deductive.[165] To this charge Spencer himself replied that "though by some I am characterized as an *a priori* thinker, it will be manifest to any one who does not set out with an *a priori* conception of me, that my beliefs, when not suggested *a posteriori*, are habitually verified *a posteriori*."[166] Spencer maintained the same position repeatedly. Thus in *Principles of Sociology* he wrote, "before deductive interpretation of the general truths must come inductive establishment of them."[167]

However, Spencer did regard deduction as permitting a more complete and coherent explanation of things than induction, and therefore employed it wherever he could. "Though my conclusions have usually been reached inductively, yet I have never been satisfied without finding how they could be reached deductively."[168] In his last published essay he wrote: ". . . leaving a truth in an inductive form is, in a sense, leaving its parts with loose ends; and the bringing it to a deductive form is, in a sense, uniting its facts as all parts of one fact."[169]

Yet Spencer's deductions about human society are not deductions pure and simple. They are derived from broad principles which are themselves inductions from a range of phenomena wider than the realm of human social life. Such propositions are therefore not a priori in any ultimate sense. Spencer held that the only basis of knowledge was experience, and that from sufficiently broad experience certain general principles could be formulated which, in turn, could be found exemplified in instances not included in the original induction.

Principles of Sociology cannot seriously be called a work of deduction. Far from being abstract and excogitative, it is, as we have noted, a veritable catalog of ethnographic data. Indeed, when it appeared, it was criticized for being "overweighted by illustrative facts"[170] that is to say, for being too inductive. In defending himself against this charge, Spencer wrote:

---

[165] For example, Melville J. Herskovits wrote that "Spencer was as complete a deductionist as science has ever seen . . ." ("A Genealogy of Ethnological Theory," in *Context and Meaning in Cultural Anthropology*, ed. Melford E. Spiro, pp. 403–15 [New York: Free Press, 1965], p. 408).

[166] *An Autobiography*, 1:304–5.

[167] *Principles of Sociology*, 3d ed., 1:443.

[168] *An Autobiography*, 2:431.

[169] "The Filiation of Ideas," in Duncan, *The Life and Letters of Herbert Spencer*, pp. 533–76, p. 535.

[170] *Principles of Sociology*, 2:vi.

"If sociological generalizations are to pass out of the stage of opinion into the stage of established truth, it can only be through extensive accumulations of instances: the inductions must be wide if the conclusions are to be accepted as valid. Especially while there continues the belief that social phenomena are not the subject-matter of a Science, it is requisite that the correlations among them should be shown to hold in multitudinous cases."[171]

The inductive foundations for the generalizations contained in *Principles of Sociology* were, as we have seen, the data compiled for *Descriptive Sociology*. In his *Autobiography* Spencer revealed the effect of this compilation of facts on the development of his ideas. When he began working on the first volume of *Principles* in 1874, "the *Descriptive Sociology* had been for seven years in progress; making me gradually acquainted with more numerous and varied groups of social phenomena, *disclosing truths of unexpected kinds, and occasionally obliging me to abandon some of my preconceptions.*"[172] Thus, contrary to common assertion,[173] facts were for Spencer more than mere illustrations for theories already conceived.

Not only was Spencer keenly aware of the necessity for induction in his own work, he was also critical of other writers for not being sufficiently inductive in theirs. He criticized Sir Henry Maine, for example, for failing to make "the area of induction wide enough."[174] Maine, Spencer contended, slighted the literature on contemporary primitive peoples, relying too heavily instead on evidence from "Barbarous" peoples like the early Germans in formulating his generalizations. Spencer likewise assailed the mythologists of his day, citing the "misinterpretation caused by analysis of the phenomena from above downwards [that is, deduction from advanced societies to simpler ones], instead of synthesis of them from below upwards [that is, induction from simpler to more complex societies]."[175]

The most common attack made against Spencer, at least during his lifetime, probably was that over his treatment of society as an organism. This criticism was voiced especially by American sociologists, notably Lester Ward and Franklin Giddings. Spencer felt that he had been misinterpreted on this point and took pains to defend himself from those "who assert that I base Sociology upon Biology . . . and who continue to do this though I have pointed out that the analogy does not in either case furnish

[171] *Ibid.*

[172] *An Autobiography,* 2:274–75; emphasis mine.

[173] Alexander Goldenweiser, for example, wrote that Spencer's assistants "scanned the available literature on human society for illustrations of customs and beliefs which Spencer had already constructed and arranged into stages . . ." ("Cultural Anthropology," in *History and Prospects of the Social Sciences,* ed. Harry Elmer Barnes, pp. 210–54 [New York: Alfred A. Knopf, 1925], pp. 214–15).

[174] *Principles of Sociology,* 1st ed., 1:714.

[175] *Ibid.,* pp. 712–13.

a foundation, but merely yields illumination."[176] In a chapter entitled "Qualifications and Summary" in Volume I of *Principles of Sociology* he stated:

"Here let it once more be distinctly asserted that there exist no analogies between the body politic and a living body, save those necessitated by that mutual dependence of parts which they display in common. Though, in foregoing chapters, sundry comparisons of social structures and functions to structures and functions in the human body, have been made, they have been made only because structures and functions in the human body furnish familiar illustrations of structures and functions in general."[177]

An even more trenchant statement of the basis and limitations of this analogy occurs in Spencer's article "Specialized Administration."

The "analogies between the phenomena presented in a physically coherent aggregate forming an individual, and the phenomena presented in a physically incoherent aggregate of individuals [forming a society] . . . cannot be analogies of a visible or sensible kind; but can only be analogies between the systems, or methods, of organization. Such analogies as exist result from the one unquestionable community between the two organizations: there is in both a mutual dependence of parts. This is the origin of all organization; and determines what similarities there are between an individual organism and a social organism."[178]

In the section of *Principles* entitled "The Inductions of Sociology" Spencer introduces countless parallels between biological organisms and human societies. One may weary of these examples, but few would deny that they are apt and instructive. Those who remain skeptical should bear in mind Spencer's remark, "I have used the analogies elaborated, but as a scaffolding to help in building up a coherent body of sociological inductions. Let us take away the scaffolding: the inductions will stand by themselves."[179]

Let us now consider some of the criticisms that have been made of Spencer's evolutionism. To begin with, it has been asserted that Spencer conceived of evolution as a kind of unfolding of immanences.[180] Spen-

---

[176] "The Filiation of Ideas," in Duncan, *The Life and Letters of Herbert Spencer*, pp. 533–76, pp. 570 n.–71 n.

[177] 3d ed.,1:592.

[178] *Fortnightly Review* 16 (1871): 627–54, p. 634. To this passage Spencer added: "Of course the similarities thus determined, are accompanied by transcendent differences, determined . . . by the unlikenesses of the aggregates" (p. 634).

[179] *Principles of Sociology*, 3d ed., 1:592–93.

[180] The sociologist E. A. Ross went so far as to avoid the very word "evolution," preferring to use "change" in its place because, "the term 'evolution,' while very properly calling attention to the *continuity* of social change . . . is apt to convey the idea that the series of social changes is the mere unfolding of characters pre-formed in the very germ or bud of society. This is misleading and should be avoided" (*Foundations of Sociology*, 5th ed. [New York: Macmillan Co., 1915], p. 185). For a similar conception of evolution see R. M. MacIver, *Society* (New York: Rinehart & Co., 1937), pp. 409–10.

cer, however, specifically rejected this interpretation of the process. Early in the first volume of *Principles of Sociology* he wrote: "Evolution is commonly conceived to imply in everything an intrinsic tendency to become something higher. This is an erroneous conception of it. In all cases it is determined by the cooperation of inner and outer factors."[181] And again, near the end of Volume III, he said, "Evolution does not imply a latent tendency to improve, everywhere in operation."[182]

Spencer and other classical evolutionists have also been criticized for holding to a theory of *rectilinear* evolution — that is to say, of viewing cultural evolution as proceeding in a straight line, without interruptions or regressions. On this point Spencer once again expressed himself unequivocally: "As with organic evolution, so with super-organic evolution. Though, taking the entire assemblage of societies, evolution may be held inevitable . . . yet it cannot be held inevitable in each particular society, or even probable."[183] And elsewhere we read: "While the current degradation theory is untenable, the theory of progression, in its ordinary form, seems to me untenable also. . . . It is possible, and, I believe, probable, that retrogression has been as frequent as progression."[184]

A closely related criticism, and the one most often lodged against nineteenth-century evolutionists, is that they believed in *unilinear* evolution.[185] Let us see where Spencer stood on this issue.

"Like other kinds of progress, social progress is not linear but divergent and re-divergent. Each differentiated product gives origin to a new set of differentiated products. While spreading over the Earth mankind have found environments of various characters, and in each case the social life fallen into, partly determined by the social life previously led, has been partly determined by the influences of the new environment; so that the multiplying groups have tended ever to acquire differences, now major and now minor: there have arisen genera and species of societies."[186]

Thus Spencer was not only not a unilinear evolutionist, he was not even a linear evolutionist. As the foregoing passage shows, he saw evolution as a process of successive branchings in which increased heterogeneity goes hand in hand with increased adaptation. This view of evolution stands in direct contrast to that which sees evolution as a single series of stages.[187]

---

[181] *Principles of Sociology*, 3d ed., 1:95.
[182] *Ibid.*, 3:609.
[183] *Ibid.*, 3d ed., 1:96.
[184] *Ibid.*, p. 95.
[185] Howard Becker, for instance, spoke of "the notion of unilinear stage-sequences attributable to social evolutionists such as Spencer, Morgan, and the like" ("Historical Sociology," in *Contemporary Social Theory*, ed. Harry Elmer Barnes and Howard Becker, pp. 491–542 [New York: D. Appleton-Century Co., 1940], p. 525).
[186] *Principles of Sociology*, 3:331.
[187] "The early exponents of the [comparative] method [in anthropology] are accused of having assumed that all institutions take their rise in one form and pass through a

Indeed, the more one reads of *Principles of Sociology* the clearer it becomes that Spencer was far more concerned with *process* than with *stages*.

This emphasis on process, in which societies were seen in large measure as developing in response to their particular social and natural environments, at times placed Spencer in opposition to other social evolutionists of his day. Unlike McLennan, for example, Spencer did not consider polyandry to have been a "transitional form once passed through by every race."[188] Forms of marriage, he maintained, did not succeed each other in a uniform and universal sequence of stages, but, instead, arose as adaptations to specific cultural and ecological conditions.[189] Thus, Spencer accounted for the assumed spread of polygyny at the expense of monogamy by pointing out that where warfare is prevalent and the loss of warriors high, a society with polygyny would be better able to replenish its numbers than a monogamous one and therefore would be in a stronger position than societies which remained monogamous. Clearly, this is a *functional* rather than a *stadial* explanation.[190]

In stressing process instead of stages, Spencer differed also from Morgan. From Tylor, Spencer can be distinguished by the fact that Tylor was more interested in the origin, distribution, and diffusion of discrete culture traits, whereas Spencer rarely concerned himself with the history of particular traits, but instead directed his attention to the operation of sociocultural systems. Spencer was, in short, more of a scientist and less of a culture historian than Tylor.[191] This difference in attitude helps to explain why Spencer always called his study sociology rather than anthropology. At the time he was writing, the term "anthropology" connoted something of a particularistic and antiquarian interest in artifacts, customs, and beliefs rather than the systematic, scientific study of society to which Spencer was completely dedicated.

Considerable reproach has been directed at Spencer for his advocacy of "Social Darwinism." It is true that he espoused all of the ideas generally associated with this philosophy, and that in fact the doctrine might more accurately be known as "Social Spencerism." However, it is usually overlooked that "Social Darwinism" is not a single doctrine but three distinguishable doctrines, which need to be considered and evaluated separately.

---

series of graded changes in a uniform direction. On a re-reading of Tylor and Spencer I find it hard to discover on what these charges are based" (Morris Ginsberg, *Evolution and Progress* [London: William Heinemann, 1961], p. 198).

[188] *Principles of Sociology*, 3d ed., 1:660.

[189] *Ibid.*, 1st ed., 1:678–81.

[190] *Ibid.*, p. 690; but cf. pp. 695–96.

[191] "When compared with the first volume of Spencer's *Sociology*, Tylor's classic work, *Primitive Culture*, was less a contribution to evolutionary thinking than an attempt to trace the life history of a particular belief, namely, animism" (Alexander Goldenweiser, "Cultural Anthropology," in *The History and Prospects of the Social Sciences*, ed. Harry Elmer Barnes, pp. 210–54 [New York: Alfred A. Knopf, 1925], p. 216).

Social Darwinism, in one of its forms, holds that the rapid elimination of "unfit" individuals from society through the operation of natural selection will benefit the race biologically, and that consequently the state should do nothing to relieve the condition of the poor and the needy, who are presumed to be the less fit.

A second form of Social Darwinism maintains that a society's economic system works best if each individual is allowed to seek his own private interests, and that therefore the state should not intervene in the economy except to enforce contracts and to see to it that no one infringes upon the rights of others. In the ensuing competition, the theory runs, the fittest business enterprises and economic institutions will survive and the unfit will go under. This is the familiar doctrine of laissez faire, fortified with the principle of natural selection. Spencer's defense of this view in *Social Statics* and later in *The Man versus the State* made him its leading exponent in the nineteenth century. The doctrine proved to be very congenial to private entrepreneurs and captains of industry, especially in the United States, where capitalism was vigorous and expanding and opposed any interference by the state.[192]

About both of these forms of Social Darwinism the same can be said: since they proclaim what ought (or ought not) to be done, they are tenets of political philosophy rather than scientific statements. As such, one may freely reject them as being out of harmony with one's own feelings and opinions without thereby discrediting any aspect of Spencer's sociology.

A third position held by Spencer, which is sometimes included under Social Darwinism, does involve a factual proposition, and so does fall within the realm of social science. As we have already noted, Spencer maintained that natural selection operated not only on biological organisms but on societies of organisms as well,[193] and that the chief mode of operation of this form of natural selection was through warfare. Those societies best able to endure this mode of competition survived and flourished, while those less able to do so declined or disappeared. To the agency of warfare Spencer attributed the rise of the state as well as the elaboration of many features of social, political, economic, and religious organi-

[192] Acting in consonance with this philosophy, the U.S. Supreme Court in 1905 declared unconstitutional a New York State statute establishing maximum working hours for bakers. In one of his famous dissents from the majority opinion, Justice Oliver Wendell Holmes objected that "The Fourteenth Amendment does not enact Mr. Herbert Spencer's *Social Statics*" (William Seagle, *The History of Law* [New York: Tudor Publishing Co., 1946], p. 417 n.).

[193] Tylor had already noted the operation of this process among culture traits. He argued that "the institutions which can best hold their own in the world gradually supersede the less fit ones, and that this incessant conflict determines the general resultant course of culture" (*Primitive Culture*, 2 vols. [London: John Murray, 1871], 1:62).

zation. Several of the chapters of *Principles of Sociology* marshal in impressive array the evidence of the profound effect that war has had on societies.

Modern social scientists are often reluctant to attribute to warfare any constructive role, but a cold reading of history shows that to a very considerable degree large and complex nations have acquired their size and organization through war. Even William James, an archfoe of Spencer on most issues, felt compelled to admit that "if we think how many things besides frontiers of states the wars of history have decided, we must feel some respectful awe, in spite of all the horrors. Our actual civilization, good and bad alike, has had past wars for its determining condition."[194]

Another charge commonly leveled against English cultural evolutionists of the latter half of the nineteenth century is that they were "Victorian" in their ideas and attitudes. From this accusation Spencer can be partially cleared although not completely exonerated. Ethnocentrism does at times appear in his writings. In discussing wife lending, for example, he refers to the "prevalence in rude societies of practices which are to us in the highest degree repugnant";[195] and in speaking of societies in which brother-sister and other close consanguineal unions occurred, he spoke of "the most degraded relations of the sexes."[196]

But Spencer maintained that no matter how aberrant or repellent one might find the beliefs and practices of primitive peoples, they could and should be viewed objectively when they became the subject matter of science. He expressed this view repeatedly, perhaps most succinctly in the following passage:

". . . trustworthy interpretations of social arrangements imply an almost passionless consciousness. Though feeling cannot and ought not to be excluded from the mind when otherwise contemplating them, yet it ought to be excluded when contemplating them as natural phenomena. . . ."[197]

It is true that Spencer considered monogamy to be the highest form of marriage, but not because it was the form that prevailed in Victorian England, as has so often been alleged. On the contrary, he offered a number of ingenious and plausible explanations — all of them functional rather than moral — to account for the supposed superiority of monogamy over

[194] *The Philosophy of William James*, ed. Horace M. Kallen (New York: Modern Library, n.d.), p. 265. In the same vein, Karl Pearson wrote that "the intense struggle which is ever waging between society and society . . . is an . . . important factor of evolution and one too often forgotten when the doctrines of Darwin are applied to human history" (*The Grammar of Science*, Everyman's Library [London: J. M. Dent & Sons, 1937], p. 306).

[195] *Principles of Sociology*, 3d ed., 1:616.

[196] *Ibid.*, p. 619; see also p. 612.

[197] *Ibid.*, 2:232; see also *An Autobiography*, 2:253–54.

other forms of marriage under certain conditions.[198] These explanations were consistent with his general belief that social institutions develop as responses to the prevailing conditions of existence rather than from any inherent tendency toward perfection.

Spencer proved to be something less than a proper Victorian on yet another score. Whereas a typical Englishman of the Victorian period presumably was ready to support the policies of queen and country, right or wrong, Spencer repeatedly and outspokenly criticized the militancy and colonialism that Great Britain was then manifesting. He noted and decried the tendency for the flag to follow the Bible — "the aggressive tendencies displayed by us all over the world — sending, as pioneers, missionaries of 'the religion of love,' and then picking quarrels with native races and taking possession of their lands."[199] England's instigation of the Boer War at the close of the nineteenth century saddened Spencer and led him to remark, more than once, "I am ashamed of my country."[200]

It is evident then that Spencer's sociology, especially his evolutionism, has been criticized in ways that were unjustified and misinformed. To redress the balance on Spencer, however, does not mean that we must overlook his errors or deny his shortcomings. In fact, let us now consider a few of Spencer's postulates which today must be regarded as inadequate or unsound.

To the end of his life Spencer staunchly supported the theory of the inheritance of acquired characteristics. As late as the 1890's, although old and in ill health, he engaged in a protracted controversy with August Weismann over this issue.[201] Spencer's belief in the transmission of acquired traits, while essentially a biological notion, did not leave his social theory unaffected. He argued, for example that "the constitutional energy needed for continuous labour, without which there cannot be civilized life . . . is an energy to be acquired only by inherited modifications slowly accumulated."[202]

Spencer cannot be classed among the believers in the "psychic unity" of man. Certain peculiar traits found among some peoples of the world he attributed to innate psychological differences. For example, he spoke of "the independence of the Greek nature," which he thought to be "unlike Oriental natures," and held that it was because of this nature that the ancient Greeks "did not readily submit to the extension of sacerdotal control over civil affairs."[203] Very much impressed by the honesty attributed

[198] *Principles of Sociology*, 3d ed., 1:681–85.
[199] *An Autobiography*, 2:375.
[200] Duncan, *The Life and Letters of Herbert Spencer*, p. 449.
[201] In the pages of the *Contemporary Review* for 1893 and 1894.
[202] *Principles of Sociology*, 2:270.
[203] *Ibid.*, 3:265.

by travelers and officials to peoples like the Todas, Santals, and Sowrahs, he remarked: "Surviving remnants of some primitive races in India have natures in which truthfulness seems to be organic."[204] Speaking more generally, Spencer maintained that "the innate feelings and aptitudes of a race have large shares in determining the sizes and cohesions of the social groups it forms. . . ."[205]

Yet, despite the pronouncements quoted above, Spencer only rarely resorted to the use of inherent psychological differences to explain different forms of culture. In the vast majority of cases, the explanations of culture he proposed were ones that involved the interplay of cultural and environmental factors.

It should also be borne in mind that Spencer did not believe that "racial" differences involved any truly fundamental differences in psychology. He did not impute to preliterate peoples anything like a prelogical mentality. On the contrary, he declared that "the laws of thought are everywhere the same: . . . given the data as known to him, the primitive man's inference is the reasonable inference."[206]

His treatment of society as an organism, on the one hand, and his championing of laissez faire and political individualism, on the other, led Spencer into a serious inconsistency.[207] He had of course recognized that among biological organisms the interests of the parts are subordinate to the interests of the whole, since only in this way can the organism achieve the integration and cohesion necessary for survival. But when it came to social organisms — to human societies specifically — the basis of Spencer's argument changed. He began by noting that while in biological organisms only the organism as a whole is capable of consciousness and therefore of experiencing pleasure and pain, in a social organism this ability resides in each of the individuals which constitute its units.[208] This, Spencer declared, is why "the welfare of citizens cannot rightly be sacrificed to some supposed benefit of the State; but why, on the other hand, the State is to be maintained solely for the benefit of citizens." Consequently, he con-

---

[204] *Ibid.*, 2:234.

[205] *Ibid.*, p. 366; see also p. 368.

[206] *Ibid.*, 3d ed., 1:100.

[207] This inconsistency has struck a number of writers. Ernest Barker, for example, observed of Spencer that "the fundamental confusion which he never surmounts is due to the fact that the *a priori* conceptions of individual rights with which he starts do not and cannot accord with the organic and evolutionary conceptions of the State which he attains . . ." (*Political Thought in England 1848–1914*, 2d ed. [London: Oxford University Press, 1959], p. 71).

[208] Already we find here an assertion that is subject to dispute: ". . . social consciousness — consciousness of the interests and processes of the group — is as centralized in society as personal consciousness is in the individual; very few of us have any 'sense of the state' " (Will Durant, *The Story of Philosophy*, new rev. ed. [Garden City: Garden City Publishing Co., 1933], p. 430).

cluded, in human society "the corporate life must . . . be subservient to the lives of the parts, instead of the lives of the parts being subservient to the corporate life."[209]

This argument did not long go unchallenged. Huxley, in an article entitled "Administrative Nihilism," insisted that if Spencer's analogy between biological and social organisms had any value, it should be followed here as well, and that if one did so, just the opposite conclusion emerged:

"The fact is that the sovereign power of the body thinks for the physiological organism, acts for it, and rules the individual components with a rod of iron. Even the blood corpuscles can't hold a public meeting without being accused of 'congestion' — and the brain, like other despots whom we have known, calls out at once for the use of sharp steel against them. . . . Hence, if the analogy of the body politic with the body physiological counts for anything, it seems to me to be in favour of a much larger amount of governmental interference than exists at present. . . ."[210]

Another telling attack on Spencer's views on this issue was made by Benjamin Kidd, who argued:

". . . in social evolution, the interests of the individual, *qua* individual, ceases to be a matter of first importance. It is by development in the individual of the qualities which will contribute most to the efficiency of society, that natural selection will in the long run produce its distinctive results. . . ." This evolutionary process involves "the subordination of the interests of the units to the higher corporate efficiency of society." Moreover, Kidd maintained:

"Societies in which the individuals resist the process quickly reach the limits of their progress, and have to give way in the struggle for existence before others . . . in which the process of subordination continues to be developed. In the end it is the social organizations in which the interests of the individual are most effectively included in and rendered subservient to the interests of society . . . that, from their higher efficiency, are naturally selected."

Concluding his critique of Spencer, Kidd remarked: ". . . for the evolutionist, whose great triumph it has been to reveal to us the principles of natural selection in universal operation throughout life elsewhere, to have to regard them as suspended in human society would be an absurd anticlimax."[211]

---

[209] "The Social Organism," in Herbert Spencer, *Essays: Scientific, Political, and Speculative*, 1:265–307 (New York: D. Appleton & Co., 1892), pp. 276–77, 277.

[210] *Fortnightly Review*, 16 (1871): 525–43, p. 535.

[211] "Sociology," *Encyclopaedia Britannica*, 11th ed., 1911, 25:322–31, pp. 325, 326, 325, 326. Frank H. Hankins argued along the same lines: ". . . no society has ever recognized the validity of Spencer's argument as to individual rights or the supremacy of private ends. Every social group sets itself up as supreme; in all matters of group

And so it would. But curiously enough, in most of his concrete analyses of the process of social evolution, Spencer did perceive that the interests of the individual were subordinated to the interests of society as a whole. In fact, in a number of places he states this quite categorically. For example, at one point he wrote: "Habitual war, requiring prompt combination in the actions of parts, necessitates subordination. Societies in which there is little subordination disappear, and leave outstanding those in which subordination is great. . . ."[212]

From a detailed examination of his sociological and anthropological writings, Spencer re-emerges as a towering figure in the history of social science. If Auguste Comte gave to the science of society its name and manifesto, it was Herbert Spencer who laid its foundations and began to erect its superstructure. Yet many social scientists today regard Spencer as having only historical significance. They concede that his impact on the social science of his time was very great but argue that this influence soon began to wane and has now disappeared altogether.

Careful analysis, however, does not sustain this interpretation. Although Spencer's direct influence on contemporary anthropology and sociology must be regarded as small, his indirect influence is by no means negligible. Let us try to piece together the threads of this influence.

We have already noted that Spencer's writings were what opened Sumner's eyes to a systematic science of society along comparative lines. In *Folkways*, his most influential work, Sumner followed these lines, drawing extensively on material from non-Western societies. Sumner's foremost student and successor at Yale was Albert G. Keller, who undertook the task of completing Sumner's even more broadly comparative treatise, *The Science of Society*. In part at least this work was inspired by and modeled after Spencer's *Principles of Sociology*.[213]

Like his teacher, Keller was a strong proponent of the comparative study of society, and in turn was extraordinarily successful in imparting this approach to his students. Among the latter, Maurice R. Davie, George P. Murdock, Leo W. Simmons, John W. M. Whiting, and Clellan S. Ford have made significant contributions to systematic cross-cultural research. The Human Relations Area Files, which may be regarded as a lineal descend-

concern it insists on regulating and subordinating individual action and claims; and in times of group crisis the individual finds that he has no rights which he can successfully assert against group domination" ("Sociology," in *History and Prospects of the Social Sciences*, ed. Harry Elmer Barnes, pp. 255–332, p. 300).

[212] *Principles of Sociology*, 3d ed., 1:595; see also 2:600–601.

[213] Bernhard J. Stern, "William Graham Sumner," *Encyclopedia of the Social Sciences*, 14:463–64 (New York: Macmillan Co., 1934), p. 463.

ant of Spencer's *Descriptive Sociology*,[214] was a culmination of their work in systematic studies of this type.

Another important link between Spencer and contemporary social science is Émile Durkheim. While it is perfectly true that in his treatment of Spencer in *The Rules of Sociological Method*[215] and again in *The Division of Labor in Society*[216] Durkheim criticized Spencer far more than he extolled him, it is undeniable that Durkheim learned a great deal from Spencer and that he built extensively on what he learned. The idea of a comparative sociology, an interest in typologies of human society, concern with the division of labor, discussions of structure, function, aggregation, and integration, all of which are found in Durkheim, occurred earlier in works by Spencer with which Durkheim was thoroughly familiar. Even when Durkheim found himself at odds with Spencer, the latter's views often served him as a springboard to launch his own new interpretation.

That Durkheim in turn exerted considerable influence on A. R. Radcliffe-Brown is well known, since the latter freely acknowledged it.[217] Moreover, the core of what Radcliffe-Brown derived from Durkheim — the concept of society as a functioning system, susceptible of scientific study — was in essence what Durkheim derived from Spencer. Radcliffe-Brown's exposure to Spencer's ideas was not, however, entirely secondhand. In a few of his articles Radcliffe-Brown discussed some of Spencer's ideas in a way that indicated not only direct familiarity but also appreciation and approval.[218]

Some of Radcliffe-Brown's followers and successors have remained aware of Spencer's pioneer contribution to social anthropology. E. E. Evans-Pritchard, for example, has noted: "Spencer's use of the biological analogy of organism . . . did much to further the use of the concepts of structure and function in social anthropology, for he constantly stressed that at every stage in social evolution there is a necessary functional inter-

---

[214] According to Murdock, *Descriptive Sociology* "clearly foreshadowed the development of the present Human Relations Area Files" ("Sociology and Anthropology," in *For a Science of Social Man*, ed. John Gillin, pp. 14–21 [New York: Macmillan Co., 1954], p. 16; see also Harris E. Starr, *William Graham Sumner* [New York: Henry Holt & Co., 1925], p. 345).

[215] Edited by George E. G. Catlin (Glencoe: Free Press, 1950). See especially pp. 20–21, 80–83.

[216] Translated by George Simpson, (Glencoe: Free Press, 1933). See especially pp. 149–50, 193–94, 200–06, 257, 260, 263–66.

[217] A. R. Radcliffe-Brown, *Method in Social Anthropology*, ed. M. N. Srinivas (Chicago: University of Chicago Press, 1958), p. 161.

[218] *Structure and Function in Primitive Society* (Glencoe: Free Press, 1952), pp. 7–9; *Method in Social Anthropology*, pp. 178–89. In the latter work Radcliffe-Brown describes himself as "one who has all his life accepted the hypothesis of social evolution as formulated by Spencer as a useful working hypothesis in the study of human society" (p. 189).

dependence between the institutions of a society. . . ."[219] And C. Daryll Forde has remarked that Spencer "formulated with admirable comprehensiveness the scientific validity and methodological importance . . . of the comparative method for isolating and estimating the effects of various factors determining particular features of [social] morphology and function."[220]

But even those few living social anthropologists of the older generation who give evidence of having delved into Spencer's works often show themselves to be insufficiently acquainted with his views on major anthropological issues. Thus, in the same article quoted above, Forde also states that Spencer drew only upon primitive societies for his factual evidence, that he held to an a priori and unilinear scheme of social evolution, and that he posited an evolution of marriage which began with promiscuity and proceeded through polyandry, polygyny, and wife capture before arriving at monogamy.[221] As we have seen, none of these assertions is true.

In view of the lack of full familiarity with Spencer's work displayed by older social anthropologists, it is not surprising that when they in turn began to train students, the latter should have failed to receive a full and accurate picture of Spencer's role in the development of functionalism. Indeed, it is probably safe to say that younger social anthropologists today have little awareness of the ultimate derivation of functional analysis in their science.

One of the few social scientists to trace the academic pedigree of functionalism back to its source was Howard Becker, who wrote: "From Spencer to Durkheim to British and British-influenced functional anthropology to structural-functional sociology in the United States' . . . may not be a drastic distortion of the actual 'who to whom' sequence."[222]

Although the thread of functionalism leading from Spencer to the present was never broken, the same cannot be said for Spencer's other great contribution to ethnology, the principle of evolution. The wide acceptance which cultural evolution enjoyed during the nineteenth century did not long withstand the sharp attacks made against it in the twentieth. In a few places it managed to survive for a time. At Yale, for example, it was kept alive by A. G. Keller, but only as a rather narrow type of Darwinian social evolution — "adaptation to environment, secured through the operation of variation, selection, and transmission. . . ."[223] Spencerian evo-

[219] *Social Anthropology* (London: Cohen & West, 1951), p. 51.
[220] "The Anthropological Approach in Social Science," *The Advancement of Science*, 4 (1947): 213–24, p. 217.
[221] *Ibid.*, p. 217.
[222] "Anthropology and Sociology," in *For a Science of Social Man*, ed. John Gillin, pp. 102–59, p. 132.
[223] Albert Galloway Keller, *Societal Evolution* (New York: Macmillan Co., 1915), p. 329.

lution, the broad-gauged process of increasing heterogeneity, integration, and definiteness, Keller found of no use and abandoned.[224] Once anti-evolutionism became firmly entrenched in cultural anthropology, its sway remained unbroken for decades.

But, as Leslie A. White observed, "The concept of evolution has proved itself to be too fundamental and fruitful to be ignored indefinitely by anything calling itself a science."[225] With White himself playing a leading role, evolutionism has once more reasserted itself as a valid and fruitful way of looking at and organizing the data of cultural anthropology. While in his own discussions of evolution White has stressed the contributions of Morgan and Tylor more than those of Spencer, the terms in which he describes the evolutionary process – as an increase in structural differentiation and functional specialization – are essentially Spencerian.

In characterizing his approach to evolution, White has rejected the label of "neo-evolutionism," maintaining, that it is a continuation and extension of the evolutionism that began in the nineteenth century and not something categorically new and different.[226] Marshall Sahlins and Elman Service, former students of White and like him evolutionists, acknowledge in their own contribution to cultural evolutionary theory that "our dependence has been largely on the classical evolutionists, Herbert Spencer, Lewis H. Morgan, and E. B. Tylor."[227]

In a recent major work in the related field of art history, Thomas Munro has made a very careful study of Spencer's evolutionism, particularly as it applies to the development of the arts. He concludes his analysis by saying that Spencer's theory of evolution in art "retains some valid and suggestive ideas. As a whole, it has not been disproved, and in many respects it has been confirmed by later research. . . . After a hundred years, the trend of opinion seems to be turning again toward a more favorable estimate of Spencer."[228]

Perhaps the most striking confirmation of the resurgence that Spencer's evolutionism appears to be undergoing is provided by Talcott Parsons, who, as we have noted, once concurred in the opinion that Spencer was dead. Writing in the introduction to a reissue of Spencer's *The Study of Sociology*, Parsons said: "Whereas evolutionary thinking in the social sciences has suffered more than a generation of eclipse since Spencer's day,

[224] *Ibid.*, pp. 7–8.
[225] Foreword to *Evolution and Culture*, ed. Marshall D. Sahlins and Elman R. Service, pp. v–xii (Ann Arbor: University of Michigan Press, 1960), p. vii.
[226] *The Evolution of Culture* (New York: McGraw-Hill Book Co., 1959), p. ix.
[227] *Evolution and Culture*, pp. 123–24.
[228] *Evolution in the Arts and Other Theories of Culture History* (Cleveland: Cleveland Museum of Art, 1963), p. 72.

there is currently a notable revival going on, which again testifies to Spencer's importance."[229]

Thus we find, unexpectedly perhaps, that three of the anthropological approaches being pursued most vigorously today — cross-cultural comparisons, functionalism, and evolutionism — have roots that lead back to Herbert Spencer.

We come now to the problem of fixing Spencer's position in the intellectual firmament. Was he a philosopher or was he a scientist? Much difference of opinion has surrounded this question. According to A. L. Kroeber, although Spencer employed "masses of data compiled from science, [he] remains a philosopher."[230] Similarly, Harris E. Starr, the biographer of William Graham Sumner, speaks of Spencer as "a philosopher rather than a scientist."[231] And Jacques Barzun not only failed to look upon Spencer as a scientist, but even contended that he had an "unscientific mind."[232] On the other hand, J. Arthur Thomson, himself a distinguished biologist, regarded Spencer as "one of the most scientific minds that ever lived,"[233] and Raphael Meldola, also a biologist, said of Spencer's work that "no more heroic and . . . successful attempt to wield single-handed such a mighty weapon as unified science has ever been made."[234]

What, then, are we to conclude? Spencer's own discussion of the matter provides an enlarged perspective for deciding the issue.

Spencer saw the task of philosophy as the complete integration of knowledge. But this knowledge he viewed as consisting of empirical generalizations derived from the various sciences. Each science integrated its own findings, but it remained for the philosopher to integrate the findings of all the sciences.

"The truths of Philosophy . . . bear the same relation to the highest scientific truths, that each of these bears to lower scientific truths. As each widest generalization of Science comprehends and consolidates the narrower generalizations of its own division; so the generalizations of Philosophy comprehend and consolidate the widest generalizations of Science."[235]

Thus, as Spencer envisioned him, the philosopher was in a very real sense a "super-scientist," and philosophy became, as Youmans noted, "a

[229] (Ann Arbor: University of Michigan Press, 1961), p. viii.

[230] *Configurations of Culture Growth* (Berkeley and Los Angeles: University of California Press, 1944), p. 98.

[231] *William Graham Sumner*, p. 394.

[232] *Darwin, Marx, Wagner: Critique of a Heritage*, rev. 2d ed. (Garden City: Doubleday & Co., 1958), p. 110.

[233] *Herbert Spencer* (London: J. M. Dent & Co., 1906), p. vii.

[234] *Evolution: Darwinian and Spencerian*, The Herbert Spencer Lecture for 1910 (Oxford: Clarendon Press, 1910), p. 13.

[235] *First Principles*, 6th ed. The Thinker's Library, No. 62 (London: Watts & Co., 1937), p. 115.

science of the sciences."[236] In *First Principles* Spencer did in fact attempt that complete integration of the findings of science which he considered to be the true function of philosophy, so that by his own definition we may properly regard him as a philosopher. Of course, he was a philosopher of science rather than a speculative philosopher. "Herbert Spencer's significance in the history of English thought," observed F. S. C. Schiller, "depends on his position as the philosopher of the great scientific movement of the second half of the 19th century. . . ."[237]

Placing Spencer in the ranks of philosophy, however, does not thereby exclude him from the lists of science. We have already seen that he made many original and significant contributions to the sciences, especially to biology and sociology. It is sometimes alleged that Spencer cannot be called a scientist because he did not himself discover or establish the facts which he brought together and integrated. But surely this is not a valid criterion for debarring anyone from the status of a scientist. As Henry Holt remarked in dismissing this argument, it would be like requiring a cook to grub his own potatoes![238]

Another writer who insisted that it was perfectly legitimate to consider Spencer's broad syntheses as falling within the realm of science was Edward Youmans, who observed:

"In the scientific world, the accumulation of facts has outstripped the work of valid generalization. For, while men of moderate ability can observe, experiment, and multiply details in special departments, it requires men of breadth to arrange them into groups, to educe principles and arrive at comprehensive laws. The great mass of scientific specialists, confined to their departments, and little trained to the work of generalization, are apt to regard lightly the logical processes of science, and to decry mere theorizing. . . . They forget that facts of themselves are not science, and only become so by being placed in true relations, and that the function of the thinker is therefore supreme. . . . [In science] the work of organizing facts and establishing general truths is, after all, just as much a specialty as that of observation or experiment. . . ."[239]

But Spencer was a scientist in the more restricted as well as in the larger sense. The idea that he disdained observation and experimentation, that in fact they were alien to his nature, a notion which has grown commonplace by repetition, is dispelled by the facts. Being primarily a synthesizer

[236] "Herbert Spencer and the Doctrine of Evolution," *Popular Science Monthly*, 6 (1874–75): 20–48, p. 42.

[237] "Herbert Spencer," *Encyclopaedia Britannica*, 11th ed., 1911, 25:634–37, p. 635; Philipp Frank, in his *Modern Science and Its Philosophy*, refers to Spencer as "the leader of nineteenth-century British empiricism" (Cambridge: Harvard University Press, 1949), p. 302.

[238] *Garrulities of an Octogenarian Editor*, p. 53.

[239] "Herbert Spencer and the Doctrine of Evolution," pp. 44–45.

and integrator of knowledge, Spencer could hardly have been expected to pursue his work in the field or in a laboratory, but he was nevertheless a careful observer of nature and sometimes supplemented his observations with experiments. It is not generally known but over a period of years Spencer studied the circulation of fluids in plants experimentally and reached some important conclusions on the subject. The distinguished botanist Joseph Hooker, whom Spencer consulted about these researches, was struck by "the skill with which he seized upon facts and suggestions and the patient labour with which he sought to test them by experiments, often devised and carried out by himself unaided."[240]

Of course, not all of Spencer's work fell either into the category of philosophy (in the sense of integrated knowledge) or into the category of science. Much of it was devoted to questions of politics and ethics, and later critics have generally chosen to stress Spencer's political and ethical writings to the neglect of his scientific works. In the article about Spencer in the *Encyclopedia of the Social Sciences*, for example, C. E. M. Joad restricts himself to discussing Spencer's political theories, virtually ignoring his evolutionism and sociology.[241] Even Harry Elmer Barnes, whose long chapter on Spencer in his *Introduction to the History of Sociology* might well have been expected to focus on Spencer's contribution to historical sociology, lays heavy emphasis on his individualism and his espousal of laissez faire.[242]

Thus fate has not dealt equitably with Herbert Spencer. His illuminating and synthesizing ideas we find, as Fiske noted, "running like the weft through all the warp of modern thought,"[243] yet with scarcely a recollection of their source.[244] On the other hand, those ideas of Spencer's now regarded as erroneous or outdated are still remembered as having come from his pen.

In this Introduction we have dealt primarily with Spencer's contributions to anthropology and sociology. But important as these are, it would

[240] Joseph Hooker to Raphael Meldola, October 14, 1910, quoted in Meldola, *Evolution: Darwinian and Spencerian*, p. 44. Spencer's botanical researches were published under the title "On Circulation and the Formation of Wood in Plants" in *The Transactions of the Linnean Society*, 25 (1866): 405–29.

[241] 14:295–96 (New York: Macmillan Co., 1934).

[242] "Herbert Spencer and the Evolutionary Defense of Individualism," pp. 110–37 (Chicago: University of Chicago Press, 1948).

[243] John Fiske, *Excursions of an Evolutionist* (Boston: Houghton Mifflin & Co., 1894), p. 181.

[244] In discussing Herbert Spencer's collection of essays on *Education*, published in 1861, Helen Keller observed: "It is the highest praise that can be bestowed upon this treatise, that it seems now a book of obvious if not commonplace philosophy, whereas, when it was published, it was recognized as revolutionary in the extreme" (*The Reader's Digest of Books*, new and greatly enlarged ed. [New York: Macmillan Co., 1945], p. 250).

be unfair to judge him on the basis of them alone. Spencer also formulated concepts and principles which advanced the frontiers of understanding in zoology, botany, and psychology,[245] and he contributed as well to such fields as astronomy[246] and education.[247]

Still, were we to choose the greatest achievement of Spencer's life, it would not be his contribution to any single science. Instead, it would be his formulation and application of the principle of evolution to all of them. This principle has justly been called "the most momentous idea in the history of human thought"[248] and "the most effective organon of thought that the world has known."[249] And it was Herbert Spencer who first developed the concept in its comprehensive form, who applied it to the entire range of cosmic phenomena, and who, in the words of Ralph Barton Perry, "was the appointed vehicle by which the general idea of evolution . . . was implanted in the minds" of the general public.[250]

In popular opinion it is the name of Charles Darwin that is most often associated with the idea of evolution. But Darwin applied it only to organic life. It was Spencer — whom Darwin himself called "the great expounder of the principle of Evolution"[251] — who extended the principle to include all of nature.

Armed with this master concept, Spencer deliberately set out to survey all orders of phenomena and to show that they were the determinate results of the operation of a universal process. To this endeavor he brought an extraordinary command of scientific fact and unrivaled powers of synthesis and generalization. With great architectonic skill and sustained force of execution he took up the data of one science after another and welded them into a fully integrated structure. No other thinker before or since

[245] "Herbert Spencer was the first to make a thoroughgoing attempt to describe the evolution of mind" (William McDougall, "Mental Evolution," in *Evolution in the Light of Modern Knowledge, A Collective Work*, pp. 321–54 [London: Blackie & Son, 1925], pp. 336–37).

[246] Alfred Russel Wallace, *Man's Place in the Universe* (London: Chapman & Hall, 1908), pp. 102–3.

[247] The remarkable breadth of his interests and the scope of his ideas and innovations can best be gathered from a passage in his *Autobiography*. They ranged "from a doctrine of State-functions to a levelling-staff; from the genesis of religious ideas to a watch escapement; from the circulation in plants to an invalid bed; from the law of organic symmetry to planing machinery; from principles of ethics to a velocimeter from a metaphysical doctrine to a binding-pin; from a classification of the sciences to an improved fishing-rod joint; from the general Law of Evolution to a better mode of dressing artificial flies" (2:435–36).

[248] Harry Elmer Barnes, *An Intellectual and Cultural History of the Western World* (New York[?]: Cordon Co., 1937), p. 959.

[249] Thomson, *Herbert Spencer*, pp. 143–44.

[250] *The Thought and Character of William James*, 2 vols. (Boston: Little, Brown, & Co., 1935), 1:474.

[251] *The Expression of the Emotions in Man and Animals*, 2d ed., ed. Francis Darwin (London: John Murray, 1890), p. 10.

has known so large a proportion of the scientific knowledge of his day, or has pieced it together into so all-embracing and rigorous a system. Details have been added and here and there conceptions and interpretations have been changed; but by and large the picture of the cosmos we have today, in which evolution is seen as giving rise successively to inorganic, organic, and superorganic phenomena, was first presented to the world by Herbert Spencer.

CHAPTER 1

WHAT IS A SOCIETY?

This question has to be asked and answered at the outset. Until we have decided whether or not to regard a society as an entity, and until we have decided whether, if regarded as an entity, a society is to be classed as absolutely unlike all other entities or as like some others, our conception of the subject matter before us remains vague.

It may be said that a society is but a collective name for a number of individuals. Carrying the controversy between nominalism and realism into another sphere, a nominalist might affirm that just as there exist only the members of a species while the species considered apart from them has no existence, so the units of a society alone exist, while the existence of the society is but verbal. Instancing a lecturer's audience as an aggregate which by disappearing at the close of the lecture proves itself to be not a thing but only a certain arrangement of persons, he might argue that the like holds of the citizens forming a nation.

But without disputing the other steps of his argument, the last step may be denied. The arrangement, temporary in the one case, is permanent in the other; and it is the permanence of the relations among component parts which constitutes the individuality of a whole as distinguished from the individualities of its parts. A mass broken into fragments ceases to be a thing, while conversely, the stones, bricks, and wood, previously separate, become the thing called a house if connected in fixed ways.

Thus we consistently regard a society as an entity because, though formed of discrete units, a certain concreteness in the aggregate of them is implied by the general persistence of the arrangements among them throughout the area occupied. And it is this trait which yields our idea of a society. . . .

But now, regarding a society as a thing, what kind of thing must we call it? It seems totally unlike every object with which our senses acquaint us. Any likeness it may possibly have to other objects cannot be manifest to perception, but can be discerned only by reason. If the constant relations among its parts make it an entity, the question arises whether these constant relations among its parts are akin to the constant relations among the parts of other entities. Between a society and anything else, the only conceivable resemblance must be one due to *parallelism of principle in the arrangement of components.*

1

There are two great classes of aggregates with which the social aggregate may be compared — the inorganic and the organic. Are the attributes of a society in any way like those of a non-living body — or are they in any way like those of a living body? or are they entirely unlike those of both?

The first of these questions needs only to be asked to be answered in the negative. A whole of which the parts are alive, cannot, in its general characters, be like lifeless wholes. The second question, not to be thus promptly answered, is to be answered in the affirmative. The reasons for asserting that the permanent relations among the parts of a society are analogous to the permanent relations among the parts of a living body we have now to consider.

CHAPTER 2

A SOCIETY IS AN ORGANISM

When we say that growth is common to social aggregates and organic aggregates we do not thus entirely exclude community with inorganic aggregates. Some of these, as crystals, grow in a visible manner, and all of them, on the hypothesis of evolution, have arisen by integration at some time or other. Nevertheless, compared with things we call inanimate, living bodies and societies so conspicuously exhibit augmentation of mass that we may fairly regard this as characterizing them both. Many organisms grow throughout their lives and the rest grow throughout considerable parts of their lives. Social growth usually continues either up to times when the societies divide or up to times when they are overwhelmed.

Here, then, is the first trait by which societies ally themselves with the organic world and substantially distinguish themselves from the inorganic world.

It is also a character of social bodies, as of living bodies, that while they increase in size they increase in structure. Like a low animal, the embryo of a high one has few distinguishable parts, but while it is acquiring greater mass, its parts multiply and differentiate. It is thus with a society. At first the unlikenesses among its groups of units are inconspicuous in number and degree, but as population augments, divisions and subdivisions become more numerous and more decided. Further, in the social organism as in the individual organism, differentiations cease only with that completion of the type which marks maturity and precedes decay.

Though in inorganic aggregates also, as in the entire solar system and in each of its members, structural differentiations accompany the integrations, yet these are so relatively slow and so relatively simple, that they may be disregarded. The multiplication of contrasted parts in bodies politic and in living bodies is so great that it substantially constitutes another common character which marks them off from inorganic bodies.

This community will be more fully appreciated on observing that progressive differentiation of structures is accompanied by progressive differentiation of functions.

The divisions, primary, secondary, and tertiary, which arise in a developing animal, do not assume their major and minor unlikenesses to no purpose. Along with diversities in their shapes and compositions go diver-

3

sities in the actions they perform: they grow into unlike organs having unlike duties. Assuming the entire function of absorbing nutriment at the same time that it takes on its structural characters, the alimentary system becomes gradually marked off into contrasted portions, each of which has a special function forming part of the general function. A limb, instrumental to locomotion or prehension, acquires divisions and subdivisions which perform their leading and their subsidiary shares in this office.

So is it with the parts into which a society divides. A dominant class arising does not simply become unlike the rest, but assumes control over the rest; when this class separates into the more and the less dominant, these again begin to discharge distinct parts of the entire control. With the classes whose actions are controlled it is the same. The various groups into which they fall have various occupations: each of such groups also, within itself, acquiring minor contrasts of parts along with minor contrasts of duties.

And here we see more clearly how the two classes of things we are comparing distinguish themselves from things of other classes, for such differences of structure as slowly arise in inorganic aggregates are not accompanied by what we can fairly call differences of function.

Why in a body politic and in a living body these unlike actions of unlike parts are properly regarded by us as functions, while we cannot so regard the unlike actions of unlike parts in an inorganic body, we shall perceive on turning to the next and most distinctive common trait.

Evolution establishes in them both, not differences simply, but definitely connected differences — differences such that each makes the others possible. The parts of an inorganic aggregate are so related that one may change greatly without appreciably affecting the rest. It is otherwise with the parts of an organic aggregate or of a social aggregate. In either of these, the changes in the parts are mutually determined, and the changed actions of the parts are mutually dependent. In both, too, this mutuality increases as the evolution advances. The lowest type of animal is all stomach, all respiratory surface, all limb. Development of a type having appendages by which to move about or lay hold of food can take place only if these appendages, losing power to absorb nutriment directly from surrounding bodies, are supplied with nutriment by parts which retain the power of absorption. A respiratory surface to which the circulating fluids are brought to be aerated can be formed only on condition that the concomitant loss of ability to supply itself with materials for repair and growth is made good by the development of a structure bringing these materials.

Similarly in a society. What we call with perfect propriety its organization, necessarily implies traits of the same kind. While rudimentary, a society is all warrior, all hunter, all hut-builder, all tool-maker: every part fulfils for itself all needs. Progress to a stage characterized by a permanent army can go on only as there arise arrangements for supplying that army with food, clothes, and munitions of war by the rest. If here the population occupies itself solely with agriculture and there with mining — if these manufacture goods while those distribute them — it must be on condition that in exchange for a special kind of service rendered by each part to other parts, these other parts severally give due proportions of their services.

This division of labor, first dwelt on by political economists as a social phenomenon, and thereupon recognized by biologists as a phenomenon of living bodies, which they called the "physiological division of labor," is that which in the society, as in the animal, makes it a living whole. Scarcely can I emphasize enough the truth that in respect of this fundamental trait a social organism and an individual organism are entirely alike. When we see that in a mammal arresting the lungs quickly brings the heart to a stand, that if the stomach fails absolutely in its office all other parts by-and-by cease to act, that paralysis of its limbs entails on the body at large death from want of food or inability to escape, that loss of even such small organs as the eyes deprives the rest of a service essential to their preservation, we cannot but admit that mutual dependence of parts is an essential characteristic. And when, in a society, we see that the workers in iron stop if the miners do not supply materials, that makers of clothes cannot carry on their business in the absence of those who spin and weave textile fabrics, that the manufacturing community will cease to act unless the food-producing and food-distributing agencies are acting, that the controlling powers, governments, bureaus, judicial officers, police, must fail to keep order when the necessaries of life are not supplied to them by the parts kept in order, we are obliged to say that this mutual dependence of parts is similarly rigorous. Unlike as the two kinds of aggregate otherwise are, they are alike in respect of this fundamental character, and the characters implied by it.

How the combined actions of mutually dependent parts constitute life of the whole, and how there hence results a parallelism between social life and animal life, we see still more clearly on learning that the life of every visible organism is constituted by the lives of units too minute to be seen by the unaided eye.

An undeniable illustration is furnished by the strange order *Myxomycetes*. The spores or germs produced by one of these forms become ciliated monads which, after a time of active locomotion, change into shapes like those of amoebae, move about, take in nutriment, grow, multiply by fission. Then these amoeba-form individuals swarm together, begin to coalesce into groups, and these groups to coalesce with one another, making a mass sometimes barely visible, sometimes as big as the hand. This *plasmodium*, irregular, mostly reticulated, and in substance gelatinous, itself exhibits movements of its parts like those of a gigantic rhizopod, creeping slowly over surfaces of decaying matters, and even up the stems of plants. Here, then, union of many minute living individuals to form a relatively vast aggregate in which their individualities are apparently lost but the life of which results from combination of their lives, is demonstrable. . . .

The relation between the lives of the units and the life of the aggregate has a further character common to the two cases. By a catastrophe the life of the aggregate may be destroyed without immediately destroying the lives of all its units, while, on the other hand, if no catastrophe abridges it, the life of the aggregate is far longer than the lives of its units.

In a cold-blooded animal, ciliated cells perform their motions with perfect regularity long after the creature they are part of has become motionless. Muscular fibers retain their power of contracting under stimulation. The cells of secreting organs go on pouring out their product if blood is artificially supplied to them. And the components of an entire organ, as the heart, continue their cooperation for many hours after its detachment.

Similarly, arrest of those commercial activities, governmental coordinations, etc., which constitute the corporate life of a nation may be caused, say by an inroad of barbarians, without immediately stopping the actions of all the units. Certain classes of these, especially the widely diffused ones engaged in food-production, may long survive and carry on their individual occupations.

On the other hand, the minute living elements composing a developed animal severally evolve, play their parts, decay, and are replaced, while the animal as a whole continues. In the deep layer of the skin, cells are formed by fission which, as they enlarge, are thrust outwards, and, becoming flattened to form the epidermis, eventually exfoliate, while the younger ones beneath take their places. Liver-cells, growing by imbibition of matters from which they separate the bile, presently die, and their vacant seats are occupied by another generation. Even bone, though so dense and seemingly inert, is permeated by blood vessels carrying materials to replace old components by new ones. And the replacement, rapid in some tissues and in others slow, goes on at such rate that during the continued existence of the entire body each portion of it has been many times over produced and destroyed.

Thus it is also with a society and its units. Integrity of the whole as of each large division is perennially maintained, notwithstanding the deaths of component citizens. The fabric of living persons which, in a manufacturing town, produces some commodity for national use, remains after a century as large a fabric, though all the masters and workers who a century ago composed it have long since disappeared. Even with minor parts of this industrial structure the like holds. A firm that dates from past generations, still carrying on business in the name of its founder, has had all its members and employees changed one by one, perhaps several times over, while the firm has continued to occupy the same place and to maintain like relations with buyers and sellers. Throughout we find this. Governing bodies, general and local, ecclesiastical corporations, armies, institutions of all orders down to guilds, clubs, philanthropic associations, etc., show us a continuity of life exceeding that of the persons constituting them. Nay, more. As part of the same law, we see that the existence of the society at large exceeds in duration that of some of the compound parts. Private unions, local public bodies, secondary national institutions, towns carrying on special industries, may decay, while the nation, maintaining its integrity, evolves in mass and structure.

In both cases, too, the mutually dependent functions of the various divisions, being severally made up of the actions of many units, it results that these units dying one by one, are replaced without the function in which they share being sensibly affected. In a muscle, each sarcous element wearing out in its turn, is removed and a substitution made while the rest carry on their combined contractions as usual; the retirement of a public official or death of a shopman, perturbs inappreciably the business of the department, or activity of the industry, in which he had a share.

Hence arises in the social organism, as in the individual organism, a life of the whole quite unlike the lives of the units, though it is a life produced by them.

From these likenesses between the social organism and the individual organism we must now turn to an extreme unlikeness. The parts of an animal form a concrete whole, but the parts of a society form a whole which is discrete. While the living units composing the one are bound together in close contact, the living units composing the other are free, are not in contact, and are more or less widely dispersed. How, then, can there be any parallelism? . . .

Though coherence among its parts is a prerequisite to that cooperation by which the life of an individual organism is carried on, and though the members of a social organism, not forming a concrete whole, cannot maintain cooperation by means of physical influences directly propagated from part to part, yet they can and do maintain cooperation by another agency. Not in contact, they nevertheless affect one another through intervening spaces, both by emotional language and by the language, oral and written, of the intellect. For carrying on mutually dependent actions it is requisite that impulses, adjusted in their kinds, amounts, and times, shall be conveyed from part to part. This requisite is fulfilled in living bodies by molecular waves that are indefinitely diffused in low types and in high types are carried along definite channels (the function of which has been significantly called *internuncial*). It is fulfilled in societies by the signs of feelings and thoughts conveyed from person to person, at first in vague ways and only through short distances, but afterwards more definitely and through greater distances. That is to say, the internuncial function, not achievable by stimuli physically transferred, is nevertheless achieved by language — emotional and intellectual.

That mutual dependence of parts which constitutes organization is thus effectually established. Though discrete instead of concrete, the social aggregate is rendered a living whole. . . .

Summary

Let us now . . . sum up the reasons for regarding a society as an organism.

It undergoes continuous growth. As it grows, its parts become unlike: it exhibits increase of structure. The unlike parts simultaneously assume activities of unlike kinds. These activities are not simply different, but their differences are so related as to make one another possible. The reciprocal aid thus given causes mutual dependence of the parts. And the mutually dependent parts, living by and for one another, form an aggregate constituted on the same general principle as is an individual organism. The analogy of a society to an organism becomes still clearer on learning that every organism of appreciable size is a society, and on further learning that in both, the lives of the units continue for some time if the life of the aggregate is suddenly arrested, while if the aggregate is not destroyed by violence, its life greatly exceeds in duration the lives of its units. Though the two are contrasted as respectively discrete and concrete, and though there results a difference in the ends subserved by the organization, there does not result a difference in the laws of the organization: the required mutual influences of the parts, not transmissible in a direct way, being, in a society, transmitted in an indirect way.

Having thus considered in their most general forms the reasons for regarding a society as an organism, we are prepared for following out the comparison in detail.

CHAPTER 3

SOCIAL GROWTH

Societies, like living bodies, begin as germs — originate from masses which are extremely minute in comparison with the masses some of them eventually reach. That out of small wandering hordes have arisen the largest societies, is a conclusion not to be contested. The implements of prehistoric peoples, ruder even than existing savages use, imply absence of those arts by which alone great aggregations of men are made possible. Religious ceremonies that survived among ancient historic races pointed back to a time when the progenitors of those races had flint knives, and got fire by rubbing together pieces of wood, and must have lived in such small clusters as are alone possible before the rise of agriculture.

The implication is that by integrations, direct and indirect, there have in course of time been produced social aggregates a million times in size the aggregates which alone existed in the remote past. Here, then, is a growth reminding us, by its degree, of growth in living bodies.

Between this trait of organic evolution and the answering trait of super-organic evolution, there is a further parallelism: the growths in aggregates of different classes are extremely various in their amounts.

Glancing over the entire assemblage of animal types, we see that the members of one large class, the *Protozoa*, rarely increase beyond the microscopic size with which every higher animal begins. Among the multitudinous kinds of *Coelenterata*, the masses range from that of the small hydra to that of the large medusa. The annulose and molluscous types respectively show us immense contrasts between their superior and inferior members. And the vertebrate animals, much larger on the average than the rest, display among themselves enormous differences.

Kindred unlikenesses of size strike us when we contemplate the entire assemblage of human societies. Scattered over many regions there are minute hordes — still extant samples of the primordial type of society. We have Wood Veddas living sometimes in pairs, and only now and then assembling; we have Bushmen wandering about in families, and forming larger groups but occasionally; we have Fuegians clustered by the dozen or the score. Tribes of Australians, of Tasmanians, of Andamanese, are variable within the limits of perhaps twenty to fifty. And similarly, if the region is inhospitable, as with the Eskimos, or if the arts of life are undeveloped, as with the Digger Indians, or if adjacent higher races are obstacles to growth, as with Indian Hill tribes like the Juangs, this limitation to primitive size continues. Where a fruitful soil affords much food, and where a more settled life, leading to agriculture, again increases the supply of food, we meet with larger social aggregates: instance those in the Polynesian Islands and in many parts of Africa. Here a hundred or two, here several thousands, here many thousands, are held together more or less completely as one mass. And then in the highest societies, instead of partially aggregated thousands, we have completely aggregated millions.

The growths of individual and social organisms are allied in another respect. In each case size augments by two processes which go on sometimes separately, sometimes together. There is increase by simple multiplication of units, causing enlargement of the group; there is increase by union of groups, and again by union of groups of groups. The first parallelism is too simple to need illustration but the facts which show us the second must be set forth.

Organic integration, treated of at length in the *Principles of Biology*, §§ 180–211, must be here summarized to make the comparison intelligible. . . . The smallest animal, like the smallest plant, is essentially a minute group of living molecules. There are many forms and stages showing us the clustering of such smallest animals. Sometimes, as in the compound *Vorticellae* and in the sponges, their individualities are scarcely at all masked; but as evolution of the composite aggregate advances, the individualities of the component aggregates become less distinct. In some *Coelenterata*, though they retain considerable independence, which they show by moving about like amoebae when separated, they have their individualities mainly merged in that of the aggregate formed of them: instance the common hydra. Tertiary aggregates similarly result from the massing of secondary ones. . . .

Social growth proceeds by an analogous compounding and recompounding. The primitive social group, like the primitive group of living molecules with which organic evolution begins, never attains any considerable size by simple increase. Where, as among Fuegians, the supplies of wild food yielded by an inclement habitat will not enable more than a score or so to live in the same place -- where, as among Andamanese, limited to a strip of shore backed by impenetrable bush, forty is about the number of individuals who can find prey without going too far from their temporary abode [Mouat 1863, p. 300] -- where, as among Bushmen, wandering over barren tracts, small hordes are alone possible and even families "are sometimes obliged to separate, since the same spot will not afford sufficient sustenance for all" [Lichtenstein 1812–15, II, 194], we have extreme instances of the limitation of simple groups, and the formation of migrating groups when the limit is passed.

Even in tolerably productive habitats, fission of the groups is eventually necessitated in a kindred manner. Spreading as its number increases, a primitive tribe presently reaches a diffusion at which its parts become incoherent, and it then gradually separates into tribes that become distinct as fast as their continually diverging dialects pass into different languages. Often nothing further happens than repetition of this. Conflicts of tribes, dwindlings or extinctions of some, growths and spontaneous divisions of others, continue.

The formation of a larger society results only by the joining of such smaller societies, which occurs without obliterating the divisions previously caused by separations. This process may be seen now going on among uncivilized races, as it once went on among the ancestors of the civilized races. Instead of absolute independence of small hordes, such as the lowest savages show us, more advanced savages show us slight cohesions among larger hordes. In North America each of the three great tribes of Comanches consists of various bands having such feeble combination only as results from the personal character of the great chief [Schoolcraft 1853–56, I, 260; Bollaert 1850, II, 267]. So of the Dakotas there are, according to Burton [1861, p. 116], seven principal bands, each including minor bands, numbering altogether, according to Catlin, forty-two [1876, I, 209]. And in like manner the five Iroquois nations had severally eight tribes.

Closer unions of these slightly coherent original groups arise under favorable conditions, but they only now and then become permanent. A common form of the process is that described by Mason as occurring among the Karens [1868, p. 130]. "Each village, with its scant domain, is an independent state, and every chief a prince; but now and then a little Napoleon arises, who subdues a kingdom to himself, and builds up an empire. The dynasties, however, last only with the controlling mind." The like happens in Africa. Livingstone says, "Formerly all the Maganja were united under the government of their great Chief, Undi; . . . but after Undi's death it fell to pieces. . . . This has been the inevitable fate of every African Empire from time immemorial" [ref. lost].

Only occasionally does there result a compound social aggregate that endures for a considerable period, as Dahomey or as Ashanti, which is "an assemblage of states owing a kind of feudal obedience to the sovereign" [Beecham 1841, p. 86]. The histories of Madagascar and of sundry Polynesian islands also display these transitory compound groups, out of which at length come in some cases permanent ones. During the earliest times of the extinct civilized races, like stages were passed through. In the words of Maspero, Egypt was "divided at first into a great number of tribes, which at several points simultaneously began to establish small independent states, every one of which had its laws and its worship" [1878, p. 18]. The compound groups of Greeks first formed were those minor ones result-

ing from the subjugation of weaker towns by stronger neighboring towns.
And in northern Europe during pagan days the numerous German tribes,
each with its cantonal divisions, illustrated this second stage of aggregation.

After such compound societies are consolidated, repetition of the process
on a larger scale produces doubly compound societies which, usually co-
hering but feebly, become in some cases quite coherent. Maspero infers
that the Egyptian nomes described above as resulting from integrations of
tribes, coalesced into the two great principalities, Upper Egypt and Lower
Egypt, which were eventually united, the small states becoming provinces.
The boasting records of Mesopotamian kings similarly show us this union
of unions going on. So, too, in Greece the integration at first occurring
locally, began afterwards to combine the minor societies into two confederacies. During Roman days there arose for defensive purposes federations of tribes which eventually consolidated, and subsequently these were
compounded into still larger aggregates. Before and after the Christian
era, the like happened throughout Northern Europe. Then after a period
of vague and varying combinations, there came, in later times, as is well
illustrated by French history, a massing of small feudal territories into
provinces, and a subsequent massing of these into kingdoms.

So that in both organic and superorganic growths we see a process of
compounding and recompounding carried to various stages. In both cases,
after some consolidation of the smallest aggregates there comes the process
of forming larger aggregates by union of them; in both cases repetition of
this process makes secondary aggregates into tertiary ones.

Organic growth and superorganic growth have yet another analogy. As
above said, increase by multiplication of individuals in a group and increase by union of groups may go on simultaneously, and it does this in
both cases.

The original clusters, animal and social, are not only small, but they lack
density. Creatures of low types occupy large spaces considering the small
quantities of animal substance they contain, and low-type societies spread
over areas that are wide relatively to the numbers of their component individuals. But as integration in animals is shown by concentration as well as
by increase of bulk, so that social integration which results from the clustering of clusters is joined with augmentation of the number contained
by each cluster. If we contrast the sprinklings in regions inhabited by wild
tribes with the crowds filling equal regions in Europe or if we contrast the
density of population in England under the Heptarchy with its present
density, we see that besides the growth produced by union of groups there
has gone on interstitial growth. Just as the higher animal has become not
only larger than the lower but more solid, so, too, has the higher society.

Social growth, then, equally with the growth of a living body, shows us the fundamental trait of evolution under a twofold aspect. Integration is displayed both in the formation of a larger mass and in the progress of such mass towards that coherence due to closeness of parts.

It is proper to add, however, that there is a model of social growth to which organic growth affords no parallel — that caused by the migration of units from one society to another. Among many primitive groups and a few developed ones this is a considerable factor but, generally, its effect bears so small a ratio to the effects of growth by increase of population and coalescence of groups that it does not much qualify the analogy.

CHAPTER 4

SOCIAL STRUCTURES

In societies, as in living bodies, increase of mass is habitually accompanied by increase of structure. Along with that integration which is the primary trait of evolution, both exhibit in high degrees the secondary trait, differentiation.

The association of these two characters in animals was described in the *Principles of Biology*, § 44. Excluding certain low kinds of them whose activities are little above those of plants, we recognized the general law that large aggregates have high organizations. The qualifications of this law which go along with differences of medium, of habitat, of type, are numerous but when made they leave intact the truth that for carrying on the combined life of an extensive mass, involved arrangements are required.

So, too, is it with societies. As we progress from small groups to larger, from simple groups to compound groups, from compound groups to doubly compound ones, the unlikenesses of parts increase. The social aggregate, homogeneous when minute, habitually gains in heterogeneity along with each increment of growth, and to reach great size must acquire great complexity. Let us glance at the leading stages.

Naturally in a state like that of the Cayaguas or Wood-Indians of South America, so little social that "one family lives at a distance from another," social organization is impossible and even where there is some slight association of families, organization does not arise while they are few and wandering [Southey 1810–19, II, 373]. Groups of Eskimos, of Australians, of Bushmen, of Fuegians, are without even that primary contrast of parts implied by settled chieftainship. Their members are subject to no control but such as is temporarily acquired by the stronger, or more cunning, or more experienced; not even a permanent nucleus is present. Habitually where larger simple groups exist, we find some kind of head. Though not a uniform rule (for, as we shall hereafter see, the genesis of a controlling agency depends on the nature of the social activities), this is a general rule. The headless clusters, wholly ungoverned, are incoherent, and separate before they acquire considerable sizes; but along with maintenance of an aggregate approaching to, or exceeding, a hundred, we ordinarily find a simple or compound ruling agency — one or more men claiming and exercising authority that is natural, or supernatural, or both. This is the first social differentiation.

Soon after it there frequently comes another, tending to form a division between regulative and operative parts. In the lowest tribes this is rudely represented only by the contrast in status between the sexes: the men, having unchecked control, carry on such external activities as the tribe shows us, chiefly in war, while the women are made drudges who perform the less skilled parts of the process of sustentation. But that tribal growth, and establishment of chieftainship, which gives military superiority, presently causes enlargement of the operative part by adding captives to it. This begins unobtrusively. While in battle the men are killed, and often afterwards eaten, the noncombatants are enslaved. Patagonians, for example, make slaves of women and children taken in war [Fitzroy 1839, II, 166]. Later, and especially when cannibalism ceases, comes the enslavement of male captives, whence results, in some cases, an operative part clearly marked off from the regulative part. Among the Chinooks, "slaves do all the laborious work" [Ross 1849, p. 92]. We read that the Beluchi, avoiding the hard labor of cultivation, impose it on the Jutts, the ancient inhabitants whom they have subjugated [Postans 1848, p. 112]. Beecham says it is usual on the Gold Coast to make the slaves clear the ground for cultivation [1841, p. 136]. And among the Felatahs "slaves are numerous: the males are employed in weaving, collecting wood or grass, or on any other kind of work; some of the women are engaged in spinning . . . in preparing the yarn for the loom, others in pounding and grinding corn, etc" [Denham, *et al.* 1828, II, 94].

Along with that increase of mass caused by union of primary social aggregates into a secondary one, a further unlikeness of parts arises. The holding together of the compound cluster implies a head of the whole as well as heads of the parts, and a differentiation analogous to that which originally produced a chief, now produces a chief of chiefs. Sometimes the combination is made for defense against a common foe, and sometimes it results from conquest by one tribe of the rest. In this last case the predominant tribe, in maintaining its supremacy, develops more highly its military character, thus becoming unlike the others.

After such clusters of clusters have been so consolidated that their united powers can be wielded by one governing agency, there come alliances with, or subjugations of, other clusters of clusters, ending from time to time in coalescence. When this happens there results still greater complexity in the governing agency, with its king, local rulers, and petty chiefs; and at the same time, there arise more marked divisions of classes — military, priestly, slave, etc. Clearly, then, complication of structure accompanies increase of mass.

This increase of heterogeneity, which in both classes of aggregates goes along with growth, presents another trait in common. Beyond unlikenesses of parts due to development of the coordinating agencies, there presently follow unlikenesses among the agencies coordinated — the organs of alimentation, etc., in the one case, and the industrial structures in the other.

When animal-aggregates of the lowest order unite to form one of a higher order, and when, again, these secondary aggregates are compounded into tertiary aggregates, each component is at first similar to the other components, but in the course of evolution dissimilarities arise and become more and more decided. Among the *Coelenterata* the stages are clearly indicated. From the sides of a common hydra, bud out young ones which, when fully developed, separate from their parent. In the compound hydroids the young polyps produced in like manner remain permanently attached and, themselves repeating the process, presently form a branched aggregate. When the members of the compound group lead similar and almost independent lives, as in various rooted genera, they remain similar, save those of them which become reproductive organs. But in the floating and swimming clusters, formed by a kindred process, the differently conditioned members become different, while assuming different functions.

It is thus with the minor social groups combined into a major social group. Each tribe originally had within itself such feebly marked industrial divisions as sufficed for its low kind of life, and these were like those of each other tribe. But union facilitates exchange of commodities and if, as mostly happens, the component tribes severally occupy localities favorable to unlike kinds of production, unlike occupations are initiated, and there result unlikenesses of industrial structures. Even between tribes not united, as those of Australia, barter of products furnished by their respective habitats goes on so long as war does not hinder. And evidently when there is reached such a stage of integration as in Madagascar, or as in the chief Negro states of Africa, the internal peace that follows subordination to one government makes commercial intercourse easy. The like parts being permanently held together, mutual dependence becomes possible and along with growing mutual dependence the parts grow unlike.

The advance of organization which thus follows the advance of aggregation, alike in individual organisms and in social organisms, conforms in both cases to the same general law: differentiations proceed from the more general to the more special. First broad and simple contrasts of parts, then within each of the parts primarily contrasted, changes which make unlike divisions of them, then within each of these unlike divisions, minor unlikenesses, and so on continually.

The successive stages in the development of a vertebrate column illustrate this law in animals. At the outset an elongated depression of the blastoderm, called the "primitive groove," represents the entire cerebrospinal axis; as yet there are no marks of vertebrae, nor even a contrast between the part which is to become head and the part which is to become backbone. Presently the ridges bounding this groove, growing up and folding over more rapidly at the anterior end, which at the same time widens, begin to make the skull distinguishable from the spine, and the commencement of segmentation in the spinal part, while the cephalic part remains unsegmented, strengthens the contrast. Within each of these main divisions minor divisions soon arise. The rudimentary cranium, bending forward, simultaneously acquires three dilatations indicating the contained nervous centers, while the segmentation of the spinal column, spreading to its ends, produces an almost-uniform series of "proto-vertebrae." At first these proto-vertebrae not only differ very little from one another, but each is relatively simple — a quadrate mass. Gradually this almost-uniform series falls into unlike divisions — the cervical group, the dorsal group, the lumbar group; and while the series of vertebrae is thus becoming specialized in its different regions, each vertebra is changing from that general form which it at first had in common with the rest, to the more special form eventually distinguishing it from the rest. Throughout the embryo there are, at the same time, going on kindred processes which, first making each large part unlike all other large parts, then make the parts of that part unlike one another.

During social evolution analogous metamorphoses may everywhere be traced. The rise of the structure exercising religious control will serve as an example. In simple tribes, and in clusters of tribes during their early stages of aggregation, we find men who are at once sorcerers, priests, diviners, exorcists, doctors — men who deal with supposed supernatural beings in all the various possible ways: propitiating them, seeking knowledge and aid from them, commanding them, subduing them. Along with advance in social integration, there come both differences of function and differences of rank. In Tanna "there are rain makers . . . and a host of other 'sacred men'" [Turner 1861, p. 89]; in Fiji there are not only priests, but seers [Williams and Calvert 1858, I, 229]; among the Hawaiian Islanders there are diviners as well as priests [Ellis 1826, p. 118], among the New Zealanders, Thomson distinguishes between priests and sorcerers [1859, I, 116]; and among the Kaffirs, besides diviners and rain makers, there are two classes of doctors who respectively rely on supernatural and on natural agents in curing their patients [Backhouse 1844, p. 230].

More advanced societies, as those of ancient America, show us still greater multiformity of this once-uniform group. In Mexico, for example, the medical class, descending from a class of sorcerers who dealt antagonistically with the supernatural agents supposed to cause disease, were distinct from the priests, whose dealings with supernatural agents were propitiatory. Further, the sacerdotal class included several kinds, dividing the religious offices among them — sacrificers, diviners, singers, composers of hymns, instructors of youth; and then there were also gradations of ranks in each [Clavigero 1787, I, 272].

This progress from general to special in priesthoods, has, in the higher nations, led to such marked distinctions that the original kinships are forgotten. The priest–astrologers of ancient races were initiators of the scientific class, now variously specialized; from the priest-doctors of old have come the medical class with its chief division and minor divisions; while within the clerical class proper, have arisen not only various ranks from pope down to acolyte, but various kinds of functionaries — dean, priest, deacon, chorister, as well as others classed as curates and chaplains. Similarly if we trace the genesis of any industrial structure, as that which from primitive blacksmiths who smelt their own iron as well as make implements from it, brings us to our iron-manufacturing districts, where preparation of the metal is separated into smelting, refining, puddling, rolling, and where turning this metal into implements is divided into various businesses.

The transformation here illustrated is, indeed, an aspect of that transformation of the homogeneous into the heterogeneous which everywhere characterizes evolution; but the truth to be noted is that it characterizes the evolution of individual organisms and of social organisms in especially high degrees.

Closer study of the facts shows us another striking parallelism. Organs in animals and organs in societies have internal arrangements framed on the same principle.

Differing from one another as the viscera of a living creature do in many respects, they have several traits in common. Each viscus contains appliances for conveying nutriment to its parts, for bringing it materials on which to operate, for carrying away the product, for draining off waste matters, as also for regulating its activity. Though liver and kidneys are unlike in their general appearances and minute structures, as well as in the offices they fulfil, the one as much as the other has a system of arteries, a system of veins, a system of lymphatics — has branched channels through which its excretions escape, and nerves for exciting and checking it. In large measure the like is true of those higher organs which, instead of elaborating and purifying and distributing the blood, aid the general life by carrying on external actions — the nervous and muscular organs. These, too, have their ducts for bringing prepared materials, ducts for drafting off vitiated materials, ducts for carrying away effete matters; as also their controlling nerve cells and fibers. So that, along with the many marked differences of structure, there are these marked communities of structure.

It is the same in a society. The clustered citizens forming an organ which produces some commodity for national use, or which otherwise satisfies national wants, has within it subservient structures substantially like those of each other organ carrying on each other function. Be it a cotton-weaving district or a district where cutlery is made, it has a set of agencies which bring the raw material, and a set of agencies which collect and send away the manufactured articles; it has an apparatus of major and minor channels through which the necessaries of life are drafted out of the general stocks circulating through the kingdom, and brought home to the local workers and those who direct them; it has appliances, postal and other, for bringing those impulses by which the industry of the place is excited or checked; it has local controlling powers, political and ecclesiastical, by which order is maintained and healthful action furthered. So, too, when, from a district which secretes certain goods we turn to a seaport which absorbs and sends out goods, we find the distributing and restraining agencies are mostly the same. Even where the social organ, instead of carrying on a material activity, has, like a university, the office of preparing certain classes of units for social functions of particular kinds, this general type of structure is repeated: the appliances for local sustentation and regulation, differing in some respects, are similar in essentials — there are like classes of distributors, like classes for civil control, and a specially-developed class for ecclesiastical control.

On observing that this community of structure among social organs, like the community of structure among organs in a living body, necessarily accompanies mutual dependence, we shall see even more clearly than hitherto how great is the likeness of nature between individual organization and social organization.

One more structural analogy must be named. The formation of organs in a living body proceeds in ways which we may distinguish as primary, secondary, and tertiary, and, paralleling them, there are primary, secondary, and tertiary ways in which social organs are formed. We will look at each of the three parallelisms by itself.

In animals of low types, bile is secreted, not by a liver, but by separate cells imbedded in the wall of the intestine at one part. These cells individually perform their function of separating certain matters from the blood, and individually pour out what they separate. No organ, strictly so-called, exists, but only a number of units not yet aggregated into an organ.

This is analogous to the incipient form of an industrial structure in a society. At first each worker carries on his occupation alone, and himself disposes of the product to consumers. The arrangement still extant in our villages, where the cobbler at his own fireside makes and sells boots, and where the blacksmith single-handed does what iron-work is needed by his neighbors, exemplifies the primitive type of every producing structure. Among savages slight differentiations arise from individual aptitudes. Even of the degraded Fuegians, Fitzroy tells us that "one becomes an adept with the spear; another with the sling; another with a bow and arrow" [1839, II, 186]. As like differences of skill among members of primitive tribes cause some to become makers of special things, it results that necessarily the industrial organ begins as a social unit. Where, as among the Shasta Indians of California, arrow-making is a distinct profession, it is clear that manipulative superiority being the cause of the differentiation, the worker is at first single [Bancroft 1875–76, I, 343]. And during subsequent periods of growth, even in small settled communities, this type continues. The statement that among the Coast Negroes "the most ingenious man in the village is usually the blacksmith, joiner, architect, and weaver" [Winterbottom 1803, I, 89], while it shows us artisan functions in an undifferentiated stage, also shows us how completely individual is the artisan structure; the implication being that as the society grows, it is by the addition of more such individuals, severally carrying on their occupations independently, that the additional demand is met.

By two simultaneous changes an incipient secreting organ in an animal reaches that higher structure with which our next comparison may be made. The cells pass from a scattered cluster into a compact cluster, and they severally become compound. In place of a single cell elaborating and emitting its special product we now have a small elongated sac containing a family of cells, and this, through an opening at one end, gives exit to their products. At the same time there is formed an integrated group of such follicles, each containing secreting units and having its separate orifice of discharge.

To this type of individual organ we find, in semi-civilized societies, a type of social organ closely corresponding. In one of these settled and growing communities the demands upon individual workers, now more specialized in their occupations, have become unceasing, and each worker, occasionally pressed by work, makes helpers of his children. This practice, beginning incidentally, establishes itself, and eventually it grows into an imperative custom that each man shall bring up his boys to his own trade. Illustrations of this stage are numerous. Skilled occupation, "like every other calling and office in Peru, always descended from father to son. The division of castes, in this particular, was as precise as that which existed in Egypt or Hindostan" [Prescott 1847, I, 138]. In Mexico, too, "the sons in general learned the trades of their fathers, and embraced their professions" [Clavigero 1787, I, 338]. The like was true of the industrial structures of European nations in early times. By the Theodosian code a Roman youth "was compelled to follow the employment of his father . . . and the suitor who sought the hand of the daughter could only obtain his bride by becoming wedded to the calling of her family" [Palgrave, F. 1832, I, 332].

In medieval France handicrafts were inherited, and the old English periods were characterized by a like usage. Branching of the family through generations into a number of kindred families carrying on the same occupation, produced the germ of the guild, and the related families who monopolized each industry formed a cluster habitually occupying the same quarter. Hence the still extant names of many streets in English towns — "Fellmonger, Horsemonger, and Fleshmonger, Shoewright and Shieldwright, Turner and Salter Streets" [Kemble 1849, II, 340), a segregation like that which still persists in Oriental bazaars.

And now, on observing how one of these industrial quarters was composed of many allied families, each containing sons working under direction of a father, who while sharing in the work sold the produce, and who, if the family and business were large, became mainly a channel taking in raw material and giving out the manufactured article, we see that there existed an analogy to the kind of glandular organ described above, which consists of a number of adjacent cell-containing follicles having separate mouths.

A third stage of the analogy may be traced. Along with that increase of a glandular organ necessitated by the more active functions of a more developed animal there goes a change of structure consequent on augmentation of bulk. If the follicles multiply while their ducts have all to be brought to one spot, it results that their orifices, increasingly numerous, occupy a larger area of the wall of the cavity which receives the discharge, and if lateral extension of this area is negatived by the functional requirements, it results that the needful area is gained by formation of a caecum. Further need of the same kind leads to secondary caeca diverging from this main caecum, which hence becomes, in part, a duct. Thus is at length evolved a large viscus, such as a liver, having a single main duct with ramifying branches running throughout its mass.

Now we rise from the above-described kind of industrial organ by parallel stages to a higher kind. There is no sudden leap from the household type to the factory type, but a gradual transition. The first step is shown us in those rules of trade guilds under which, to the members of the family, might be added an apprentice (possibly at first a relation) who, as Brentano [1870, pp. 129–30] says, "became a member of the family of his master, who instructed him in his trade, and who, like a father, had to watch over his morals, as well as his work;" practically an adopted son. This modification having been established, there followed the employing of apprentices who had changed into journeymen. With development of this modified household group the master grew into a seller of goods made, not by his own family only, but by others and, as his business enlarged, necessarily ceased to be a worker, and became wholly a distributor — a channel through which went out the products, not of a few sons, but of many unrelated artisans. This led the way to establishments in which the employed far outnumber the members of the family, until at length, with the use of mechanical power, came the factory — a series of rooms, each containing a crowd of producing units, and sending its tributary stream of product to join other streams before reaching the single place of exit. Finally, in greatly developed industrial organs, we see many factories clustered in the same town, and others in adjacent towns, to and from which, along branching roads, come the raw materials and go the bales of cloth, calico, etc.

There are instances in which a new industry passes through these stages in the course of a few generations, as happened with the stocking-manufacture. In the Midland counties, fifty years ago, the rattle and burr of a solitary stocking-frame came from a roadside cottage every here and there; the single worker made and sold his product. Presently arose workshops in which several such looms might be heard going: there was the father and his sons, with perhaps a journeyman. At length grew up the large building containing many looms driven by a steam engine; and finally many such large buildings in the same town.

These structural analogies reach a final phase that is still more striking. In both cases there is a contrast between the original mode of development and a substituted later mode.

In the general course of organic evolution from low types to high, there have been passed through by insensible modifications all the stages above described; but now, in the individual evolution of an organism of high type, these stages are greatly abridged, and an organ is produced by a comparatively direct process. Thus the liver of a mammalian embryo is formed by the accumulation of numerous cells, which presently grow into a mass projecting from the wall of the intestine, while simultaneously there dips down into it a caecum from the intestine. Transformation of this caecum into the hepatic duct takes place at the same time that within the mass of cells there arise minor ducts, connected with this main duct and there meanwhile go on other changes which, during evolution of the organ through successively higher types, came one after another.

In the formation of industrial organs the like happens. Now that the factory system is well-established — now that it has become ingrained in the social constitution — we see direct assumptions of it in all industries for which its fitness has been shown. If at one place the discovery of ore prompts the setting up of iron-works, or at another a special kind of water facilitates brewing, there is no passing through the early stages of single worker, family, clustered families, and so on, but there is a sudden drafting of materials and men to the spot, followed by formation of a producing structure on the advanced type. Nay, not one large establishment only is thus evolved after the direct manner, but a cluster of large establishments. At Barrow-in-Furness we see a town with its iron works, its importing and exporting businesses, its extensive docks and means of communication, all in the space of a few years framed after that type which it has taken centuries to develop through successive modifications.

An allied but even more marked change in the evolutionary process is also common to both cases. Just as in the embryo of a high animal various organs have their important parts laid down out of their original order, in anticipation, as it were, so, with the body at large, it happens that entire organs which, during the serial genesis of the type, came comparatively late, come in the evolving individual comparatively soon. This, which Prof. Haeckel has called heterochrony, is shown us in the early marking out of the brain in a mammalian embryo, though in the lowest vertebrate animal no brain ever exists; or, again, in the segmentation of the spinal column before any alimentary system is formed, though, in a proto-vertebrate, even when its alimentary system is completed, there are but feeble signs of segmentation.

The analogous change of order in social evolution is shown us by new societies which inherit the confirmed habits of old ones. Instance the United States, where a town in the far west, laid down in its streets and plots, has its hotel, church, post-office, built while there are but few houses, and where a railway is run through the wilderness in anticipation of settlements. Or instance Australia, where a few years after the huts of gold diggers begin to cluster round new mines there is established a printing-office and journal, though, in the mother-country, centuries passed before a town of like size developed a like agency.

CHAPTER 5

SOCIAL FUNCTIONS

Changes of structures cannot occur without changes of functions. Much that was said in the last chapter might, therefore, be said here with substituted terms. Indeed, as in societies many changes of structure are more indicated by changes of function than directly seen, it may be said that these last have been already described by implication.

There are, however, certain functional traits not manifestly implied by traits of structure. To these a few pages must be devoted.

If organization consists in such a construction of the whole that its parts can carry on mutually dependent actions, then in proportion as organization is high there must go a dependence of each part upon the rest so great that separation is fatal; and conversely. This truth is equally well shown in the individual organism and in the social organism.

The lowest animal-aggregates are so constituted that each portion, similar to every other in appearance, carries on similar actions, and here spontaneous or artificial separation interferes scarcely at all with the life of either separated portion. When the faintly differentiated speck of protoplasm forming a rhizopod is accidently divided, each division goes on as before. So, too, is it with those aggregates of the second order in which the components remain substantially alike. The ciliated monads clothing the horny fibers of a living sponge need one another's aid so little that, when the sponge is cut in two, each half carries on its processes without interruption. Even where some unlikeness has arisen among the units, as in the familiar polyp, the perturbation caused by division is but temporary: the two or more portions resulting need only a little time for the units to rearrange themselves into fit forms before resuming their ordinary simple actions.

The like happens for the like reason with the lowest social aggregates. A headless wandering group of primitive men divides without any inconvenience. Each man, at once warrior, hunter, and maker of his own weapons, hut, etc., with a squaw who has in every case the like drudgeries to carry on, needs concert with his fellows only in war and to some extent in the chase, and, except for fighting, concert with half the tribe is as good as concert with the whole. Even where the slight differentiation implied by chieftainship exists, little inconvenience results from voluntary or enforced separation. Either before or after a part of the tribe migrates, some man becomes head, and such low social life as is possible recommences.

With highly organized aggregates of either kind it is very different. We cannot cut a mammal in two without causing immediate death. Twisting off the head of a fowl is fatal. Not even a reptile, though it may survive the loss of its tail, can live when its body is divided. And among annulose creatures it similarly happens that though in some inferior genera bisection does not kill either half, it kills both in an insect, an arachnid, or a crustacean.

If in high societies the effect of mutilation is less than in high animals, still it is great. Middlesex separated from its surroundings would in a few days have all its social processes stopped by lack of supplies. Cut off the cotton-district from Liverpool and other ports and there would come arrest of its industry followed by mortality of its people. Let a division be made between the coal-mining populations and adjacent populations which smelt metals or make broadcloth by machinery, and both, forthwith dying socially by arrest of their actions, would begin to die individually. Though when a civilized society is so divided that part of it is left without a central controlling agency it may presently evolve one, yet there is meanwhile much risk of dissolution, and before reorganization is efficient, a long period of disorder and weakness must be passed through.

So that the consensus of functions becomes closer as evolution advances. In low aggregates, both individual and social, the actions of the parts are but little dependent on one another, whereas in developed aggregates of both kinds that combination of actions which constitutes the life of the whole makes possible the component actions which constitute the lives of the parts.

Another corollary, manifest a priori and proved a posteriori, must be named. Where parts are little differentiated they can readily perform one another's functions, but where much differentiated they can perform one another's functions very imperfectly, or not at all.

Again the common polyp furnishes a clear illustration. One of these sack-shaped creatures admits of being turned inside out, so that the skin becomes stomach and the stomach becomes skin, each thereupon beginning to do the work of the other. The higher we rise in the scale of organization the less practicable do we find such exchanges. Still, to some extent, substitutions of functions remain possible in highly developed creatures. Even in man the skin shows a trace of its original absorptive power, now monopolized by the alimentary canal: it takes into the system certain small amounts of matter rubbed on to it. Such vicarious actions are, however, most manifest between parts having functions that are still allied. If, for instance, the bile-excreting function of the liver is impeded, other excretory organs, the kidneys and the skin, become channels through which bile is got rid of. If a cancer in the esophagus prevents swallowing, the arrested food, dilating the esophagus, forms a pouch in which imperfect digestion is set up. But these small abilities of the differentiated parts to discharge one another's duties are not displayed where they have diverged more widely. Though mucous membrane, continuous with skin at various orifices, will, if everted, assume to a considerable extent the characters and powers of skin, yet serous membrane will not; nor can bone or muscle undertake, for any of the viscera, portions of their functions if they fail.

In social organisms, low and high, we find these relatively great and relatively small powers of substitution. Of course, where each member of the tribe repeats every other in his mode of life, there are no unlike functions to be exchanged; and where there has arisen only that small differentiation implied by the barter of weapons for other articles, between one member of the tribe skilled in weapon-making and others less skilled, the destruction of this specially-skilled member entails no great evil, since the rest can severally do for themselves that which he did for them, though not quite so well. Even in settled societies of considerable sizes we find the like holds to a great degree. Of the ancient Mexicans, Zurita says, "Every Indian knows all handicrafts which do not require great skill or delicate instruments" [1840, p. 183], and in Peru each man "was expected to be acquainted with the various handicrafts essential to domestic comfort" [Prescott 1847, I, 138]: the parts of the societies were so slightly differentiated in their occupations that assumption of one another's occupations remained practicable.

But in societies like our own, specialized industrially and otherwise in high degrees, the actions of one part which fails in its function cannot be assumed by other parts. Even the relatively unskilled farm laborers, were they to strike, would have their duties very inadequately performed by the urban population; and our iron manufactures would be stopped if their trained artisans, refusing to work, had to be replaced by peasants or hands from cotton factories. Still less could the higher functions, legislative, judicial, etc., be effectually performed by coal miners and navvies.

Evidently the same reason for this contrast holds in the two cases. In proportion as the units forming any part of an individual organism are limited to one kind of action, as that of absorbing, or secreting, or contracting, or conveying an impulse, and become adapted to that action, they lose adaptation to other actions; and in the social organism the discipline required for effectually discharging a special duty causes unfitness for discharging special duties widely unlike it.

Beyond these two chief functional analogies between individual organisms and social organisms, that when they are little evolved, division or mutilation causes small inconvenience, but when they are much evolved it causes great perturbation or death, and that in low types of either kind the parts can assume one another's functions, but cannot in high types, sundry consequent functional analogies might be enlarged on did space permit.

There is the truth that in both kinds of organisms the vitality increases as fast as the functions become specialized. In either case, before there exist structures severally adapted for the unlike actions, these are ill-performed and in the absence of developed appliances for furthering it, the utilization of one another's services is but slight. But along with advance of organization, every part, more limited in its office, performs its office better; the means of exchanging benefits become greater; each aids all, and all aid each with increasing efficiency; and the total activity we call life, individual or national, augments.

Much, too, remains to be said about the parallelism between the changes by which the functions become specialized, but this, along with other parallelisms, will best be seen on following out, as we will now do, the evolution of the several great systems of organs, individual and social, considering their respective structural and functional traits together.

CHAPTER 6

SYSTEMS OF ORGANS

The hypothesis of evolution implies a truth which was established independently of it — the truth that all animals, however unlike they finally become, begin their developments in like ways. The first structural changes, once passed through in common by divergent types, are repeated in the early changes undergone by every new individual of each type. Admitting some exceptions, chiefly among parasites, this is recognized as a general law.

This common method of development among individual organisms we may expect to find paralleled by some common method among social organisms, and our expectation will be verified.

In *First Principles* (§§ 149–152) and in the *Principles of Biology* (§§ 287–289) were described the primary organic differentiations which arise in correspondence with the primary contrast of conditions among the parts, as outer and inner. Neglecting earlier stages, let us pass to those which show us the resulting systems of organs in their simple forms.

The aggregated units composing the lowest coelenterate animal have become so arranged that there is an outer layer of them directly exposed to the surrounding medium with its inhabitants, and an inner layer lining the digestive cavity directly exposed only to the food. From units of the outer layer are formed those tentacles by which small creatures are caught, and those thread-cells, as they are called, whence are ejected minute weapons against invading larger creatures, while by units of the inner layer is poured out the solvent which prepares the food for that absorption afterwards effected by them, both for their own sustentation and for the sustentation of the rest. Here we have in its first stage the fundamental distinction which pervades the animal kingdom, between the external parts which deal with environing existences — earth, air, prey, enemies — and the internal parts which utilize for the benefit of the entire body the nutritious substances which the external parts have secured. . . .

Early stages which are in principle analogous, occur in the evolution of social organisms. When from low tribes entirely undifferentiated we pass to tribes next above them, we find classes of masters and slaves — masters who, as warriors, carry on the offensive and defensive activities and thus especially stand in relations to environing agencies, and slaves who carry on inner activities for the general sustentation, primarily of their masters and secondarily of themselves. Of course this contrast is at first vague.

Where the tribe subsists mainly on wild animals, its dominant men, being hunters as well as warriors, take a large share in procuring food, and such few captives as are made by war become men who discharge the less skilled and more laborious parts of the process of sustentation. But along with establishment of the agricultural state the differentiation grows more appreciable. Though members of the dominant class, superintending the labor of their slaves in the fields, sometimes join in it, yet the subject class is habitually the one immediately in contact with the food supply, and the dominant class, more remote from the food supply, is becoming directive only, with respect to internal actions, while it is both executive and directive with respect to external actions, offensive and defensive.

A society thus composed of two strata in contact, complicates by the rise of grades within each stratum. For small tribes the structure just described suffices, but where there are formed aggregates of tribes, necessarily having more-developed governmental and militant agencies, with accompanying more-developed industrial agencies supporting them, the higher and lower strata severally begin to differentiate internally. The superior class, besides minor distinctions which arise locally, originates everywhere a supplementary class of personal adherents who are mostly also warriors, while the inferior class begins to separate into bond and free. Various of the Malayo-Polynesian societies show us this stage. Among the East Africans, the Congo people, the Coast Negroes, the Inland Negroes, we find the same general subdivision — the king with his relatives, the class of chiefs, the common people, the slaves, of which the first two with their immediate dependents carry on the corporate actions of the society, and the second two those actions of a relatively-separate order which yield it all the necessaries of life.

In both individual and social organisms, after the outer and inner systems have been marked off from one another, there begins to arise a third system, lying between the two and facilitating their cooperation. Mutual dependence of the primarily-contrasted parts implies intermediation, and in proportion as they develop, the apparatus for exchanging products and influences must develop too. This we find it does.

In the low coelenterate animal first described, consisting of inner and outer layers with intervening protoplasm, the nutritive matter which members of the inner layer have absorbed from prey caught by members of the outer layer is transmitted almost directly to these members of the outer layer. Not so, however, in the superior type. Between the double-layered body wall and the double-layered alimentary cavity there is now a partially separate perivisceral sac, and this serves as a reservoir for the digested matters from which the surrounding tissues take up their shares of prepared food. Here we have the rudiment of a distributing system. Higher in the animal series, as in *Mollusca*, this perivisceral sac, quite shut off, has ramifications running throughout the body, carrying nutriment to its chief organs, and in the central part of the sac is a contractile tube which, by its occasional pulses, causes irregular movements in the nutritive fluid. Further advances are shown by the lengthening and branching of this tube, until, dividing and subdividing, it becomes a set of blood vessels, while its central part becomes a heart. As this change progresses, the nutriment taken up by the alimentary structures is better distributed by these vascular structures to the outer and inner organs in proportion to their needs. Evidently this distributing system must arise between the two pre-existing systems, and it necessarily ramifies in proportion as the parts to which it carries materials become more remote, more numerous, and severally more complex.

The like happens in societies. The lowest types have no distributing systems — no roads or traders exist. The two original classes are in contact. Any slaves possessed by a member of the dominant class stand in such direct relation to him that the transfer of products takes place without intervening persons; and each family being self-sufficing, there need [be] no agents through whom to effect exchanges of products between families. Even after these two primary divisions become partially subdivided, we find that so long as the social aggregate is a congeries of tribes severally carrying on within themselves the needful productive activities, a distributing system is scarcely traceable; occasional assemblings for barter alone occur. But as fast as consolidation of such tribes makes possible the localization of industries, there begins to show itself an appliance for transferring commodities consisting now of single hawkers, now of traveling companies of traders, and growing with the formation of roads into an organized system of wholesale and retail distribution which spreads everywhere.

There are, then, parallelisms between these three great systems in the two kinds of organisms. Moreover, they arise in the social organism in the same order as in the individual organism and for the same reasons.

A society lives by appropriating matters from the earth — the mineral matters used for buildings, fuel, etc., the vegetal matters raised on its surface for food and clothing, the animal matters elaborated from these with or without human regulation; and the lowest social stratum is the one through which such matters are taken up and delivered to agents who pass them into the general current of commodities, the higher part of this lowest stratum being that which, in workshops and factories, elaborates some of these materials before they go to consumers. Clearly, then, the classes engaged in manual occupations play the same part in the function of social sustentation as is played by the components of the alimentary organs in the sustentation of a living body.

No less certain is it that the entire class of men engaged in buying and selling commodities of all kinds, on large and small scales, and in sending them along gradually-formed channels to all districts, towns, and individuals, so enabling them to make good the waste caused by action, is, along with those channels, fulfilling an office essentially like that fulfilled in a living body by the vascular system, which, to every structure and every unit of it, brings a current of nutritive matters proportionate to its activity. And it is equally manifest that while in the living body, the brain, the organs of sense, and the limbs guided by them, distant in position from the alimentary surfaces, are fed through the tortuous channels of the vascular system, so the controlling parts of a society, most remote from the operative parts, have brought to them through courses of distribution often extremely indirect, the needful supplies of consumable articles.

That the order of evolution is necessarily the same in the two cases is just as clear. In a creature which is both very small and very inactive, like a hydra, direct passage of nutriment from the inner layer to the outer layer by absorption suffices. But in proportion as the outer structures, becoming more active, expend more, simple absorption from adjacent tissues no longer meets the resulting waste and in proportion as the mass becomes larger, and the parts which prepare nutriment consequently more remote from the parts which consume it, there arises the need for a means of transfer. Until the two original systems have been marked off from one another, this tertiary system has no function; and when the two original systems arise, they cannot develop far without corresponding development of this tertiary system.

In the evolution of the social organism we see the like. Where there exist only a class of masters and a class of slaves, in direct contact, an appliance for transferring products has no place; but a larger society having classes exercising various regulative functions, and localities devoted to different industries, not only affords a place for a transferring system, but can grow and complicate only on condition that this transferring system makes proportionate advances. . . .

CHAPTER 7

THE REGULATING SYSTEM

When observing how the great systems of organs, individual and social, are originally marked off from one another, we recognized the truth that the inner and outer parts become respectively adapted to those functions which their respective positions necessitate — the one having to deal with environing actions and agents, the other having to use internally placed materials. . . . We have now to see how the evolution of the structures carrying on outer actions is determined by the characters of things existing around.

Stated in a more concrete form, the general fact to be here set forth is that while the alimentary systems of animals and the industrial systems of societies are developed into fitness for dealing with the substances, organic and inorganic, used for sustentation, the regulating and expending systems (nervo-motor in the one, and governmental-military in the other) are developed into fitness for dealing with surrounding organisms, individual or social — other animals to be caught or escaped from, hostile societies to be conquered or resisted. In both cases that organization which fits the aggregate for acting as a whole in conflict with other aggregates, indirectly results from the carrying on of conflicts with other aggregates.

To be slow of speed is to be caught by an enemy; to be wanting in swiftness is to fail in catching prey, death being in either case the result. Sharp sight saves the herbivorous animal from a distant carnivore, and is an essential aid to the eagle's successful swoop on a creature far below. Obviously it is the same with quickness of hearing and delicacy of scent; the same with all improvements of limbs that increase the power, the agility, the accuracy of movements; the same with all appliances for attack and defense — claws, teeth, horns, etc. And equally true must it be that each advance in that nervous system which, using the information coming through the senses, excites and guides these external organs, becomes established by giving an advantage to its possessor in presence of prey, enemies and competitors. On glancing up from low types of animals having but rudimentary eyes and small powers of motion, to high types of animals having wide vision, considerable intelligence, and great activity, it becomes undeniable that where loss of life is entailed on the first of these defects, life is preserved in the last by these superiorities. The implication, then, is that successive improvements of the organs of sense and motion, and of the internal coordinating apparatus which uses them, have indirectly resulted from the antagonisms and competitions of organisms with one another.

A parallel truth is disclosed on watching how there evolves the regulating system of a political aggregate, and how there are developed those appliances for offense and defense put in action by it. Everywhere the wars between societies originate governmental structures, and are causes of all such improvements in those structures as increase the efficiency of corporate action against environing societies. Observe, first, the conditions under which there is an absence of this agency furthering combination, and then observe the conditions under which this agency begins to show itself.

Where food is scarce, diffusion great, and cooperation consequently hindered, there is no established chieftainship. The Fuegians, the Cayaguas or Wood-Indians of South America, the Jungle-Veddas of Ceylon, the Bushmen of South Africa, are instances. They do not form unions for defense, and have no recognized authorities: personal predominance of a temporary kind, such as tends to arise in every group, being the only approach to it. So of the Eskimos, necessarily much scattered, Hearne says, "they live in a state of perfect freedom; no one apparently claiming the superiority over, or acknowledging the least subordination to, another" [1795, p. 161], joined with which fact stands the fact that they do not know what war means. In like manner where barrenness of territory negatives anything more than occasional assemblings, as with the Chippewyans, there is nothing like chieftainship beyond the effect due to character, and this is very small. . . .

But it is not only in cases like these that governmental coordination is absent. It is absent also among tribes which are settled and considerably more advanced, provided they are not given to war. Among such Papuans as the Arafuras and the Dalrymple Islanders, there are but nominal chiefs, the people living "in such peace and brotherly love with one another" that they need no control but the decisions of their elders [Kolff 1840, p. 161]. The Todas, too, wholly without military organization, and described as peaceable, mild, friendly, have no political headships [Marshall 1873, pp. 41–5; Shortt 1868, p. 241] . . .

Now observe how the headless state is changed and political coordination initiated. Edwards says the Caribs in time of peace admitted no supremacy but, he adds, "in war, experience had taught them that subordination was as requisite as courage" [1801–19, I, 49]. So, too, describing the confederations of tribes among the Caribs, Humboldt compares them with "those warlike hordes who see no advantage in the ties of society but for common defence" [1852–53, III, 89]. Of the Creeks, whose subordination to authority is but slight, Schoolcraft says, "it would be difficult, if not impossible, to impress on the community at large the necessity of any social compact, that should be binding upon it longer than common danger threatened them" [1853–56, V, 279]. Again, Bonwick says: "Chieftains undoubtedly did exist among the Tasmanians, though they were neither hereditary nor elective. They were, nevertheless, recognized, especially in time of war, as leaders of the tribes. . . . After the cessation of hostilities they retired . . . to the quietude of everyday forest life" [1870, p. 81].

In other cases we find a permanent change produced. Kotzebue says the Kamchadals "acknowledged no chief" [1830, II, 13], while another statement is that the principal authority was that of "the old men, or those who were remarkable for their bravery" [Krasheninnikov 1764, p. 175]. And then it is remarked that these statements refer to the time before the Russian conquest — before there has been combined opposition to an enemy. This development of simple headship in a tribe by conflict with other tribes we find advancing into compound headship along with larger antagonisms of race with race. Of the Patagonians Falkner tells us that though the tribes "are at continual variance among themselves, yet they often join together against the Spaniards" [1774, p. 123]. It was the same with the North American Indians. The confederacy of the six nations, which cohered under a settled system of cooperation, resulted from a war with the English. Stages in the genesis of a compound controlling agency by conflict with other societies are shown us by the Polynesians. In Samoa eight or ten village communities, which are in other respects independent,

> "unite by common consent, and form a district, or state, for mutual protection. . . . When war is threatened by another district, no single village can act alone; . . . Some of these districts or states have their king; others cannot agree on the choice of one; . . . there is no such thing as a king, or even a district, whose power extends all over the group." Yet in case of war, they sometimes combine in twos or three [Turner 1861, pp. 287, 291].

Early histories of the civilized similarly show us how union of smaller social aggregates for offensive or defensive purposes, necessitating coordination of their actions, tends to initiate a central coordinating agency. Instance the Hebrew monarchy: the previously-separate tribes of Israelites became a nation subordinate to Saul and David during wars with the Moabites, Ammonites, Edomites and Philistines. Instance the case of the Greeks: the growth of the Athenian hegemony into mastership, and the organization, political and naval, which accompanied it, was a concomitant of the continued activity of the confederacy against external enemies. Instance in later times the development of governments among Teutonic peoples. At the beginning of the Christian era there were only chieftainships of separate tribes and, during wars, temporary greater chieftainships of allied forces. Between the first and the fifth centuries the federations made to resist or invade the Roman empire did not evolve permanent heads, but in the fifth century the prolonged military activities of these federations ended in transforming these military leaders into kings over consolidated states.

As this differentiation by which there arises first a temporary and then a permanent military head, who passes insensibly into a political head, is initiated by conflict with adjacent societies, it naturally happens that his political power increases as military activity continues. Everywhere, providing extreme diffusion does not prevent, we find this connection between predatory activity and submission to despotic rule. Asia shows it in the Kirghiz tribes, who are slave hunters and robbers, and of whose manaps, once elective but now hereditary, the Michells say, "The word Manap literally means a tyrant, in the ancient Greek sense. It was at first the proper name of an elder distinguished for his cruelty and unrelenting spirit; from him the appellation became general to all Kirghiz rulers" [Valikhanov 1865, pp. 278–9]. Africa shows it in the cannibal Niam-niams, whose king is unlimited lord of persons and things [Schweinfurth 1873, II, 22] or again in the sanguinary Dahomeans with their Amazon army and in the warlike Ashantis, all trained to arms, both of them under governments so absolute that the highest officials are slaves to the king [Beecham 1841, p. 96]. Polynesia shows it in the ferocious Fijians, whose tribes are ever fighting with one another, and among whom loyalty to absolute rulers is the extremest imaginable — even so extreme that people of a slave district "said it was their duty to become food and sacrifices for the chiefs" [Erskine 1853, p. 464].

This relation between the degree of power in the political head and the degree of militancy, has, indeed, been made familiar to us in the histories of ancient and modern civilized races. The connection is implied in the Assyrian inscriptions as well as in the frescoes and papyri of Egypt. The case of Pausanias and other such cases were regarded by the Spartans themselves as showing the tendency of generals to become despots — as showing, that is, the tendency of active operations against adjacent societies to generate centralized political power. How the imperativeness fostered by continuous command of armies thus passes into political imperativeness has been again and again shown us in later histories.

Here, then, the induction we have to carry with us is that as in the individual organism that nervo-muscular apparatus which carries on conflict with environing organisms, begins with, and is developed by, that conflict, so the governmental-military organization of a society, is initiated by, and evolves along with, the warfare between societies. Or, to speak more strictly, there is thus evolved that part of its governmental organization which conduces to efficient cooperation against other societies.

The development of the regulating system may now be dealt with. Let us first trace the governmental agency through its stages of complication.

In small and little-differentiated aggregates, individual and social, the structure which coordinates does not become complex: neither the need for it nor the materials for forming and supporting it exist. But complexity begins in compound aggregates. In either case its commencement is seen in the rise of a superior coordinating center exercising control over inferior centers. Among animals the *Annulosa* illustrate this most clearly. In an annelid the like nervous structures of the like successive segments are but little subordinated to any chief ganglion or group of ganglia. But along with that evolution which, integrating and differentiating the segments, produces a higher annulose animal, there arise at the end which moves foremost, more developed senses and appendages for action, as well as a cluster of ganglia connected with them; and along with formation of this goes an increasing control exercised by it over the ganglia of the posterior segments. Not very strongly marked in such little-integrated types as centipedes, a nervous centralization of this kind becomes great in such integrated types as the higher crustaceans and the arachnida.

So is it in the progress from compound social aggregates that are loosely coherent to those that are consolidated. Manifestly, during those early stages in which the chief of a conquering tribe succeeds only in making the chiefs of adjacent tribes tributary while he lives, the political centralization is but slight, and hence, as in cases before referred to in Africa and elsewhere, the powers of the local centers re-assert themselves when they can throw off their temporary subordination. Many races which have got beyond the stage of separate simple tribes show us, along with various degrees of cohesion, various stages in the subjection of local governing centers to a general governing center. When first visited, the Hawaiian Islanders had a king with turbulent chiefs, formerly independent [Ellis 1826, p. 392], and in Tahiti there was similarly a monarch with secondary rulers but little subordinate [Forster 1778, p. 355]. So was it with the New Zealanders; and so was it with the Malagasy until a century since.

The nature of the political organization during such stages is shown us by the relative degrees of power which the general and special centers exercise over the people of each division. Thus of the Tahitians we read that the power of the chief was supreme in his own district, and greater than that of the king over the whole [Ellis 1829, II, 366–7]. Lichtenstein tells us of the Xosa that "they are all vassals of the king, chiefs, as well as those under them; but the subjects are generally so blindly attached to their chiefs, that they will follow them against the king" [1812–15, I, 286]. "Scarcely would the slave of an Ashanti chief," says Cruickshank, "obey the mandate of his king, without the special concurrence of his immediate master" [1853, II, 242]. And concerning the three grades of chiefs among the Araucanians, Thompson says of those who rule the smallest divisions that "their authority is less precarious" than that of the higher officers [1812,

I, 405]. These few instances, which might readily be multiplied, remind us of the relations between major and minor political centers in feudal times, when there were long periods during which the subjection of barons to kings was being established — during which failures of cohesion and re-assertions of local authority occurred — during which there was loyalty to the district ruler greater than that to the general ruler.

And now let us note deliberately what was before implied, that this subordination of local governing centers to a general governing center accompanies cooperation of the components of the compound aggregate in its conflicts with other like aggregates. Between such superior *Annulosa* as the winged insects and clawed crustaceans above described as having centralized nervous systems, and the inferior *Annulosa* composed of many similar segments with feeble limbs, the contrast is not only in the absence from these last of centralized nervous systems but also in the absence of offensive and defensive appliances of efficient kinds. In the high types, nervous subordination of the posterior segments to the anterior has accompanied the growth of those anterior appendages which preserve the aggregate of segments in its dealings with prey and enemies and this centralization of the nervous structure has resulted from the cooperation of these external organs.

It is thus also with the political centralizations which become permanent. So long as the subordination is established by internal conflict of the divisions with one another and hence involves antagonism among them, it remains unstable; but it tends towards stability in proportion as the regulating agents, major and minor, are habituated to combined action against external enemies. The recent changes in Germany have re-illustrated under our eyes this political centralization by combination in war, which was so abundantly illustrated in the Middle Ages by the rise of monarchical governments over numerous fiefs.

How this compound regulating agency for internal control results from combined external actions of the compound aggregate in war we may understand on remembering that at first the army and the nation are substantially the same. As in each primitive tribe the men are all warriors, so, during early stages of civilization the military body is co-extensive with the adult male population excluding only the slaves — co-extensive with all that part of the society which has political life. In fact the army is the nation mobilized, and the nation the quiescent army. Hence men who are local rulers while at home and leaders of their respective bands of dependents when fighting a common foe under direction of a general leader, become minor heads disciplined in subordination to the major head and as they carry more or less of this subordination home with them, the military organization developed during war survives as the political organization during peace.

Chiefly, however, we have here to note that in the compound regulating system evolved during the formation of a compound social aggregate, what were originally independent local centers of regulation become dependent local centers, serving as deputies under command of the general center, just as the local ganglia above described become agents acting under direction of the cephalic ganglia.

This formation of a compound regulating system characterized by a dominant center and subordinate centers is accompanied, in both individual organisms and social organisms, by increasing size and complexity of the dominant center.

In an animal, along with development of senses to yield information and limbs to be guided in conformity with it, so that by their cooperation prey may be caught and enemies escaped, there must arise one place to which the various kinds of information are brought and from which are issued the adjusted motor impulses, and, in proportion as evolution of the senses and limbs progresses, this center which utilizes increasingly varied information and directs better-combined movements, necessarily comes to have more numerous unlike parts and a greater total mass. Ascending through the annulose subkingdom, we find a growing aggregation of optic, auditory, and other ganglia receiving stimuli, together with the ganglia controlling the chief legs, claws, etc. And so in the vertebrate series, beginning in its lowest member with an almost uniform cord formed of local centers undirected by a brain, we rise finally to a cord appended to an integrated cluster of minor centers through which are issued the commands of certain supreme centers growing out of them.

In a society it similarly happens that the political agency which gains predominance is gradually augmented and complicated by additional parts for additional functions. The chief of chiefs begins to require helpers in carrying on control. He gathers round him some who get information, some with whom he consults, some who execute his commands. No longer a governing unit, he becomes the nucleus in a cluster of governing units. Various stages in this compounding, proceeding generally from the temporary to the permanent, may be observed. In the Hawaiian Islands the king and governor have each a number of chiefs who attend on them and execute their orders [Ellis 1826, p. 402]. The Tahitian king had a prime minister, as well as a few chiefs to give advice [Ellis 1829, II, 363], and in Samoa, too, each village chief has a sort of prime minister [Turner 1861, p. 284].

Africa shows us stages in this progress from simple personal government to government through agents. Among the Beetjuans (a Bechuana people) the king executes "his own sentence, even when the criminal is condemned to death," and Lichtenstein [1812–15, II, 329, 298] tells us of another group of Bechuanas (the Maatjaping) that, his people being disorderly, the monarch "swung his tremendous *sjambok* of rhinoceros leather, striking on all sides, till he fairly drove the whole multitude before him" being thereupon imitated by his courtiers. And then of the Bachapin government, belonging to this same race, we learn that the duty of the chief's brother "was to convey the chief's orders wherever the case demanded, and to see them put in execution" [Burchell 1822–24, II, 431]. Among the Xosa, governed by a king and vassal chiefs, every chief has councillors, and "the great council of the king is composed of the chiefs of particular kraals" [Lichtenstein 1812–15, I, 286]. Again, the Zulu sovereign shares his power with two soldiers of his choice, and these form the supreme judges of the country [Arboussett and Daumas 1846, p. 140].

The appendages which add to the size and complexity of the governing center in the larger African kingdoms are many and fully established. In Dahomey, besides two premiers and various functionaries surrounding the king, there are two judges, of whom one or other is "almost constantly with the king, informing him of every circumstance that passes" [Dalzel 1793, p. 121], and, according to Burton, every official is provided with a second in command, who is in reality a spy [1864, I, 53, 276]. Though the king joins in judging causes, and though when his executioners bungle he himself shows them how to cut off heads, yet he has agents around him into whose hands these functions are gradually lapsing, as, in the compound nervous structures above described, there are appended centers through which information is communicated, and appended centers through which the decisions pass into execution.

How in civilized nations analogous developments have taken place — how among ourselves William the Conqueror made his "justiciar" supreme administrator of law and finance, having under him a body of Secretaries of whom the chief was called Chancellor; how the justiciar became Prime Minister and his staff a supreme court, employed alike on financial and judicial affairs and in revision of laws; how this in course of time became specialized and complicated by appendages; needs not to be shown in detail [Stubbs 1870, pp. 16–7]. Always the central governing agency while being enlarged is made increasingly heterogeneous by the multiplication of parts having specialized functions. . . .

One further concomitant may be added. During evolution of the supreme regulating centers, individual and social, the older parts become relatively automatic. A simple ganglion with its afferent and efferent fibers receives stimuli and issues impulses unhelped and unchecked; but when there gather round it ganglia through which different kinds of impressions come to it, and others through which go from it impulses causing different motions, it becomes dependent on these, and in part an agent for transforming the sensory excitements of the first into the motor discharges of the last. As the supplementary parts multiply, and the impressions sent by them to the original center, increasing in number and variety, involve multiplied impulses sent through the appended motor centers, this original center becomes more and more a channel through which, in an increasingly mechanical way, special stimuli lead to appropriate actions.

Take, for example, three stages in the vertebrate animal. We have first an almost uniform spinal cord, to the successive portions of which are joined the sensory and motor nerves supplying the successive portions of the body: the spinal cord is here the supreme regulator. Then in the nervous system of vertebrates somewhat more advanced, the medulla oblongata and the sensory ganglia at the anterior part of this spinal cord, taking a relatively large share in receiving those guiding impressions which lead to motor discharges from its posterior part, tend to make this subordinate and its actions mechanical: the sensory ganglia have now become the chief rulers. And when in the course of evolution the cerebrum and cerebellum grow, the sensory ganglia, with the coordinating motor center to which they were joined, lapse into mere receivers of stimuli and conveyers of impulses; the last-formed centers acquire supremacy, and those preceding them are their servants.

Thus is it with kings, ministries, and legislative bodies. As the original political head, acquiring larger functions, gathers agents around him who bring data for decisions and undertake execution of them, he falls more and more into the hands of these agents — has his judgments in great degree made for him by informers and advisers, and his deputed acts modified by executive officers: the ministry begins to rule through the original ruler. At a later stage the evolution of legislative bodies is followed by the subordination of ministries, who, holding their places by the support of majorities, are substantially the agents executing the wills of those majorities. And while the ministry is thus becoming less deliberative and more executive, as the monarch did previously, the monarch is becoming more automatic: royal functions are performed by commission, royal speeches are but nominally such, royal assents are practically matters of form. This general truth, which our own constitutional history so well illustrates, was illustrated in another way during the development of Athenian institutions, political, judicial, and administrative: the older classes of functionaries survived, but fell into subordinate positions, performing duties of a comparatively routine kind.

From the general structures of regulating systems, and from the structures of their great centers of control, we must now turn to the appliances through which control is exercised. For coordinating the actions of an aggregate, individual or social, there must be not only a governing center, but there must also be media of communication through which this center may affect the parts.

Ascending stages of animal organization carry us from types in which this requirement is scarcely at all fulfilled, to types in which it is fulfilled effectually. Aggregates of very humble orders, as sponges, *Thallassicollae*, etc., without coordinating centers of any kind, are also without means of transferring impulses from part to part, and there is no cooperation of parts to meet an outer action. In *Hydrozoa* and *Actinozoa*, not possessing visible centers of coordination, slow adjustments result from the diffusion of molecular changes from part to part through the body: contraction of the whole creature presently follows rough handling of the tentacles, while contact of the tentacles with nutritive matter causes a gradual closing of them around it. Here, by the propagation of some influence among them, the parts are made to cooperate for the general good, feebly and sluggishly. In *Polyzoa*, along with the rise of distinct nerve centers, there is a rise of distinct nerve fibers, conveying impulses rapidly along definite lines, instead of slowly through the substance in general. Hence comes a relatively prompt cooperation of parts to deal with sudden external actions. And as these internuncial lines multiply, becoming at the same time well adjusted in their connections, they make possible those varied coordinations which developed nervous centers direct.

Analogous stages in social evolution are sufficiently manifest. Over a territory covered by groups devoid of political organization, news of an inroad spreads from person to person, taking long to diffuse over the whole area, and the inability of the scattered mass to cooperate is involved as much by the absence of internuncial agencies as by the absence of regulating centers. But along with such slight political coordination as union for defense produces, there arise appliances for influencing the actions of distant allies. Even the Fuegians light fires to communicate intelligence [Darwin 1839, p. 238]. The Tasmanians, too, made use of signal fires [Bonwick 1870, p. 21], as do the Tannese [Turner 1871, p. 326]; and this method of producing a vague coordination among the parts in certain emergencies is found among other uncivilized races.

As we advance, and as more definite combinations of more varied kinds have to be effected for offense and defense, messengers are employed. Among the Fijians, for instance, men are sent with news and commands, and use certain mnemonic aids [Wilkes 1845, III, 332]. The New Zealanders "occasionally conveyed information to distant tribes during war by marks on gourds" [Thomson 1859, I, 77]. In such comparatively advanced states as those of ancient America, this method of sending news was greatly developed. The Mexicans had couriers who at full speed ran six-mile stages, and so carried intelligence, it is said, even three hundred miles in a day [Clavigero 1787, I, 345], and the Peruvians, besides their fire and smoke signals in time of rebellion, had runners of the same kind [Garcilasso de la Vega 1869–71, II, 119–20]. So, too, was it with the Persians. Herodotus writes:

Nothing mortal travels so fast as these Persian messengers. The entire plan is a Persian invention; and this is the method of it. Along the whole line of road there are men (they say) stationed with horses, and the message is borne from hand to hand along the whole line, like the light in the torch-race, which the Greeks celebrate to Vulcan [1858, IV, 344].

Thus what is in its early stage a slow propagation of impulses from unit to unit throughout a society, becomes, as we advance, a more rapid propagation along settled lines, so making quick and definitely-adjusted combinations possible. Moreover, we must note that this part of the regulating system, like its other parts, is initiated by the necessities of cooperation against alien societies. As in later times among Highland clans the fast runner, bearing the fiery cross, carried a command to arm, so, in early English times the messages were primarily those between rulers and their agents and habitually concerned military affairs. Save in these cases (and even state messengers could not move swiftly along the bad roads of early days) the propagation of intelligence through the body politic was very slow. The slowness continued down to comparatively late periods. Queen Elizabeth's death was not known in some parts of Devon until after the Court had gone out of mourning, and the news of the appointment of Cromwell as Protector took nineteen days to reach Bridgewater [Smiles 1861–62, I, 185].

Nor have we to remark only the tardy spread of the influences required for cooperation of parts. The smallness and uniformity of these influences have also to be noted in contrast with their subsequent greatness and multiformity. Instead of the courier bearing a single despatch, military or political, from one ruling agent to another, at irregular intervals in few places, there come eventually, through despatches of multitudinous letters daily and several times a day, in all directions through every class, swift transits of impulses, no less voluminous than varied, all instrumental to cooperation.

Two other internuncial agencies of more developed kinds are afterwards added. Out of the letter, when it had become comparatively frequent among the educated classes, there came the newsletter: at first a partially printed sheet issued on the occurrence of an important event, and having an unprinted space left for a written letter. From this, dropping its blank part, and passing from the occasional into the periodic, came the newspaper. And the newspaper has grown in size, in multitudinousness, in variety, in frequency, until the feeble and slow waves of intelligence at long and irregular intervals, have become the powerful, regular, rapid waves by which, twice and thrice daily, millions of people receive throughout the kingdom stimulations and checks of all kinds, furthering quick and balanced adjustments of conduct.

Finally there arises a far swifter propagation of stimuli serving to coordinate social actions, political, military, commercial, etc. Beginning with the semaphore telegraph, which, reminding us in principle of the signal fires of savages, differed by its ability to convey not single vague ideas only, but numerous, complex, and distinct ideas, we end with the electric telegraph, immeasurably more rapid, through which go quite definite messages, infinite in variety and of every degree of complexity. And in place of a few such semaphore telegraphs, transmitting, chiefly for governmental purposes, impulses in a few directions, there has come a multiplicity of lines of instant communication in all directions, subserving all purposes. Moreover, by the agency of these latest internuncial structures the social organism, though discrete, has acquired a promptness of coordination equal to, and indeed exceeding, the promptness of coordination in concrete organisms. It was before pointed out that social units, though forming a discontinuous aggregate, achieve by language a transmission of impulses which, in individual aggregates, is achieved by nerves. But now, utilizing the molecular continuity of wires, the impulses are conveyed throughout the body politic much faster than they would be were it a solid living whole. Including times occupied by taking messages to and from the offices in each place, any citizen in Edinburgh may give motion to any citizen in London in less than one-fourth of the time a nervous discharge would take to pass from one to the other, were they joined by living tissue.

Nor should we omit the fact that parallelism in the requirements has caused something like parallelism in the arrangements of the internuncial lines. Out of great social centers emerge many large clusters of wires, from which, as they get further away, diverge at intervals minor clusters, and these presently give off re-diverging clusters, just as main bundles of nerves on their way towards the periphery, from time to time emit lateral bundles, and these again others. . . .

The general result, then, is that in societies, as in living bodies, the increasing mutual dependence of parts, implying an increasingly efficient regulating system, therefore implies not only developed regulating centers, but also means by which the influences of such centers may be propagated. And we see that as, under one of its aspects, organic evolution shows us more and more efficient internuncial appliances subserving regulation, so, too, does social evolution. . . .

The general law of organization, abundantly illustrated in foregoing chapters, is that distinct duties entail distinct structures; that from the strongest functional contrasts come the greatest structural differences and that within each of the leading systems of organs first divided from one another in conformity with this principle, secondary divisions arise in conformity with the same principle. The implication is, then, that if in an organism, individual or social, the function of regulation falls into two divisions which are widely unlike, the regulating apparatus will differentiate into correspondingly unlike parts, carrying on their unlike functions in great measure independently. This we shall find it does.

The fundamental division in a developed animal we have seen to be that between the outer set of organs which deal with the environment and the inner set of organs which carry on sustentation. . . . A parallel contrast of duties produces a parallel differentiation of structures during the evolution of social organisms. Single in low societies as in low animals, the regulating system in high societies as in high animals becomes divided into two systems, which, though they perpetually affect one another, carry on their respective controls with substantial independence. Observe the like causes for these like effects.

Success in conflicts with other societies implies quickness, combination, and special adjustments to ever varying circumstances. Information of an enemy's movements must be swiftly conveyed, forces must be rapidly drafted to particular spots, supplies fit in kinds and quantities must be provided, military maneuvers must be harmonized, and to these ends there must be a centralized agency that is instantly obeyed. Quite otherwise is it with the structures carrying on sustentation. Though the actions of these have to be somewhat varied upon occasion, especially to meet war demands, yet their general actions are comparatively uniform. The several kinds of food raised have to meet a consumption which changes within moderate limits only; for clothing the demands are tolerably constant, and alter in their proportions not suddenly but slowly; and so with commodities of less necessary kinds: rapidity, speciality, and exactness, do not characterize the required coordinations. Hence a place for another kind of regulating system. Such a system evolves as fast as the sustaining system itself evolves. Let us note its progress.

In early stages the occupations are often such as to prevent division between the control of defensive actions and the control of sustaining actions, because the two are closely allied. Among the Mandans the families joined in hunting and divided the spoil equally, showing us that the war with beasts carried on for joint benefit was so nearly allied to the war with men carried on for joint benefit that both remained public affairs [Lewis and Clarke 1814, p. 113]. Similarly with the Comanches, the guarding of a tribe's cattle is carried on in the same manner as military guarding and since the community of individual interests in this protection of cattle from enemies is like the community of interests in personal protection, unity in the two kinds of government continues [Marcy 1866, p. 29]. Moreover in simple tribes which are under rulers of any kinds, what authority exists is unlimited in range and includes industrial actions as well as others. If there are merely wives for slaves, or if there is a slave class, the dominant individuals who carry on outer attack and defense also direct in person such labor as is performed, and where a chief having considerable power has arisen, he not only leads in war but orders the daily activities during peace. The Gonds, the Bhils, the Nagas, the Mishmis, the Kalmucks, and many other simple tribes show us this identity of the political and industrial governments.

A partial advance, leading to some distinction, does not separate the two in a definite way. Thus among the Kukis the rajah claims and regulates work, superintends village removals, and apportions the land each family has to clear on a new site [Stewart 1855, p. 635]; among the Santals the head man partially controls the people's labor [Hunter 1868, p. 217]; and among the Khonds he acts as chief merchant. Polynesia presents like facts. The New Zealand chiefs superintend agricultural and building operations [Angas 1847, II, 50]; the Hawaiian Islanders have a market, in which "the price is regulated by the chiefs" [Ellis 1826, p. 292]; trade in Tonga also "is evidently under [the chief's] supervision" [Wilkes 1845, III, 22], and the Kadayan chiefs "settle the price of rice" [St. John 1862, II, 269]. So again in Celebes the days for working in the plantations are decided by the political agency, and the people go at beat of gong [Wallace 1869, I, 387]; so again in East Africa the times of sowing and harvest depend on the chief's will [Burton, R. 1860, p. 365], and among the Inland Negroes the "market is arranged according to the directions of the chiefs" [Allen 1848, I, 321]; so again in some parts of ancient America, as El Salvador, where the cacique directed the plantings [Palacio 1860, p. 83]. . . .

In other societies, and especially in those which are considerably developed, we find this union of political and industrial rule becoming modified; the agency, otherwise the same, is doubled. Thus among the Sakarran Dyaks there is a "trading chief" in addition to two principal chiefs [Low 1848, p. 184]; among the Dahomeans there is a commercial chief in Whydah [Burton, R. 1864, I, 52], and there are industrial chiefs in Fiji, where, in other respects, social organization is considerably advanced. At a later stage the commercial chief passes into the government officer exercising stringent supervision. In ancient Guatemala a state functionary fixed the price of the markets [Ximénez 1857, p. 203], and in Mexico, agents of the state saw that lands did not remain uncultivated [Zurita 1840, pp. 56–7].

Facts of this kind introduce us to the stages passed through by European societies. Up to the tenth century each domain in France had its bond, or only partially free, workmen and artisans, directed by the seigneur and paid in meals and goods; between the eleventh and fourteenth centuries the feudal superiors, ecclesiastical or lay, regulated production and distribution to such extent that industrial and commercial licences had to be purchased from them; in the subsequent monarchical stage, it was a legal maxim that "the right to labor is a royal right, which the prince may sell and subjects can buy;" and onwards to the time of the Revolution the country swarmed with officials who authorized occupations, dictated processes, examined products, . . . [Levasseur 1859, I, 167; Bourquelot 1865, Pt. II, 208–9].

Still better does our own history show us this progressive differentiation. In the Old English period the heads of guilds were identical with the local political heads — ealdormen, wick-, port-, or burgh-reeves — and the guild was itself in part a political body. Purchases and bargains had to be made in presence of officials. Agricultural and manufacturing processes were prescribed by law. Dictations of kindred kinds, though decreasing, continued to late times. Down to the sixteenth century there were metropolitan and local councils, politically authorized, which determined prices, fixed wages, etc. [Lappenberg 1845, II, 352–3, 355–6; Hallam 1867, I, Ch. 8; Macaulay 1849–61, I, 416]. . . .

Summary

Thus the increasing mutual dependence of parts, which both kinds of organisms display as they evolve, necessitates a further series of remarkable parallelisms. Cooperation being in either case impossible without appliances by which the cooperating parts shall have their actions adjusted, it inevitably happens that in the body politic, as in the living body, there arises a regulating system and within itself this differentiates as the sets of organs evolve.

The cooperation most urgent from the outset is that required for dealing with environing enemies and prey. Hence the first regulating center, individual and social, is initiated as a means to this cooperation, and its development progresses with the activity of this cooperation. As compound aggregates are formed by integration of simple ones, there arise in either case supreme regulating centers and subordinate ones and the supreme centers begin to enlarge and complicate. While doubly compound and trebly compound aggregates show us further developments in complication and subordination, they show us, also, better internuncial appliances, ending in those which convey instant information and instant command.

To this chief regulating system, controlling the organs which carry on outer actions, there is, in either case, added during the progress of evolution, a regulating system for the inner organs carrying on sustentation and this gradually establishes itself as independent. Naturally it comes later than the other. Complete utilization of materials for sustentation being less urgent, and implying coordination relatively simple, [it] has its controlling appliances less rapidly developed than those which are concerned with the catching of prey and the defense against enemies.

And then the third or distributing system, which, though necessarily arising after the others, is indispensable to the considerable development of them, eventually gets a regulating apparatus peculiar to itself.

(Here let it . . . be distinctly asserted that there exist no analogies between the body politic and a living body save those necessitated by that mutual dependence of parts which they display in common. Though, in foregoing chapters, sundry comparisons of social structures and functions to structures and functions in the human body have been made, they have been made only because structures and functions in the human body furnish familiar illustrations of structures and functions in general. The social organism, discrete instead of concrete, asymmetrical instead of symmetrical, sensitive in all its units instead of having a single sensitive center, is not comparable to any particular type of individual organism, animal or vegetal. All kinds of creatures are alike in so far as each exhibits cooperation among its components for the benefit of the whole and this trait, common to them, is a trait common also to societies. Further, among individual organisms, the degree of cooperation measures the degree of evolution and this general truth, too, holds among social organisms. Once more, to effect increasing cooperation, creatures of every order show us increasingly complex appliances for transfer and mutual influence and to this general characteristic societies of every order furnish a corresponding characteristic. These, then, are the analogies alleged; community in the fundamental principles of organization is the only community asserted.)

CHAPTER 8

SOCIAL TYPES

A glance at the respective antecedents of individual organisms and social organisms shows why the last admit of no such definite classification as the first. Through a thousand generations a species of plant or animal leads substantially the same kind of life, and its successive members inherit the acquired adaptations.* When changed conditions cause divergences of forms once alike, the accumulating differences arising in descendants only superficially disguise the original identity — do not prevent the grouping of the several species into a genus; nor do wider divergences that began earlier prevent the grouping of genera into orders and orders into classes. It is otherwise with societies. Hordes of primitive men, dividing and subdividing, do, indeed, show us successions of small social aggregates leading like lives, inheriting such low structures as had resulted, and repeating those structures. But higher social aggregates propagate their respective types in much less decided ways. Though colonies tend to grow like their parent-societies, yet the parent-societies are so comparatively plastic and the influences of new habitats on the derived societies are so great, that divergences of structure are inevitable. In the absence of definite organizations established during the similar lives of many societies descending one from another, there cannot be the precise distinctions implied by complete classification.

Two cardinal kinds of differences there are, however, of which we may avail ourselves for grouping societies in a natural manner. Primarily we may arrange them according to their degrees of composition, as simple, compound, doubly compound, trebly compound; and secondarily, though in a less specific way, we may divide them into the predominantly militant and the predominantly industrial — those in which the organization for offense and defense is most largely developed and those in which the sustaining organization is most largely developed.

We have seen that social evolution begins with small simple aggregates, that it progresses by the clustering of these into larger aggregates, and that after being consolidated, such clusters are united with others like themselves into still larger aggregates. Our classification, then, must begin with societies of the first or simplest order.

We cannot in all cases say with precision what constitutes a simple

* [The inheritance of acquired characteristics, still a subject of controversy at the time Spencer wrote, is today denied by biologists.—ED.]

society, for, in common with products of evolution generally, societies present transitional stages which negative sharp divisions. As the multiplying members of a group spread and diverge gradually, it is not always easy to decide when the groups into which they fall become distinct. Here, inhabiting a barren region, the descendants of common ancestors have to divide while yet the constituent families are near akin, and there, in a more fertile region, the group may hold together until clusters of families remotely akin are formed — clusters which, diffusing slowly, are held by a common bond that slowly weakens. By and by comes the complication arising from the presence of slaves not of the same ancestry, or of an ancestry but distantly allied and these, though they may not be political units, must be recognized as units sociologically considered. Then there is the kindred complication arising where an invading tribe becomes a dominant class. Our only course is to regard as a simple society one which forms a single working whole unsubjected to any other, and of which the parts cooperate, with or without a regulating center, for certain public ends. Here is a table [Table 1] presenting with as much definiteness as may be the chief divisions and subdivisions of such simple societies.

On contemplating these uncivilized societies which, though alike as being uncompounded differ in their sizes and structures, certain generally associated traits may be noted. Of the groups without political organization, or with but vague traces of it, the lowest are those small wandering ones which live on the wild food sparsely distributed in forests, over barren tracts, or along seashores. Where small simple societies remain without chiefs though settled, it is where circumstances allow them to be habitually peaceful. Glancing down the table we find reason for inferring that the changes from the hunting life to the pastoral, and from the pastoral to the agricultural, favor increase of population, the development of political organization, of industrial organization, and of the arts, though these causes do not of themselves produce these results.

[Table 2] contains societies which have passed to a slight extent, or considerably, or wholly, into a state in which the simple groups have their respective chiefs under a supreme chief. The stability or instability alleged of the headship in these cases refers to the headship of the composite group and not to the headships of the component groups. As might be expected, stability of this compound headship becomes more marked as the original unsettled state passes into the completely settled state, the nomadic life obviously making it difficult to keep the heads of groups subordinate to a general head. Though not in all cases accompanied by considerable organization, this coalescence evidently conduces to organization. The completely settled compound societies are mostly characterized by division into ranks, four, five, or six, clearly marked off; by established ecclesiastical arrangements; by industrial structures that show

TABLE 1

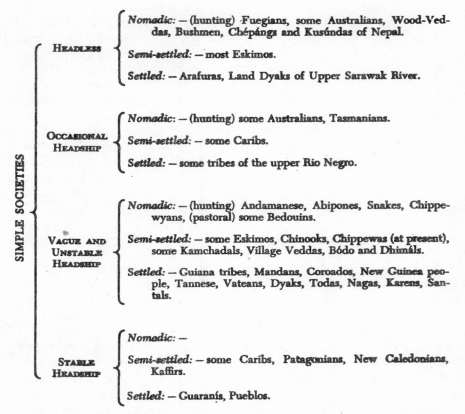

SIMPLE SOCIETIES

HEADLESS

Nomadic: — (hunting) Fuegians, some Australians, Wood-Veddas, Bushmen, Chépángs and Kusúndas of Nepal.

Semi-settled: — most Eskimos.

Settled: — Arafuras, Land Dyaks of Upper Sarawak River.

OCCASIONAL HEADSHIP

Nomadic: — (hunting) some Australians, Tasmanians.

Semi-settled: — some Caribs.

Settled: — some tribes of the upper Rio Negro.

VAGUE AND UNSTABLE HEADSHIP

Nomadic: — (hunting) Andamanese, Abipones, Snakes, Chippewyans, (pastoral) some Bedouins.

Semi-settled: — some Eskimos, Chinooks, Chippewas (at present), some Kamchadals, Village Veddas, Bódo and Dhimáls.

Settled: — Guiana tribes, Mandans, Coroados, New Guinea people, Tannese, Vateans, Dyaks, Todas, Nagas, Karens, Santals.

STABLE HEADSHIP

Nomadic: —

Semi-settled: — some Caribs, Patagonians, New Caledonians, Kaffirs.

Settled: — Guaranís, Pueblos.

advancing division of labor, general and local; by buildings of some permanence clustered into places of some size; and by improved appliances of life generally.

In the succeeding table [Table 3] are placed societies formed by the recompounding of these compound groups, or in which many governments of the types tabulated above have become subject to a still higher government. The first notable fact is that these doubly compound societies are all completely settled. Along with their greater integration we see in many cases, though not uniformly, a more elaborate and stringent political organization. Where complete stability of political headship over these doubly compound societies has been established, there is mostly, too, a developed ecclesiastical hierarchy. While becoming more complex by division of labor, the industrial organization has in many cases assumed a caste structure. To a greater or less extent, custom has passed into positive law and religious observances have grown definite, rigid, and com-

TABLE 2

<table>
<tr><td rowspan="9">COMPOUND SOCIETIES</td></tr>
</table>

COMPOUND SOCIETIES

OCCASIONAL HEADSHIP
- *Nomadic:* — (pastoral) some Bedouins.
- *Semi-settled:* — Tannese.
- *Settled:* —

UNSTABLE HEADSHIP
- *Nomadic:* — (hunting) Dakotas, (hunting and pastoral) Comanches, (pastoral) Kalmucks.
- *Semi-settled:* — Ostyaks, Beluchis, Kukis, Bhils, Congo-people (passing into doubly compound), Teutons before 5th century.
- *Settled:* — Chippewas (in past times), Creeks, Mundurucús, Tupís, Khonds, some New Guinea people, Sumatrans, Malagasy (till recently), Coast Negroes, Inland Negroes, some Abyssinians, Homeric Greeks, Kingdoms of the Heptarchy, Teutons in 5th century, Fiefs of 10th century.

STABLE HEADSHIP
- *Nomadic:* — (pastoral) Kirghiz.
- *Semi-settled:* — Bechuanas, Zulus.
- *Settled:* Fijians (when first visited), New Zealanders, Hawaiian Islanders (in Cook's time), Javans, Hottentots, Dahomeans, Ashantis, some Abyssinians, Ancient Yucatanese, New Granada people, Honduras people, Chibchas, some town Arabs.

TABLE 3

DOUBLY COMPOUND SOCIETIES

OCCASIONAL HEADSHIP
- *Semi-settled:* —
- *Settled:* — Samoans.

UNSTABLE HEADSHIP
- *Semi-settled:* —
- *Settled:* — Tahitians, Tongans, Javans (occasionally), Fijians, (since fire-arms), Malagasy (in recent times), Athenian Confederacy, Spartan Confederacy, Teutonic Kingdoms from 6th to 9th centuries, Greater Fiefs in France of the 13th century.

STABLE HEADSHIP
- *Semi-settled:* —
- *Settled:* — Iroquois, Araucanians, Hawaiian Islanders (since Cook's time), Ancient Vera Paz and Bogotá peoples, Guatemalans, Ancient Peruvians, Wahhàbees (Arab), Oman (Arab), Ancient Egyptian Kingdom, England after the 10th century.

plex. Towns and roads have become general and considerable progress in knowledge and the arts has taken place.

There remain to be added the great civilized nations which need no tabular form, since they mostly fall under one head — trebly compound. Ancient Mexico, the Assyrian Empire, the Egyptian Empire, the Roman Empire, Great Britain, France, Germany, Italy, Russia, may severally be regarded as having reached this stage of composition, or perhaps, in some cases, a still higher stage. Only in respect of the stabilities of their governments may they possibly require classing apart — not their political stabilities in the ordinary sense, but their stabilities in the sense of continuing to be the supreme centers of these great aggregates. So defining this trait, the ancient trebly compound societies have mostly to be classed as unstable; of the modern, the Kingdom of Italy and the German Empire have to be tested by time.

As already indicated, this classification must not be taken as more than an approximation to the truth. In some cases the data furnished by travellers and others are inadequate; in some cases their accounts are conflicting; in some cases the composition is so far transitional that it is difficult to say under which of two heads it should come. Here the gens or the phratry may be distinguished as a local community, and here these groups of near or remote kinsmen are so mingled with other such groups as practically to form parts of one community. Evidently the like combination of several such communities, passing through stages of increasing cohesion, leaves it sometimes doubtful whether they are to be regarded as many or as one. And when, as with the larger social aggregates, there have been successive conquests, resulting unions, subsequent dissolutions, and re-unions otherwise composed, the original lines of structure become so confused or lost that it is difficult to class the ultimate product.

But there emerge certain generalizations which we may safely accept. The stages of compounding and re-compounding have to be passed through in succession. No tribe becomes a nation by simple growth, and no great society is formed by the direct union of the smallest societies. Above the simple group the first stage is a compound group inconsiderable in size. The mutual dependence of parts which constitutes it a working whole cannot exist without some development of lines of intercourse and appliances for combined action and this must be achieved over a narrow area before it can be achieved over a wide one. When a compound society has been consolidated by the cooperation of its component groups in war under a single head — when it has simultaneously differentiated somewhat its social ranks and industries and proportionately developed its arts, which all of them conduce in some way to better cooperation, the compound society becomes practically a single one. Other societies of the same order, each having similarly reached a stage of organization alike required and made possible by this coordination of actions throughout a larger mass, now form bodies from which, by conquest or by federation in war, may be formed societies of the doubly compound type. The consolidation of these has again an accompanying advance of organization distinctive of it — an organization for which it affords the scope and which makes it practicable — an organization having a higher complexity in its regulative, distributive, and industrial systems. And at later stages, by kindred steps, arise still larger aggregates having still more complex structures. In this order has social evolution gone on, and only in this order does it appear to be possible. Whatever imperfections and incongruities the above classification has, do not hide these general facts — that there are societies of these different grades of composition; that those of the same grade have general resemblances in their structures; and that they arise in the order shown.

We pass now to the classification based on unlikenesses between the kinds of social activity which predominate and on the resulting unlikenesses of organization. The two social types thus essentially contrasted are the militant and the industrial.

It is doubtless true that no definite separation of these can be made. Excluding a few simple groups such as the Eskimos, inhabiting places where they are safe from invasion, all societies, simple and compound, are occasionally or habitually in antagonism with other societies and, as we have seen, tend to evolve structures for carrying on offensive and defensive actions. At the same time sustentation is necessary and there is always an organization, slight or decided, for achieving it. But while the two systems in social organisms, as in individual organisms, co-exist in all but the rudimentary forms, they vary immensely in the ratios they bear to one another. In some cases the structures carrying on external actions are largely developed, the sustaining system exists solely for their benefit, and the activities are militant. In other cases there is predominance of the structures carrying on sustentation, offensive and defensive structures are maintained only to protect them, and the activities are industrial. At the one extreme we have those warlike tribes which, subsisting mainly by the chase, make the appliances for dealing with enemies serve also for procuring food, and have sustaining systems represented only by their women, who are their slave classes; while at the other extreme we have the type, as yet only partially evolved, in which the agricultural, manufacturing, and commercial organizations form the chief part of the society, and, in the absence of external enemies, the appliances for offense and defense are either rudimentary or absent. Transitional as are nearly all

the societies we have to study, we may yet clearly distinguish the constitutional traits of these opposite types, characterized by predominance of
the outer and inner systems respectively.

Having glanced at the two thus placed in contrast it will be most convenient to contemplate each by itself.

As before pointed out, the militant type is one in which the army is
the nation mobilized while the nation is the quiescent army and which,
therefore, acquires a structure common to army and nation. We shall most
clearly understand its nature by observing in detail this parallelism between the military organization and the social organization at large.

Already we have had ample proof that centralized control is the primary
trait acquired by every body of fighting men, be it horde of savages, band
of brigands, or mass of soldiers. And this centralized control, necessitated
during war, characterizes the government during peace. Among the uncivilized there is a marked tendency for the military chief to become also
the political head (the medicine man being his only competitor) and in
a conquering race of savages his political headship becomes fixed. In
semi-civilized societies the conquering commander and the despotic king
are the same and they remain the same in civilized societies down to late
times. The connection is well shown where in the same race, along with
a contrast between the habitual activities, we find contrasted forms of
government. Thus the powers of the patriarchal chiefs of Kaffir tribes are
not great but the Zulus, who have become a conquering division of the
Kaffirs, are under an absolute monarch [Shooter 1857, p. 268; Gardiner
1836, p. 34]. Of advanced savages the Fijians may be named as well showing this relation between habitual war and despotic rule: the persons and
property of subjects are entirely at the king's or chief's disposal [Erskine
1853, p. 431]. We have seen that it is the same in the warlike African states,
Dahomey and Ashanti. The ancient Mexicans, again, whose highest profession was that of arms and whose eligible prince became king only by
feats in war, had an autocratic government, which, according to Clavigero
became more stringent as the territory was enlarged by conquest [1787,
I, 342]. Similarly, the unmitigated despotism under which the Peruvians
lived had been established during the spread of the Inca conquests. And
that race is not the cause we are shown by this recurrence in ancient
America of a relation so familiar in ancient states of the Old World.

The absoluteness of a commander in chief goes along with absolute
control exercised by his generals over their subordinates and by their subordinates over the men under them: all are slaves to those above and
despots to those below. This structure repeats itself in the accompanying
social arrangements. There are precise gradations of rank in the community and complete submission of each rank to the ranks above it. We
see this in the society already instanced as showing among advanced

savages the development of the militant type. In Fiji six classes are enumerated, from king down to slaves, as sharply marked off [Williams and Calvert 1858, I, 32]. Similarly in Madagascar, where despotism has been in late times established by war, there are several grades and castes [Ellis 1838, I, 346–9]. Among the Dahomeans, given in so great a degree to bloodshed of all kinds, "the army, or, what is nearly synonymous, the nation," says Burton, "is divided, both male and female, into two wings" [1864, I, 220], and then, of the various ranks enumerated, all are characterized as legally slaves of the king. In Ashanti, too, where his officers are required to die when the king dies, we have a kindred condition [Bastian 1860, II, 333]. Of old, among the aggressive Persians, grades were strongly marked. So was it in warlike ancient Mexico: besides three classes of nobility, and besides the mercantile classes, there were three agricultural classes down to the serfs — all in precise subordination [Sahagún 1829–30, III, 1]. In Peru, also, below the Inca there were grades of nobility — lords over lords. Moreover, in each town the inhabitants were registered in decades under a decurion, five of these under a superior, two such under a higher one, five of these centurions under a head, two of these heads under one who thus ruled a thousand men, and for every ten thousand there was a governor of Inca race, the political rule being thus completely regimental [Garcilasso de la Vega 1869–71, I, 143]. Till lately, another illustration was furnished by Japan.

That there were kindred, if less elaborate, structures in ancient militant states of the Old World scarcely needs saying and that like structures were repeated in medieval times, when a large nation like France had under the monarch several grades of feudal lords, vassals to those above, and suzerains to those below, with serfs under the lowest, again shows us that everywhere the militant type has sharply marked social gradations as it has sharply marked military gradations.

Along with this natural government there goes a like form of supernatural government. I do not mean merely that in the ideal other worlds of militant societies the ranks and powers are conceived as like those of the real world around, though this also is to be noted, but I refer to the militant character of the religion. Ever in antagonism with other societies, the life is a life of enmity and the religion a religion of enmity. The duty of blood revenge, most sacred of all with the savage, continues to be the dominant duty as the militant type of society evolves. The chief, balked of his vengeance, dies enjoining his successors to avenge him; his ghost is propitiated by fulfilling his commands; the slaying of his enemies becomes the highest action; trophies are brought to his grave in token of fulfilment and, as tradition grows, he becomes the god worshipped with bloody sacrifices. Everywhere we find evidence. The Fijians offer the bodies of their victims killed in war to the war-god before cooking them

[Williams and Calvert 1858, I, 208]. In Dahomey, where the militant type is so far developed that women are warriors, men are almost daily sacrificed by the monarch to please his dead father, and the ghosts of old kings are invoked for aid in war by blood sprinkled on their tombs [Burton, R. 1864, II, 19, 167]. The war-god of the Mexicans (originally a conqueror), the most revered of their gods, had his idol fed with human flesh, wars being undertaken to supply him with victims [Herrera 1725–26, IV, 213]. And similarly in Peru, where there were habitual human sacrifices, men taken captive were immolated to the father of the Incas, the Sun [Markham 1873, pp. 54–6].

How militant societies of old in the East similarly evolved deities who were similarly propitiated by bloody rites needs merely indicating. Habitually their mythologies represent gods as conquerors; habitually their gods are named "the strong one," "the destroyer," "the avenger," "god of battles," "lord of hosts," "man of war," and so forth. As we read in Assyrian inscriptions, wars were commenced by their alleged will and, as we read elsewhere, peoples were massacred wholesale in professed obedience to them. How its theological government, like its political government, is essentially military we see even in late and qualified forms of the militant type, for down to the present time absolute subordination, like that of soldier to commander, is the supreme virtue, and disobedience the crime for which eternal torture is threatened.

Similarly with the accompanying ecclesiastical organization. Generally where the militant type is highly developed, the political head and the ecclesiastical head are identical — the king, chief descendant of his ancestor who has become a god, is also chief propitiator of him. It was so in ancient Peru [Garcilasso de la Vega 1869–71, I, 132], and in Acolhuacán (Mexico) the high priest was the king's second son [Clavigero 1787, I, 271]. The Egyptian wall paintings show us kings performing sacrifices, as do also the Assyrian. Babylonian records harmonize with Hebrew traditions in telling us of priest-kings. In Lydia it was the same: Croesus was king and priest. In Sparta, too, the kings, while military chiefs, were also high priests and a trace of the like original relation existed in Rome. A system of subordination essentially akin to the military has habitually characterized the accompanying priesthoods. The Fijians have an hereditary priesthood forming a hierarchy [Erskine 1853, p. 250]. In Tahiti, where the high priest was often royal, there were grades of hereditary priests belonging to each social rank [Ellis 1829, II, 208; Hawkesworth 1773, II, 240]. In ancient Mexico the priesthoods of different gods had different ranks and there were three ranks within each priesthood [Clavigero 1787, I, 270; Sahagún 1829–30, I, 277]; in ancient Peru, besides the royal chief priest, there were priests of the conquering race set over various classes of inferior priests [Garcilasso de la Vega 1869–71, I, 132]. A like type of

structure, with subjection of rank to rank, has characterized priesthoods in
the ancient and modern belligerent societies of the Old World.

A kind of government essentially the same is traceable throughout the
sustaining organization also, so long as the social type remains predominantly militant. Beginning with simple societies in which the slave class
furnishes the warrior class with the necessaries of life, we have already
seen that during subsequent stages of evolution the industrial part of the
society continues to be essentially a permanent commissariat, existing
solely to supply the needs of the government-military structures, and having left over for itself only enough for bare maintenance. Hence the development of political regulation over its activities has been in fact the
extension throughout it of that military rule which, as a permanent commissariat, it naturally had. An extreme instance is furnished us by the
ancient Peruvians, whose political and industrial governments were identical — whose kinds and quantities of labor for every class in every locality
were prescribed by laws enforced by state officers — who had work legally
dictated even for their young children, their blind, and their lame, and
who were publicly chastised for idleness, regimental discipline being
applied to industry just as our modern advocate of strong government
would have it now [Garcilasso de la Vega 1869–71, II, 34]. The late Japanese system, completely military in origin and nature, similarly permeated
industry: great and small things — houses, ships, down even to mats —
were prescribed in their structures. In the warlike monarchy of Madagascar the artisan classes are in the employ of government, and no man can
change his occupation or locality under pain of death [Ellis 1838, I, 197].
Without multiplication of cases, these typical ones, reminding the reader
of the extent to which even in modern fighting states industrial activities
are officially regulated, will sufficiently show the principle.

Not industry only, but life at large, is, in militant societies, subject to
kindred discipline. Before its recent collapse the government of Japan
enforced sumptuary laws on each class, mercantile and other, up to the
provincial governors, who must rise, dine, go out, give audience, and
retire to rest at prescribed hours, and the native literature specifies regulations of a scarcely credible minuteness. In ancient Peru officers "minutely
inspected the houses, to see that the man, as well as his wife, kept the
household in proper order, and preserved a due state of discipline among
their children" and householders were rewarded or chastised accordingly
[Garcilasso de la Vega 1869–71, II, 34]. Among the Egyptians of old each
person had, at fixed intervals, to report to the local authority his name,
abode, and mode of living [Wilkinson 1878, I, 299]. Sparta, too, yields an
example of a society specially organized for offense and defense in which
the private conduct of citizens in all its details was under public control,
enforced by spies and censors.

Though regulations so stringent have not characterized the militant type in more recent ages, yet we need but recall the laws regulating food and dress, the restraints on locomotion, the prohibitions of some games and dictation of others, to indicate the parallelism of principle. Even now where the military organization has been kept in vigor by military activities, as in France, we are shown by the peremptory control of journals and suppression of meetings, by the regimental uniformity of education, by the official administration of the fine arts, the way in which its characteristic regulating system ramifies everywhere.

And then, lastly, is to be noted the theory concerning the relation between the state and the individual, with its accompanying sentiment. This structure, which adapts a society for combined action against other societies, is associated with the belief that its members exist for the benefit of the whole and not the whole for the benefit of its members. As in an army the liberty of the soldier is denied and only his duty as a member of the mass insisted on, as in a permanently encamped army like the Spartan nation, the laws recognize no personal interests, but patriotic ones only, so in the militant type throughout, the claims of the unit are nothing and the claims of the aggregate everything. Absolute subjection to authority is the supreme virtue and resistance to it a crime. Other offenses may be condoned but disloyalty is an unpardonable offense. If we take the sentiments of the sanguinary Fijians, among whom loyalty is so intense that a man stands unbound to be knocked on the head, himself saying that what the king wills must be done [Williams and Calvert 1858, I, 30], or those of the Dahomeans, among whom the highest officials are the king's slaves and on his decease his women sacrifice one another that they may all follow him, or those of the ancient Peruvians, among whom with a dead Inca, or great Curaca, were buried alive his favorite attendants and wives that they might go to serve him in the other world [Garcilasso de la Vega 1869–71, II, 113], or those of the ancient Persians, among whom a father, seeing his innocent son shot by the king in pure wantonness, "felicitated" the king "on the excellence of his archery," and among whom bastinadoed subjects "declared themselves delighted because his majesty had condescended to recollect them" [ref. lost], we are sufficiently shown that in this social type the sentiment which prompts assertion of personal rights in opposition to a ruling power, scarcely exists.

Thus the trait characterizing the militant structure throughout is that its units are coerced into their various combined actions. As the soldier's will is so suspended that he becomes in everything the agent of his officer's will, so is the will of the citizen in all transactions, private and public, overruled by that of the government. The cooperation by which the life of the militant society is maintained is a *compulsory* cooperation. The social structure adapted for dealing with surrounding hostile societies is under a centralized regulating system, to which all the parts are completely subject, just as in the individual organism the outer organs are completely subject to the chief nervous center.

The traits of the industrial type have to be generalized from inadequate and entangled data. Antagonism more or less constant with other societies, having been almost everywhere and always the condition of each society, a social structure fitted for offense and defense exists in nearly all cases and disguises the structure which social sustentation alone otherwise originates. Such conception as may be formed of it has to be formed from what we find in the few simple societies which have been habitually peaceful, and in the advanced compound societies which, though once habitually militant, have become gradually less so.

Already I have referred to the chiefless Arafuras living in "peace and brotherly love with one another," of whom we are told that "they recognize the right of property in the fullest sense of the word, without there being any authority among them than the decisions of their elders, according to the customs of their forefathers" [Kolff 1840, p. 161]. That is, there has grown up a recognition of mutual claims and personal rights, with voluntary submission to a tacitly elected representative government formed of the most experienced. Among the Todas, "who lead a peaceful, tranquil life," disputes are "settled either by arbitration" or by "a council of five" [Shortt 1868, pp. 239, 241]. The amiable Bódo and Dhimáls, said to be wholly unmilitary, display an essentially free social form. They have nothing but powerless head men and are without slaves or servants but they give mutual assistance in clearing ground and housebuilding: there is voluntary exchange of services — giving of equivalents of labor [Hodgson 1849, p. 741]. The Mishmis again, described as quiet, inoffensive, not warlike, and only occasionally uniting in self-defense, have scarcely any political organization. Their village communities under merely nominal chiefs acknowledge no common chief of the tribe and the rule is democratic; crimes are judged by an assembly [Rowlatt 1845, p. 491; Griffith 1837, p. 332].

Naturally few, if any, cases occur in which societies of this type have evolved into larger societies without passing into the militant type, for, as we have seen, the consolidation of simple aggregates into a compound aggregate habitually results from war, defensive or offensive, which, if continued, evolves a centralized authority with its coercive institutions. The Pueblos, however, industrious and peaceful agriculturists, who, building their unique villages, or compound houses containing two thousand people, in such ways as to "wall out black barbarism," fight only when invaded, show us a democratic form of government: "the governor and his council are elected annually by the people" [Bancroft 1875–76, I, 536,

546]. The case of Samoa, too, may be named as showing to some extent how in one of these compound communities where the warlike activity is now not considerable, decline in the rigidity of political control has gone along with some evolution of the industrial type. Chiefs and minor heads, partly hereditary, partly elective, are held responsible for the conduct of affairs; there are village parliaments and district parliaments. Along with this we find a considerably developed sustaining organization separate from the political — masters who have apprentices, employ journeymen, and pay wages, and when payment for work is inadequate, there are even strikes upheld by a tacit trades-unionism [Turner 1861, p. 287].

Passing to more evolved societies it must be observed, first, that the distinctive traits of the industrial type do not become marked, even where the industrial activity is considerable, so long as the industrial government remains identified with the political. In Phoenicia, for example, the foreign wholesale trade seems to have belonged mostly to the state, the kings, and the nobles. Ezekiel describes the king of Tyre as a prudent commercial prince who finds out the precious metals in their hidden seats, enriches himself by getting them, and increases these riches by traffic [Cook 1871–81, Ezk. XXVIII, 3, 4, 5]. Clearly, where the political and military heads have thus themselves become the heads of the industrial organization, the traits distinctive of it are prevented from showing themselves.

Of ancient societies to be named in connection with the relation between industrial activities and free institutions, Athens will be at once thought of and, by contrast with other Greek states, it showed this relation as clearly as can be expected. Up to the time of Solon all these communities were under either oligarchies or despots. Those of them in which war continued to be the honored occupation while industry was despised, retained this political type; but in Athens, where industry was regarded with comparative respect, where it was encouraged by Solon, and where immigrant artisans found a home, there grew up an industrial organization which distinguished the Athenian society from adjacent societies while it was also distinguished from them by those democratic institutions that simultaneously developed.

Turning to later times, the relation between a social regime predominantly industrial and a less coercive form of rule is shown us by the Hanse towns, by the towns of the Low Countries out of which the Dutch Republic arose, and in high degrees by ourselves, by the United States, and by our colonies. Along with wars less frequent and these carried on at a distance, and along with an accompanying growth of agriculture, manufactures, and commerce, beyond that of continental states more military in habit, there has gone in England a development of free institutions.

As further implying that the two are related as cause and consequence there may be noted the fact that the regions whence changes towards greater political liberty have come are the leading industrial regions and that rural districts, less characterized by constant trading transactions, have retained longer the earlier type with its appropriate sentiments and ideas.

In the form of ecclesiastical government we see parallel changes. Where the industrial activities and structures evolve, this branch of the regulating system, no longer as in the militant type a rigid hierarchy, little by little loses strength, while there grows up one of a different kind, sentiments and institutions both relaxing. Right of private judgment in religious matters gradually establishes itself along with establishment of political rights. In place of a uniform belief imperatively enforced, there come multiform beliefs voluntarily accepted, and the ever-multiplying bodies espousing these beliefs, instead of being governed despotically, govern themselves after a manner more or less representative. Military conformity coercively maintained gives place to a varied nonconformity maintained by willing union.

The industrial organization itself, which thus as it becomes predominant affects all the rest, of course shows us in an especial degree this change of structure. From the primitive condition under which the master maintains slaves to work for him there is a transition through stages of increasing freedom to a condition like our own, in which all who work and employ, buy and sell, are entirely independent, and in which there is an unchecked power of forming unions that rule themselves on democratic principles. Combinations of workmen and countercombinations of employers, no less than political societies and leagues for carrying on this or that agitation, show us the representative mode of government. . . .

Along with all which traits there go sentiments and ideas concerning the relation between the citizen and the state, opposite to those accompanying the militant type. In place of the doctrine that the duty of obedience to the governing agent is unqualified, there arises the doctrine that the will of the citizens is supreme and the governing agent exists merely to carry out their will. Thus subordinated in position, the regulating power is also restricted in range. Instead of having an authority extending over actions of all kinds, it is shut out from large classes of actions. Its control over ways of living in respect to food, clothing, amusements, is repudiated; it is not allowed to dictate modes of production nor to regulate trade. . . . The cooperation by which the multiform activities of the society are carried on becomes a *voluntary* cooperation. And while the developed sustaining system which gives to a social organism the industrial type, acquires for itself, like the developed sustaining system of an animal, a regulating apparatus of a diffused or uncentralized kind, it tends also to decentralize the primary regulating apparatus by making it derive from more numerous classes its deputed powers. . . .

Summary

We class societies, then, in two ways, both having to be kept in mind when interpreting social phenomena.

First, they have to be arranged, in the order of their integration, as simple, compound, doubly compound, trebly compound. And along with the increasing degrees of evolution implied by these ascending stages of composition we have to recognize the increasing degrees of evolution implied by growing heterogeneity, general and local.

Much less definite is the division to be made among societies according as one or other of their great systems of organs is supreme. Omitting those lowest types which show no differentiations at all, we have but few exceptions to the rule that each society has structures for carrying on conflict with other societies and structures for carrying on sustentation, and as the ratios between these admit of all gradations, it results that no specific classification can be based on their relative developments. Nevertheless, as the militant type, characterized by predominance of the one, is framed on the principle of compulsory cooperation, while the industrial type, characterized by predominance of the other, is framed on the principle of voluntary cooperation, the two types, when severally evolved to their extreme forms, are diametrically opposed and the contrasts between their traits are among the most important with which sociology has to deal. . . .

CHAPTER 9

POLITICAL ORGANIZATION IN GENERAL

The mere gathering of individuals into a group does not constitute them a society. A society, in the sociological sense, is formed only when, besides juxtaposition there is cooperation. So long as members of the group do not combine their energies to achieve some common end or ends, there is little to keep them together. They are prevented from separating only when the wants of each are better satisfied by uniting his efforts with those of others than they would be if he acted alone.

Cooperation, then, is at once that which cannot exist without a society and that for which a society exists. It may be a joining of many strengths to affect something which the strength of no single man can effect or it may be an apportioning of different activities to different persons who severally participate in the benefits of one another's activities. The motive for acting together, originally the dominant one, may be defense against enemies, or it may be the easier obtainment of food, by the chase or otherwise, or it may be, and commonly is, both of these. In any case, however, the units pass from the state of perfect independence to the state of mutual dependence and as fast as they do this they become united into a society rightly so called.

But cooperation implies organization. If acts are to be effectually combined, there must be arrangements under which they are adjusted in their times, amounts, and characters.

This social organization, necessary as a means to concerted action, is of two kinds. Though these two kinds generally co-exist, and are more or less interfused, yet they are distinct in their origins and natures. There is a spontaneous cooperation which grows up without thought during the pursuit of private ends, and there is a cooperation which, consciously devised, implies distinct recognition of public ends. The ways in which the two are respectively established and carried on present marked contrasts.

Whenever, in a primitive group, there begins that cooperation which is effected by exchange of services — whenever individuals find their wants better satisfied by giving certain products which they can make best in return for other products they are less skilled in making, or not so well circumstanced for making — there is initiated a kind of organization which then and throughout its higher stages, results from endeavors to meet personal needs. Division of labor, to the last as at first, grows by experience of mutual facilitations in living. Each new specialization of industry arises from the effort of one who commences it to get profit and establishes itself by conducing in some way to the profit of others. So that there is a kind of concerted action with an elaborate social organization developed by it which does not originate in deliberate concert. Though within the small subdivisions of this organization we find everywhere repeated the relation of employer and employed, of whom the one directs the actions of the other, yet this relation, spontaneously formed in aid of private ends and continued only at will, is not formed with conscious reference to achievement of public ends: these are not thought of. And though, for regulating trading activities, there arise agencies serving to adjust the supplies of commodities to the demands, yet such agencies do this not by direct stimulations or restraints but by communicating information which serves to stimulate or restrain; further, these agencies grow up not for the avowed purpose of thus regulating but in the pursuit of gain by individuals. So unintentionally has there arisen the elaborate division of labor by which production and distribution are now carried on that only in modern days has there come a recognition of the fact that it has all along been arising.

On the other hand, cooperation for a purpose immediately concerning the whole society is a conscious cooperation and is carried on by an organization of another kind, formed in a different way. When the primitive group has to defend itself against other groups, its members act together under further stimuli than those constituted by purely personal desires. Even at the outset, before any control by a chief exists, there is the control exercised by the group over its members, each of whom is obliged by public opinion to join in the general defense. Very soon the warrior of recognized superiority begins to exercise over each, during war, an influence additional to that exercised by the group, and when his authority becomes established, it greatly furthers combined action.

From the beginning, therefore, this kind of social cooperation is a conscious cooperation, and a cooperation which is not wholly a matter of choice — is often at variance with private wishes. As the organization initiated by it develops, we see that, in the first place, the fighting division of the society displays in the highest degree these same traits: the grades and divisions constituting an army cooperate more and more under the regulation, consciously established, of agencies which override individual volitions — or, to speak strictly, control individuals by motives which prevent them from acting as they would spontaneously act. In the second place, we see that throughout the society as a whole there spreads a kindred form of organization — kindred in so far that, for the purpose of maintaining the militant body and the government which directs it, there are established over citizens agencies which force them to labor more or less largely for public ends instead of private ends. And, simultaneously, there develops a further organization, still akin in its fundamental principle, which restrains individual actions in such wise that social safety shall not be endangered by the disorder consequent on unchecked pursuit of personal ends. So that this kind of social organization is distinguished from the other as arising through conscious pursuit of public ends, in furtherance of which individual wills are constrained, first by the joint wills of the entire group and afterwards more definitely by the will of a regulative agency which the group evolves.

Most clearly shall we perceive the contrast between these two kinds of organization on observing that, while they are both instrumental to social welfare, they are instrumental in converse ways. That organization shown us by the division of labor for industrial purposes exhibits combined action but it is a combined action which directly seeks and subserves the welfares of individuals, and indirectly subserves the welfare of society as a whole by preserving individuals. Conversely, that organization evolved for governmental and defensive purposes exhibits combined action but it is a combined action which directly seeks and subserves the welfare of the society as a whole and indirectly subserves the welfares of individuals by protecting the society. Efforts for self-preservation by the units originate the one form of organization, while efforts for self-preservation by the aggregate originate the other form of organization. In the first case there is conscious pursuit of private ends only and the correlative organization resulting from this pursuit of private ends, growing up unconsciously, is without coercive power. In the second case there is conscious pursuit of public ends and the correlative organization, consciously established, exercises coercion.

Of these two kinds of cooperation and the structures effecting them we are here concerned only with one. Political organization is to be understood as that part of social organization which constantly carries on directive and restraining functions for public ends. It is true, as already hinted and as we shall see presently, that the two kinds are mingled in various ways — that each ramifies through the other more or less according to their respective degrees of predominance. But they are essentially different in origin and nature and for the present we must, so far as may be, limit our attention to the last.

That the cooperation into which men have gradually risen secures to them benefits which could not be secured while, in their primitive state, they acted singly, and that, as an indispensable means to this cooperation political organization has been, and is, advantageous, we shall see on contrasting the states of men who are not politically organized with the states of men who are politically organized in less or greater degrees.

There are, indeed, conditions under which as good an individual life is possible without political organization as with it. Where, as in the habitat of the Eskimos, there are but few persons and these widely scattered, where there is no war, probably because the physical impediments to it are great and the motives to it feeble, and where circumstances make the occupations so uniform that there is little scope for division of labor, mutual dependence can have no place, and the arrangements which effect it are not needed. Recognizing this exceptional case, let us consider the cases which are not exceptional.

The Digger Indians, "very few degrees removed from the ourang-outang," who, scattered among the mountains of the Sierra Nevada, sheltering in holes and living on roots and vermin, "drag out a miserable existence in a state of nature, amid the most loathsome and disgusting squalor," differ from the other divisions of the Shoshones by their entire lack of social organization. The river-haunting and plain-haunting divisions of the race, under some, though but slight, governmental control, lead more satisfactory lives [Kelly 1851, I, 252–3]. In South America the Chaco Indians, low in type as are the Diggers, and like them degraded and wretched in their lives, are similarly contrasted with the superior and more comfortable savages around them in being dissociated [Hutchinson 1865, p. 280]. Among the Bedouin tribes, the Sherarat are unlike the rest in being divided and subdivided into countless bands which have no common chief and they are described as being the most miserable of the Bedouins. More decided still is the contrast noted by Baker between certain adjacent African peoples [1867, pp. 234–5]. Passing suddenly, he says, from the unclothed, ungoverned tribes — from the "wildest savagedom to semi-civilisation" — we come, in Unyoro, to a country ruled by "an unflinching despot," inflicting "death or torture" for "the most trivial offences," but where they have developed administration, subgovernors, taxes, good clothing, arts, agriculture, architecture. So, too, concerning New Zealand when first discovered, Cook remarked that there seemed to be greater prosperity and populousness in the regions subject to a king [Hawkesworth 1773, III, 470].

These last cases introduce us to a further truth. Not only does that first step in political organization which places individuals under the control of a tribal chief bring the advantages gained by better cooperation but such advantages are increased when minor political heads become subject to a major political head. As typifying the evils which are thereby avoided I may name the fact that among the Beluchis, whose tribes, unsubordinated to a general ruler, are constantly at war with one another, it is the habit to erect a small mud tower in each field, where the possessor and his retainers guard his produce, a state of things allied to, but worse than, that of the Highland clans, with their strongholds for sheltering women and cattle from the inroads of their neighbors in days when they were not under the control of a central power [Postans 1848, p. 109].

The benefits derived from such wider control, whether of a simple head or of a compound head, were felt by the early Greeks when an Amphictyonic council established the laws that "no Hellenic tribe is to lay the habitations of another level with the ground; and from no Hellenic city is the water to be cut off during a siege" [Curtius 1868–73, I, 115–6]. How that advance of political structure which unites smaller communities into larger ones furthers welfare was shown in our own country when, by the Roman conquest, the incessant fights between tribes were stopped, and again in later days when feudal nobles, becoming subject to a monarch, were debarred from private wars. Under its converse aspect the same truth was illustrated when, amidst the anarchy which followed the collapse of the Carolingian empire, dukes and counts, resuming their independence, became active enemies to one another, their state being such that "when they were not at war they lived by open plunder" [Dunham 1837, I, 101]. And the history of Europe has repeatedly, in many places and times, furnished kindred illustrations.

While political organization, as it extends itself throughout masses of increasing size, directly furthers welfare by removing that impediment to cooperation which the antagonisms of individuals and of tribes cause, it indirectly furthers it in another way. Nothing beyond a rudimentary division of labor can arise in a small social group. Before commodities can be multiplied in their kinds there must be multiplied kinds of producers, and before each commodity can be produced in the most economical way the different stages in the production of it must be apportioned among special hands. Nor is this all. Neither the required complex combinations of individuals, nor the elaborate mechanical appliances which facilitate manufacture, can arise in the absence of a large community, generating a great demand. . . .

As was pointed out . . . [earlier], "complication of structure accompanies increase of mass," in social organisms as in individual organisms. When small societies are compounded into a larger society, the controlling agencies needed in the several component societies must be subordinated to a central controlling agency: new structures are required. Recompounding necessitates a kindred further complexity in the governmental arrangements, and at each of such stages of increase all other arrangements must become more complicated. As Duruy remarks, "By becoming a world in place of a town, Rome could not conserve institutions established for a single city and a small territory. . . . How was it possible for sixty millions of provincials to enter the narrow and rigid circle of municipal institutions?" [Duruy 1870–79, III, 126–7]. The like holds where, instead of extension of territory, there is only increase of population. The contrast between the simple administrative system which sufficed in old English times for a million people and the complex administrative system at present needed for many millions sufficiently indicates this general truth.

But now mark a corollary. If, on the one hand, further growth implies more complex structure, on the other hand, changeableness of structure is a condition to further growth; conversely, unchangeableness of structure is a concomitant of arrested growth. Like the correlative law just noted, this law is clearly seen in individual organisms. Necessarily, transition from the small immature form to the large mature form in a living creature implies that all the parts have to be changed in their sizes and connections: every detail of every organ has to be modified, and this implies the retention of plasticity. Necessarily, also, when, on approaching maturity, the organs are assuming their final arrangement, their increasing definiteness and firmness constitute an increasing impediment to growth; the unbuilding and rebuilding required before there can be readjustment, become more and more difficult. So is it with a society. Augmentation of its mass necessitates change of the pre-existing structures, either by incorporation of the increment with them or by their extension through it. Every further elaboration of the arrangements entails an additional obstacle to this, and when rigidity is reached, such modifications of them as increase of mass would involve are impossible, and increase is prevented. . . .

The stones composing a house cannot be otherwise used until the house has been pulled down. If the stones are united by mortar there must be extra trouble in destroying their present combination before they can be recombined. And if the mortar has had centuries in which to consolidate, the breaking up of the masses formed is a matter of such difficulty that building with new materials becomes more economical than rebuilding with the old.

I name these facts to illustrate the truth that any arrangement stands in the way of rearrangement, and that this must be true of organization, which is one kind of arrangement. When, during the evolution of a living body, its component substance, at first relatively homogeneous, has been transformed into a combination of heterogeneous parts, there results an obstacle, always great and often insuperable, to any considerable further change, the more elaborate and definite the structure the greater being the resistance it opposes to alteration. And this, which is conspicuously true of an individual organism, is true, if less conspicuously, of a social organism. Though a society, formed of discrete units and not having had its type fixed by inheritance from countless like societies, is much more plastic, yet the same principle holds. As fast as its parts are differentiated — as fast as there arise classes, bodies of functionaries, established administrations — these, becoming coherent within themselves and with one another, struggle against such forces as tend to modify them. The conservatism of every long-settled institution daily exemplifies this law. Be it in the antagonism of a church to legislation interfering with its discipline, be it in the opposition of an army to abolition of the purchase-system, be it in the disfavor with which the legal profession at large has regarded law-reform, we see that neither in their structures nor in their modes of action are parts that have once been specialized easily changed.

As it is true of a living body that its various acts have as their common end self-preservation, so it is true of its component organs that they severally tend to preserve themselves in their integrity. And, similarly, as it is true of a society that maintenance of its existence is the aim of its combined actions, so it is true of its separate classes, its sets of officials, its other specialized parts, that the dominant aim of each is to maintain itself. Not the function to be performed, but the sustentation of those who perform the function, becomes the object in view, the result being that when the function is needless or even detrimental, the structure still keeps itself intact as long as it can. In early days the history of the Knights Templars furnished an illustration of this tendency. Down to the present time we have before us the familiar instance of trade-guilds in London, which having ceased to perform their original duties, nevertheless jealously defend their possessions and privileges. The convention of Royal Burghs in Scotland, which once regulated the internal municipal laws, still meets annually though it has no longer any work to do. . . .

The extent to which an organization resists reorganization we shall not fully appreciate until we observe that its resistance increases in a compound progression. For while each new part is an additional obstacle to change, the formation of it involves a deduction from the forces causing change. If, other things remaining the same, the political structures of a society are further developed — if existing institutions are extended or fresh ones set up — if for directing social activities in greater detail, extra staffs of officials are appointed — the simultaneous results are an increase in the aggregate of those who form the regulating part and a corresponding decrease in the aggregate of those who form the part regulated. In various ways all who compose the controlling and administrative organization become united with one another and separated from the rest. Whatever be their particular duties they are similarly related to the governing centers of their departments, and, through them, to the supreme governing center and are habituated to like sentiments and ideas respecting the set of institutions in which they are incorporated. . . .

No matter what their previous political opinions may have been, men cannot become public agents of any kind without being biased towards opinions congruous with their functions. So that, inevitably, each further growth of the instrumentalities which control, or administer, or inspect, or in any way direct social forces, increases the impediment to future modifications, both positively by strengthening that which has to be modified, and negatively, by weakening the remainder, until at length the rigidity becomes so great that change is impossible and the type becomes fixed. . . .

Nor is this all. Controlling and administrative instrumentalities antagonize growth by absorbing the materials for growth. . . . Governmental expenditure . . . has for its ulterior result deducting from the life of the community; depletion of the units entails depletion of the aggregate. Where the abstraction of private means for public purposes is excessive, the impoverishment leads to decrease of population, and where it is less excessive, to arrest of population. Clearly those members of a society who form the regulative parts, together with all their dependents, have to be supplied with the means of living by the parts which carry on the processes of production and distribution, and if the regulative parts go on increasing relatively to the other parts, there must eventually be reached a point at which they absorb the entire surplus, and multiplication is stopped by innutrition.

Hence a significant relation between the structure of a society and its growth. Organization in excess of need prevents the attainment of that larger size and accompanying higher type which might else have arisen.

Summary

To aid our interpretations of the special facts presently to be dealt with we must keep in mind the foregoing general facts. They may be summed up as follows:

Cooperation is made possible by society, and makes society possible. It presupposes associated men, and men remain associated because of the benefits cooperation yields them.

But there cannot be concerted actions without agencies by which actions are adjusted in their times, amounts, and kinds, and the actions cannot be of various kinds without the cooperators undertaking different duties. That is to say, the cooperators must become organized, either voluntarily or involuntarily.

The organization which cooperation implies is of two kinds, distinct in origin and nature. The one, arising directly from the pursuit of individual ends, and indirectly conducing to social welfare, develops unconsciously and is noncoercive. The other, arising directly from the pursuit of social ends, and indirectly conducing to individual welfare, develops consciously and is coercive.

While by making cooperation possible political organization achieves benefits, deductions from these benefits are entailed by the organization. Maintenance of it is costly and the cost may become a greater evil than the evils escaped. . . .

An established organization is an obstacle to reorganization. Self-sustentation is the primary aim of each part as of the whole, and hence parts once formed tend to continue, whether they are or are not useful. Moreover, each addition to the regulative structures, implying, other things equal, a simultaneous deduction from the rest of the society which is regulated, it results that while the obstacles to change are increased, the forces causing change are decreased. . . .

Though, to make cooperation possible, and therefore to facilitate social growth, there must be organization, yet the organization formed impedes further growth, since further growth implies reorganization, which the existing organization resists, and since the existing organization absorbs part of the material for growth. So that while, at each stage, better immediate results may be achieved by completing organization, they must be at the expense of better ultimate results.

CHAPTER 10

POLITICAL INTEGRATION

The analogy between individual organisms and social organisms, which holds in so many respects, holds in respect to the actions which cause growth. We shall find it instructive to glance at political integration in the light of this analogy.

Every animal sustains itself and grows by incorporating either the materials composing other animals or those composing plants, and from microscopic *Protozoa* upwards, it has been through success in the struggle thus to incorporate that animals of the greatest sizes and highest structures have been evolved. This process is carried on by creatures of the lowest kinds in a purely physical or insentient way. Without nervous system or fixed distribution of parts, the rhizopod draws in fragments of nutritive matter by actions which we are obliged to regard as unconscious. So is it, too, with simple aggregates formed by the massing of such minute creatures. The sponge, for example, in that framework of fibers familiar to us in its dead state, holds together, when living, a multitude of separate monads and the activities which go on in the sponge are such as directly further the separate lives of these monads and indirectly further the life of the whole, the whole having neither sentiency nor power of movement.

At a higher stage, however, the process of taking in nutritive materials by a composite organism comes to be carried on in a sentient way and in a way differing from the primitive way in this, that it directly furthers the life of the whole and indirectly furthers the lives of the component units. Eventually, the well consolidated and organized aggregate, which originally had no other life than was constituted by the separate lives of these minute creatures massed together, acquires a corporate life predominating over their lives and also acquires desires by which its activities are guided to acts of incorporation. To which add the obvious corollary that as, in the course of evolution, its size increases, it incorporates with itself larger and larger aggregates as prey.

Analogous stages may be traced in the growth of social organisms and in the accompanying forms of action. At first there is no other life in the group than that seen in the lives of its members, and only as organization increases does the group as a whole come to have that joint life constituted by mutually-dependent actions. The members of a primitive horde, loosely aggregated and without distinctions of power, cooperate for immediate furtherance of individual sustentation, and in a comparatively small degree for corporate sustentation. Even when, the interests of all being simultaneously endangered, they simultaneously fight, they still fight separately — their actions are uncoordinated; the only spoils of successful battle are such as can be individually appropriated. But in the course of the struggles for existence between groups thus unorganized there comes, with the development of such political organization as gives tribal individuality, the struggle to incorporate one another, first partially and then wholly. Tribes which are larger or better organized or both, conquer adjacent tribes and annex them, so that they form parts of a compound whole. And as political evolution advances, it becomes a trait of the larger and stronger societies that they acquire appetites prompting them to subjugate and incorporate weaker societies.

Full perception of this difference will be gained on looking more closely at the contrast between the wars of small groups and those of large nations. As, even among dogs, the fights that arise between individuals when one attempts to take another's food grow into fights between packs if one trespasses upon the feeding haunts of another (as is seen in Constantinople), so among primitive men, individual conflicts for food pass into conflicts between hordes, when, in pursuit of food, one encroaches on another's territory.

After the pastoral state is reached, such motives continue with a difference. "Retaliation for past robberies" is the habitual plea for war among the Bechuanas, "their real object being always the acquisition of cattle" [Burchell 1822–24, II, 532]. Similarly among European peoples in ancient days. Achilles says of the Trojans — "They are blameless as respects me, since they have never driven away my oxen, nor my horses" [Homer 1883, Bk. I]. And the fact that in Scotland during early times cattle raids were habitual causes of intertribal fights shows us how persistent have been these struggles for the means of individual sustentation. Even where the life is agricultural, the like happens at the outset. "A field or a farrow's breadth of land is disputed upon the border of a district, and gives rise to rustic strife between the parties and their respective hamlets," says Macpherson of the Khonds, and "should the tribes to which the disputants belong be disposed to hostility, they speedily embrace quarrel" [1842, p. 43]. So that competition in social growth is still restricted to competition for the means to that personal welfare indirectly conducive to social growth.

In yet another way do we see exemplified this general truth. The furthering of growth by that which furthers the multiplication of units is shown us in the stealing of women — a second cause of primitive war. Men of one tribe who abduct the women of another, not only by so doing directly increase the number of their own tribe, but, in a greater degree, indirectly conduce to its increase by afterwards adding to the number of children.

In which mode of growing at one another's expense, common among existing tribes of savages and once common among tribes from which civilized nations have descended, we still see the same trait: any augmentation of the group which takes place is an indirect result of individual appropriations and reproductions.

Contrariwise, in more advanced stages the struggle between societies is, not to appropriate one another's means of sustentation and multiplication, but to appropriate one another bodily. Which society shall incorporate other societies with itself becomes the question. Under one aspect, the history of large nations is a history of successes in such struggles, and down to our own day nations are being thus enlarged. Part of Italy is incorporated by France; part of France is incorporated by Germany; part of Turkey is incorporated by Russia, and between Russia and England there appears to be a competition which shall increase most by absorbing uncivilized and semi-civilized peoples.

Thus, then, with social organisms as with individual organisms, it is through the struggle for existence, first, by appropriating one another's means of growth, and then by devouring one another, that there arise those great aggregates which at once make possible high organization, and require high organization.

Political integration is in some cases furthered, and in other cases hindered, by conditions, external and internal. . . .

How political integration is prevented by an inclemency of climate, or an infertility of soil, which keeps down population, was shown . . . [earlier]. To the instances . . . named may be added . . . that of certain Snake Indians of whom Schoolcraft says, "the paucity of game in this region is, I have little doubt, the cause of the almost entire absence of social organization" [1853–56, V, 260]. We saw, too, that great uniformity of surface, of mineral products, of flora, of fauna, are impediments, and that on the special characters of the flora and fauna, as containing species favorable or unfavorable to human welfare, in part depends the individual prosperity required for social growth.

It was also pointed out that structure of the habitat, as facilitating or impeding communication, and as rendering escape easy or hard, has much to do with the size of the social aggregate formed. To the illustrations before given, showing that mountain-haunting peoples and peoples living in deserts and marshes are difficult to consolidate, while peoples penned in by barriers are consolidated with facility, I may here add two significant ones not before noticed. One occurs in the Polynesian islands — Tahiti, Hawaii, Tonga, Samoa, and the rest — where, restrained within limits by surrounding seas, the inhabitants have become united more or less closely into aggregates of considerable sizes. The other is furnished by ancient Peru, where, before the time of the Incas, semi-civilized communities had been formed in valleys separated from each other "on the coast, by hot, and almost impassable deserts, and in the interior by lofty mountains, or cold and trackless *punas*" [Squier 1870, p. 19]. And to the implied inability of these peoples to escape governmental coercion, thus indicated by Squier as a factor in their civilization, is ascribed, by the ancient Spanish writer Cieza, the difference between them and the neighboring Indians of Popayán, who could retreat, "whenever attacked, to other fertile regions" [Cieza de León 1864, Ch. XIII].

How, conversely, the massing of men together is furthered by ease of internal communication within the area occupied is sufficiently manifest. The importance of it is implied by the remark of Grant concerning Equatorial Africa that "no jurisdiction extends over a district which cannot be crossed in three or four days" [Grant 1864, p. ref. lost]. And such facts, implying that political integration may increase as the means of going from place to place become better, remind us how from Roman times downwards the formation of roads has made larger social aggregates possible. . . .

. . . Social union requires a considerable homogeneity of nature among . . . [individuals]. At the outset, this needful likeness of kind is insured by greater or less kinship in blood. Evidence meets us everywhere among the uncivilized. Of the Bushmen, Lichtenstein says, "families alone form associations in single small hordes — sexual feelings, the instinctive love to children, or the customary attachment among relations, are the only ties that keep them in any sort of union" [1812–15, II, 194]. Again, "the Rock Veddahs are divided into small clans or families associated for relationship, who agree in partitioning the forest among themselves for hunting grounds" [Tennent 1859, II, 440]. And this rise of the society out of the family, seen in these least organized groups, reappears in the considerably organized groups of more advanced savages. Instance the New Zealanders, of whom we read that "eighteen historical nations occupy the country, each being subdivided into many tribes, originally families, as the prefix Ngati, signifying offspring (equivalent to O or Mac) obviously indicates" [Thomson 1859, I, 92–3]. This connection between blood relationship and social union is well shown by Humboldt's remarks concerning South American Indians [1852–53, II, 412]. "Savages," he says, "know only their own family, and a tribe appears to them but a more numerous assemblage of relations." When Indians who inhabit the missions see those of the forest, who are unknown to them, they say — "They are no doubt my relations; I understand them when they speak to me." But these same savages detest all who are not of their tribe. "They know the duties of family ties and of relationship, but not those of humanity."

When treating of the domestic relations, reasons were given for concluding that social stability increases as kinships become more definite
and extended, since development of kinships, while insuring the likeness
of nature which furthers cooperation, involves the strengthening and
multiplication of those family bonds which check disruption. . . . If local
circumstances bring together several . . . tribes, which are . . . allied
in blood though . . . remotely, it results that when, seated side by side,
they are gradually fused, partly by interspersion and partly by intermar-
riage, the compound society formed, united by numerous and complicated
links of kinship as well as by political interests, is more strongly bound
together than it would otherwise be. Dominant ancient societies illustrate
this truth. Says Grote, "All that we hear of the most ancient Athenian
laws is based upon the gentile and phratric divisions, which are treated
throughout as extensions of the family" [1846–56, III, 88]. Similarly, according to Mommsen, on the "Roman Household was based the Roman
State, both as respected its constituent elements and its form. The community of the Roman people arose out of the junction (in whatever
way brought about) of such ancient clanships as the Romilii, Voltinii,
Fabii etc." [1862, I, 65]. And Sir Henry Maine [1876] has shown in detail
the ways in which the simple family passes into the house-community,
and eventually the village-community. . . .

One of the laws of evolution at large is that integration results when
like units are subject to the same force or to like forces (*First Principles*,
§ 169), and from the first stages of political integration up to the last we
find this law illustrated. Joint exposure to uniform external actions and
joint reactions against them have from the beginning been the leading
causes of union among members of societies.

Already . . . there has been indirectly implied the truth that coherence is first given to small hordes of primitive men during combined
opposition to enemies. Subject to the same danger and joining to meet
this danger, the members of the horde become, in the course of their
cooperation against it, more bound together. In the first stages this relation of cause and effect is clearly seen in the fact that such union as arises
during a war disappears when the war is over; there is loss of all such
slight political combination as was beginning to show itself. But it is by
the integration of simple groups into compound groups in the course of
common resistance to foes, and attacks upon them, that this process is
best exemplified. The cases before given may be reinforced by others.
Of the Karens, Mason says, "Each village, being an independent community, had always an old feud to settle with nearly every other village
among their own people. But the common danger from more powerful
enemies, or having common injuries to requite, often led to several villages uniting together for defence or attack" [1868, p. 152]. According to

Kolb, "smaller nations of Hottentots, which may be near some powerful nation, frequently enter into an alliance, offensive and defensive, against the stronger nation" [1731, I, 287]. Among the New Caledonians of Tanna, "six, or eight, or more of their villages unite, and form what may be called a district, or county, and all league together for mutual protection. . . . In war two or more of these districts unite" [Turner 1861, pp. 85–6]. Samoan "villages, in numbers of eight or ten, unite by common consent, and form a district or state for mutual protection" and during hostilities these districts themselves sometimes unite in twos and threes [Turner 1861, p. 291].

The like has happened with historic peoples. It was during the wars of the Israelites in David's time that they passed from the state of separate tribes into the state of a consolidated ruling nation. The scattered Greek communities, previously aggregated into minor confederacies by minor wars, were prompted to the Pan-Hellenic congress and to the subsequent cooperation when the invasion of Xerxes was impending; and of the Spartan and Athenian confederacies afterwards formed, that of Athens acquired the hegemony, and finally the empire, during continued operations against the Persians [Grote 1846–56, IV, 430; II, 359].

So, too, was it with the Teutonic races. The German tribes, originally without federal bonds, formed occasional alliances for opposing enemies. Between the first and fifth centuries these tribes massed themselves into great groups for resistance against, or attack upon, Rome. During the subsequent century the prolonged military confederations of peoples "of the same blood" had grown into states, which afterwards became aggregated into still larger states. And, to take a comparatively modern instance, the wars between France and England aided each in passing from that condition in which its feudal divisions were in considerable degrees independent to the condition of a consolidated nation.

As further showing how integration of smaller societies into larger ones is thus initiated, it may be added that at first the unions exist only for military purposes. Each component society retains for a long time its independent internal administration, and it is only when joint action in war has become habitual that the cohesion is made permanent by a common political organization.

This compounding of smaller communities into larger by military cooperation is insured by the disappearance of such smaller communities as do not cooperate. Barth [1857–58, II, 510] remarks that "the Fúlbe [Fulahs] are continually advancing, as they have not to do with one strong enemy, but with a number of small tribes without any bond of union." Of the Damaras, Galton [1852, p. 159] says, "If one werft is plundered, the adjacent ones rarely rise to defend it, and thus the Namaquas have destroyed or enslaved piecemeal about one-half of the whole Damara population." Similarly with the Inca conquests in Peru: "there was no general opposition to their advance, for each province merely defended its land without aid from any other" [Polo de Ondegardo 1873, pp. 152–3]. This process, so obvious and familiar, I name because it has a meaning which needs emphasizing. For we here see that in the struggle for existence among societies, the survival of the fittest is the survival of those in which the power of military cooperation is the greatest, and military cooperation is that primary kind of cooperation which prepares the way for other kinds. So that this formation of larger societies by the union of smaller ones in war, and this destruction or absorption of the smaller un-united societies by the united larger ones, is an inevitable process through which the varieties of men most adapted for social life supplant the less adapted varieties.

Respecting the integration thus effected, it remains only to remark that it necessarily follows this course — necessarily begins with the formation of simple groups and advances by the compounding and recompounding of them. Impulsive in conduct and with rudimentary powers of concerted action, savages cohere so slightly that only small bodies of them can maintain their integrity. Not until such small bodies have severally had their members bound to one another by some slight political organization does it become possible to unite them into larger bodies, since the cohesion of these implies greater fitness for concerted action and more developed organization for achieving it. And similarly, these composite clusters must be to some extent consolidated before the composition can be carried a stage further.

Passing over the multitudinous illustrations among the uncivilized, it will suffice if I refer to those given . . . [earlier], and reinforce them by some which historic peoples have supplied. There is the fact that in primitive Egypt the numerous small societies (which eventually became the "nomes") first united into the two aggregates, Upper Egypt and Lower Egypt, which were afterwards joined into one, and the fact that in ancient Greece villages became united to form towns before the towns became united into states, while this change preceded the change which united the states with one another, and the fact that in the old English period small principalities were massed into the divisions constituting the Heptarchy, before these passed into something like a whole.

It is a principle in physics that, since the force with which a body resists strains increases as the squares of its dimensions while the strains which its own weight subject it to increase as the cubes of its dimensions, its power of maintaining its integrity becomes relatively less as its mass becomes greater. Something analogous may be said of societies. Small aggregates only can hold together while cohesion is feeble, and successively larger aggregates become possible only as the greater strains implied are met by that greater cohesion which results from an adapted human nature and a resulting development of social organization.

As social integration advances, the increasing aggregates exercise increasing restraints over their units — a truth which is the obverse of the one just set forth, that the maintenance of its integrity by a larger aggregate implies greater cohesion. The forces by which aggregates keep their units together are at first feeble, and becoming strenuous at a certain stage of social evolution, afterwards relax — or rather, change their forms.

Originally the individual savage gravitates to one group or other, prompted by sundry motives, but mainly by the desire for protection. Concerning the Patagonians we read that no one can live apart: "if any of them attempted to do it, they would undoubtedly be killed, or carried away as slaves, as soon as they were discovered" [Falkner 1774, p. 123]. In North America, among the Chinooks, "on the coast a custom prevails which authorizes the seizure and enslavement, unless ransomed by his friends, of every Indian met with at a distance from his tribe, although they may not be at war with each other" [Kane 1859, p. 215]. At first, however, though it is necessary to join some group, it is not necessary to continue in the same group. When oppressed by their chief, Kalmucks and Mongols desert him and go over to other chiefs. Of the Abipones Dobrizhoffer says, "Without leave asked on their part, or displeasure evinced on his, they remove with their families whithersoever it suits them, and join some other cacique, and when tired of the second, return with impunity to the horde of the first" [1822, II, 105]. Similarly in South Africa, "the frequent instances which occur [among the Balonda] of people changing from one part of the country to another, show that the great chiefs possess only a limited power" [Livingstone 1861, p. 208]. And how through this process some tribes grow while others dwindle, we are shown by McCulloch's remark respecting the Kukis that "a village, having around it plenty of land suited for cultivation and a popular chief, is sure soon, by accessions from less favoured ones, to become large" [1857, p. 58] . . .

Kindred motives produced kindred results within more modern societies during times when their parts were so imperfectly integrated that there remained antagonisms among them. Thus we have the fact that in medieval England, while local rule was incompletely subordinated to general rule, every free man had to attach himself to a lord, a burgh, or a guild, being otherwise "a friendless man," and in a danger like that which the savage is in when not belonging to a tribe [Burton, J. 1873, II, 72]. . . .

These last illustrations introduce us to the truth that while at first there is little cohesion and great mobility of the units forming a group, advance in integration is habitually accompanied not only by decreasing ability to go from group to group but also by decreasing ability to go from place to place within the group. Of course the transition from the nomadic to the settled state partially implies this, since each person becomes in a considerable degree tied by his material interests. Slavery, too, effects in another way this binding of individuals to locally placed members of the society, and therefore to particular parts to it, and where serfdom exists, the same thing is shown with a difference. But in highly integrated societies, not simply those in bondage but others also are tied to their localities. Of the ancient Mexicans, Zurita [1840, p. 51] says, "The Indians never changed their village nor even their quarter. This custom was observed as a law." In ancient Peru "it was not lawful for any one to remove from one province, or village, to another," and "any who traveled without just cause were punished as vagabonds" [Garcilasso de la Vega 1869–71, Bk. IV, ch. 8; Bk. V, ch. 9]. Elsewhere, along with that development of the militant type accompanying aggregation, there have been imposed restraints on transit under other forms. Ancient Egypt had a system of registration, and all citizens periodically reported themselves to local officers. "Every Japanese is registered, and whenever he removes his residence, the Nanushi, or head man of the temple gives a certificate" [Dickson 1869, p. 305]. And then in despotically governed European countries we have passport systems, hindering the journeys of citizens from place to place, and in some cases preventing them from going abroad. . . .

Summary

Thus, saying nothing for the present of that political evolution manifested by increase of structure, and restricting ourselves to that political evolution manifested by increase of mass here distinguished as political integration, we find that this has the following traits.

While the aggregates are small, the incorporation of materials for growth is carried on at one another's expense in feeble ways — by taking one another's game, by robbing one another of women, and, occasionally by adopting one another's men. As larger aggregates are formed, incorporations proceed in more wholesale ways: first by enslaving the separate members of conquered tribes, and presently by the bodily annexation of such tribes, with their territory. And as compound aggregates pass into doubly and trebly compound ones, there arise increasing desires to absorb adjacent smaller societies and so to form still larger aggregates.

Conditions of several kinds further or hinder social growth and consolidation. The habitat may be fitted or unfitted for supporting a large population or it may, by great or small facilities for intercourse within its area, favor or impede cooperation or it may, by presence or absence of natural barriers, make easy or difficult the keeping together of the individuals under that coercion which is at first needful. . . .

Likeness in the units forming a social group being one condition to their integration, a further condition is their joint reaction against external action: cooperation in war is the chief cause of social integration. The temporary unions of savages for offense and defense show us the initiatory step. When many tribes unite against a common enemy, long continuance of their combined action makes them coherent under some common control. And so it is subsequently with still larger aggregates.

Progress in social integration is both a cause and a consequence of a decreasing separableness among the units. Primitive wandering hordes exercise no such restraints over their members as prevent them individually from leaving one horde and joining another at will. Where tribes are more developed, desertion of one and admission into another are less easy — the assemblages are not so loose in composition. And throughout those long stages during which societies are being enlarged and consolidated by militancy, the mobility of the units becomes more and more restricted. . . .

A remaining truth to be named is that political integration, as it advances, obliterates the original divisions among the united parts. In the first place there is the slow disappearance of those non-topographical divisions arising from relationship, as seen in separate gentes and tribes; gradual intermingling destroys them. In the second place, the smaller local societies united into a larger one, which at first retain their separate organizations, lose them by long cooperation; a common organization begins to ramify through them. And in the third place, there simultaneously results a fading of their topographical bounds and a replacing of these by the new administrative bounds of the common organization.

Hence naturally results the converse truth that in the course of social dissolution the great groups separate first, and afterwards, if dissolution continues, these separate into their component smaller groups. Instance the ancient empires successively formed in the East, the united kingdoms of which severally resumed their autonomies when the coercion keeping them together ceased. Instance, again, the Carolingian empire, which, first parting into its large divisions, became in course of time further disintegrated by subdivision of these. And where, as in this last case, the process of dissolution goes very far, there is a return to something like the primitive condition under which small predatory societies are engaged in continuous warfare with like small societies around them.

CHAPTER 11

POLITICAL DIFFERENTIATION

As was pointed out in *First Principles*, § 154, it is true of a social aggregate, as of every other aggregate, that the state of homogeneity is an unstable state and that where there is already some heterogeneity, the tendency is towards greater heterogeneity.

Lapse from homogeneity, however, or rather, the increase of such heterogeneity as usually exists, requires that the parts shall be heterogeneously conditioned, and whatever prevents the rise of contrasts among the conditions, prevents increase of heterogeneity. One of the implications is that there must not be continual changes in the distribution of the parts. If now one part and now another occupies the same position in relation to the whole, permanent structural differences cannot be produced. There must be such cohesion among the parts as prevents easy transposition.

We see this truth exemplified in the simplest individual organisms. A low rhizopod, of which the substance has a mobility approaching to that of a liquid, remains almost homogeneous because each part is from moment to moment assuming new relations to other parts and to the environment. And the like holds with the simplest societies. Concerning the members of the small unsettled groups of Fuegians, Cook remarks that "none was more respected than another" [Hawkesworth 1773, II, 58]. The Veddas, the Andamanese, the Australians, the Tasmanians, may also be instanced as loose assemblages which present no permanent unlikenesses of social position, or if unlikeness exist, as some travellers allege, they are so vague that they are denied by others. And in such wandering hordes as the Coroados of South America, formed of individuals held together so feebly that they severally join one or other horde at will, the distinctions of parts are but nominal [Spix and Martius 1824, II, 244].

Conversely, it is to be anticipated that where the several parts of a social aggregate are heterogeneously conditioned in a permanent way, they will become proportionately heterogeneous. We shall see this more clearly on changing the point of view.

The general law that like units exposed to like forces tend to integrate was in the last chapter exemplified by the formation of social groups. Here the correlative general law, that in proportion as the like units of an aggregate are exposed to unlike forces they tend to form differentiated parts of the aggregate, has to be observed in its application to such groups, as the second step in social evolution.

The primary political differentiation originates from the primary family differentiation. Men and women being by the unlikenesses of their functions in life exposed to unlike influences, begin from the first to assume unlike positions in the community as they do in the family; very early they respectively form the two political classes of rulers and ruled. And how truly such dissimilarity of social positions as arises between them is caused by dissimilarity in their relations to surrounding actions we shall see on observing that the one is small or great according as the other is small or great. When treating of the status of women it was pointed out that to a considerable degree among the Chippewyans, and to a still greater degree among the Clatsops and Chinooks, "who live upon fish and roots, which the women are equally expert with the men in procuring, the former have a rank and influence very rarely found among Indians" [Lewis and Clarke 1814, p. 441]. We saw also that in Cueba, where the women join the men in war, "fighting by their side," their position is much higher than usual among rude peoples [Bancroft 1875–76, I, 764], and, similarly, that in Dahomey, where the women are as much warriors as the men, they are so regarded that in the political organization "the woman is officially superior" [Burton, R. 1864, II, 72n.].

On contrasting these exceptional cases with the ordinary cases in which the men, solely occupied in war and the chase, have unlimited authority, while the women, occupied in gathering miscellaneous small food and carrying burdens, are abject slaves, it becomes clear that diversity of relations to surrounding actions initiates diversity of social relations. And, as we saw . . . [earlier], this truth is further illustrated by those few uncivilized societies which are habitually peaceful, such as the Bódo and the Dhimáls of the Indian hills, and the ancient Pueblos of North America — societies in which the occupations are not or were not, broadly divided into fighting and working, and severally assigned to the two sexes, and in which, along with a comparatively small difference between the activities of the sexes, there goes, or went, small difference of social status.

So is it when we pass from the greater or less political differentiation which accompanies difference of sex to that which is independent of sex — to that which arises among men. Where the life is permanently peaceful, definite class-divisions do not exist. One of the Indian Hill tribes to which I have already referred as exhibiting the honesty, truthfulness, and amiability accompanying a purely industrial life may be instanced. Hodgson says "all Bódo and all Dhimáls are equal — absolutely so in right or law — wonderfully so in fact" [1847, p. 158].

As, at first, the domestic relation between the sexes passes into a political relation such that men and women become, in militant groups, the ruling class and the subject class, so does the relation between master and slave, originally a domestic one, pass into a political one as fast as, by habitual war, the making of slaves becomes general. It is with the formation of a slave class that there begins that political differentiation between the regulating structures and the sustaining structures which continues throughout all higher forms of social evolution.

Kane remarks that "slavery in its most cruel form exists among the Indians of the whole coast from California to Behring's Straits, the stronger tribes making slaves of all the others they can conquer. In the interior, where there is but little warfare, slavery does not exist" [1859, I, 147]. And this statement does but exhibit, in a distinct form, the truth everywhere obvious. Evidence suggests that the practice of enslavement diverged by small steps from the practice of cannibalism. Concerning the Nootkas we read that "slaves are occasionally sacrificed and feasted upon" [Bancroft 1875–76, I, 195], and if we contrast this usage with the usage common elsewhere of killing and devouring captives as soon as they are taken, we may infer that the keeping of captives too numerous to be immediately eaten, with the view of eating them subsequently, leading as it would, to the employment of them in the meantime, caused the discovery that their services might be of more value than their flesh, and so initiated the habit of preserving them as slaves. Be this as it may, however, we find that very generally among tribes to which habitual militancy has given some slight degree of the appropriate structure, the enslavement of prisoners becomes an established habit. That women and children taken in war, and such men as have not been slain, naturally fall into unqualified servitude is manifest. They belong absolutely to their captors, who might have killed them and who retain the right afterwards to kill them if they please. They become property, of which any use whatever may be made.

The acquirement of slaves, which is at first an incident of war, becomes presently an object of war. Of the Nootkas we read that "some of the smaller tribes at the north of the island are practically regarded as slave-breeding tribes, and are attacked periodically by stronger tribes" [Bancroft 1875–76, I, 195], and the like happens among the Chinooks. It was thus in ancient Vera Paz, where periodically they made "an inroad into the enemy's territory . . . and captured as many as they wanted" [Ximénez 1857, pp. 202–3], and it was so in Honduras, where, in declaring war, they gave their enemies notice "that they wanted slaves" [Herrera 1725–26, IV, 136]. Similarly with various existing peoples. St. John says that many of the Kayans "are more desirous to obtain slaves than heads, and in attacking a village kill only those who resist or attempt to escape" [1863, I, 104]. And that in Africa slave-making wars are common needs no proof.

The class division thus initiated by war afterwards maintains and strengthens itself in sundry ways. Very soon there begins the custom of purchase. The Chinooks, besides slaves who have been captured, have slaves who were bought as children from their neighbors, and, as we saw when dealing with the domestic relations, the selling of their children into slavery is by no means uncommon with savages. Then the slave class, thus early enlarged by purchase, comes afterwards to be otherwise enlarged. There is voluntary acceptance of slavery for the sake of protection; there is enslavement for debt; there is enslavement for crime.

Leaving details, we need here note only that this political differentiation which war begins is effected, not by the bodily incorporation of other societies or whole classes belonging to other societies but by the incorporation of single members of other societies and by like individual accretions. Composed of units who are detached from their original social relations and from one another, and absolutely attached to their owners, the slave class is at first but indistinctly separated as a social stratum. It acquires separateness only as fast as there arise some restrictions on the powers of the owners. Ceasing to stand in the position of domestic cattle, slaves begin to form a division of the body politic when their personal claims begin to be distinguished as limiting the claims of their masters.

It is commonly supposed that serfdom arises by mitigation of slavery, but examination of the facts shows that it arises in a different way. While during the early struggles for existence between them, primitive tribes, growing at one another's expense by incorporating separately the individuals they capture, thus form a class of absolute slaves, the formation of a servile class considerably higher and having a distinct social status accompanies that later and larger process of growth under which one society incorporates other societies bodily. Serfdom originates along with conquest and annexation. For whereas the one implies that the captured people are detached from their homes, the other implies that the subjugated people continue in their homes.

Thomson remarks that "among the New Zealanders whole tribes sometimes became nominally slaves when conquered, although permitted to live at their usual places of residence, on condition of paying tribute, in food, etc." [1859, I, 148], a statement which shows the origin of kindred arrangements in allied societies. Of the Hawaiian Islands government when first known, described as consisting of a king with turbulent chiefs, who had been subjected in comparatively recent times, Ellis writes: "The common people are generally considered as attached to the soil and are transferred with the land from one chief to another" [1826, p. 397]. Before the late changes in Fiji there were enslaved districts, and of their inhabitants we read that they had to supply the chief's houses "with daily food, and build and keep them in repair" [Erskine 1853, p. 457]. Though conquered peoples thus placed differ widely in the degrees of their subjection (being at the one extreme, as in Fiji, liable to be eaten when wanted, and at the other extreme called on only to give specified proportions of produce or labor), yet they remain alike as being undetached from their original places of residence.

That serfdom in Europe originated in an analogous way, there is good reason to believe. In Greece we have the case of Crete, where, under the conquering Dorians, there existed a vassal population formed, it would seem, partly of the aborigines and partly of preceding conquerors, of which the first were serfs attached to lands of the state and of individuals and the others had become tributary landowners. In Sparta the like relations were established by like causes. There were the helots, who lived on and cultivated the lands of their Spartan masters, and the perioeci, who had probably been, before the Dorian invasion, the superior class. So was it also in the Greek colonies afterwards founded, such as Syracuse, where the aborigines became serfs. Similarly in later times and nearer regions. When Gaul was overrun by the Romans, and again when Romanized Gaul was overrun by the Franks, there was little displacement of the actual cultivators of the soil, but these simply fell into lower positions: certainly lower political positions, and M. Guizot thinks lower industrial positions. Our own country yields illustrations.

> Among the Scottish Highlanders some entire septs or clans are stated to have been enslaved to others; and on the very threshold of Irish history we meet with a distinction between free and rent-paying tribes, which may possibly imply the same kind of superiority and subordination [Maine 1875, p. 133].

In ancient British times, writes Pearson, "it is probable that, in parts at least, there were servile villages, occupied by a kindred but conquered race, the first occupants of the soil" [1867, I, 112]. More trustworthy is the evidence which comes to us from old English days and Norman days. Professor Stubbs [1880, II, 493] says,

> The ceorl had his right in the common land of his township; his Latin name, villanus, had been a symbol of freedom, but his privileges were bound to the land, and when the Norman lord took the land he took the villein with it. Still the villein retained his customary rights, his house and land and rights of wood and hay; his lord's demesne depended for cultivation on his services, and he had in his lord's sense of self-interest the sort of protection that was shared by the horse and the ox.

And of kindred import is the following passage from Innes [1860, pp. 141–2]:

> I have said that of the inhabitants of the Grange, the lowest in the scale was the *ceorl, bond, serf,* or villein, who was transferred like the land on which he labored, and who might be caught and brought back if he attempted to

escape, like a stray ox or sheep. Their legal name of *nativus*, or *neyf*, which I have not found but in Britain, seems to point to their origin in the native race, the original possessors of the soil. . . . In the register of Dunfermline are numerous 'genealogies,' or stud-books, for enabling the lord to trace and reclaim his stock of serfs by descent. It is observable that most of them are of Celtic names.

Clearly, a subjugated territory, useless without cultivators, was left in the hands of the original cultivators because nothing was to be gained by putting others in their places, even could an adequate number of others be had. Hence while it became the conqueror's interest to tie each original cultivator to the soil, it also became his interest to let him have such an amount of produce as to maintain him and enable him to rear offspring, and it further became his interest to protect him against injuries which would incapacitate him for work.

To show how fundamental is the distinction between bondage of the primitive type and the bondage of serfdom, it needs but to add that while the one can and does exist among savages and pastoral tribes, the other becomes possible only after the agricultural stage is reached, for only then can there occur the bodily annexation of one society by another, and only then can there be any tying to the soil.

Associated men who live by hunting and to whom the area occupied is of value only as a habitat for game, cannot well have anything more than a common participation in the use of this occupied area; such ownership of it as they have must be joint ownership. Naturally, then, at the outset all the adult males, who are at once hunters and warriors, are the common possessors of the undivided land, encroachment on which by other tribes they resist. Though in the earlier pastoral state, especially where the barrenness of the region involves wide dispersion, there is no definite proprietorship of the tract wandered over, yet, as is shown us in the strife between the herdsmen of Abraham and those of Lot respecting feeding grounds, some claims to exclusive use tend to arise; and at a later half-pastoral stage, as among the ancient Germans, the wanderings of each division fall within prescribed limits.

I refer to these facts by way of showing the identity established at the outset between the militant class and the landowning class. For whether the group is one which lives by hunting or one which lives by feeding cattle, any slaves its members possess are excluded from landownership; the freemen, who are all fighting men, become, as a matter of course, the proprietors of their territory. This connection, in variously modified forms, long continues and could scarcely do otherwise. Land being, in early settled communities, the almost exclusive source of wealth, it happens inevitably that during times in which the principle that might is right remains unqualified, personal power and ownership of the soil go together. Hence the fact that where, instead of being held by the whole society, land comes to be parceled out among component village-communities, or among families, or among individuals, possession of it habitually goes along with the bearing of arms. In ancient Egypt "every soldier was a land-owner" — "had an allotment of land of about six acres" [Sharpe 1876, I, 189; Kenrick 1850, II, 42]. In Greece the invading Hellenes, wresting the country from its original holders, joined military service with territorial endowment. In Rome, too, "every freeholder from the seventeenth to the sixtieth year of his age, was under obligation of service . . . so that even the emancipated slave had to serve who, in an exceptional case, had come into possession of landed property" [Mommsen 1862, I, 95].

The like happened in the early Teutonic community. Joined with professional warriors, its army included "the mass of freemen arranged in families fighting for their homesteads and hearths" [Stubbs 1880, I, 34], such freemen, or markmen, owning land partly in common and partly as individual proprietors. Or as is said of this same arrangement among the ancient English, "their occupation of the land as *cognationes* resulted from their enrolment in the field, where each kindred was drawn up under an officer of its own lineage and appointment" [Kemble 1876, I, 69], and so close was this dependence that "a thane forfeited his hereditary freehold by misconduct in battle" [Hallam 1855, II, 295].

Beyond the original connection between militancy and landowning, which naturally arises from the joint interest which those who own the land and occupy it, either individually or collectively, have in resisting aggressors, there arises later a further connection. As, along with successful militancy, there progresses a social evolution which gives to a dominant ruler increased power, it becomes his custom to reward his leading soldiers by grants of land. Early Egyptian kings "bestowed on distinguished military officers" portions of the crown domains [Wilkinson 1878, I, 150n.]. When the barbarians were enrolled as Roman soldiers "they were paid also by assignments of land, according to a custom which prevailed in the Imperial armies. The possession of these lands was given to them on condition of the son becoming a soldier like his father" [Fustel de Coulanges 1872, p. 246]. And that kindred usages were general throughout the feudal period is a familiar truth, feudal tenancy being, indeed, thus constituted, and inability to bear arms being a reason for excluding women from succession. To exemplify the nature of the relation established, it will suffice to name the fact that "William the Conqueror . . . distributed this kingdom into about 60,000 parcels, of nearly equal value [partly left in the hands of those who previously held it, and partly made over to his followers as either owners or suzerains], from each of which the service of a soldier was due," and the further fact that one of his laws requires all owners of land to "swear that they become vassals or tenants," and will "defend their lord's territories and title as well as his person" by "knight-service on horseback" [Hallam 1855, I, Ch. II, pt. 1; Reeves 1869, I, 34–6]. . . .

Setting out with the class of warriors or men bearing arms, who in primitive communities are owners of the land, collectively or individually, or partly one and partly the other, there arises the question — How does this class differentiate into nobles and freemen?

The most general reply is, of course, that since the state of homogeneity is by necessity unstable, time inevitably brings about inequalities of positions among those whose positions were at first equal. Before the semi-civilized state is reached the differentiation cannot become decided, because there can be no larger accumulations of wealth and because the laws of descent do not favor maintenance of such accumulations as are possible. But in the pastoral, and still more in the agricultural, community, especially where descent through males has been established, several causes of differentiation come into play. There is, first, unlikeness of kin-ship to the head man. Obviously, in course of generations, the younger descendants of the younger become more and more remotely related to the eldest descendant of the eldest, and social inferiority arises. As the obligation to execute blood revenge for a murdered member of the family does not extend beyond a certain degree of relationship (in ancient France not beyond the seventh), so neither does the accompanying distinction. From the same cause comes inferiority in point of possessions. Inheritance by the eldest male from generation to generation works the effect that those who are the most distantly connected in blood with the head of the group are also the poorest.

Then there cooperates with these factors a consequent factor, namely the extra power which greater wealth gives. For when there arise disputes within the tribe, the richer are those who, by their better appliances for defense and their greater ability to purchase aid, naturally have the advantage over the poorer. Proof that this is a potent cause is found in a fact named by Sir Henry Maine. "The founders of a part of our modern European aristocracy, the Danish, are known to have been originally peasants who fortified their houses during deadly village struggles and then used their advantage" [1875, pp. 84–5].

Such superiorites of position, once initiated, are increased in another way. Already in the last chapter we have seen that communities are to a certain extent increased by the addition of fugitives from other com-munities — sometimes criminals, sometimes those who are oppressed. . . . Sometimes they yield up their freedom for the sake of protection: a man makes himself a slave by breaking a spear in the presence of his wished-for master, as among the East Africans, or by inflicting some small bodily injury upon him, as among the Fulahs. In ancient Rome the semi-slave class distinguished as clients originated by this voluntary acceptance of servitude with safety. But where his aid promises to be of value in war, the fugitive offers himself as a warrior in exchange for maintenance and refuge. Other things equal, he chooses for master someone marked by superiority of power and property, and thus enables the man already dominant to become more dominant. Such armed dependents, having as aliens no claims to the lands of the group and bound to its head only by fealty, answer in position to the *comites* as found in the early German communities and as exemplified in old English times by the "Huscarlas" (Housecarls), with whom nobles surrounded themselves. Evidently, too, followers of this kind, having certain interests in common with their protector and no interests in common with the rest of the community, become in his hands the means of usurping communal rights and elevating himself while depressing the rest.

Step by step the contrast strengthens. Beyond such as have voluntarily made themselves slaves to a headman, others have become enslaved by capture in the wars meanwhile going on, others by staking themselves in gaming, others by purchase, others by crime, others by debt. And of necessity the possession of many slaves, habitually accompanying wealth and power, tends further to increase that wealth and power and to mark off still more the higher rank from the lower.

And then, finally, the inferior freeman finds himself so much at the mercy of the superior freeman or noble, and his armed followers of alien origin, that it becomes needful for safety's sake to be also a follower, and, at first voluntary, the relation of dependence grows more and more compulsory. "The freeman might choose his Lord, he might determine to whom, in technical phrase, he should *commend* himself; but a Lord he must have, a Lord to act at once as his protector and as his surety" [Freeman 1867–79, I, 96–7]. . . .

By implying habitual war among settled societies, the foregoing interpretations have implied the formation of compound societies. Such class divisions as have been described are therefore usually complicated by further class divisions arising from the relations established between those conquerors and conquered whose respective groups already contain class divisions.

This increasing differentiation which accompanies increasing integration is clearly seen in such semi-civilized societies as that of the Hawaiian Islanders. Their ranks are:

1. King, queens, and royal family, along with the councillor or chief minister of the king. 2. The governors of the different islands, and the chiefs of several large divisions. Many of these are descendants of those who were kings of the respective islands in Cook's time, and until subdued by Tamehameha.

3. Chiefs of districts or villages, who pay a regular rent for the land, cultivating it by means of their dependants, or letting it out to tenants. This rank includes also the ancient priests. 4. The labouring classes — those renting small portions of land, those working on the land for food and clothing, mechanics, musicians, and dancers [Ellis 1826, pp. 392–3].

And, as shown elsewhere, these laboring classes are otherwise divisible into artisans who are paid wages, serfs attached to the soil, and slaves. Inspection makes it tolerably clear that the lowest chiefs, once independent, were reduced to the second rank when adjacent chiefs conquered them and became local kings and that they were reduced to the third rank at the same time that these local kings became chiefs of the second rank, when, by conquest, a kingship of the whole group was established.

Other societies in kindred stages show us kindred divisions, similarly to be accounted for. Among the New Zealanders there are six grades; there are six among the Ashantis; there are five among the Abyssinians; and other more or less compounded African states present analogous divisions. Perhaps ancient Peru furnishes as clear a case as any of the superposition of ranks resulting from subjugation. The petty kingdoms which were massed together by the conquering Incas were severally left with the rulers and their subordinates undisturbed, but over the whole empire there was a superior organization of Inca rulers of various grades. That kindred causes produced kindred effects in early Egyptian times is inferable from traditions and remains which tell us both of local struggles which ended in consolidation, and of conquests by invading races, whence would naturally result the numerous divisions and subdivisions which Egyptian society presented, an inference justified by the fact that under Roman dominion there was a recomplication caused by the superposing of Roman governing agencies upon native governing agencies.

Passing over other ancient instances and coming to the familiar case of our own country, we may note how, from the followers of the conquering Normans, there arose the two ranks of the greater and lesser barons, holding their land directly from the king, while the old English thanes were reduced to the rank of sub-feudatories. Of course where perpetual wars produce first small aggregations, and then larger ones, and then dissolutions, and then reaggregations, and then unions of them, various in their extents, as happened in medieval Europe, there result very numerous divisions. In the Merovingian kingdoms there were slaves having seven different origins, there were serfs of more than one grade, there were freedmen — men who, though emancipated, did not rank with the fully free, and there were two other classes less than free — the *liten* and the *coloni*. Of the free there were three classes — independent landowners, freemen in relations of dependence with other freemen, of whom there were two kinds, and freemen in special relations with the king, of whom there were three kinds.

And here, while observing in these various cases how greater political differentiation is made possible by greater political integration, we may also observe that in early stages, while social cohesion is small, greater political integration is made possible by greater political differentiation. For the larger the mass to be held together, while incoherent, the more numerous must be the agents standing in successive degrees of subordination to hold it together.

The political differentiations which militancy originates and which for a long time increase in definiteness so that mixture of ranks by marriage is made a crime, are at later stages and under other conditions, interfered with, traversed, and partially or wholly destroyed.

Where for ages and in varying degrees war has been producing aggregations and dissolutions, the continual breaking up and re-forming of social bonds obscures the original divisions established in the ways described: instance the state of things in the Merovingian kingdoms just named. And where, instead of conquests by kindred adjacent societies which in large measure leave standing the social positions and properties of the subjugated, there are conquests by alien races carried on more barbarously, the original grades may be practically obliterated, and in place of them there may come grades established entirely by appointment of the despotic conqueror. In parts of the East, where such over-runnings of race by race have been going on from the earliest recorded times, we see this state of things substantially realized. There is little or nothing of hereditary rank, and the only rank recognized is that of official position. Besides the different grades of appointed state-functionaries, there are no class distinctions having political meanings.

A tendency to subordination of the original ranks, and a substitution of new ranks, is otherwise caused: it accompanies the progress of political consolidation. The change which occurred in China illustrates this effect. Gützlaff [1838, II, 305–6] says:

> Mere title was afterwards (on the decay of the feudal system) the reward bestowed by the sovereign. . . . and the haughty and powerful grandees of other countries are here the dependent and penurious servants of the Crown. . . . The revolutionary principle of leveling all classes has been carried, in China, to a very great extent. . . . This is introduced for the benefit of the sovereign, to render his authority supreme.

The causes of such changes are not difficult to see. In the first place the subjugated local rulers, losing, as integration advances, more and more of their power, lose, consequently, more and more of their actual if not of their nominal rank, passing from the condition of tributary rulers to the condition of subjects. Indeed, jealousy on the part of the monarch sometimes prompts positive exclusion of them from influential positions, as in France, where "Louis XIV systematically excluded the nobility from ministerial functions" [ref. lost]. Presently their distinction is further diminished by the rise of competing ranks created by state authority. Instead of the titles inherited by the land-possessing military chiefs, which were descriptive of their attributes and positions, there come to be titles conferred by the sovereign. Certain of the classes thus established are still of military origin, as the knights made on the battlefield, sometimes in large numbers before battle, as at Agincourt when five hundred were thus created, and sometimes afterwards in reward for valor. Others of them arise from the exercise of political functions of different grades, as in France, where in the seventeenth century hereditary nobility was conferred on officers of the great council and officers of the chamber of accounts. The administration of law, too, originates titles of honor. In France in 1607, nobility was granted to doctors, regents, and professors of law, and "the superior courts obtained, in 1644, the privileges of nobility of the first degree." So that, as Warnkoenig and Stein remark, "the original conception of nobility was in the course of time so much widened that its primitive relation to the possession of a fief is no longer recognizable and the whole institution seems changed" [1846–48, I, 392–3].

These, with kindred instances which our own country and other European countries furnish, show us both how the original class divisions become blurred, and how the new class divisions are distinguished by being delocalized. They are strata which run through the integrated society, having, many of them, no reference to the land and no more connection with one place than with another. It is true that of the titles artificially conferred, the higher are habitually derived from the names of districts and towns, so simulating, but only simulating, the ancient feudal titles expressive of actual lordship over territories. The other modern titles, however, which have arisen with the growth of political, judicial, and other functions, have not even nominal references to localities. This change naturally accompanies the growing integration of the parts into a whole, and the rise of an organization of the whole which disregards the divisions among the parts.

More effective still in weakening those primitive political divisions initiated by militancy is increasing industrialism. This acts in two ways — firstly, by creating a class having power derived otherwise than from territorial possessions or official positions, and, secondly, by generating ideas and sentiments at variance with the ancient assumptions of class superiority.

As we have already seen, rank and wealth are at the outset habitually associated. Existing uncivilized peoples still show us this relation. The chief of a kraal among the Koranna Hottentots is "usually the person of greatest property" [Thompson, G. 1827, II, 30]. In the Bechuana language "the word *kosi* . . . has a double acceptation, denoting either a chief or a rich man" [Burchell 1822-24, II, 347]. Such small authority as a Chinook chief has, "rests on riches, which consists in wives, children, slaves, boats, and shells" [Waitz, G. 1860-61, III, 338]. Rude European peoples, like the Albanians, yield kindred facts: the heads of their communes "sont en général les gens les plus riches" [Boué, 1840, III, 254]. Indeed it is manifest that before the development of commerce, and while possession of land could alone give largeness of means, lordship and riches were directly connected, so that, as Sir Henry Maine remarks, "the opposition commonly set up between birth and wealth, and particularly wealth other than landed property, is entirely modern" [1875, p. 134]. When, however, with the arrival of industry at that stage in which wholesale transactions bring large profits there arise traders who vie with and exceed, many of the landed nobility in wealth, and when by conferring obligations on kings and nobles such traders gain social influence, there comes an occasional removal of the barrier between them and the titled classes. In France the process began as early as 1271 when there were issued letters ennobling Raoul the goldsmith: "the first letters conferring nobility in existence" in France [Jourdan 1822-23, II, 645]. The precedent, once established, is followed with increasing frequency, and sometimes, under pressure of financial needs, there grows up the practice of selling titles, in disguised ways or openly. In France in 1702, the king ennobled 200 persons at 3,000 livres a head; in 1706, 500 persons at 6,000 livres a head.

And then the breaking down of the ancient political divisions thus caused is furthered by that weakening of them consequent on the growing spirit of equality fostered by industrial life. In proportion as men are habituated to maintain their own claims while respecting the claims of others, which they do in every act of exchange, whether of goods for money or of services for pay, there is produced a mental attitude at variance with that which accompanies subjection, and as fast as this happens such political distinctions as imply subjection lose more and more of that respect which gives them strength.

Summary

Class distinctions, then, date back to the beginnings of social life. Omitting these small wandering assemblages which are so incoherent that their component parts are ever changing their relations to one another and to the environment, we see that wherever there is some coherence and some permanence of relation among the parts, there begin to arise political divisions. Relative superiority of power, first causing a differentiation at once domestic and social between the activities of the sexes and the consequent positions of the sexes, presently begins to cause a differentiation among males, shown in the bondage of captives: a master class and a slave class are formed.

Where men continue the wandering life in pursuit of wild food for themselves or their cattle, the groups they form are debarred from doing more by war than appropriate one another's units individually, but where men have passed into the agricultural or settled state it becomes possible for one community to take possession bodily of another community, along with the territory it occupies. When this happens there arise additional class divisions. The conquered and tribute-paying community, besides having its headmen reduced to subjection, has its people reduced to a state such that, while they continue to live on their lands, they yield up, through the intermediation of their chiefs, part of the produce to the conquerors, so foreshadowing what eventually becomes a serf class.

From the beginning the militant class, being by force of arms the dominant class, becomes the class which owns the source of food — the land. During the hunting and pastoral stages the warriors of the group hold the land collectively. On passing into the settled state, their tenures become partly collective and partly individual in sundry ways, and eventually almost wholly individual. But throughout long stages of social evolution landowning and militancy continue to be associated.

The class differentiation of which militancy is the active cause is furthered by the establishment of definite descent, and especially male descent, and by the transmission of position and property to the eldest son of the eldest continually. This conduces to inequalities of position and wealth between near kindred and remote kindred, and such inequalities once initiated, tend to increase, since it results from them that the superior get greater means of maintaining their power by accumulating appliances for offense and defense.

Such differentiation is augmented, at the same time that a new differentiation is set up, by the immigration of fugitives who attach themselves to the most powerful member of the group, now as dependants who work and now as armed followers — armed followers who form a class bound to the dominant man and unconnected with the land. And since, in clusters of such groups, fugitives ordinarily flock most to the strongest group and become adherents of its head, they are instrumental in furthering those subsequent integrations and differentiations which conquests bring about. . . .

When there come the conquests which produce compound societies, and again, doubly compound ones, there result superpositions of ranks. And the general effect is that while the ranks of the conquering society become respectively higher than those which existed before, the ranks of the conquered society become respectively lower.

The class divisions thus formed during the earlier stages of militancy are traversed and obscured as fast as many small societies are consolidated into one large society. Ranks referring to local organization are gradually replaced by ranks referring to general organization. Instead of deputy and subdeputy governing agents who are the militant owners of the subdivisions they rule, there come governing agents who more or less clearly form strata running throughout the society as a whole — a concomitant of developed political administration.

Chiefly, however, we have to note that while the higher political evolution of large social aggregates tends to break down the divisions of rank which grew up in the small component social aggregates by substituting other divisions, these original divisions are still more broken down by growing industrialism. Generating a wealth that is not connected with rank, this initiates a competing power; at the same time, by establishing the equal positions of citizens before the law in respect of trading transactions, it weakens those divisions which at the outset expressed inequalities of position before the law. . . .

CHAPTER 12

POLITICAL FORMS AND FORCES

The conceptions of biologists have been greatly enlarged by the discovery that organisms which, when adult, appear to have scarcely anything in common, were, in their first stages, very similar, and that indeed, all organisms start with a common structure. Recognition of this truth has revolutionized not only their ideas respecting the relations of organisms to one another, but also their ideas respecting the relations of the parts of each organism to one another.

If societies have evolved and if that mutual dependence of their parts which cooperation implies has been gradually reached, then the implication is that however unlike their developed structures become, there is a rudimentary structure with which they all set out. And if there can be recognized any such primitive unity, recognition of it will help us to interpret the ultimate diversity. We shall understand better how in each society the several components of the political agency have come to be what we now see them, and also how those of one society are related to those of another.

Setting out with an unorganized horde including both sexes and all ages, let us ask what must happen when some public question, as that of migration or of defense against enemies, has to be decided. The assembled individuals will fall, more or less clearly, into two divisions. The elder, the stronger, and those whose sagacity and courage have been proved by experience will form the smaller part, who carry on the discussions, while the larger part, formed of the young, the weak, and the undistinguished, will be listeners, who usually do no more than express from time to time assent or dissent. A further inference may safely be drawn. In the cluster of leading men there is sure to be one whose weight is greater than that of any other — some aged hunter, some distinguished warrior, some cunning medicine man — who will have more than his individual share in forming the resolution finally acted upon. This is to say, the entire assemblage will resolve itself into three parts. To use a biological metaphor, there will, out of the general mass, be differentiated a nucleus and a nucleolus.

These first traces of political structure which we infer a priori must spontaneously arise, we find have arisen among the rudest peoples, repetition having so strengthened them as to produce a settled order. When, among the aborigines of Victoria, a tribe plans revenge on another tribe

97

supposed to have killed one of its members, "a council is called of all the old men of the tribe. . . . The women form an outer circle round the men. . . . The chief [simply 'a native of influence'] opens the council" [Smyth 1878, I, 303]. And what we here see happening in an assemblage having no greater differences than those based on strength, age, and capacity, happens when, later, these natural distinctions have gained definiteness. . . . Of the Hill tribes of India may be instanced the Khonds, of whom we read that

> Assemblies of the whole tribe, or of any of its sub-divisions, are convened, to determine questions of general importance. The members of every society, however, have a right to be present at *all* its councils, and to give their voices on the questions mooted, although the patriarchs alone take part in their public *discussion*. . . . The federal patriarchs, in like manner, consult with the heads of tribes, and assemble when necessary the entire population of the federal group [Macpherson 1842, pp. 32, 27].

In New Zealand, too, the government was conducted in accordance with public opinion expressed in general assemblies, and the chiefs "could not declare peace or war, or do anything affecting the whole people, without the sanction of the majority of the clan" [Thomson 1859, I, 95]. Of the Tahitians, Ellis tells us that the king had a few chiefs as advisers, but that no affair of national importance could be undertaken without consulting the landholders or second rank, and also that public assemblies were held [1829, II, 363]. Similarly of the Malagasy. "The greatest national council in Madagascar is an assembly of the people of the capital, and the heads of the provinces, towns, villages, etc." The king usually presides in person [Ellis 1838, I, 378].

Though in these last cases we see considerable changes in the relative powers of the three components, so that the inner few have gained in authority at the expense of the outer many, yet all three are still present, and they continue to be present when we pass to sundry historic peoples. Even of the Phoenicians, Movers notes that "in the time of Alexander a war was decided upon by the Tyrians without the consent of the absent king, the senate acting together with the popular assembly" [1841–56, II, Pt. 1, 541]. Then there is the familiar case of the Homeric Greeks, whose Agora, presided over by the king, was "an assembly for talk, communication and discussion to a certain extent by the chiefs, in presence of the people as listeners and sympathisers," who were seated around [Grote 1846–56, II, 92]; and that the people were not always passive is shown by the story of Thersitês, who, ill-used though he was by Odysseus and derided by the crowd for interfering, had first made his harangue. Again, the king, the senate, and the freemen in early Roman times stood in relations which had manifestly grown out of those existing in the original assembly, for though the three did not simultaneously cooperate, yet on important occasions the king communicated his proposals to the assembled burgesses, who expressed their approval or disapproval, and the clan chiefs, forming the senate, though they did not debate in public, had yet such joint power that they could, on occasion, negative the decision of king and burgesses.

Concerning the primitive Germans, Tacitus, as translated by Mr. Freeman, writes:

> On smaller matters the chiefs debate, on greater matters all men; but so that those things whose final decision rests with the whole people are first handled by the chiefs. . . . The multitude sits armed in such order as it thinks good; silence is proclaimed by the priests, who have also the right of enforcing it. Presently the king or chief, according to the age of each, according to his birth, according to his glory in war or his eloquence, is listened to, speaking rather by the influence of persuasion than by the power of commanding. If their opinions give offence, they are thrust aside with a shout; if they approved, the hearers clash their spears [1876, p. 17].

Similarly among the Scandinavians, as shown us in Iceland, where, besides the general Al-thing annually held, which it was "disreputable for a freeman not to attend," and at which

> people of all classes in fact pitched their tents, there were local assemblies called Var-things attended by all the freemen of the district, with a crowd of retainers . . . both for the discussion of public affairs and the administration of justice. . . . Within the circle [formed for administering justice] sat the judges, the people standing on the outside [Mallet 1847, pp. 291–3]. . . .

This form of ruling agency is thus shown to be the fundamental form by its presence at the outset of social life and by its continuance under various conditions. Not among peoples of superior types only, such as Aryans and some Semites, do we find it, but also among sundry Malayo-Polynesians, among the red men of North America, the Dravidian tribes of the Indian hills, the aborigines of Australia. In fact, as already implied, governmental organization could not possibly begin in any other way. On the one hand, no controlling force at first exists save that of the aggregate will as manifested in the assembled horde. On the other hand, leading parts in determining this aggregate will are inevitably taken by the few whose superiority is recognized. And of these predominant few, some one is sure to be most predominant. That which we have to note as specially significant is not that a free form of government is the primitive form, though this is an implication which may be dwelt upon. Nor are we chiefly concerned with the fact that at the very beginning there shows itself that separation of the superior few from the inferior many, which becomes marked in later stages, though this, too, is a fact which may be singled out and emphasized. Nor is attention to be mainly directed to the early appearance of a man whose controlling power is greater than that of any other, though the evidence given may be cited to prove this. But here we have to note, particularly, the truth that at the outset may be discerned the vague outlines of a triune political structure.

Of course the ratios among the powers of these three components are in no two cases quite the same, and, as implied in sundry of the above examples, they everywhere undergo more or less change — change determined here by the emotional natures of the men composing the group, there by the physical circumstances as favoring or hindering independence; now by the activities as warlike or peaceful, and now by the exceptional characters of particular individuals.

Unusual sagacity, skill, or strength, habitually regarded by primitive men as supernatural, may give to some member of the tribe an influence which, transmitted to a successor supposed to inherit his supernatural character, establishes an authority subordinating both that of the other leading men and that of the mass. Or from a division of labor such that while some remain exclusively warriors the rest are in a measure otherwise occupied, it may result that the two superior components of the political agency get power to override the third. Or the members of the third, keeping up habits which make coercion of them difficult or impossible, may maintain a general predominance over the other two. And then the relations of these three governing elements to the entire community may, and ordinarily do, undergo change by the formation of a passive class excluded from their deliberations — a class at first composed of the women and afterwards containing also the slaves or other dependents.

War successfully carried on not only generates this passive class but also, implying as it does subjection to leaders, changes more or less decidedly the relative powers of these three parts of the political agency. As, other things equal, groups in which there is little subordination are subjugated by groups in which subordination is greater, there is a tendency to the survival and spread of groups in which the controlling power of the dominant few becomes relatively great. In like manner, since success in war largely depends on that promptitude and consistency of action which singleness of will gives, there must, where warfare is chronic, be a tendency for members of the ruling group to become more and more obedient to its head, failure in the struggle for existence among tribes otherwise equal being ordinarily a consequence of disobedience. And then it is also to be noted that the overrunnings of societies one by another, repeated and re-repeated as they often are, have the effect of obscuring and even obliterating the traces of the original structure.

While, however, recognizing the fact that during political evolution these three primitive components alter their proportions in various ways and degrees to the extent that some of them become mere rudiments or wholly disappear, it will greatly alter our conception of political forms if we remember that they are all derived from this primitive form — that a despotism, an oligarchy, or a democracy, is a type of government in which one of the original components has greatly developed at the expense of the other two, and that the various mixed types are to be arranged according to the degrees in which one or other of the original components has the greater influence.

Is there any fundamental unity of political forces accompanying this fundamental unity of political forms? While losing sight of the common origin of the structures have we not also become inadequately conscious of the common source of their powers? How prone we are to forget the ultimate while thinking of the proximate it may be worth while pausing a moment to observe.

One who in a storm watches the breaking up of a wreck or the tearing down of a sea wall is impressed by the immense energy of the waves. Of course, when it is pointed out that in the absence of winds no such results can be produced, he recognizes the truth that the sea is in itself powerless, and that the power enabling it to destroy vessels and piers is given by the currents of air which roughen its surface. If he stops short here, however, he fails to identify the force which works these striking changes. Intrinsically, the air is just as passive as the water is. There would be no winds were it not for the varying effects of the Sun's heat on different parts of the Earth's surface. Even when he has traced back thus far the energy which undermines cliffs and makes shingle, he has not reached its source, for in the absence of that continuous concentration of the solar mass caused by the mutual gravitation of its parts, there would be no solar radiations.

The tendency here illustrated, which all have in some degree and most in a great degree, to associate power with the visible agency exercising it rather than with its inconspicuous source, has, as above implied, a vitiating influence on conceptions at large, and among others on political ones. Though the habit, general in past times, of regarding the powers of governments as inherent, has been, by the growth of popular institutions, a good deal qualified, yet, even now, there is no clear apprehension of the fact that governments are not themselves powerful, but are the instrumentalities of a power. This power existed before governments arose; governments were themselves produced by it; and it ever continues to be that which, disguised more or less completely, works through them. [To see how this power finds expression] let us go back to the beginning.

The Greenlanders are entirely without political control, having nothing which represents it more nearly than the deference paid to the opinion of some old man skilled in seal-catching and the signs of the weather. But a Greenlander who is aggrieved by another has his remedy in what is called a singing combat. He composes a satirical poem and challenges his antagonist to a satirical duel in face of the tribe: "he who has the last word wins the trial." And then Cranz adds, "nothing so effectually restrains a Greenlander from vice as the dread of public disgrace" [1820, I, 164–5]. Here we see operating in its original unqualified way that governing influence of public sentiment which precedes more special governing influences.

The dread of social reprobation is in some cases enforced by the dread of banishment. Among the otherwise unsubordinated Australians they "punish each other for such offences as theft, sometimes by expulsion from the camp" [Sturt 1833, p. ref. lost]. Of one of the [British] Columbian tribes we read that "the Salish can hardly be said to have any regular form of government;" and then, further, we read that "criminals are sometimes punished by banishment from their tribe" [Domenech 1860, II, 343–4]. . . . Among the Bódo and the Dhimáls, whose village heads are simply respected elders with no coercive powers, those who offend against customs "are admonished, fined, or excommunicated, according to the degree of the offence" [Hodgson 1847, p. 159]. But the controlling influence of public sentiment in groups which have little or no organization is best shown in the force with which it acts on those who are bound to avenge murders. Concerning the Australian aborigines, Sir George Grey writes:

> The holiest duty a native is called on to perform is that of avenging the death of his nearest relation, for it is his peculiar duty to do so; until he has fulfilled this task, he is constantly taunted by the old women; his wives, if he is married, would soon quit him; if he is unmarried, not a single young woman would speak to him; his mother would constantly cry, and lament that she should ever have given birth to so degenerate a son; his father would treat him with contempt, and reproaches would constantly be sounded in his ear [1841, II, 240].

We have next to note that for a long time after political control has made its appearance it remains conspicuously subordinate to this control of general feeling, both because while there are no developed governmental structures the head man has but little ability to enforce his will and because such ability as he has, if unduly exercised, causes desertion. All parts of the world furnish illustrations. In America among the Snake Indians "each individual is his own master, and the only control to which his conduct is subjected, is the advice of a chief supported by his influence over the opinions of the rest of the tribe" [Lewis and Clarke 1814, p. 306]. Of a Chinook chief we are told that his ability to render service to his neighbors, and the popularity which follows it, is at once the foundation and the measure of his authority" [Lewis and Clarke 1814, p. 443]. If a Dakota "wishes to do mischief, the only way a chief can influence him is to give him something, or pay him to desist from his evil intentions. The chief has no authority to act for the tribe, and dare not do it" [Schoolcraft 1853–56, II, 182]. And among the Creeks, more advanced in political organization though they are, the authority of the elected chiefs "continues during good behavior. The disapproval of the body of the people is an effective bar to the exercise of their powers and functions" [Schoolcraft 1853–56, I, 275].

Turning to Asia, we read that the bais or chiefs of the Kirghiz "have little power over them for good or evil. In consideration of their age and blood, some deference to their opinions is shown, but nothing more" [Wood 1841, p. 338]. The Ostyaks "pay respect, in the fullest sense of the word, to their chief, if wise and valiant, but this homage is voluntary, and founded on personal regard" [Felińska 1853, II, 269]. And of the Naga chiefs Butler says, "Their orders are obeyed so far only as they accord with the wishes and convenience of the community" [1855, p. 146].

So, too, is it in parts of Africa, as instance the Koranna Hottentots. "A chief or captain presides over each clan or kraal, being usually the person of greatest property; but his authority is extremely limited, and only obeyed so far as it meets the general approbation" [Thompson, G. 1827, II, 30]. And even among the more politically organized Kaffirs there is a kindred restraint. The king "makes laws and executes them according to his sole will. Yet there is a power to balance his in the people; he governs only so long as they choose to obey" [Lichtenstein 1812–15, I, 286–7]. They leave him if he governs ill.

In its primitive form, then, political power is the feeling of the community, acting through an agency which it has either informally or formally established. Doubtless, from the beginning, the power of the chief is in part personal: his greater strength, courage, or cunning, enables him in some degree to enforce his individual will. But, as the evidence shows, his individual will is but a small factor, and the authority he wields is proportionate to the degree in which he expresses the wills of the rest.

While this public feeling, which first acts by itself and then partly through an agent, is to some extent the feeling spontaneously formed by those concerned, it is to a much larger extent the opinion imposed on them or prescribed for them. In the first place, the emotional nature prompting the general mode of conduct is derived from ancestors — is a product of all ancestral activities; in the second place, the special desires which, directly or indirectly, determine the courses pursued, are induced during early life by seniors, and enlisted on behalf of beliefs and usages which the tribe inherits. The governing sentiment is, in short, mainly the accumulated and organized sentiment of the past.

It needs but to remember the painful initiation which, at a prescribed age, each member of a tribe undergoes (submitting to circumcision, or knocking out of teeth, or gashing of the flesh or tattooing) — it needs but to remember that from these imperative customs there is no escape, to see that the directive force which exists before a political agency arises and which afterwards makes the political agency its organ is the gradually formed opinion of countless preceding generations, or rather, not the opinion which strictly speaking is an intellectual product wholly impotent, but the emotion associated with the opinion. This we everywhere find to be at the outset the chief controlling power.

The notion of the Tupís that "if they departed from the customs of their forefathers they should be destroyed," may be named as a definite manifestation of the force with which this transmitted opinion acts [Southey 1810–19, I, 250]. . . . Of the Koranna Hottentots we read that "when ancient usages are not in the way, every man seems to act as is right in his own eyes" [Thompson, G. 1827, II, 30]. Though the Damara chiefs "have the power of governing arbitrarily, yet they venerate the traditions and customs of their ancestors" [ref. lost]. Smith says, "laws the Araucanians can scarcely be said to have, though there are many ancient usages they hold sacred and strictly observe" [1855, p. 243]. According to Brooke [1866, I, 129], among the Dyaks custom simply seems to have become law, and breaking the custom leads to a fine. In the minds of some clans of the Malagasy, "innovation and injury are. . . . inseparable, and the idea of improvement altogether inadmissible [Ellis, 1838, I, 146].

This control by inherited usages is not simply as strong in groups of men who are politically unorganized, or but little organized, as it is in advanced tribes and nations, but it is stronger. As Sir John Lubbock remarks, "No savage is free. All over the world his daily life is regulated by a complicated and apparently most inconvenient set of customs (as forcible as laws), of quaint prohibitions and privileges" [1882, p. 445]. Though one of these rude societies appears structureless, yet its ideas and usages form a kind of invisible framework for it, serving rigorously to restrain certain classes of its actions. And this invisible framework has been slowly and unconsciously shaped during daily activities impelled by prevailing feelings and guided by prevailing thoughts, through generations stretching back into the far past.

In brief, then, before any definite agency for social control is developed there exists a control arising partly from the public opinion of the living, and more largely from the public opinion of the dead.

But now let us note definitely a truth implied in some of the illustrations above given — the truth that when a political agency has been evolved, its power, largely dependent on present public opinion, is otherwise almost wholly dependent on past public opinion. The ruler, in part the organ of the wills of those around, is in a still greater degree the organ of the wills of those who have passed away, and his own will, much restrained by the first, is still more restrained by the last.

For his function as regulator is mainly that of enforcing the inherited rules of conduct which embody ancestral sentiments and ideas. Everywhere we are shown this. Among the Arafuras such decisions as are given by their elders are "according to the customs of their forefathers, which are held in the highest regard" [Kolff 1840, p. 161]. So is it with the Kirghiz: "the judgments of the Bis, or esteemed elders, are based on the known and universally recognized customs" [Michie 1864, p. ref. lost]. And in Sumatra "they are governed, in their various disputes, by a set of long-established customs (*adat*), handed down to them from their ancestors. . . . The chiefs, in pronouncing their decisions, are not heard to say, 'so the law directs,' but 'such is the custom'" [Marsden 1811, p. 217].

As fast as custom passes into law, the political head becomes still more clearly an agent through whom the feelings of the dead control the actions of the living. That the power he exercises is mainly a power which acts through him we see on noting how little ability he has to resist it if he wishes to do so. His individual will is practically inoperative save where the overt or tacit injunctions of departed generations leave him free. Thus in Madagascar, "in cases where there is no law, custom, or precedent, the word of the sovereign is sufficient" [Ellis 1838, I, 377]. Among the East Africans, "the only limit to the despot's power is the Ada or precedent" [Burton, R. 1860, p. 361]. Of the Javans, Raffles writes, "the only restraint upon the will of the head of the government is the custom of the country, and the regard which he has for his character among his subjects" [1817, I, 274]. In Sumatra the people "do not acknowledge a right in the chiefs to constitute what laws they think proper, or to repeal or alter their ancient usages, of which they are extremely tenacious and jealous" [Marsden 1811, p. 217]. And how imperative is conformity to the beliefs and sentiments of progenitors is shown by the fatal results apt to occur from disregarding them.

> 'The King of Ashanti, although represented as a despotic monarch. . . . is not in all respects beyond control.' He is under an 'obligation to observe the national customs which have been handed down to the people from remote antiquity; and a practical disregard of this obligation, in the attempt to change some of the customs of their forefathers, cost Osai Quamina his throne' [Beecham 1841, pp. 90–1].

Which instance reminds us how commonly, as now among the Hottentots, as in the past among the ancient Mexicans, and as throughout the histories of civilized peoples, rulers have engaged, on succeeding to power, not to change the established order.

Doubtless the proposition that a government is in the main but an agency through which works the force of public feeling, present and past, seems at variance with the many facts showing how great may be the power of a ruling man himself. Saying nothing of a tyrant's ability to take lives for nominal reasons or none at all, to make groundless confiscations, to transfer subjects bodily from one place to another, to exact contributions of money and labor without stint, we are apparently shown by his ability to begin and carry on wars which sacrifice his subjects wholesale, that his single will may override the united wills of all others. In what way, then, must the original statement be qualified?

While holding that, in unorganized groups of men, the feeling manifested as public opinion controls political conduct, just as it controls the conduct distinguished as ceremonial and religious, and while holding that governing agencies, during their early stages, are at once the products of aggregate feeling, derive their powers from it, and are restrained by it, we must admit that these primitive relations become complicated when, by war, small groups are compounded and recompounded into great ones. Where the society is largely composed of subjugated people held down by superior force, the normal relation above described no longer exists. We must not expect to find in a rule coercively established by an invader the same traits as in a rule that has grown up from within. Societies formed by conquest may be, and frequently are, composed of two societies, which are in large measure, if not entirely, alien, and in them there cannot arise a political force from the aggregate will. Under such conditions the political head either derives his power exclusively from the feeling of the dominant class, or else, setting the diverse feelings originated in the upper and lower classes one against the other, is enabled so to make his individual will the chief factor.

After making which qualifications, however, it may still be contended that ordinarily, nearly all the force exercised by the governing agency originates from the feeling, if not of the whole community, yet of the part which is able to manifest its feeling. Though the opinion of the subjugated and unarmed lower society becomes of little account as a political factor, yet the opinion of the dominant and armed upper society continues to be the main cause of political action. What we are told of the Congo people, that "the king, who reigns as a despot over the people, is often disturbed in the exercise of his power by the princes, his vassals" [Pinkerton 1808–14, XVI, 577], what we are told of the despotically governed Dahomeans, that "the ministers, war captains, and feetishers may be, and often are, individually punished by the king: collectively they are too strong for him, and without their cordial cooperation he would soon cease to reign" [Burton, R. 1864, I, 263], is what we recognize as having been true and as being still true in various better known societies where the supreme head is nominally absolute. From the time when the Roman emperors were chosen by the soldiers and slain when they did not please them, to the present time when, as we are told in Russia, the desire of the army often determines the will of the Czar, there have been many illustrations of the truth that an autocrat is politically strong or weak according as many or few of the influential classes give him their support. . . .

Summary

A number of facts must be remembered if we are rightly to estimate the power of the aggregate will in comparison with the power of the autocrat's will. There is the fact that the autocrat is obliged to respect and maintain the great mass of institutions and laws produced by past sentiments and ideas, which have acquired a religious sanction, so that, as in ancient Egypt, dynasties of despots live and die leaving the social order essentially unchanged. There is the fact that a serious change of the social order, at variance with general feeling, is likely afterwards to be reversed, as when, in Egypt, Amenhotep IV, [in] spite of a rebellion, succeeded in establishing a new religion which was abolished in a succeeding reign; there is the allied fact that laws much at variance with the general will prove abortive, as, for instance, the sumptuary laws made by medieval kings, which, continually re-enacted, continually failed. There is the fact that, supreme as he may be, and divine as the nature ascribed to him, the all-powerful monarch is often shackled by usages which make his daily life a slavery: the opinions of the living oblige him to fulfil the dictates of the dead. There is the fact that if he does not conform, or if he otherwise produces by his acts much adverse feeling, his servants, civil and military, refuse to act, or turn against him, and in extreme cases there comes an example of "despotism tempered by assassination." And there is the final fact that habitually in societies where an offending autocrat is from time to time removed, another autocrat is set up: the implication being that the average sentiment is of a kind which not only tolerates but desires autocracy. That which some call loyalty and others call servility, both creates the absolute ruler and gives him the power he exercises.

But the cardinal truth, difficult adequately to appreciate, is that while the forms and laws of each society are the consolidated products of the emotions and ideas of those who lived throughout the past, they are made operative by the subordination of existing emotions and ideas to them. We are familiar with the thought of "the dead hand" as controlling the doings of the living in the uses made of property, but the effect of "the dead hand" in ordering life at large through the established political system is immeasurably greater. That which, from hour to hour in every country, governed despotically or otherwise, produces the obedience making political action possible is the accumulated and organized sentiment felt towards inherited institutions made sacred by tradition. Hence it is undeniable that, taken in its widest acceptation, the feeling of the community is the sole source of political power — in those communities, at least, which are not under foreign domination. It was so at the outset of social life, and it still continues substantially so. . . .

CHAPTER 13

POLITICAL HEADS—CHIEFS, KINGS, etc.

Of the three components of the triune political structure traceable at the outset, we have now to follow the development of the first. Already in the last two chapters something has been said, and more has been implied, respecting that most important differentiation which results in the establishment of a headship. What was there indicated under its general aspects has here to be elaborated under its special aspects.

"When Rink asked the Nicobarians who among them was the chief, they replied laughing, how could he believe that *one* could have power against so many?" [Bastian 1860, III, 384]. I quote this as a reminder that there is, at first, resistance to the assumption of supremacy by one member of a group — resistance which, though in some types of men small, is in most considerable, and in a few very great. To instances already given of tribes practically chiefless may be added, from America, the Haidas, among whom "the people seemed all equal," the Californian tribes, among whom "each individual does as he likes," the Navajos, among whom "each is sovereign in his own right as a warrior" [Bancroft 1875–76, I, 168, 348, 508]; and from Asia the Angamis, who "have no recognized head or chief, although they elect a spokesman, who, to all intents and purposes, is powerless and irresponsible" [Stewart 1855, p. 650].

Such small subordination as rude groups show, occurs only when the need for joint action is imperative, and control is required to make it efficient. Instead of recalling before-named examples of temporary chieftainship, I may here give some others. Of the Lower Californians we read: "In hunting and war they have one or more chiefs to lead them, who are selected only for the occasion" [Bancroft 1875–76, I, 565]. Of the Flatheads' chiefs it is said that "with the war their power ceases" [Bancroft 1875–76, I, 275]. Among the [Puget] Sound Indians the chief "has no authority, and only directs the movements of his band in warlike incursions" [Bancroft 1875–76, I, 217].

As observed under another head, this primitive insubordination has greater or less play according as the environment and the habits of life hinder or favor coercion. The Lower Californians, above instanced as chiefless, Baegert says resemble "herds of wild swine, which run about according to their own liking, being together today and scattered tomorrow, till they meet again by accident at some future time" [Bancroft 1875–76, I, 565]. "The chiefs among the Chipewyans are now totally without power," says Franklin [1823, p. 159] and these people exist as small migratory bands. Of the Abipones, who are "impatient of agriculture and a fixed home," and "are continually moving from place to place," Dobrizhoffer writes, "they neither revere their cacique as a master, nor pay him tribute or attendance as is usual with other nations" [1822, II, 102]. The like holds under like conditions with other races remote in type. Of the Bedouins Burckhardt remarks "the sheikh has no fixed authority" [1830, p. 161]; and according to another writer, "a chief, who has drawn the bond of allegiance too tight, is deposed or abandoned, and becomes a mere member of a tribe or remains without one" [Murray 1864, p. 9].

And now, having noted the original absence of political control, the resistance it meets with, and the circumstances which facilitate evasion of it, we may ask what causes aid its growth. There are several, and chieftainship becomes settled in proportion as they cooperate.

Among the members of the primitive group, slightly unlike in various ways and degrees, there is sure to be some one who has a recognized superiority. This superiority may be of several kinds which we will briefly glance at. . . .

The first to be named is that which goes with seniority. Though age, when it brings incapacity, is often among rude peoples treated with such disregard that the old are killed or left to die, yet, so long as capacity remains, the greater experience accompanying age generally insures influence. The chiefless Eskimos show "deference to seniors and strong men" [ref. lost]. Burchell says that over the Bushmen, old men seem to exercise the authority of chiefs to some extent [1822-24, I, 458], and the like holds true with the natives of Australia. Among the Fuegians "the word of an old man is accepted as law by the young people" [Fitzroy 1839, II, 179]. Each party of Rock Veddas "has a headman, the most energetic senior of the tribe," who divides the honey, etc. [Tennent 1859, II, 440]. Even with sundry peoples more advanced the like holds. The Dyaks in North Borneo, "have no established chiefs, but follow the counsels of the old man to whom they are related" [ref. lost]; and Edwards [1801–19, I, 49] says of the ungoverned Caribs that "to their old men, indeed, they allowed some kind of authority."

Naturally, in rude societies, the strong hand gives predominance. Apart from the influence of age, "bodily strength alone procures distinction among" the Bushmen [Lichtenstein 1812–15, II, 194]. The leaders of the Tasmanians were tall and powerful men: "instead of an elective or hereditary chieftaincy, the place of command was yielded up to the bully of the tribe" [Lloyd 1862, p. 56; Dove 1842, p. 253]. A remark of Sturt's implies a like origin of supremacy among the Australians. Similarly in South America. Of people on the Tapajós, Bates tells us that "the footmarks of the chief could be distinguished from the rest by their great size and the length of the stride" [1873, pp. 222–3]. And in Bedouin tribes "the fiercest, the strongest, and the craftiest obtains complete mastery over his fellows" [Burton, R. 1855–56, III, 44]. During higher stages physical vigor long continues to be an all-important qualification, as in Homeric Greece where even age did not compensate for decline of strength: "an old chief, such as Pêleus and Laërtes, cannot retain his position" [Grote 1846–56, II, 87]. Everyone knows that throughout medieval Europe, maintenance of headship largely depended on bodily prowess. And even but two centuries ago in the Western Isles of Scotland, "every Heir, or young Chieftain of a Tribe, was oblig'd in Honour to give a publick Specimen of his Valour, before he was own'd and declar'd Governor" [Martin 1716, p. 101].

Mental superiority, alone or joined with other attributes, is a common cause of predominance. With the Snake Indians the chief is no more than "the most confidential person among the warriors" [Lewis and Clarke 1814, p. 306]. Schoolcraft says of the chief acknowledged by the Creeks that "he is eminent with the people only for his superior talents and political abilities" [1853–56, V, 279], and that over the Comanches "the position of a chief is not hereditary, but the result of his own superior cunning, knowledge, or success in war" [1853–56, II, 130]. A chief of the Coroados is one "who by his strength, cunning, and courage had obtained some command over them" [Spix and Martius 1824, II, 234]. And the Ostyaks "pay respect, in the fullest sense of the word, to their chief, if wise and valiant; but this homage is voluntary, and not a prerogative of his position" [Felińska 1853, II, 269].

Yet another source of governmental power in primitive tribes is largeness of possessions, wealth being at once an indirect mark of superiority and a direct cause of influence. With the Tacullies "any person may become a *miuty* or chief who will occasionally provide a village feast" [Bancroft 1875–76, I, 123]. "Among the Tolewas, in Del Norte County, money makes the chief" [Bancroft 1875–76, I, 348]. The Spokanes have "no regularly recognized chief," "but an intelligent and rich man often controls the tribe by his influence" [Bancroft 1875–76, I, 276n.]. Of the chiefless Navajos we read that "every rich man has many dependants, and these dependants are obedient to his will, in peace and in war" [Bancroft 1875–76, I, 506]. And to other evidence that it is the same in Africa, may be added the statement of Heuglin that "a Dor chief is generally the richest and most reputable man of the village or neighbourhood" [1869, p. 195].

But, naturally, in societies not yet politically developed, acknowledged superiority is ever liable to be competed with or replaced by superiority arising afresh.

If an Arab, accompanied by his own relations only, has been successful on many predatory excursions against the enemy, he is joined by other friends; and if his success still continues, he obtains the reputation of being 'lucky;' and he thus establishes a kind of second, or inferior agydship in the tribe [Burton, R. 1855–56, III, 44].

So in Sumatra:

A commanding aspect, an insinuating manner, a ready fluency in discourse, and a penetration and sagacity in unravelling the little intricacies of their disputes, are qualities which seldom fail to procure to their possessor respect and influence, sometimes, perhaps, superior to that of an acknowledged chief [Marsden 1811, p. 211].

And supplantings of kindred kinds occur among the Tongans and the Dyaks.

At the outset then, what we before distinguished as the principle of efficiency is the sole principle of organization. Such political headship as exists, is acquired by one whose fitness asserts itself in the form of greater age, superior prowess, stronger will, wider knowledge, quicker insight, or larger wealth. But evidently supremacy which thus depends exclusively on personal attributes is but transitory. It is liable to be superseded by the supremacy of some more able man from time to time arising, and if not superseded, is ended by death. We have, then, to inquire how permanent chieftainship becomes established. Before doing this, however, we must consider more fully the two kinds of superiority which especially conduce to chieftainship, and their modes of operation.

As bodily vigor is a cause of predominance within the tribe on occasions daily occurring, still more on occasions of war is it, when joined with courage, a cause of predominance. War, therefore, tends to make more pronounced any authority of this kind which is incipient. Whatever reluctance other members of the tribe have to recognize the leadership of any one member is likely to be overridden by their desire for safety when recognition of his leadership furthers that safety.

This rise of the strongest and most courageous warrior to power is at first spontaneous, and afterwards by agreement more or less definite, sometimes joined with a process of testing. Where, as in Australia, each "is esteemed by the rest only according to his dexterity in throwing or evading a spear" [Oldfield 1864, p. 256], it is inferable that such superior capacity for war as is displayed generates of itself such temporary chieftainship as exists. Where, as among the Comanches, any one who distinguishes himself by taking many "horses or scalps, may aspire to the honors of chieftaincy, and is gradually inducted by a tacit popular consent" [Schoolcraft 1853–56, I, 231], this natural genesis is clearly shown. Very commonly, however, there is deliberate choice, as by the Flatheads, among whom, "except by the war chiefs no real authority is exercised"

[Bancroft 1875–76, I, 275]. Skill, strength, courage, and endurance are in some cases deliberately tested. The King of Tonga has to undergo a trial: three spears are thrown at him, which he must ward off. "The ability to climb up a large pole, well greased, is a necessary qualification of a fighting chief among the Sea Dyaks" [Low 1848, p. 209], and St. John [1863, I, 223] says that in some cases "it was a custom in order to settle who should be chief, for the rivals to go out in search of a head: the first in finding one being victor."

Moreover, the need for an efficient leader tends ever to re-establish chieftainship where it has become only nominal or feeble. Edwards says of the Caribs that "in war, experience had taught them that subordination was as requisite as courage; they therefore elected their captains in their general assemblies with great solemnity," and "put their pretensions to the proof with circumstances of outrageous barbarity" [1801–19, I, 49]. Similarly, "although the Abipones neither fear their cacique as a judge, nor honour him as a master, yet his fellow soldiers follow him as a leader and governor of the war, whenever the enemy is to be attacked or repelled" [Dobrizhoffer 1822, II, 103].

These and like facts, of which there are abundance, have three kindred implications. One is that continuity of war conduces to permanence of chieftainship. A second is that, with increase of his influence as successful military head, the chief gains influence as civil head. A third is that there is thus initiated a union, maintained through subsequent phases of social evolution, between military supremacy and political supremacy. Not only among the uncivilized Hottentots, Malagasy, and others, is the chief or king head of the army, not only among such semi-civilized peoples as the ancient Peruvians and Mexicans do we find the monarch one with the commander in chief, but the histories of extinct and surviving nations all over the world exemplify the connection. In Egypt "in the early ages, the offices of king and general were inseparable" [Taylor 1849, p. 16]. Assyrian sculptures and inscriptions represent the despotic ruler as also the conquering soldier, as do the records of the Hebrews. Civil and military headship were united among the Homeric Greeks, and in primitive Rome "the general was ordinarily the king himself" [Mommsen 1862, I, 79]. That throughout European history it has been so, and partially continues so even now in the more militant societies, needs no showing.

How command of a wider kind follows military command we cannot readily see in societies which have no records; we can but infer that along with increased power of coercion which the successful head warrior gains, naturally goes the exercise of a stronger rule in civil affairs. That this has been so among peoples who have known histories, there is proof. Of the primitive Germans Sohm remarks that the Roman invasions had one result:

> The kingship became united with the leadership (become permanent) of the army, and, as a consequence, raised itself to a *power* [institution] in the State. The military subordination under the king-leader furthered political subordination under the king. . . . Kingship after the invasions is a kingship clothed with supreme rights — a kingship in our sense [1871, p. 9].

In like manner it is observed by Ranke that during the wars with the English in the fifteenth century:

> The French monarchy, whilst struggling for its very existence, acquired at the same time, and as the result of the struggle, a firmer organization. The expedients adopted to carry on the contest grew, as in other important cases, to national institutions [1875, I, 75].

And modern instances of the relation between successful militancy and the strengthening of political control are furnished by the career of Napoleon and the recent history of the German Empire.

Headship of the society, then, commonly beginning with the influence gained by the warrior of greatest power, boldness, and capacity, becomes established where activity in war gives opportunity for his superiority to show itself and to generate subordination; thereafter the growth of civil governorship continues primarily related to the exercise of militant functions.

Very erroneous, however, would be the idea formed if no further origin for political headship were named. There is a kind of influence, in some cases operating alone and in other cases cooperating with that above specified, which is all-important. I mean the influence possessed by the medicine man.

That this arises as early as the other can scarcely be said, since, until the ghost theory takes shape, there is no origin for it. But when belief in the spirits of the dead becomes current, the medicine man, professing ability to control them and inspiring faith in his pretensions, is regarded with a fear which prompts obedience. When we read of the Tlingits that the "supreme feat of a conjuror's power is to throw one of his liege spirits into the body of one who refuses to believe in his power, upon which the possessed is taken with swooning and fits" [Bancroft 1875–76, III, 148], we may imagine the dread he excites and the sway he consequently gains. From some of the lowest races upwards we find illustrations. Fitzroy says of the "doctor-wizard among the Fuegians" that he is the most cunning and most deceitful of his tribe, and that he has great influence over his companions [1839, II, 178]. "Though the Tasmanians were free from the despotism of rulers, they were swayed by the counsels, governed by the arts, or terrified by the fears, of certain wise men or doctors. These could not only mitigate suffering, but inflict it" [Bonwick 1870, p. 175]. A chief of the Haidas "seems to be the principal sorcerer, and indeed to possess little authority save from the connection with the preterhuman powers" [Bancroft 1875–76, III, 150]. The Dakota medicine men:

> are the greatest rascals in the tribe, and possess immense influence over the minds of the young, who are brought up in the belief of their supernatural powers. . . .The war-chief, who leads the party to war, is always one of these medicine-men, and is believed to have the power to guide the party to success, or save it from defeat [Schoolcraft 1853–56, IV, 495].

Among more advanced peoples in Africa, supposed abilities to control invisible beings similarly give influence — strengthening authority otherwise gained. It is so with the Amazulu: a chief "practises magic on another chief before fighting with him," and his followers have great confidence in him if he has much repute as a magician [Callaway 1868–70, p. 340, note 86]. Hence the sway acquired by Langalibalele, who, as Bishop Colenso says, "knows well the composition of that *intelezi* [used for controlling the weather]; and he knows well, too, the war medicine, *i.e.*, its component parts, being himself a doctor" [ref. lost]. Still better is seen the governmental influence thus acquired in the case of the king of Obbo, who in time of drought calls his subjects together and explains to them:

> how much he regrets that their conduct has compelled him to afflict them with unfavourable weather, but that it is their own fault. . . . He must have goats and corn. 'No goats, no rain; that's our contract, my friends,' says Katchiba. . . . Should his people complain of too much rain, he threatens to pour storms and lightning upon them forever, unless they bring him so many hundred baskets of corn, &c., &c. . . . His subjects have the most thorough confidence in his power [Baker 1866, I, 318–9].

And the king is similarly supposed to exercise control over the weather among the people of Loango.

A like connection is traceable in the records of various extinct peoples in both hemispheres. Of Huitzilopochtli, the founder of the Mexican power, we read that "a great wizard he had been, and a sorcerer" [Bancroft 1875–76, III, 295], and every Mexican king on ascending the throne had to swear "to make the sun go his course, to make the clouds pour down rain, to make the rivers run, and all fruits to ripen" [Clavigero 1787, Bk. VII, ch. 7]. Reproaching his subjects for want of obedience, a Chibcha ruler told them they knew "that it was in his power to afflict them with pestilence, small-pox, rheumatism, and fever, and to make to grow as much grass, vegetables, and plants as they wanted" [Fernández de Piedrahita 1688, Bk. II, ch. 7].

Ancient Egyptian records yield indications of a similar early belief. Thothmes III, after being deified, "was considered as the luck-bringing god of the country, and a preserver against the evil influence of wicked spirits and magicians" [Brugsch 1879, I, 406]. And it was thus with the Jews:

> Rabbinical writings are never weary of enlarging upon the magical power and knowledge of Solomon. He was represented as not only king of the whole earth, but also as reigning over devils and evil spirits, and having the power of expelling them from the bodies of men and animals and also of delivering people to them [Cassels 1874, I, 117–8].

The traditions of European peoples furnish kindred evidence. As before shown, stories in the *Heims-kringla* saga imply that the Scandinavian ruler, Odin, was a medicine man, as were also Niort and Frey, his successors. And after recalling the supernatural weapons and supernatural achievements of early heroic kings we can scarcely doubt that with them were in some cases associated those ascribed magical characters whence have descended the supposed powers of kings to cure diseases by touching. We shall the less doubt this on finding that like powers were attributed to subordinate rulers of early origin. There existed certain Breton nobles whose spittle and touch were said to have curative properties.

Thus one important factor in the genesis of political headship originates with the ghost theory and the concomitant rise of a belief that some men, having acquired power over ghosts, can obtain their aid. Generally the chief and the medicine man are separate persons, and there then exists between them some conflict: they have competing authorities. But where the ruler joins with his power naturally gained this ascribed supernatural power, his authority is necessarily much increased. Recalcitrant members of his tribe who might dare to resist him if bodily prowess alone could decide the struggle do not dare if they think he can send one of his *posse comitatus* of ghosts to torment them. That rulers desire to unite the two characters, we have, in one case, distinct proof. Canon Callaway [1868–70, p. ref. lost] tells us that among the Amazulu, a chief will endeavor to discover a medicine man's secrets and afterwards kill him.

Still there recurs the question: How does permanent political headship arise? Such political headship as results from bodily power, or courage, or sagacity, even when strengthened by supposed supernatural aid, ends with the life of any savage who gains it. The principle of efficiency, physical or mental, while it tends to produce a temporary differentiation into ruler and ruled, does not suffice to produce a permanent differentiation. . . .

As was pointed out in a foregoing chapter, while succession by efficiency gives plasticity to social organization, succession by inheritance gives it stability. No settled arrangement can arise in a primitive community so long as the function of each unit is determined exclusively by his fitness, since, at his death, the arrangement, in so far as he was a part of it, must be recommenced. Only when his place is forthwith filled by one whose claim is admitted does there begin a differentiation which survives through successive generations. And evidently in the earlier stages of social evolution, while the coherence is small and the want of structure great, it is requisite that the principle of inheritance should, especially in respect of the political headship, predominate over the principle of efficiency. . . .

And now, having considered the several factors which cooperate to establish political headship, let us consider the process of cooperation through its ascending stages. The truth to be noted is that the successive phenomena which occur in the simplest groups habitually recur in the same order in compound groups, and again in doubly compound groups.

As in the simple group there is at first a state in which there is no headship, so when simple groups which have acquired political heads possessing slight authorities are associated, there is at first no headship of the cluster. The Chinooks furnish an example. Describing them Lewis and Clarke [1814, p. 443] say: "As these families gradually expand into bands, or tribes, or nations, the paternal authority is represented by the chief of each association. This chieftain, however, is not hereditary." And then comes the further fact, which here specially concerns us, that "the chiefs of the separate villages are independent of each other" [Waitz, G. 1860–61, III, 338]; there is no general chieftain.

As headship in a simple group, at first temporary, ceases when the war which initiates it ends, so in a cluster of groups which severally have recognized heads, a common headship at first results from a war and lasts no longer than the war. Falkner says, "In a general war, when many nations enter into an alliance against a common enemy," the Patagonians "chose an Apo, or Commander-in-chief, from among the oldest or most celebrated of the Caciques" [1774, p. 121]. The Indians of the Upper Orinoco live "in hordes of forty or fifty under a family government, and they recognize a common chief only in times of war" [Humboldt 1852–53, II, 360]. So it is in Borneo. "During war the chiefs of the Sarebas Dyaks give an uncertain allegiance to a head chief, or commander-in-chief" [Low 1848, p. 183]. It has been the same in Europe. Seeley [ref. lost] remarks that the Sabines "seem to have had a central government only in war time." Again, "Germany had anciently as many republics as it had tribes. Except in time of war, there was no chief common to all, or even to any given confederation" [Dunham 1837, I, 17].

This recalls the fact, indicated when treating of political integration, that the cohesion within compound groups is less than that within simple groups and that the cohesion within the doubly compound is less than that within the compound. What was there said of cohesion may here be said of the subordination conducing to it, for we find that when, by continuous war, a permanent headship of a compound group has been generated, it is less stable than the headships of the simple groups are. Often it lasts only for the life of the man who achieves it, as among the Karens and the Maganja, . . . and as among the Dyaks, of whom Boyle says:

> It is an exceptional case if a Dyak chief is raised to an acknowledged suprem-
> acy over the other chiefs. If he is so raised he can lay no claim to his power
> except that of personal merit and the consent of his former equals; and his
> death is instantly followed by the disruption of his dominions [1865, p. 183].

Even where there has arisen a headship of the compound group which lasts beyond the life of its founder, it remains for a long time not equal in stability to the headships of the component groups. Pallas, while describing the Mongol and Kalmuck chiefs as having unlimited power over their dependents, says that the khans had in general only an uncertain and weak authority over the subordinate chiefs [1788–93, I, 527]. Concerning the Araucanians, Thompson [1812, I, 405] says "the ulmenes are the lawful judges of their vassals, and for this reason their authority is less precarious than that of the higher officers" — the central rulers. Of the Kaffirs we read: "They are all vassals of the king, chiefs, as well as those under them; but the subjects are generally so blindly attached to their chiefs, that they will follow them against the king" [Lichtenstein 1812–15, I, 286]. Europe has furnished kindred examples. Of the Homeric Greeks Mr. Gladstone writes, "It is probable that the subordination of the subchief to his local sovereign was a closer tie than that of the local sovereign to the head of Greece" [1858, III, 10–1]. And during the early feudal period in the West, allegiance to the minor but proximate ruler was stronger than that to the major but remote ruler.

In the compound group, as in the simple group, the progress towards stable headship is furthered by transition from succession by choice to succession by inheritance. During early stages of the independent tribe, chieftainship, when not acquired by individual superiority tacitly yielded to, is acquired by election. In North America it is so with the Aleuts, the Comanches, and many more; in Indonesia it is so with the Land Dyaks, and, before the Mohammedan conquest, it was so in Java. Among the hill peoples of India it is so with the Nagas and others. In sundry regions the change to hereditary succession is shown by different tribes of the same race. Of the Karens we read that "in many districts the chieftain-ship is considered hereditary, but in more it is elective" [Mason 1868, p. 131]. Some Chinook villages have chiefs who inherit their powers, though mostly they are chosen.

Similarly, the doubly compound group is at first ruled by an elected head. Several examples come to us from Africa. Bastian tells us that "in many parts of the Congo region the king is chosen by the petty princes" [1859, p. 58]. The crown of Yariba is not hereditary: "the chiefs invariably electing, from the wisest and most sagacious of their own body" [Lander 1830, II, 223]. And the king of Ibo, say Allen and Thomson, seems to be "elected by a council of sixty elders, or chiefs of large villages" [1848, I, 234]. In Asia it is thus with the Kukis:

> One, among all the Rajahs of each class, is chosen to be the Prudham or chief Rajah of that clan. The dignity is not hereditary, as is the case with the minor Rajahships, but is enjoyed by each Rajah of the clan in rotation [Butler 1855, p. 91].

So has it been in Europe. Though by the early Greeks hereditary right was in a considerable measure recognized, yet the case of Telemachus implies "that a practice, either approaching to election, or in some way involving a voluntary action on the part of the subjects, or of a portion of them, had to be gone through" [Gladstone 1858, III, 51–2]. The like is true of ancient Rome. That its monarchy was elective "is proved by the existence in later times of an office of *interrex*, which implies that the kingly power did not devolve naturally upon an hereditary successor" [ref. lost]. Later on it was thus with Western peoples. Up to the beginning of the tenth century "the formality of election subsisted . . . in every European kingdom; and the imperfect right of birth required a ratification by public assent" [ref. lost]. And it was once thus with ourselves. Among the early English the Bretwaldship, or supreme headship over the minor kingdoms, was at first elective, and the form of election continued long traceable in our history. Moreover, it is observable that the change to hereditary succession is by assent, as in France. "The first six kings of this dynasty [the Capetian] procured the *co-optation* of their sons, by having them crowned during their own lives. And this was not done without the consent of the chief vassals" [Hallam 1855, I, Ch. 1].

The stability of the compound headship, made greater by efficient leadership in war and by establishment of hereditary succession, is further increased when there cooperates the additional factor — supposed supernatural origin or supernatural sanction. Everywhere, up from a New Zealand king, who is strictly *tapu* or sacred, we may trace this influence, and occasionally, where divine descent or magical powers are not claimed, there is a claim to origin that is extraordinary. Asia yields an example in the Fodli dynasty, which reigned 150 years in South Arabia — a six-fingered dynasty, regarded with awe by the people because of its continuously inherited malformation. Europe of the Merovingian period yields an example. In pagan times the king's race had an alleged divine origin, but in Christian times, says Waitz, when they could no longer mount back to the gods, a more than natural origin was alleged:

"a sea-monster ravished the wife of Chlogio as she sat by the seashore, and from this embrace Merovech sprang" [1865–70, II, 45–6]. Later days show us the gradual acquisition of a sacred or semi-supernatural character where it did not originally exist. Divine assent to their supremacy was asserted by the Carolingian kings. During the later feudal age, rare exceptions apart, kings "were not far removed from believing themselves near relatives of the masters of heaven. Kings and gods were colleagues" [Méray 1873, p. 45]. In the 17th century this belief was endorsed by divines. "Kings," says Bossuet, "are gods, and share in a manner the divine independence" [1865, II, 56; Saint-Simon 1857, III, 69].

So that the headship of a compound group, arising temporarily during war, then becoming, with frequent cooperation of the groups, settled for life by election, passing presently into the hereditary form and gaining permanence as fast as the law of succession grows well defined and undisputed, acquires its greatest stability only when the king is regarded as a deputy god, or when, if he is not supposed to inherit a divine nature, he is supposed to have a divine commission.

Ascribed divine nature, or divine descent, or divine commission, naturally gives to the political head unlimited sway. In theory, and often to a large extent in practice, he is owner of his subjects and of the territory they occupy.

Where militancy is pronounced and the claims of a conqueror unqualified, it is indeed to a considerable degree thus with those uncivilized peoples who do not ascribe supernatural characters to their rulers. Among the Zulu Kaffirs the chief "exercises supreme power over the lives of his people" [Mann 1866, p. 291]; the Bhil chiefs "have a power over the lives and property of their own subjects" [Malcolm 1832, I, 551]; and in Fiji the subject is property. But it is still more thus where the ruler is considered more than human. Astley [1745–47, III, 223] tells us that in Loango the king is "called *samba* and *pongo*, that is, god," and according to Proyart, the Loango people "say their lives and goods belong to the king" [Pinkerton 1808–14, XVI, 557]. In Wasoro (East Africa) "the king has unlimited power of life and death . . . in some tribes . . . he is almost worshipped" [Burton, R. 1860, p. 361]. In Msambara the people say "we are all slaves of the Zumbe (king), who is our Mulungu [god]" [Krapf 1860, p. 384n.]. "By the state law of Dahomey, as at Benin, all men are slaves to the king, and most women are his wives," and in Dahomey the king is called "the spirit" [Burton 1864, I, 226]. The Malagasy speak of their king as "our god," and he is lord of the soil, owner of all property, and master of his subjects. Their time and services are at his command [Ellis 1838, I, 341]. In the Hawaiian Islands the king, personating the god, utters oracular responses, and his power "extends over the property, liberty, and lives of his people" [Ellis 1826, p. 401].

Various Asiatic rulers, whose titles ascribe to them divine descent and nature, stand in like relations to their peoples. In Siam "the king is master not only of the persons but really of the property of his subjects: he disposes of their labour and directs their movements at will" [Bowring 1857, I, 422–3]. Of the Burmese we read: "their goods likewise, and even their persons are reputed his [the king's] property, and on this ground it is that he selects for his concubine any female that may chance to please his eye" [Sangermano 1833, p. 58]. In China "there is only one who possesses authority — the Emperor. . . . A wang, or king, has no hereditary possessions, and lives upon the salary vouchsafed by the Emperor. . . . He is the only possessor of the landed property" [Gützlaff 1838, II, 251]. And the like is alleged of the divinely descended Japanese Mikado: "his majesty, although often but a child a few years old, still dispensed ranks and dignitaries, and the ownership of the soil always in reality resided in him" [Adams 1874–75, I, 11].

Of course, where the political head has unlimited power, where, as victorious invader, his subjects lie at his mercy, or where, as divinely descended, his will may not be questioned without impiety, or where he unites the characters of conqueror and god, he naturally absorbs every kind of authority. He is at once military head, legislative head, judicial head, ecclesiastical head. The fully developed king is the supreme center of every social structure and director of every social function.

In a small tribe it is practicable for the chief personally to discharge all the duties of his office. Besides leading the other warriors in battle, he has time to settle disputes, he can sacrifice to the ancestral ghost, he can keep the village in order, he can inflict punishments, he can regulate trading transactions, for those governed by him are but few, and they live within a narrow space. When he acquires the headship of many united tribes, both the increased amount of business and the wider area covered by his subjects put difficulties in the way of exclusively personal administration. It becomes necessary to employ others for the purposes of gaining information, conveying commands, seeing them executed, and in course of time the assistants thus employed grow into established heads of departments with deputed authorities.

While this development of governmental structures increases the ruler's power by enabling him to deal with more numerous affairs, it, in another way, decreases his power, for his actions are more and more modified by the instrumentalities through which they are effected. Those who watch the working of administrations, no matter of what kind, have forced upon them the truth that a head regulative agency is at once helped and hampered by its subordinate agencies. In a philanthropic association, a scientific society, or a club, those who govern find that the organized officialism which they have created often impedes and not infrequently defeats their aims. Still more is it so with the immensely larger administrations of the state. Through deputies the ruler receives his information, by them his orders are executed, and as fast as his connection with affairs becomes indirect, his control over affairs diminishes until, in extreme cases, he either dwindles into a puppet in the hands of his chief deputy or has his place usurped by him.

Strange as it seems, the two causes which conspire to give permanence to political headship also, at a later stage, conspire to reduce the political head to an automaton, executing the wills of the agents he has created. In the first place, when hereditary succession is finally settled in some line of descent rigorously prescribed, the possession of supreme power becomes independent of capacity for exercising it. The heir to a vacant throne may be, and often is, too young for discharging his duties, or he may be, and often is, too feeble in intellect, too deficient in energy, or too much occupied with the pleasures which his position offers in unlimited amounts. The result is that in the one case the regent, and in the other the chief minister, becomes the actual ruler. In the second place, that sacredness which supposed divine origin gives, makes him inaccessible to the ruled. All intercourse between him and them must be through the agents he surrounds himself with. Hence it becomes difficult or impossible for him to learn more than they choose him to know, and there follows inability to adapt his commands to the requirements, and inability to discover whether his commands have been fulfilled. His authority is consequently used to give effect to the purposes of his agents.

Even in so relatively simple a society as that of Tonga, we find an example. There is an hereditary sacred chief who "was originally the sole chief, possessing temporal as well as spiritual power, and regarded as of divine origin," but who is now politically powerless [Erskine 1853, p. 126]. Abyssinia shows us something analogous. Holding no direct communication with his subjects and having a sacredness such that even in council he sits unseen, the monarch is a mere dummy. In Gondar, one of the divisions of Abyssinia, the king must belong to the royal house of Solomon, but any one of the turbulent chiefs who has obtained ascendency by force of arms becomes a Ras — a prime minister or real monarch — though he requires "a titular emperor to perform the indispensable ceremony of nominating a Ras," since the name, at least, of emperor "is deemed essential to render valid the title of Ras" [Harris 1844, III, 10, 34]. The case of Tibet may be named as one in which the sacredness of the original political head is dissociated from the claim based on hereditary descent, for the Grand Lama considered as "God the Father," in-

carnate afresh in each new occupant of the throne, is discovered among
the people at large by certain indications of his godhood. But with his
divinity, involving disconnection with temporal matters, there goes absence of political power. A like state of things exists in Bhutan.

> The Dhurma Raja is looked upon by the Bhotanese in the same light as the
> Grand Lama of Thibet is viewed by his subjects — namely as a perpetual
> incarnation of the Deity, or Bhudda himself in a corporeal form. During the
> interval between his death and reappearance, or, more properly speaking,
> until he has reached an age sufficiently mature to ascend his spiritual throne,
> the office of Dhurma Raja is filled by proxy from amongst the priesthood
> [Rennie 1866, pp. 16–7].

And then along with this sacred ruler there co-exists a secular ruler.
Bhutan "has two nominal heads, known to us and to the neighbouring
hill tribes under the Hindoostanee names of the Dhurma and the Deb
Rajas. . . . The former is the spiritual head, the latter the temporal
one" [Rennie 1866, p. 17]. Though in this case the temporal head has not
great influence (probably because the priest-regent, whose celibacy prevents him from founding a line, stands in the way of unchecked assumption of power by the temporal head), still the existence of a temporal
head implies a partial lapsing of political functions out of the hands of
the original political head.

But the most remarkable, and at the same time most familiar, example,
is that furnished by Japan. Here the supplanting of inherited authority
by deputed authority is exemplified, not in the central government alone,
but in the local governments.

> Next to the prince and his family came the *karos* or 'elders.' Their office be-
> came hereditary, and, like the princes, they in many instances became effete.
> The business of what we may call the clan would thus fall into the hands
> of any clever man or set of men of the lower ranks, who, joining ability to
> daring and unscrupulousness, kept the princes and the *karos* out of sight,
> but surrounded with empty dignity, and, commanding the opinion of the
> bulk of the *samurai* or military class, wielded the real power themselves. They
> took care, however, to perform every act in the name of the *fainéants*, their
> lords, and thus we hear of . . . daimios, just as in the case of the Emperors,
> accomplishing deeds . . . of which they were perhaps wholly ignorant
> [Adams 1874–75, I, 74, 17].

This lapsing of political power into the hands of ministers was, in the
case of the central government, doubly illustrated. Successors as they
were of a god-descended conqueror whose rule was real, the Japanese
Emperors gradually became only nominal rulers, partly because of the
sacredness which separated them from the nation and partly because
of the early age at which the law of succession frequently enthroned
them. Their deputies consequently gained predominance. The regency
in the ninth century "became hereditary in the Fujiwara [sprung from

the imperial house], and these regents ultimately became all-powerful. They obtained the privilege of opening all petitions addressed to the sovereign, and of presenting or rejecting them at their pleasure" [Titsingh 1834, p. 223]. And then, in course of time, this usurping agency had its own authority usurped in like manner. Again succession by fixed rule was rigorously adhered to and again seclusion entailed loss of hold on affairs. "High descent was the only qualification for office, and unfitness for functions was not regarded in the choice of officials." Besides the Shôgun's four confidential officers, "no one else could approach him. Whatever might be the crimes committed at Kama Koura, it was impossible through the intrigues of these favourites, to complain of them to the Seogoun." The result was that "subsequently this family . . . gave way to military commanders, who, however, often became the instruments of other chiefs" [Adams 1874–75, I, 11, 70].

Though less definitely, this process was exemplified during early times in Europe. The Merovingian kings, to whom there clung a tradition of supernatural origin, and whose order of succession was so far settled that minors reigned, fell under the control of those who had become chief ministers. Long before Childeric, the Merovingian family had ceased to govern.

> The treasures and the power of the kingdom had passed into the hands of the prefects of the palace, who were called 'mayors of the palace,' and to whom the supreme power really belonged. The prince was obliged to content himself with bearing the name of king, having flowing locks and a long beard, sitting on the chair of State, and representing the image of the monarch [Eginhardus 1877, pp. 123–4].

From the evolution standpoint we are thus enabled to discern the relative beneficence of institutions which, considered absolutely, are not beneficent, and are taught to approve as temporary that which, as permanent, we abhor. The evidence obliges us to admit that subjection to despots has been largely instrumental in advancing civilization. Induction and deduction alike prove this.

If, on the one hand, we group together those wandering headless hordes which are found here and there over the earth, they show us that, in the absence of political organization, little progress has taken place, and if we contemplate those settled simple groups which have but nominal heads, we are shown that though there is some development of the industrial arts and some cooperation, the advance is but small. If, on the other hand, we glance at those ancient societies in which considerable heights of civilization were first reached, we see them under autocratic rule. In America, purely personal government, restricted only by settled customs, characterized the Mexican, Central American, and Chibcha states, and in Peru, the absolutism of the divine king was unqualified. In Africa, ancient

Egypt exhibited very conspicuously this connection between despotic control and social evolution. Throughout the distant past it was repeatedly displayed in Asia, from the Accadian civilization downwards, and the still-extant civilizations of Siam, Burma, China, and Japan, re-illustrate it. Early European societies, too, where not characterized by centralized despotism, were still characterized by diffused patriarchal despotism. Only among modern peoples, whose ancestors passed through the discipline given under this social form, and who have inherited its effects, is civilization being dissociated from subjection to individual will.

The necessity there has been for absolutism is best seen on observing that during intertribal and international conflicts those have conquered who, other things equal, were the more obedient to their chiefs and kings. And since in early stages military subordination and social subordination go together, it results that, for a long time, the conquering societies continued to be the despotically governed societies. Such exceptions as histories appear to show us, really prove the rule. In the conflict between Persia and Greece, the Greeks, but for a mere accident, would have been ruined by the division of councils which results from absence of subjection to a single head. And their habit of appointing a dictator when in great danger from enemies implies that the Romans had discovered that efficiency in war requires undivided control.

Thus, leaving open the question whether, in the absence of war, wandering primitive groups could ever have developed into settled civilized communities, we conclude that, under such conditions as there have been, those struggles for existence among societies which have gone on consolidating smaller into larger until great nations have been produced, necessitated the development of a social type characterized by personal rule of a stringent kind.

Summary

To make clear the genesis of this leading political institution, let us set down in brief the several influences which have conspired to effect it, and the several stages passed through.

In the rudest groups resistance to the assumption of supremacy by any individual usually prevents the establishment of settled headship, though some influence is commonly acquired by superiority of strength, or courage, or sagacity, or possessions, or the experience accompanying age.

In such groups and in tribes somewhat more advanced, two kinds of superiority conduce more than all others to predominance — that of the warrior and that of the medicine man. Usually separate but sometimes united in the same person, and then greatly strengthening him, both of these superiorities, tending to initiate political headship, continue thereafter to be important factors in developing it.

At first, however, the supremacy acquired by great natural power, or supposed supernatural power, or both, is transitory — ceases with the life of one who has acquired it. So long as the principle of efficiency alone operates, political headship does not become settled. It becomes settled only when there cooperates the principle of inheritance. . . .

The processes by which political headships are established repeat themselves at successively higher stages. In simple groups chieftainship is at first temporary — ceases with the war which initiated it. When simple groups that have acquired permanent political heads unite for military purposes, the general chieftainship is originally but temporary. As in simple groups chieftainship is at the outset habitually elective and becomes hereditary at a later stage, so chieftainship of the compound group is habitually elective at the outset and only later passes into the hereditary. Similarly in some cases where a doubly compound society is formed. Further, this later-established power of a supreme ruler, at first given by election and presently gained by descent, is commonly less than that of the local rulers in their own localities, and when it becomes greater it is usually by the help of ascribed divine origin or ascribed divine commission.

Where, in virtue of supposed supernatural genesis or authority, the king has become absolute and, owning both subjects and territory, exercises all powers, he is obliged by the multiplicity of his affairs to depute his powers. There follows a reactive restraint due to the political machinery he creates, and this machinery ever tends to become too strong for him. Especially where rigorous adhesion to the rule of inheritance brings incapables to the throne, or where ascribed divine nature causes inaccessibility save through agents, or where both causes conspire, power passes into the hands of deputies. The legitimate ruler becomes an automaton and his chief agent the real ruler, and this agent, again, in some cases passing through parallel stages, himself becomes an automaton and his subordinates the rulers.

Lastly, by colligation and comparison of the facts, we are led to recognize the indirectly achieved benefits which have followed the directly inflicted evils of personal government. Headship of the conquering chief has been a normal accompaniment of that political integration without which any high degree of social evolution would probably have been impossible. Only by imperative need for combination in war were primitive men led into cooperation. Only by subjection to imperative command was such cooperation made efficient. And only by the cooperation thus initiated were made possible those other forms of cooperation characterizing civilized life.

CHAPTER 14

COMPOUND POLITICAL HEADS

In the preceding chapter we traced the development of the first element in that triune political structure which everywhere shows itself at the outset. We pass now to the development of the second element — the group of leading men among whom the chief is, at first, merely the most conspicuous. Under what conditions this so evolves as to subordinate the other two, what causes make it narrower, and what causes widen it until it passes into the third, we have here to observe. . . .

We saw . . . [earlier] that it is relatively easy to form a large society if the country is one within which all parts are readily accessible, while it has barriers through which exit is difficult; and that, conversely, formation of a large society is prevented, or greatly delayed, by difficulties of communication within the occupied area, and by facilities of escape from it. Here we see, further, that not only is political integration under its primary aspect of increasing mass hindered by these last-named physical conditions, but that there is hindrance to the development of a more integrated form of government. The circumstances which impede social consolidation also impede the concentration of political power. . . .

. . . Where groups of the patriarchal type fall into regions permitting considerable growth of population but having physical structures which impede the centralization of power, compound political heads will arise, and for a time sustain themselves through cooperation of the two factors — independence of local groups and need for union in war. Let us consider some examples.

The island of Crete has numerous high mountain valleys containing good pasturage, and provides many seats for strongholds — seats which ruins prove that the ancient inhabitants utilized. Similarly with the mainland of Greece. A complicated mountain system cuts off its parts from one another and renders each difficult of access. Especially is this so in the Peloponnesus, and above all, in the part occupied by the Spartans. It has been remarked that the state which possesses both sides of Taygetus has it in its power to be master of the peninsula: "it is the Acropolis of the Peloponnese, as that country is of the rest of Greece" [Tozer 1873, pp. 284–5].

When, over the earlier inhabitants, there came successive waves of Hellenic conquerors, these brought with them the type of nature and organization common to the Aryans. . . . Such a people taking possession of such a land inevitably fell in course of time "into as many independent clans as the country itself was divided by its mountain chains into valleys and districts" [Hermann 1836, p. 14]. From separation resulted alienation, so that those remote from one another, becoming strangers, became enemies. In early Greek times the clans, occupying mountain villages, were so liable to incursions from one another that the planting of fruit trees was a waste of labor. There existed a state like that seen at present among such Indian hill tribes as the Nagas.

Though preserving the tradition of a common descent and owning allegiance to the oldest male representative of the patriarch, a people spreading over a region which thus cut off from one another even adjacent small groups, and still more those remoter cluster of groups arising in course of generations, would inevitably become disunited in government; subjection to a general head would be more and more difficult to maintain, and subjection to local heads would alone continue practicable. At the same time there would arise, under such conditions, increasing causes of insubordination. When the various branches of a common family are so separated as to prevent intercourse, their respective histories and the lines of descent of their respective heads must become unknown, or but partially known, to one another, and claims to supremacy made now by this local head and now by that are certain to be disputed. If we remember how, even in settled societies having records, there have been perpetual conflicts about rights of succession, and how, down to our own day, there are frequent lawsuits to decide on heirships to titles and properties, we cannot but infer that in a state like that of the early Greeks the difficulty of establishing the legitimacy of general headships, conspiring with the desire to assert independence and the ability to maintain it, inevitably entailed lapse into numerous local headships.

Of course, under conditions varying in each locality, splittings-up of wider governments into narrower went to different extents, and naturally, too, re-establishments of wider governments or extensions of narrower ones in some cases took place. But generally, the tendency under such conditions was to form small independent groups, severally having the patriarchal type of organization. Hence, then, the decay of such kingships as are implied in the *Iliad*. As Grote [1846–56, II, 103] writes: "When we approach historical Greece, we find that (with the exception of Sparta) the primitive, hereditary, unresponsible monarch, uniting in himself all the functions of government, has ceased to reign."●

Let us now ask what will happen when a cluster of clans of common

---

● While I am writing, the just-issued third volume of Mr. Skene's *Celtic Scotland*, supplies me with an illustration of the process above indicated. It appears that the original Celtic tribes which formed the earldoms of Moray, Buchan, Athol, Angus, Menteith, became broken up into clans, and how influential was the physical character descent, which have become independent and hostile, are simultaneously endangered by enemies to whom they are not at all akin, or but remotely akin. Habitually they will sink their differences and cooperate for defense. But on what terms will they cooperate? Even among friendly groups joint action would be hindered if some claimed supremacy, and among groups having outstanding feuds there could be no joint action save on a footing of equality. The common defense would, therefore, be directed by a body formed of the heads of the cooperating small societies, and if the cooperation for defense was prolonged or became changed into cooperation for offense, this temporary controlling body would naturally grow into a permanent one, holding the small societies together.

The special characters of this compound head would, of course, vary with the circumstances. Where the traditions of the united clans agreed in identifying some one chief as the lineal representative of the original patriarch or hero, from whom all descended, precedence and some extra authority would be permitted to him. Where claims derived from descent were disputed, personal superiority or election would determine which member of the compound head should take the lead. If within each of the component groups chiefly power was unqualified, there would result from union of chiefs a close oligarchy, while the closeness of the oligarchy would become less in proportion as recognition of the authority of each chief diminished. And in cases where there came to be incorporated numerous aliens, owing allegiance to the heads of none of the component groups, there would arise influences tending still more to widen the oligarchy.

Such, we may conclude, were the origins of those compound headships of the Greek states which existed at the beginning of the historic period. In Crete, where there survived the tradition of primitive kingship but where dispersion and subdivision of clans had brought about a condition in which "different towns carried on open feuds," there were "patrician houses, deriving their right from the early ages of royal government," who continued "to retain possession of the administration" [Curtius 1868–73, I, 182, 178–9]. In Corinth the line of Heracleid kings "subsides gradually, through a series of empty names, into the oligarchy denominated Bac-chiadæ. . . . The persons so named were all accounted descendants of Hêraklês, and formed the governing caste in the city" [Grote 1846–56, III, 2]. So was it with Megara. According to tradition, this arose by com-bination of several villages inhabited by kindred tribes, which, originally in antagonism with Corinth, had, probably in the course of this antago-nism, become consolidated into an independent state. . . .

---

of the country in producing this result we are shown by the fact that this change took place in the parts of them which fell within the highland country [Skene 1876–80, III, 323–4].

Sparta, too, "always maintained, down to the times of the despot Nabis, its primitive aspect of a group of adjacent hill villages rather than a regular city." Though in Sparta kingship had survived under an anomalous form, yet the joint representatives of the primitive king, still reverenced because the tradition of their divine descent was preserved, had become little more than members of the governing oligarchy, retaining certain prerogatives. And though it is true that in its earliest historically known stage the Spartan oligarchy did not present the form which would spontaneously arise from the union of chiefs of clans for cooperation in war — though it had become elective within a limited class of persons — yet the fact that an age of not less than sixty was a qualification harmonizes with the belief that it at first consisted of the heads of the respective groups, who were always the eldest sons of the eldest, and that these groups with their heads, described as having been in pre-Lycurgean times, "the most lawless of all the Greeks," became united by that continuous militant life which distinguished them [Grote 1846–56, II, *passim*].

The Romans exemplify the rise of a compound headship under conditions which, though partially different from those the Greeks were subject to, were allied fundamentally. In its earliest-known state, Latium was occupied by village communities which were united into cantons, while these cantons formed a league headed by Alba — a canton regarded as the oldest and most eminent. This combination was for joint defense, as is shown by the fact that each group of clan villages composing a canton had an elevated stronghold in common, and also by the fact that the league of cantons had for its center and place of refuge, Alba, the most strongly placed as well as the oldest. The component cantons of the league were so far independent that there were wars between them; hence we may infer that when they cooperated for joint defense it was on substantially equal terms.

Thus before Rome existed, the people who formed it had been habituated to a kind of life such that, with great subordination in each family and clan and partial subordination within each canton (which was governed by a prince, council of elders, and assembly of warriors), there went a union of heads of cantons who were in no degree subordinate one to another. When the inhabitants of three of these cantons, the Ramnians, Tities, and Luceres, began to occupy the tract on which Rome stands, they brought with them their political organization. The oldest Roman patricians bore the names of rural clans belonging to these cantons. Whether, when seating themselves on the Palatine hills and on the Quirinal they preserved their cantonal divisions, is not clear, though it seems probable a priori. But however this may be, there is proof that they fortified themselves against one another as well as against outer enemies. The "mount-men" of the Palatine and the "hill-men" of the Quirinal were habitually at feud, and even among the minor divisions of those who occupied the Palatine there were dissensions. As Mommsen says, primitive Rome was "rather an aggregate of urban settlements than a single city" [1862, I, 30]. And that the clans who formed these settlements brought with them their enmities is to be inferred from the fact that not only did they fortify the hills on which they fixed themselves, but even "the houses of the old and powerful families were constituted somewhat after the manner of fortresses" [Mommsen 1862, I, 80].

So that again, in the case of Rome, we see a cluster of small independent communities, allied in blood but partially antagonistic, which had to cooperate against enemies on such terms as all would agree to. In early Greece the means of defense were, as Grote remarks, greater than the means of attack, and it was the same in early Rome. Hence, while coercive rule within the family and the group of related families was easy, there was difficulty in extending coercion over many such groups, fortified as they were against one another. Moreover, the stringency of government within each of the communities constituting the primitive city was diminished by facility of escape from one and admission into another. As we have seen among simple tribes, desertions take place when the rule is harsh; we may infer that, in primitive Rome there was a check on exercise of force by the more powerful families in each settlement over the less powerful caused by the fear that migration might weaken the settlement and strengthen an adjacent one. Thus the circumstances were such that when, for defense of the city, cooperation became needful, the heads of the clans included in its several divisions came to have substantially equal powers. The original senate was the collective body of clan-elders, and "this assembly of elders was the ultimate holder of the ruling power;" it was "an assembly of kings" [Mommsen 1862, I, 87].

At the same time, the heads of families in each clan, forming the body of burgesses, stood, for like reasons, on equal footing. Primarily for command in war there was an elected head who was also chief magistrate. Though not having the authority given by alleged divine descent, he had the authority given by supposed divine approval, and, himself bearing the insignia of a god, he retained till death the absoluteness appropriate to one. But besides the fact that the choice, originally made by the senate, had to be again practically made by it in case of sudden vacancy, and besides the fact that each king, nominated by his predecessor, had to be approved by the assembled burgesses, there is the fact that the king's power was executive only. The assembly of burgesses "was in law superior to, rather than coordinate with, the king" [Mommsen 1862, I, 84]. Further, in the last resort was exercised the supreme power of the senate, which was the guardian of the law and could veto the joint decision of king and burgesses. Thus the constitution was in essence an oligarchy of heads of clans, included in an oligarchy of heads of houses — a compound oligarchy which became unqualified when kingship was suppressed.

And here should be emphasized the truth, sufficiently obvious and yet continually ignored, that the Roman Republic which remained when the regal power ended differed utterly in nature from those popular governments with which it has been commonly classed. The heads of clans, of whom the narrower governing body was formed, as well as the heads of families who formed the wider governing body, were indeed jealous of one another's powers, and in so far simulated the citizens of a free state who individually maintain their equal rights. But these heads severally exercised unlimited powers over the members of their households and over their clusters of dependents. A community of which the component groups severally retained their internal autonomies, with the result that the rule within each remained absolute, was nothing but an aggregate of small despotisms. Institutions under which the head of each group, besides owning slaves, had such supremacy that his wife and children, including even married sons, had no more legal rights than cattle, and were at his mercy in life and limb, or could be sold into slavery, can be called free institutions only by those who confound similarity of external outline with similarity of internal structure.

The formation of compound political heads in later times repeats this process in essentials if not in details. In one way or other the result arises when a common need for defense compels cooperation while there exists no means of securing cooperation save voluntary agreement. . . .

Over the area, half land, half water, formed of the sediment brought down by the Rhine and adjacent rivers, there early existed scattered families. Living on isolated sand hills, or in huts raised on piles, they were so secure amid their creeks and mud banks and marshes that they remained unsubdued by the Romans. Subsisting at first by fishing, with here and there such small agriculture as was possible, and eventually becoming maritime and commercial, these people, in course of time, rendered their land more habitable by damming out the sea, and they long enjoyed a partial if not complete independence. In the third century, "the low countries contained the only free people of the German race." Especially the Frisians, more remote than the rest from invaders, "associated themselves with the tribes settled on the limits of the German Ocean, and formed with them a connection celebrated under the title of the 'Saxon League.'" Though at a later time the inhabitants of the low countries fell under Frankish invaders, yet the nature of their habitat continued to give them such advantages in resisting foreign control that they organized themselves after their own fashion notwithstanding interdicts. "From the time of Charlemagne, the people of the ancient Menapia, now become a prosperous commonwealth, formed political associations to raise a barrier against the despotic violence of the Franks." Meanwhile the Frisians, who after centuries of resistance to the Franks were obliged to yield and render small tributary services, retained their internal autonomy. They formed "a confederation of rude but self-governed maritime provinces," each of these seven provinces being divided into districts severally governed by elective heads with their councils, and the whole being under a general elective head and a general council [Grattan 1830, pp. 10, 11, 20; Motley 1855, I, 38].

Of illustrations which modern times have furnished must be named those which again show us the effects of a mountainous region. The most notable is, of course, that of Switzerland. Surrounded by forests, "among marshes, and rocks, and glaciers, tribes of scattered shepherds had, from the early times of the Roman conquest, found a land of refuge from the successive invaders of the rest of Helvetia" [Vieusseux 1840, p. 39]. In the labyrinths of the Alps, accessible to those only who knew the ways to them, their cattle fed unseen, and against straggling bands of marauders who might discover their retreats, they had great facilities for defense. These districts — which eventually became the cantons of Schweitz, Uri, and Unterwalden, originally having but one center of meeting, but eventually, as population increased, getting three, and forming separate political organizations — long preserved complete independence. With the spread of feudal subordination throughout Europe they became nominally subject to the Emperor, but, refusing obedience to the superiors set over them, they entered into a solemn alliance, renewed from time to time, to resist outer enemies.

Details of their history need not detain us. The fact of moment is that in these three cantons, which physically favored in so great a degree the maintenance of independence by individuals and by groups, the people, while framing for themselves free governments, united on equal terms for joint defense. And it was these typical "Swiss," as they were the first to be called, whose union formed the nucleus of the larger unions which, through varied fortunes, eventually grew up. Severally independent as were the cantons composing these larger unions, there at first existed feuds among them which were suspended during times of joint defense. Only gradually did the league pass from temporary and unsettled forms to a permanent and settled form. . . .

One noteworthy difference between the compound heads arising under physical conditions of the kinds exemplified must not be overlooked — the difference between the oligarchic form and the popular form. As shown at the outset of this section, if each of the groups united by militant cooperation is despotically ruled — if the groups are severally framed on the patriarchal type, or are severally governed by men of supposed divine descent — then the compound head becomes one in which the people at large have no share. But if . . . patriarchal authority has decayed, or if belief in divine descent of rulers has been undermined by a creed at variance with it, or if peaceful habits have weakened that coercive authority which war ever strengthens, then the compound head is no longer an assembly of petty despots. With the progress of these changes it becomes more and more a head formed of those who exercise power not by right of position but by right of appointment.

There are other conditions which favor the rise of compound heads, temporary if not permanent, those, namely, which occur at the dissolutions of preceding organizations. Among peoples habituated for ages to personal rule, having sentiments appropriate to it and no conception of anything else, the fall of one despot is at once followed by the rise of another; or, if a large personally governed empire collapses, its parts severally generate governments for themselves of like kind. But among less servile peoples the breaking up of political systems having single heads is apt to be followed by the establishment of others having compound heads, especially where there is a simultaneous separation into parts which have not local governments of stable kinds. Under such circumstances there is a return to the primitive state. The pre-existing regulative system having fallen, the members of the community are left without any controlling power save the aggregate will; and political organization having to commence afresh, the form first assumed is akin to that which we see in the assembly of the savage horde or in the modern public meeting. Whence there presently results the rule of a select few subject to the approval of the many.

In illustration may first be taken the rise of the Italian republics. When, during the ninth and tenth centuries, the German Emperors, who had long been losing their power to restrain local antagonisms in Italy and the outrages of wandering robber bands, failed more than ever to protect their subject communities, and, as a simultaneous result, exercised diminished control over them, it became at once necessary and practicable for the Italian towns to develop political organizations of their own. Though in these towns there were remnants of the old Roman organization, this had obviously become effete, for, in time of danger, there was an assembling of "citizens at the sound of a great bell, to concert together the means for their common defence" [Sismondi 1832, p. 21]. Doubtless on such occasions were marked out the rudiments of those republican constitutions which afterwards arose. Though it is alleged that the German Emperors allowed the towns to form these constitutions, yet we may reasonably conclude, rather, that having no care further than to get their tribute, they made no efforts to prevent the towns from forming them. And though Sismondi [1826, I, 371] says of the townspeople: "ils cherchèrent à se constituer sur le modèle de la république romaine," yet we may question whether, in those dark days, the people knew enough of Roman institutions to be influenced by their knowledge. With more probability may we infer that "this meeting of all the men of the state capable of bearing arms . . . in the great square" [Sismondi 1832, p. 22], originally called to take measures for repelling aggressors — a meeting which must, at the very outset, have been swayed by a group of dominant citizens and must have chosen leaders — was itself the republican government in its incipient state.

Meetings of this kind, first held on occasions of emergency, would gradually come into use for deciding all important public questions. Repetition would bring greater regularity in the modes of procedure and greater definiteness in the divisions formed, ending in compound political heads, presided over by elected chiefs. And that this was the case in those early stages of which there remain but vague accounts is shown by the fact that a similar, though somewhat more definite, process afterwards occurred at Florence when the usurping nobles were overthrown. Records tell us that in 1250 "the citizens assembled at the same moment in the square of Santa Croce; they divided themselves into fifty groups, of which each group chose a captain, and thus formed companies of militia: a council of these officers was the first-born authority of this newly revived republic" [Sismondi 1832, p. 83]. Clearly, that sovereignty of the people which for a time characterized these small governments would inevitably arise if the political form grew out of the original public meeting, while it would be unlikely to have arisen had the political form been artificially devised by a limited class.

That this interpretation harmonizes with the facts which modern times have furnished, scarcely needs pointing out. On an immensely larger scale and in ways variously modified, here by the slow collapse of an old regime and there by combination for war, the rise of the first French Republic and of the American Republic have similarly shown us this tendency towards resumption of the primitive form of political organization when a decayed or otherwise incapable government collapses. Obscured by complicating circumstances and special incidents as these transformations were, we may recognize in them the play of the same general causes.

In the last chapter we saw that, as conditions determine, the first element of the triune political structure may be differentiated from the second in various degrees, beginning with the warrior-chief, slightly predominant over other warriors, and ending with the divine and absolute king widely. distinguished from the select few next to him. By the foregoing examples we are shown that the second element is, as conditions determine, variously differentiated from the third, being at the one extreme qualitatively distinguished in a high degree and divided from it by an impassable barrier, and at the other extreme almost merged into it.

Here we are introduced to the truth next to be dealt with, that not only do conditions determine the various forms which compound heads assume, but that conditions determine the various changes they undergo. There are two leading kinds of such changes — those through which the compound head passes towards a less popular form, and those through which it passes towards a more popular form. We will glance at them in this order.

Progressive narrowing of the compound head is one of the concomitants of continued military activity. Setting out with the case of Sparta, the constitution of which in its early form differed but little from that which the *Iliad* shows us existed among the Homeric Greeks, we first see the tendency towards concentration of power in the regulation, made a century after Lycurgus, that "in case the people decided crookedly, the senate with the kings should reverse their decisions" [ref. lost], and then we see that later, in consequence of the gravitation of property into fewer hands, "the number of qualified citizens went on continually diminishing" [Grote 1846–56, II, 90], the implication being not only a relatively increased power of the oligarchy but, probably, a growing supremacy of the wealthier members within the oligarchy itself.

Turning to the case of Rome, ever militant, we find that in course of time inequalities increased to the extent that the senate became "an order of lords, filling up its ranks by hereditary succession, and exercising collegiate misrule." Moreover, "out of the evil of oligarchy there emerged the still worse evil of usurpation of power by particular families" [Mommsen 1862, II, 326]. In the Italian Republics, again, perpetually at war one with another, there resulted a kindred narrowing of the governing body. The nobility, deserting their castles, began to direct "the municipal government of the cities, which consequently, during this period of the Republics, fell chiefly into the hands of the superior families" [Hallam 1855, I, 368]. Then at a later stage, when industrial progress had generated wealthy commercial classes, these, competing with the nobles for power and finally displacing them, repeated within their respective bodies this same process. The richer guilds deprived the poorer of their shares in the choice of the ruling agencies; the privileged class was continually diminished by disqualifying regulations; and newly risen

families were excluded by those of long standing. So that, as Sismondi
points out, those of the numerous Italian Republics which remained
nominally such at the close of the fifteenth century, were, like "Sienna
and Lucca, each governed by a single caste of citizens . . . had no longer
popular governments" [1832, p. 280]. . . .

We have next to note as a cause of progressive modification in compound heads that, like simple heads, they are apt to be subordinated
by their administrative agents. The earliest case to be named is one in
which this effect is exemplified along with the last — the case of Sparta.
Originally appointed by the kings to perform prescribed duties, the
ephors first made the kings subordinate and eventually subordinated
the senate, so that they became substantially the rulers. From this we
may pass to the instance supplied by Venice, where power once exercised by the people gradually lapsed into the hands of an executive body
the members of which, habitually re-elected, and at death replaced by
their children, became an aristocracy, whence there eventually grew the
council of ten, who were, like the Spartan ephors, "charged to guard the
security of the state with a power higher than the law," and who thus,
"restrained by no rule," constituted the actual government [ref. lost]. . . .

But the liability of the compound political head to become subject to
its civil agents is far less than its liability to become subject to its military
agents. From the earliest times this liability has been exemplified and
commented upon, and, familiar though it is, I must here illustrate and
emphasize it because it directly bears on one of the cardinal truths of
political theory.

Setting out with the Greeks, we observe that the tyrants, by whom
oligarchies were so often overthrown, had armed forces at their disposal.
Either the tyrant was "the executive magistrate, upon whom the oligarchy
themselves had devolved important administrative powers" [Grote 1846–
56, III, 25], or he was a demagogue who pleaded the alleged interests of the
community "in order to surround" himself "with armed defenders," soldiers being in either case the agents of his usurpation [Curtius 1868–73,
I, 250]. And then, in Rome, we see the like done by the successful general. As Machiavelli remarks:

> For the further abroad they [the generals] carried their arms, the more neces-
> sary such prolongations [of their commissions] appeared, and the more
> common they became; hence it arose, in the first place, that but a few of
> their Citizens could be employed in the command of armies, and conse-
> quently few were capable of acquiring any considerable degree of experi-
> ence or reputation; and in the next, that when a Commander in chief was
> continued for a long time in that post, he had an opportunity of corrupting
> his army to such a degree that the Soldiers entirely threw off their obedience
> to the Senate, and acknowledged no authority but his. To this it was owing

that Sylla and Marius found means to debauch their armies and make them fight against their country; and that Julius Caesar was enabled to make himself absolute in Rome [1775, III, 429].

The Italian Republics, again, furnish many illustrations. By the beginning of the fourteenth century those of Lombardy "all submitted themselves to the military power of some nobles to whom they had entrusted the command of their militias, and thus all lost their liberty" [Sismondi 1832, p. 80]. Later times and nearer regions yield instances. At home, Cromwell showed how the successful general tends to become autocrat. In the Netherlands the same thing was exemplified by the Van Arteveldes, father and son, and again by Maurice of Nassau; and, but for form's sake, it would be needless to name the case of Napoleon.

It should be added that not only by command of armed forces is the military chief enabled to seize on supreme power, but acquired popularity, especially in a militant nation, places him in a position which makes it relatively easy to do this. Neither their own experience nor the experiences of other nations throughout the past prevented the French from lately making Marshal MacMahon executive head, and even the Americans, in more than once choosing General Grant for president, proved that, predominantly industrial though their society is, militant activity promptly caused an incipient change towards the militant type, of which an essential trait is the union of civil headship with military headship.

From the influences which narrow compound political headships or change them into single ones let us pass to the influences which widen them. The case of Athens is, of course, the first to be considered. To understand this we must remember that up to the time of Solon democratic government did not exist in Greece. The only actual forms were the oligarchic and the despotic, and in those early days before political speculation began it is unlikely that there was recognized in theory a social form entirely unknown in practice. We have, therefore, to exclude the notion that popular government arose in Athens under the guidance of any preconceived idea. As having the same implication should be added the fact that (Athens being governed by an oligarchy at the time) the Solonian legislation served but to qualify and broaden the oligarchy and remove crying injustices.

In seeking the causes of change which worked through Solon and also made practicable the reorganization he initiated, we shall find them to lie in the direct and indirect influences of trade. Grote comments on "the anxiety, both of Solon and of Drako, to enforce among their fellow citizens industrious and self-maintaining habits," a proof that even before

Solon's time there was in Attica little or no reprobation of "sedentary industry, which in most other parts of Greece was regarded as comparatively dishonourable." Moreover, Solon was himself in early life a trader and his legislation "provided for traders and artizans a new home at Athens, giving the first encouragement to that numerous town population, both in the city and in the Peiraeus, which we find actually residing there in the succeeding century."

The immigrants who flocked into Attica because of its greater security Solon was anxious to turn rather to manufacturing industry than to cultivation of a soil naturally poor, and one result was "a departure from the primitive temper of Atticism, which tended both to cantonal residence and rural occupation," while another result was to increase the number of people who stood outside those gentile and phratic divisions which were concomitants of the patriarchal type and of personal rule. And then the constitutional changes made by Solon were in leading respects towards industrial organization. The introduction of a property qualification for classes, instead of a birth qualification, diminished the rigidity of the political form, since acquirement of wealth by industry or otherwise, made possible an admission into the oligarchy, or among others of the privileged. By forbidding self-enslavement of the debtor and by emancipating those who had been self-enslaved, his laws added largely to the enfranchised class as distinguished from the slave class. Otherwise regarded, this change, leaving equitable contracts untouched, prevented those inequitable contracts under which, by a lien on himself, a man gave more than an equivalent for the sum he borrowed. And with a decreasing number of cases in which there existed the relation of master and slave went an increasing number of cases in which benefits were exchanged under agreement. The odium attaching to that lending at interest which ended in slavery of the debtor having disappeared, legitimate lending became general and unopposed; the rate of interest was free, and accumulated capital was made available.

Then, as cooperating cause, and as ever-increasing consequence, came the growth of a population favorably circumstanced for acting in concert. Urban people who, daily in contact, gather one another's ideas and feelings, and who, by quickly diffused intelligence are rapidly assembled, can cooperate far more readily than people scattered through rural districts. With all which direct and indirect results of industrial development must be joined the ultimate result on character produced by daily fulfilling and enforcing contracts — a discipline which, while requiring each man to recognize the claims of others, also requires him to maintain his own. In Solon himself this attitude, which joins assertion of personal rights with respect for the rights of others, was well exemplified, since, when his influence was great he refused to become a despot, though pressed to do so, and in his latter days he resisted at the risk of death the establishment of a despotism [Grote 1846–56, III, 181–5].

In various ways, then, increasing industrial activity tended to widen the original oligarchic structure. And though these effects of industrialism, joined with subsequently accumulated effects, were for a long time held in check by the usurping Peisistratidae, yet, being ready to show themselves when, some time after the expulsion of these tyrants, there came the Cleisthenian revolution, they were doubtless instrumental in then initiating the popular form of government.

Though not in so great a degree, yet in some degree, the same causes operated in liberalizing the Roman oligarchy. Rome "was indebted for the commencement of its importance to international commerce," and, as Mommsen points out, "the distinction between Rome and the mass of the other Latin towns, must certainly be traced back to its commercial position and to the type of character produced by that position . . . Rome was the emporium of the Latin districts" [1862, Bk. I, ch. 4, *passim*]. Moreover, as in Athens, though doubtless to a smaller extent, trade brought an increasing settlement of strangers to whom rights were given and who, joined with emancipated slaves and with clients, formed an industrial population the eventual inclusion of which in the burgess-body caused that widening of the constitution effected by Servius Tullius.

The Italian Republics of later days again show us in numerous cases this connection between trading activities and a freer form of rule. The towns were industrial centers.

> The merchants of Genoa, Pisa, Florence, and Venice supplied Europe with the products of the Mediterranean and of the East: the bankers of Lombardy instructed the world in the mysteries of finance, and foreign exchanges: Italian artificers taught the workmen of other countries the highest skill in the manufacture of steel, iron, bronze, silk, glass, porcelain, and jewelry. Italian shops, with their dazzling array of luxuries, excited the admiration and envy of foreigners from less favoured lands [May 1877, I, 281–2].

Then, on looking into their histories, we find that industrial guilds were the bases of their political organizations; that the upper mercantile classes became the rulers, in some cases excluding the nobles, and that while external wars and internal feuds tended continually to revive narrower or more personal forms of rule, rebellions of the industrial citizens, occasionally happening, tended to re-establish popular rule.

When we join with these the like general connections that arose in the Netherlands and in the Hanse towns — when we remember the liberalization of our own political institutions which has gone along with growing industrialism — when we observe that the towns more than the country and the great industrial centers more than the small ones, have given the impulses to these changes it becomes unquestionable that while by increase of militant activities compound headships are narrowed, they are widened in proportion as industrial activities become predominant.

Summary

In common with the results reached in preceding chapters, the results above reached show that types of political organization are not matters of deliberate choice. It is common to speak of a society as though it had, once upon a time, decided on the form of government which thereafter existed in it. Even Mr. Grote, in his comparison between the institutions of ancient Greece and those of medieval Europe tacitly implies that conceptions of the advantages or disadvantages of this or that arrangement furnished motives for establishing or maintaining it [1846–56, III, 10–2]. But, as gathered together in the foregoing sections, the facts show that as with the genesis of simple political heads so with the genesis of compound political heads, conditions and not intentions determine.

Recognizing the truth that independence of character is a factor, but ascribing this independence of character to the continued existence of a race in a habitat which facilitates evasion of control, we saw that with such a nature so conditioned, cooperation in war causes the union on equal terms of groups whose heads are joined to form a directive council. And according as the component groups are governed more or less autocratically, the directive council is more or less oligarchic. We have seen that in localities differing so widely as do mountain regions, marshes or mud islands, and jungles, men of different races have developed political heads of this compound kind. And on observing that the localities otherwise so unlike are alike in being severally made up of parts difficult of access, we cannot question that to this is mainly due the governmental form under which their inhabitants unite.

Besides the compound heads which are thus indigenous in places favoring them, there are other compound heads which arise after the breakup of preceding political organizations. Especially apt are they so to arise where the people, not scattered through a wide district but concentrated in a town, can easily assemble bodily. Control of every kind having disappeared, it happens in such cases that the aggregate will has free play, and there establishes itself for a time that relatively popular form with which all government begins; but, regularly or irregularly, a superior few become differentiated from the many, and of predominant men some one is made, directly or indirectly, most predominant.

Compound heads habitually become, in course of time, either narrower or wider. They are narrowed by militancy, which tends ever to concentrate directive power in fewer hands, and, if continued, almost certainly changes them into simple heads. Conversely, they are widened by indus-trialism. This, by gathering together aliens detached from the restraints imposed by patriarchal, feudal, or other such organizations, by increas-ing the number of those to be coerced in comparison with the number of those who have to coerce them, by placing this larger number in condi-tions favoring concerted action, by substituting for daily enforced obedi-ence the daily fulfilment of voluntary obligations and daily maintenance of claims, tends ever towards equalization of citizenship.

CHAPTER 15

LOCAL GOVERNING AGENCIES

. . . Of the local governing agencies to which family headships and political headships give origin as groups become compounded and recompounded, we will consider first the political as being most directly related to the central governing agencies hitherto dealt with.

According to the relative powers of conqueror and conquered, war establishes various degrees of subordination. Here the payment of tribute and occasional expression of homage interfere but little with political independence and there political independence is almost or quite lost. Generally, however, at the outset the victor either finds it necessary to respect the substantial autonomies of the vanquished societies, or finds it his best policy to do this. Hence, before integration has proceeded far, local governments are usually nothing more than those governments of the parts which existed before they were united into a whole.

We find instances of undecided subordination everywhere. In Tahiti "the actual influence of the king over the haughty and despotic district chieftains, was neither powerful nor permanent" [Ellis 1829, II, 367]. Of our own political organization in old English times Kemble [1876, II, 142] writes: "the whole executive government may be considered as a great aristocratic association, of which the ealdormen were the constituent earls, and the king little more than president." Similarly during early feudal times, as, for example, in France. "Under the first Capetians, we find scarcely any general act of legislation. . . . Everything was local, and all the possessors of fiefs first, and afterwards all the great suzerains, possessed the legislative power within their domain" [Guizot 1856, III, 233–4]. This is the kind of relation habitually seen during the initial stages of those clustered groups in which one group has acquired power over the rest.

In cases where the successful invader, external to the cluster instead of internal, is powerful enough completely to subjugate all the groups, it still happens that the pre-existing local organizations commonly survive. Ancient American states yield examples. "When the kings of Mexico, Tezcuco, and Tacuba conquered a province, they used to maintain in their authority all the natural chiefs, the highest as well as the lower ones" [Zurita 1840, pp. 66–7]. Concerning certain rulers of Chibcha communities who became subject to Bogotá, we read that the Zipa subdued them but left them their jursidiction and left the succession to the caciqueship in their families [Acosta 1848, pp. 188–90]. And as was pointed out under another head, the victorious Incas left outstanding the political headships and administrations of the many small societies they consolidated. Such is, in fact, the most convenient policy. As is remarked by Sir Henry Maine [1876, pp. 235–6], "certain institutions of a primitive people, their corporations and village communities, will always be preserved by a suzerain state governing them, on account of the facilities which they afford to civil and fiscal administration," and the like may be said of the larger regulative structures. Indeed the difficulty of suddenly replacing an old local organization by an entirely new one is so great that almost of necessity the old one is in large measure retained.

The autonomies of local governments, thus sometimes scarcely at all interfered with and in other cases but partially suppressed, manifest themselves in various ways. The original independence of groups continues to be shown by the right of private war between them. They retain their local gods, their ecclesiastical organizations, their religious festivals. And in time of general war the contingents they severally furnish remain separate. Egyptian nomes, Greek cities, feudal lordships, yield illustrations.

The gradual disappearance of local autonomies is a usual outcome of the struggle between the governments of the parts, which try to retain their powers, and the central government, which tries to diminish their powers.

In proportion as his hands are strengthened, chiefly by successful wars, the major political head increases his restraints over the minor political heads: first by stopping private wars among them, then by interfering as arbitrator, then by acquiring an appellate jurisdiction. Where the local rulers have been impoverished by their struggles with one another, or by futile attempts to recover their independence, or by drafts made on their resources for external wars; where, also, followers of the central ruler have grown into a new order of nobles, with gifts of conquered or usurped lands as rewards for services, the way is prepared for administrative agencies centrally appointed. Thus in France, when the monarch became dominant, the seigneurs were gradually deprived of legislative authority. Royal confirmation became requisite to make signorial acts valid, and the crown acquired the exclusive right of granting charters, the exclusive right of ennobling, the exclusive right of coining. Then with decline in the power of the original local rulers came deputies of the king overlooking them; provincial governors holding office at the king's pleasure were nominated. In subsequent periods grew up the administration of intendants and their sub-delegates, acting as agents of the crown, and whatever small local powers remained were exercised under central supervision.

English history at various stages yields kindred illustrations. When

Mercia was formed out of petty kingdoms, the local kings became ealdormen, and a like change took place afterwards on a large scale. "From the time of Ecgberht onwards there is a marked distinction between the King and the Ealdorman. The King is a sovereign, the Ealdorman is only a magistrate" [Freeman 1867–79, I, 80]. Just noting that under Cnut, ealdormen became subordinated by the appointment of earls, and again that under William I earldoms were filled up afresh, we observe that after the War of the Roses had weakened them the hereditary nobles had their local powers interfered with by those of centrally appointed lords-lieutenant.

Not only provincial governing agencies of a personal kind come to be thus subordinated as the integration furthered by war progresses, but also those of a popular kind. The old English Scirgeréfa, who presided over the Sciregemot, was at first elective but was afterwards nominated by the king [Fischel 1863, p. 301]. Under a later regime there occurred a kindred change: "Edward II abolished the popular right to election" to the office of sheriff. And similarly, "from the beginning of Edward III's reign, the appointment of conservators" of the peace, who were originally elected, "was vested in the crown," "and their title changed to that of justices" [Hallam 1855, Ch. VIII].

With sufficient distinctness such facts show us that rapidly where a cluster of small societies is subjugated by an invader, and slowly where one among them acquires an established supremacy, the local rulers lose their directive powers and become executive agents only, discharging whatever duties they retain as the servants of newer local agents. In the course of political integration the original governing centers of the component parts become relatively automatic in their functions.

A further truth to be noted is that there habitually exists a kinship in structure between the general government and the local governments. Several causes conspire to produce this kinship.

Where one of a cluster of groups has acquired power over the rest, either directly by the victories of its ruler over them, or indirectly by his successful leadership of the confederation in war, this kinship becomes a matter of course. For under such conditions the general government is but a development of that which was previously one of the local governments. We have a familiar illustration furnished by old English times in the likeness between the hundred moot (a small local governing assembly), the shire moot (constituted in an analogous way, but having military, judicial, and fiscal duties of a wider kind, and headed by a chief originally elected), and the national witanagemot (containing originally the same class elements, though in different proportions, headed by a king, also at first elected, and discharging like functions on a larger scale. This similarity recurs under another phase. Sir Henry Maine says:

It has often, indeed, been noticed that a Feudal Monarchy was an exact counterpart of a Feudal Manor, but the reason of the correspondence is only now beginning to dawn upon us, which is, that both of them were in their origin bodies of assumed kinsmen settled on land and undergoing the same transmutation of ideas through the fact of settlement [1875, p. 77].

Of France in the early feudal period Maury says, "the court of every great feudatory was the image, of course slightly reduced, of that of the king," and the facts he names curiously show that locally, as generally, there was a development of servants into ministerial officers [1878, p. 584]. Kindred evidence comes from other parts of the world — Japan, several African states, sundry Polynesian islands, ancient Mexico, Medieval India, etc., where forms of society essentially similar to those of the feudal system exist or have existed.

Where the local autonomy has been almost or quite destroyed, as by a powerful invading race bringing with it another type of organization, we still see the same thing, for its tendency is to modify the institutions locally as it modifies them generally. From early times eastern kingdoms have shown us this, as instance the provincial rulers, or satraps, of the Persians. "While . . . they remained in office they were despotic — they represented the Great King, and were clothed with a portion of his majesty. . . . They wielded the power of life and death" [Rawlinson 1862–67, III, 418]. And down to the present day this union of central chief-despot with local sub-despots survives, as is implied by Rawlinson's remark that these ancient satraps had "that full and complete authority which is possessed by Turkish pashas and modern Persian khans or beys — an authority practically uncontrolled" [1862–67, III, 426]. Other ancient societies of quite other types displayed this tendency to assimilate the structures of the incorporated parts to that of the incorporating whole. Grecian history shows us that oligarchic Sparta sought to propagate oligarchy as a form of government in dependent territories, while democratic Athens propagated the democratic form. And, similarly, where Rome conquered and colonized there followed the Roman municipal system.

This last instance reminds us that as the character of the general government changes, the character of the local government changes too. In the Roman empire that progress towards a more concentrated form of rule which continued militancy brought, spread from center to periphery. "Under the Republic every town had, like Rome, a popular assembly which was sovereign for making the law and 'creating' magistrates," but with the change towards oligarchic and personal rule in Rome, popular power in the provinces decreased; "the municipal organization, from being democratic, became aristocratic" [Duruy 1870–79, V, 83–4]. In

France, as monarchical power approached absoluteness, similar changes were effected in another way. The government seized on municipal offices, "erecting them into hereditary offices, and . . . selling them at the highest price: . . . a permanent mayor and assessors were imposed upon all the municipalities of the kingdom, which ceased to be elective" [Thierry 1859, I, 365–6], and then these magistrates began to assume royal airs — spoke of the sanctity of their magistracy, the veneration of the people, etc. [Chéruel 1855, II, 138–9].

Our own history interestingly shows simultaneous movements now towards freer, and now towards less free forms, locally and generally. When, under King John, the central government was liberalized, towns acquired the power to elect their own magistrates. Conversely when at the Restoration monarchical power increased, there was a framing of the "municipalities on a more oligarchical model" [Hallam 1854, Ch. XII]. And then comes the familiar case of the kindred liberalizations of the central government and the local governments which have occurred in our own time.

From those local governing agencies which have acquired a political character we turn now to those which have retained the primitive family character. Though with the massing of groups political organization and rule become separate from, and predominant over, family organization and rule, locally as well as generally, yet family organization and rule do not disappear but in some cases retaining their original nature, in some cases give origin to other local organizations of a governmental kind. Let us first note how widespread is the presence of the family cluster considered as a component of the political society.

Among the uncivilized Bedouins we see it existing separately, "every large family with its relations constituting a small tribe by itself" [Burckhardt 1830, p. 5]. But, says Palgrave, "though the clan and the family form the basis and are the ultimate expression of the civilized Arab society, they do not, as is the case among the Bedouins, sum it up altogether" [1875, p. 249]. That is, political union has left outstanding the family organization but has added something to it. And it was thus with Semitic societies of early days, as those of the Hebrews. Everywhere it has been thus with the Aryans.

"The [Irish] Sept is a body of kinsmen whose progenitor is no longer living, but whose descent from him is a reality. . . . An association of this sort is well known to the law of India as the Joint Undivided Family. . . . The family thus formed by the continuance of several generations in union, is identical in outline with a group very familiar to the students of the older Roman law — the Agnatic Kindred" [Maine 1875, pp. 105–6].

Not only where descent in the male line has been established but also where the system of descent through females continues, this development of the family into gens, phratry, and tribe, is found. It was so with such ancient American peoples as those of Yucatan, where, within each town, tribal divisions were maintained, and, according to Mr. Morgan and Major Powell, it is still so with such American tribes as the Iroquois and the Wyandottes.

After its conclusion in a political aggregate, as before its inclusion, the family group evolves a government quasi-political in nature. According to the type of race and the system of descent this family government may be, as among ancient Semites and Aryans, an unqualified patriarchal despotism; or it may be, as among the Hindus at present, a personal rule arising by selection of a head from the leading family of the group (a selection usually falling on the eldest); or it may be, as in American tribes like those mentioned, the government of an elected council of the gens, which elects its chief. That is to say, the triune structure which tends to arise in any incorporated assembly is traceable in the compound family group as in the political group, the respective components of it being variously developed according to the nature of the people and the conditions.

The government of each aggregate of kinsmen repeats, on a small scale, functions like those of the government of the political aggregate. As the entire society revenges itself on other such societies for injury to its members, so does the family-cluster revenge itself on other family-clusters included in the same society. This fact is too familiar to need illustration, but it may be pointed out that even now, in parts of Europe where the family organization survives, the family vendettas persist. "L'Albanais vous dira froidement . . . Akeni-Dgiak? avez-vous du sang à venger dans votre famille" [Boué 1840, II, 86], and then, asking the name of your tribe, he puts his hand on his pistol. With this obligation to take vengeance goes, of course, reciprocal responsibility. The family in all its branches is liable as a whole, and in each part, for the injuries done by its members to members of other families, just as the entire society is held liable by other entire societies. This responsibility holds not alone for lives taken by members of the family group but also for damages they do to property, and for pecuniary claims.

Dans les districts Albanais libres, les dettes sont contractées à terme. En cas de non-paiement, on a recours aux chefs de la tribu du débiteur, et si ceux-ci refusent de faire droit, on arrête le premier venu qui appartient à cette tribu, et on l'accable de mauvais traitements jusqu'à ce qu'il s'entende avec le véritable débiteur, ou qu'il paie lui-même ses dettes, risque à se pouvoir ensuite devant les anciens de sa tribu ou de poursuivre par les armes celui qui lui a valu ce dommage [Boué 1840, III, 359].

And of the old English maegth we read that "if any one was imprisoned for theft, witchcraft, etc., his kindred must pay the fine . . . and must become surety for his good conduct on his release" [Young 1876, p. 147].

While within the political aggregate each compound family group thus stood towards other such included groups in quasi-political relations, its government exercised internal control. In the gens as constituted among the American peoples above named there is administration of affairs by its council. The gentile divisions among historic peoples were ruled by their patriarchs, as are still those of the Hindus by their chosen elders. And then besides this judicial organization within the assemblage of kindred there is the religious organization, arising from worship of a common ancestor, which entails periodic joint observances.

Thus the evidence shows us that while the massing together of groups by war has for its concomitant, development of a political organization which dominates over the organizations of communities of kindred, yet these communities of kindred long survive and partially retain their autonomies and their constitutions.

Social progress, however, transforms them in sundry ways, differentiating them into groups which gradually lose their family characters. One cause is change from the wandering life to the settled life, with the implied establishment of definite relations to the land, and the resulting multiplication and interfusion.

To show that this process and its consequences are general, I may name the calpulli of the ancient Mexicans, which "means a district inhabited by a family . . . of ancient origin," whose members hold estates which "belong not to each inhabitant, but to the calpulli," who have chiefs chosen out of the tribe, and who "meet for dealing with the common interests, and regulating the apportionment of taxes, and also what concerns the festivals" [Zurita 1840, pp. 50, 62]. And then I may name as being remote in place, time, and race, the still-existing Russian mir, or village commune, which is constituted by descendants of the same family group of nomads who became settled, which is "a judicial corporation . . . proprietor of the soil, of which individual members have but the usufruct or temporary enjoyment," which is governed by the "heads of families, assembled in council under the presidency of the *starosta* or mayor, whom they have elected" [Laveleye 1878, pp. 8, 9].

Just noting these allied examples, we may deal more especially with the Teutonic mark, which was "formed by a primitive settlement of a family or kindred" [Stubbs 1880, I, 56], when, as said by Caesar of the Suevi, the land was divided among "gentes et cognationes hominum" [Caesar 1863, Bk. VI, ch. 22]. In the words of Kemble, marks were:

> great family-unions, comprising households of various degrees of wealth, rank, and authority; some in direct descent from the common ancestors, or

from the hero of the particular tribe; others, more distantly connected. . . . ; some, admitted into communion by marriage, others by adoption, others by emancipation; but all recognizing a brotherhood, a kinsmanship or *sibsceaft*; all standing together as one unit in respect of other similar communities; all governed by the same judges and led by the same captains; all sharing in the same religious rites; and all known to themselves and to their neighbours by one general name [1876, I, 56–7].

To which add that, in common with family groups as already described, the cluster of kindred constituting the mark had, like both smaller and larger clusters, a joint obligation to defend and avenge its members and a joint responsibility for their actions.

And now we are prepared for observing sundry influences which conspire to change the grouping of kindred into political grouping, locally as well as generally. In the first place, there is that admission of strangers into the family, gens, or tribe, which we have before recognized as a normal process from savage life upwards. Livingstone, remarking of the Bakwains that "the government is patriarchal," describes each chief man as having his hut encircled by the huts of his wives, relatives, and dependents, forming a kotla: "a poor man attaches himself to the kotla of a rich one and is considered a child of the latter" [1861, p. 14]. Here we see being done informally that which was formally done in the Roman household and the Teutonic mark. In proportion as the adopted strangers increase, and in proportion also as the cluster becomes diluted by incorporating with itself emancipated dependents, the links among its members become weakened and its character altered. In the second place, when, by concentration and multiplication, different clusters of kindred placed side by side become interspersed, and there ceases to be a direct connection between locality and kinship, the family or gentile bonds are further weakened. And then there eventually results, both for military and fiscal purposes, the need for a grouping based on locality instead of on relationship. An early illustration is furnished by the Cleisthenian revolution in Attica, which made a division of the territory into demes, replacing for public purposes tribal divisions by topographical divisions, the inhabitants of each of which had local administrative powers and public responsibilities.

We are here brought to the vexed question about the origin of tithings and hundreds. It was pointed out that the ancient Peruvians had civil as well as military divisions into tens and hundreds, with their respective officers. In China, where there is pushed to an extreme the principle of making groups responsible for their members, the clan divisions are not acknowledged by the government, but only the tithings and hundreds, the implication being that these last were results of political organization as distinguished from family organization. In parts of Japan, too, "there is a sort of subordinate system of wards, and heads of tens and hundreds, in the *Otonos* of towns and villages, severally and collectively responsible for each other's good conduct" [Alcock 1863, II, 241]. We have seen that in Rome the groupings into hundreds and tens, civil as well as military, became political substitutes for the gentile groupings. Under the Frankish law, "the tithing-man is *Decanus*, the hundred-man *Centenarius*" [Kemble 1876, I, 238]; and whatever may have been their indigenous names, divisions into tens and hundreds appear to have had (judging from the statements of Tacitus) an independent origin among the Germanic races.

And now remembering that these hundreds and tithings, formed within the marks or other large divisions, still answered in considerable degrees to groups based on kinship (since the heads of families of which they were constituted as local groups were ordinarily closer akin to one another than to the heads of families similarly grouped in other parts of the mark), we go on to observe that there survived in them, or were redeveloped in them, the family organization, rights and obligations. I do not mean merely that by their hundred-moots, etc., they had their internal administrations, but I mean chiefly that they became groups which had towards other groups the same joint claims and duties which family groups had. Responsibility for its members, previously attaching exclusively to the cluster of kindred irrespective of locality, was in a large measure transferred to the local cluster formed but partially of kindred.

For this transfer of responsibility an obvious cause arose as the gentes and tribes spread and became mingled. While the family community was small and closely aggregated, an offense committed by one of its members against another such community could usually be brought home to it bodily, if not to the sinning members, and as a whole it had to take the consequences. But when the family community, multiplying, began to occupy a wide area, and also became interfused with other family communities, the transgressor, while often traceable to some one locality within the area, was often not identifiable as of this or that kindred, and the consequences of his act, when they could not be visited on his family, which was not known, were apt to be visited on the inhabitants of the locality, who were known. Hence the genesis of a system of suretyship which is so ancient and so widespread. Here are illustrations:

This then is my will, that every man be in surety, both within the towns and without the towns. — Eádg. ii. Supp. § 3 [Thorpe 1865, I, 274].

And we will that every freeman be brought into a hundred and into a tithing, who desires to be entitled to *lád* or *wer*, in case any one should slay him after he have reached the age of xii years: or let him not otherwise be entitled to any free rights, be he householder, be he follower. — Cnut, ii § xx [Thorpe 1865, I, 386].

. . . in all the vills throughout the kingdom, all men are bound to be in a guarantee by tens, so that if one of the ten men offend, the other nine may hold him to right. — Edw. Conf., xx [Thorpe 1865, I, 450].

Speaking generally of this system of mutual guarantee as exhibited among the Russians, as well as among the Franks, Kutorga says:

Tout membre de la société devait entrer dans une décanie, laquelle avait pour mission la défence et la garantie de tous en général et de chacun en particulier; c'est-à-dire que la décanie devait venger le citoyen qui lui appartenait et exiger le wehrgeld, s'il avait été tué; mais en même temps elle se portait caution pour tous les seins [1839, p. 229].

In brief, then, this form of local governing agency, developing out of and partially replacing the primitive family form, was a natural concomitant of the multiplication and mixture resulting from a settled life. . . .

Summary

Involved and obscure as the process has been, the evolution of local governing agencies is thus fairly comprehensible. We divide them into two kinds, which, starting from a common root, have diverged as fast as small societies have been integrated into large ones.

Through successive stages of consolidation the political heads of the once-separate parts pass from independence to dependence, and end in being provincial agents — first partially conquered chiefs paying tribute, then fully conquered chiefs governing under command, then local governors who are appointed by the central governor and hold power under approval, becoming eventually executive officers.

There is habitually a kinship in character between the controlling systems of the parts and the controlling system of the whole. . . . With a central despotism there goes local despotic rule; with a freer form of the major government there goes a freer form of the minor governments; and a change either way in the one is followed by a kindred change in the other.

While with the compounding of small societies into large ones the political ruling agencies which develop locally as well as generally become separate from and predominant over the ruling agencies of family origin, these last do not disappear, but surviving in their first forms, also give origin to differentiated forms. The assemblage of kindred long continues to have a qualified semi-political autonomy, with internal government and external obligations and claims. And while family clusters, losing their definiteness by interfusion, slowly lose their traits as separate independent societies, there descend from them clusters which, in some cases united chiefly by locality and in others chiefly by occupation, inherit their traits and constitute governing agencies supplementing the purely political ones. . . .

CHAPTER 16

MILITARY SYSTEMS

Indirectly, much has already been said concerning the subject now to be dealt with. Originally identical as is the political organization with the military organization, it has been impossible to treat of the first without touching on the second. After exhibiting the facts under one aspect we have here to exhibit another aspect of them, and at the same time to bring into view classes of related facts thus far unobserved. But, first, let us dwell a moment on the alleged original identity.

In rude societies all adult males are warriors and consequently the army is the mobilized community, and the community is the army at rest. . . . With this general truth we may join the general truth that the primitive military gathering is also the primitive political gathering. Alike in savage tribes and in communities like those of our rude ancestors, the assemblies which are summoned for purposes of defense and offense are the assemblies in which public questions at large are decided.

Next stands the fact, so often named, that in the normal course of social evolution the military head grows into the political head. This double character of leading warrior and civil ruler, early arising, ordinarily continues through long stages, and where, as not infrequently happens, military headship becomes in a measure separated from political headship, continued warfare is apt to cause a re-identification of them.

As societies become compounded and recompounded, coincidence of military authority with political authority is shown in detail as well as in general — in the parts as in the whole. The minor war chiefs are also minor civil rulers in their several localities, and the commanding of their respective groups of soldiers in the field is of like nature with the governing of their respective groups of dependents at home.

Once more, there is the general fact that the economic organizations of primitive communities coincide with their military organizations. In savage tribes war and hunting are carried on by the same men, while their wives (and their slaves where they have any) do the drudgery of domestic life. And, similarly, in rude societies that have become settled, the military unit and the economic unit are the same. The soldier is also the landowner.

Such then, being the primitive identity of the political organization with military organization, we have in this chapter to note the ways in which the two differentiate.

We may most conveniently initiate the inquiry by observing the change which, during social evolution, takes place in the incidence of military obligations, and by recognizing the accompanying separation of the fighting body from the rest of the community.

Though there are some tribes in which military service (for aggressive war at any rate) is not compulsory, as the Comanches, Dakotas, Chippewas, whose war chiefs go about enlisting volunteers for their expeditions, yet habitually where political subordination is established, every man not privately possessed as a chattel is bound to fight when called on. There have been, and are, some societies of considerably advanced structures in which this state of things continues. In ancient Peru the common men were all either actually in the army or formed a reserve occupied in labor, and in modern Siam the people "are all soldiers, and owe six months' service yearly to their prince" [La Loubère 1691, I, 237]. But, usually, social progress is accompanied by a narrowed incidence of military obligation.

When the enslavement of captives is followed by the rearing of their children as slaves, as well as by the consigning of criminals and debtors to slavery—when, as in some cases, there is joined with the slave class a serf class composed of subjugated people not detached from their homes—the community becomes divided into two parts, on one of which only does military duty fall. Whereas in previous stages the division of the whole society had been into men as fighters and women as workers, the division of workers now begins to include men, and these continue to form an increasing part of the total male population. Though we are told that in Ashanti (where everyone is in fact owned by the king) the slave population "principally constitutes the military force" [Beecham 1841, p. 129], and that in Rabbah (among the Fulahs) the army is composed of slaves liberated "on consideration of their taking up arms" [Laird and Oldfield 1837, II, 87], yet, generally, those in bondage are not liable to military service, the causes being partly distrust of them (as was shown among the Spartans when forced to employ the helots), partly contempt for them as defeated men or the offspring of defeated men, and partly a desire to devolve on others, labors at once necessary and repugnant. Causes aside, however, the evidence proves that the army at this early stage usually coincides with the body of freemen, who are also the body of landowners. This . . . was the case in Egypt, Greece, Rome, and Germany. How natural is this incidence of military obligation we see in the facts that in ancient Japan and medieval India there were systems of military tenure like that of the middle ages in Europe, and that a kindred connection had arisen even in societies like those of Tahiti and Samoa.

Extent of estate being a measure of its owner's ability to bear burdens, there grows up a connection between the amount of land held and the amount of military aid to be rendered. Thus in Greece under Solon those whose properties yielded less than a certain revenue were exempt from duty as soldiers, save in emergencies. In Rome, with a view to better adjustment of the relation between means and requirements, there was a periodic "revision of the register of landed property, which was at the same time the levy-role" [Mommsen 1862, I, 99–100]. Throughout the middle ages this principle was acted upon by proportioning the numbers of warriors demanded to the sizes of the fiefs, and again afterwards, by requiring from parishes their respective contingents.

A dissociation of military duty from landownership begins when land ceases to be the only source of wealth. The growth of a class of free workers, accumulating property by trade, is followed by the imposing on them, also, of obligations to fight or to provide fighters. Though, as apparently in the cases of Greece and Rome, the possessions in virtue of which citizens of this order at first become liable are lands in which they have invested, yet, at later stages, they become liable as possessors of other property. Such, at least, is the interpretation we may give to the practice of making industrial populations furnish their specified numbers of warriors, whether, as during the Roman conquests, it took the shape of requiring "rich and populous" towns to maintain cohorts of infantry or divisions of cavalry, or whether, as with chartered towns in medieval days, there was a contract with the king as suzerain to supply him with stated numbers of men duly armed.

Later on, the same cause initiates a further change. As fast as industry increases the relative quantity of transferable property, it becomes easier to compound for service in war, either by providing a deputy or by paying to the ruler a sum which enables him to provide one. Originally the penalty for non-fulfilment of military obligation was loss of lands; then a heavy fine, which, once accepted, it became more frequently the custom to bear; then an habitual compounding for the special services demanded; then a levying of dues, such as those called scutages, in place of special compositions. Evidently industrial growth made this change possible, both by increasing the population from which the required numbers of substitutes could be obtained, and by producing the needful floating capital.

So that whereas in savage and semi-civilized communities of warlike kinds the incidence of military obligation is such that each free man has to serve personally, and also to provide his own arms and provisions, the progress from this state in which industry does but occupy the intervals between wars to a state in which war does but occasionally break the habitual industry brings an increasing dissociation of military obligation from free citizenship, military obligation at the same time tending to become a pecuniary burden levied in proportion to property of whatever kind. Though where there is a conscription personal service is theoretically due from each on whom the lot falls, yet the ability to buy a substitute brings the obligation back to a pecuniary one. And though we have an instance in our own day of universal military obligation not thus to be compounded for, we see that it is part of a reversion to the condition of predominant militancy.

An aspect of this change not yet noted is the simultaneous decrease in the ratio which the fighting part of the community bears to the rest. With the transition from nomadic habits to settled habits there begins an economic resistance to militant action which increases as industrial life develops, and diminishes the relative size of the military body.

Though in tribes of hunters the men are as ready for war at one time as at another, yet in agricultural societies there obviously exists an impediment to unceasing warfare. In the exceptional case of the Spartans the carrying on of rural industry was not allowed to prevent daily occupation of all freemen in warlike exercises, but, speaking generally, the sowing and reaping of crops hinder the gathering together of freemen for offensive or defensive purposes. Hence in course of time come decreased calls on them. The ancient Suevi divided themselves so as alternately to share war duties and farm work: each season the active warriors returned to till the land, while their places were "supplied by the husbandmen of the previous year" [Stubbs 1880, I, 15]. Alfred established in England a kindred alternation between military service and cultivation of the soil. In feudal times, again, the same tendency was shown by restrictions on the duration and amount of the armed aid which a feudal tenant and his retainers had to give — now for sixty, for forty, for twenty days, down even to four; now alone, and again with specified numbers of followers; here without limit of distance, and there within the bounds of a county. Doubtless, insubordination often caused resistances to service, and consequent limitations of this kind. But manifestly, absorption of the energies in industry directly and indirectly antagonized militant action, with the result that separation of the fighting body from the general body of citizens was accompanied by a decrease in its relative mass.

There are two cooperating causes for this decrease of its relative mass which are of much significance. One is the increasing costliness of the soldier and of war appliances, which goes along with that social progress made possible by industrial growth. In the savage state each warrior provides his own weapons, and, on war excursions, depends on himself for sustenance. At a higher stage this ceases to be the case. When chariots of war and armor and siege implements come to be used, there are presupposed sundry specialized and skilled artisan-classes, implying a higher ratio of the industrial part of the community to the militant part. And when later on there are introduced firearms, artillery, ironclads, torpedoes, and the like, we see that there must co-exist a large and highly organized body of producers and distributors, alike to furnish the required powers and bear the entailed cost. That is to say, the war-machinery, both living and dead, cannot be raised in efficiency without lowering the ratio it bears to those sustaining structures which give it efficiency.

The other cooperating cause which simultaneously comes into play is directly due to the compounding and recompounding of societies. The larger nations become, and the greater the distances over which their military actions range, the more expensive do those actions grow. It is with an army as with a limb, the effort to put forth is costly in proportion to the remoteness of the acting parts from the base of operations. Though it is true that a body of victorious invaders may raise some, or the whole, of its supplies from the conquered society, yet before it has effected conquest it cannot do this, but is dependent for maintenance on its own society, of which it then forms an integral part; where it ceases to form an integral part and wanders far away, living on spoils, like Tartar hordes in past ages, we are no longer dealing with social organization and its laws, but with social destruction. Limiting ourselves to societies which, permanently localized, preserve their individualities, it is clear that the larger the integrations formed, the greater is the social strain consequent on the distances at which fighting has to be done, and the greater the amount of industrial population required to bear the strain. Doubtless, improved means of communication may all at once alter the ratio, but this does not conflict with the proposition when qualified by saying — other things equal.

In three ways, therefore, does settled life and the development of civilization so increase the economic resistance to militant action as to cause decrease of the ratio borne by the militant part to the non-militant part.

With those changes in the incidence of military obligation which tend to separate the body of soldiers from the body of workers, and with those other changes which tend to diminish its relative size, there go changes which tend to differentiate it in a further way. The first of these to be noted is the parting of military headship from political headship.

We have seen that the commencement of social organization is the growth of the leading warrior into the civil governor. To illustrative facts before named may be added the fact that an old English ruler, as instance Hengist, was originally called "Here-toga" — literally army-leader, and the office developed into that of king only after settlement in Britain. But with establishment of hereditary succession to political headship there comes into play an influence which tends to make the chief of the state distinct from the chief of the army. That antagonism between the principle of inheritance and the principle of efficiency, everywhere at work, has from the beginning been conspicuous in this relation because of the imperative need for efficient generalship. Often . . . there is an endeavor to unite the two qualifications, as, for example, in ancient Mexico, where the king, before being crowned, had to fill successfully the position of commander in chief. But from quite early stages we find that where hereditary succession has been established and there does not happen to be inheritance of military capacity along with political supremacy, it is common for headship of the warriors to become a separate post filled by election. Says Waitz, "among the Guaranis the chieftainship generally goes from father to first-born son. The leader in war is, however, elected" [1860–61, III, 422]. In ancient Nicaragua "the war chief was elected by the warriors to lead them, on account of his ability and bravery in battle; but the civil or hereditary chief often accompanies the army" [Squier 1852, II, 342]. Of the New Zealanders we read that "hereditary chiefs were generally the leaders," but not always, others being chosen on account of bravery [ref. lost]. And among the Sakarran Dyaks there is a war chief in addition to the ordinary chief. In the case of the Bedouins the original motive has been defeated in a curious way.

> During a campaign in actual warfare, the authority of the sheikh of the tribe is completely set aside, and the soldiers are wholly under the command of the agyd. . . . The office of agyd is hereditary in a certain family, from father to son; and the Arabs submit to the commands of an agyd whom they know to be deficient both in bravery and judgment, rather than yield to the orders of their sheikh during the actual expedition; for they say that expeditions headed by the sheikh, are always unsuccessful [Burckhardt 1830, p. 168].

It should be added that in some cases we see coming into play further motives. Forster [1778, p. 377] tells us that in Tahiti the king sometimes resigns the post of commander in chief of the fighting force to one of his chiefs, conscious either of his own unfitness or desirous of avoiding danger. And then in some cases the anxiety of subjects to escape the evils following the loss of the political head leads to this separation, as when among the Hebrews, "the men of David sware unto him, saying, Thou shalt go no more out with us to battle, that thou quench not the light of Israel" [Cook 1871–81, 2 Sam. XXI, 17], or as when in France in 923, the king was besought by the ecclesiastics and nobles who surrounded him to take no part in the impending fight.

At the same time the ruler, conscious that military command gives great power to its holder, frequently appoints as army leader his son or other near relative, thus trying to prevent the usurpation so apt to occur (as, to add another instance, it occurred among the Hebrews, whose throne was several times seized by captains of the host). The *Iliad* shows that it was usual for a Greek king to delegate to his heir the duty of commanding his troops. In Merovingian times kings' sons frequently led their fathers' armies, and of the Carolingians we read that while the king commanded the main levy, "over other armies his sons were placed, and to them the business of commanding was afterwards increasingly transferred" [Waitz, G. 1860–61, IV, 522]. It was thus in ancient Japan. When the emperor did not himself command his troops, "this charge was only committed to members of the Imperial house," and "the power thus remained with the sovereign" [Adams 1874–75, I, 15]. In ancient Peru there was a like alternative. "The army was put under the direction of some experienced chief of the royal blood, or, more frequently, headed by the Inca in person" [Prescott 1847, I, 35].

The widening civil functions of the political head obviously prompt this delegation of military functions. But while the discharge of both becomes increasingly difficult as the nation enlarges, and while the attempt to discharge both is dangerous, there is also danger in doing either by deputy. At the same time that there is risk in giving supreme command of a distant army to a general, there is also risk in going with the army and leaving the government in the hands of a vice-regent; and the catastrophes from the one or the other cause, which, in spite of precautions have taken place, show us alike that there is, during social evolution, an inevitable tendency to the differentiation of the military headship from the political headship, but that this differentiation can become permanent only under certain conditions.

The general fact would appear to be that while militant activity is great, and the whole society has the organization appropriate to it, the state of equilibrium is one in which the political head continues to be also the militant head; that in proportion as there grows up, along with industrial life, a civil administration distinguishable from the military administration, the political head tends to become increasingly civil in his functions and to delegate, now occasionally, now generally, his militant functions; that if there is a return to great militant activity, with consequent reversion to militant structure, there is liable to occur a reestablishment of the primitive type of headship by usurpation on the part of the successful general — either practical usurpation, where the king is too sacred to be displaced, or complete usurpation where he is not too sacred — but that where, along with decreasing militancy, there goes increasing civil life and administration, headship of the army becomes permanently differentiated from political headship, and subordinated to it.

While, in the course of social evolution, there has been going on this

separation of the fighting body from the community at large, this diminu-
tion in its relative mass, and this establishment of a distinct headship to
it, there has been going on an internal organization of it.

The fighting body is at first wholly without structure. Among savages
a battle is a number of single combats, the chief, if there is one, being but
the warrior of most mark, who fights like the rest. Through long stages
this disunited action continues. The *Iliad* tells of little more than the personal encounters of heroes, which were doubtless multiplied in detail by
their unmentioned followers, and after the decay of that higher military
organization which accompanied Greek and Roman civilization, this
chaotic kind of fighting recurred throughout medieval Europe. During
the early feudal period everything turned on the prowess of individuals.
War, says Gautier, consisted of "bloody duels" [ref. lost]; and even much
later the idea of personal action dominated over that of combined action.
But along with political progress, the subjection of individuals to their
chief is increasingly shown by fulfilling his commands in battle. Action in
the field becomes in a higher degree concerted by the absorption of their
wills in his will.

A like change presently shows itself on a larger scale. While the members of each component group have their actions more and more combined, the groups themselves, of which an army is composed, pass from
disunited action to united action. When small societies are compounded
into a larger one, their joint body of warriors at first consists of the tribal
clusters and family clusters assembled together but retaining their respective individualities. The head of each Hottentot kraal "has the command, under the chief of his nation, of the troops furnished out by his
kraal" [Kolb 1731, I, 85]. Similarly, the Malagasy "kept their own respective clans, and every clan had its own leader" [Ellis 1838, II, 253]. Among
the Chibchas, "each cazique and tribe came with different signs on their
tents, fitted out with the mantles by which they distinguished themselves
from each other" [Simón 1830, p. 269]. A kindred arrangement existed in
early Roman times: the city army was "distributed into tribes, curiae, and
families" [Fustel de Coulanges 1864, p. 158]. It was so, too, with the
Germanic peoples, who, in the field, "arranged themselves, when not
otherwise tied, in families and affinities" [Stubbs 1880, I, 34], or, as is said
by Kemble of our ancestors in old English times, "each kindred was drawn
up under an officer of its own lineage and appointment, and the several
members of the family served together" [1876, I, 69]. This organization,
or lack of organization, continued throughout the feudal period. In France
in the 14th century the army was a "horde of independent chiefs, each
with his own following, each doing his own will" [Kitchin 1873–77, I, 399],

and, according to Froissart [1839, I, 168], the different groups "were so ill-formed" that they did not always know of a discomfiture of the main body.

Besides that increased subordination of local heads to the general head which accompanies political integration and which must of course precede a more centralized and combined mode of military action, two special causes may be recognized as preparing the way for it.

One of these is unlikeness of kinds in the arms used. Sometimes the cooperating tribes, having habituated themselves to different weapons, come to battle already marked off from one another. In such cases the divisions by weapons correspond with the tribal divisions, as seems to have been to some extent the case with the Hebrews, among whom the men of Benjamin, of Gad, and of Judah, were partially thus distinguished. But, usually, the unlikenesses of arms consequent on unlikenesses of rank initiate these military divisions which tend to traverse the divisions arising from tribal organization. The army of the ancient Egyptians included bodies of charioteers, of cavalry, and of foot, and the respective accouterments of men forming these bodies, differing in their costliness, implied differences of social position. The like may be said of the Assyrians. Similarly, the *Iliad* shows us among the early Greeks a state in which the contrasts in weapons due to contrasts in wealth had not yet resulted in differently armed bodies, such as are formed at later stages with decreasing regard for tribal or local divisions. And it was so in Western Europe during times when each feudal superior led his own knights and his followers of inferior grades and weapons. Though within each group there were men differing alike in their rank and in their arms, yet what we may call the vertical divisions between groups were not traversed by those horizontal divisions throughout the whole army which unite all who are similarly armed.

This wider segregation it is, however, which we observe taking place with the advance of military organization. The supremacy acquired by the Spartans was largely due to the fact that Lycurgus "established military divisions quite distinct from the civil divisions, whereas in the other states of Greece, until a period much later . . . the two were confounded — the hoplites or horsemen of the same tribe or ward being marshalled together on the field of battle" [Grote 1846–56, p. ref. lost]. With the progress of the Roman arms there occurred kindred changes. The divisions came to be related less to rank as dependent on tribal organization, and more to social position as determined by property, so that the kinds of arms to be borne and the services to be rendered were regulated by the sizes of estates, with the result of "merging all distinctions of a gentile and local nature in the one common levy of the community." In the field, divisions so established stood thus:

> The four first ranks of each phalanx were formed of the full-armed hoplites of the first class, the holders of an entire hide [?]; in the fifth and sixth were placed the less completely equipped farmers of the second 'and third class; the two last classes were annexed as rear ranks to the phalanx [Mommsen 1862, I, 98–9].

And though political distinctions of clan origin were not thus directly disregarded in the cavalry, yet they were indirectly interfered with by the addition of a larger troop of non-burgess cavalry. That a system of divisions which tends to obliterate those of rank and locality has been reproduced during the redevelopment of military organizations in modern times is a familiar fact.

A concomitant cause of this change has all along been that interfusion of the gentile and tribal groups entailed by aggregation of large numbers. As before pointed out, the Cleisthenian reorganization in Attica and the Servian reorganization in Rome were largely determined by the impracticability of maintaining the correspondence between tribal divisions and military obligations, and a redistribution of military obligations naturally proceeded on a numerical basis. By various peoples, we find this step in organization taken for civil purposes or military purposes, or both. To cases named . . . may be added that of the Hebrews, who were grouped into tens, fifties, hundreds, and thousands. Even the barbarous Araucanians divided themselves into regiments of a thousand, subdivided into companies of a hundred. Evidently numerical grouping conspires with classing by arms to obliterate the primitive divisions.

This transition from the state of incoherent clusters, each having its own rude organization, to the state of a coherent whole held together by an elaborate organization running throughout it, of course implies a concomitant progress in the centralization of command. As the primitive horde becomes more efficient for war in proportion as its members grow obedient to the orders of its chief, so the army, formed of aggregated hordes, becomes more efficient in proportion as the chiefs of the hordes fall under the power of one supreme chief. And the above-described transition from aggregated tribal and local groups to an army formed of regular divisions and subdivisions goes along with the development of grades of commanders, successively subordinated one to another. A controlling system of this kind is developed by the uncivilized where considerable military efficiency has been reached, as at present among the Araucanians, the Zulus, [and] the Uganda people, who have severally three grades of officers; as in the past among the ancient Peruvians and ancient Mexicans, who had respectively several grades, and as also among the ancient Hebrews.

One further general change has to be noticed — the change from a state in which the army now assembles and now disperses as required, to a state in which it becomes permanently established.

While, as among savages, the male adults are all warriors, the fighting body existing in its combined form only during war, becomes during peace a dispersed body carrying on in parties or separately, hunting and other occupations; similarly, as we have seen, during early stages of settled life the armed freemen, owning land jointly or separately, all having to serve as soldiers when called on, return to their farming when war is over; there is no standing army. But though after the compounding of small societies into larger ones by war, and the rise of a central power, a kindred system long continues, there come the beginnings of another system. Of course, irrespective of form of government, frequent wars generate permanent military forces, as they did in early times among the Spartans, as later among the Athenians, and as among the Romans, when extension of territory brought frequent needs for repressing rebellions.

Recognizing these cases, we may pass to the more usual cases in which a permanent military force originates from the body of armed attendants surrounding the ruler. Early stages show us this nucleus. In Tahiti the king or chief had warriors among his attendants, and the king of Ashanti has a bodyguard clad in skins of wild beasts — leopards, panthers, etc. As was pointed out when tracing the process of political differentiation, there tend everywhere to gather round a predominant chieftain, refugees and others who exchange armed service for support and protection, and so enable the predominant chieftain to become more predominant. Hence the *comites* attached to the *princeps* in the early German community, the huscarlas or housecarls surrounding old English kings, and the antrustions of the Merovingian rulers. These armed followers displayed in little the characters of a standing army, not simply as being permanently united, but also as being severally bound to their prince or lord by relations of personal fealty, and as being subject to internal government under a code of martial law, apart from the government of the freemen, as was especially shown in the large assemblage of them, amounting to 6,000, which was formed by Cnut.

In this last case we see how small bodyguards, growing as the conquering chief or king draws to his standard adventurers, fugitive criminals, men who have fled from injustice, etc., pass unobtrusively into troops of soldiers who fight for pay. The employment of mercenaries goes back to the earliest times, being traceable in the records of the Egyptians at all periods, and it continues to reappear under certain conditions, a primary condition being that the ruler shall have acquired a considerable revenue. Whether of home origin or foreign origin, these large bodies of professional soldiers can be maintained only by large pecuniary means, and, ordinarily, possession of these means goes along with such power as enables the king to exact dues and fines. In early stages the members of the fighting body, when summoned for service, have severally to provide themselves not only with their appropriate arms, but also with the needful supplies of all kinds, there being, while political organization is little developed, neither the resources nor the administrative machinery required for another system. But the economic resistance to militant action, which, as we have seen, increases as agricultural life spreads, leading to occasional non-attendance, to confiscations, to heavy fines in place of confiscations, then to fixed money payments in place of personal services, results in the growth of a revenue which serves to pay professional soldiers in place of the vassals who have compounded. And it then becomes possible, instead of hiring many such substitutes for short times, to hire a smaller number continuously — so adding to the original nucleus of a permanent armed force. Every further increase of royal power, increasing the ability to raise money, furthers this differentiation. As Ranke remarks of France, "standing armies, imposts, and loans, all originated together" [1852, I, 83].

Of course the primitive military obligation falling on all freemen long continues to be shown in modified ways. Among ourselves, for instance, there were the various laws under which men were bound, according to their incomes to have in readiness specified supplies of horses, weapons, and accouterments for themselves and others when demanded. Afterwards came the militia laws, under which there fell on men in proportion to their means, the obligations to provide duly armed horse soldiers or foot soldiers, personally or by substitute, to be called out for exercise at specified intervals for specified numbers of days, and to be provided with subsistence. There may be instanced, again, such laws as those under which in France, in the 15th century, a corps of horsemen was formed by requiring all the parishes to furnish one each. And there are the various more modern forms of conscription, used now to raise temporary forces and now to maintain a permanent army. Everywhere, indeed, freemen remain potential soldiers when not actual soldiers.

Summary

Setting out with that undifferentiated state of the body politic in which the army is co-extensive with the adult male population, we thus observe several ways in which there goes on the evolution which makes it a specialized part.

There is the restriction in relative mass, which, first seen in the growth of a slave population engaged in work instead of war, becomes more decided as a settled agricultural life occupies freemen and increases the obstacles to military service. There is, again, the restriction caused by that growing costliness of the individual soldier accompanying the development of arms, accouterments, and ancillary appliances of warfare. And there is the yet additional restriction caused by the intenser strain which military action puts on the resources of a nation in proportion as it is carried on at a greater distance.

With separation of the fighting body from the body politic at large there very generally goes acquirement of a separate head. Active militancy ever tends to maintain union of civil rule with military rule, and often causes re-union of them where they have become separate; but with the primary differentiation of civil from military structures is commonly associated a tendency to the rise of distinct controlling centers for them. This tendency, often defeated by usurpation where wars are frequent, takes effect under opposite conditions and then produces a military head subordinate to the civil head.

While the whole society is being developed by differentiation of the army from the rest, there goes on a development within the army itself. As in the primitive horde the progress is from the uncombined fighting of individuals to combined fighting under direction of a chief, so on a larger scale, when small societies are united into great ones, the progress is from the independent fighting of tribal and local groups to fighting under direction of a general commander. And to effect a centralized control there arises a graduated system of officers, replacing the set of primitive heads of groups, and a system of divisions which, traversing the original divisions of groups, establish regularly organized masses having different functions.

With developed structure of the fighting body comes permanence of it. While, as in early times, men are gathered together for small wars and then again dispersed, efficient organization of them is impracticable. It becomes practicable only among men who are constantly kept together by wars or preparations for wars, and bodies of such men growing up, replace the temporarily summoned bodies.

Lastly, we must not omit to note that while the army becomes otherwise distinguished, it becomes distinguished by retaining and elaborating the system of status, though in the rest of the community, as it advances, the system of contract is spreading and growing definite. Compulsory cooperation continues to be the principle of the military part, however widely the principle of voluntary cooperation comes into play throughout the civil part.

CHAPTER 17

JUDICIAL AND EXECUTIVE SYSTEMS

That we may be prepared for recognizing the primitive identity of military institutions with institutions for administering justice, let us observe how close is the kinship between the modes of dealing with external aggression and internal aggression respectively.

We have the facts, already more than once emphasized, that at first the responsibilities of communities to one another are paralleled by the responsibilities to one another of family groups within each community, and that the kindred claims are enforced in kindred ways. Various savage tribes show us that, originally, external war has to effect an equalization of injuries, either directly in kind or indirectly by compensations. Among the Chinooks, "has the one party a larger number of dead than the other, indemnification must be made by the latter, or the war is continued" [Waitz, T. 1859–72, III, 338], and among the Arabs "when peace is to be made, both parties count up their dead, and the usual blood money is paid for excess on either side" [Burton, R. 1855–56, III, 47]. By which instances we are shown that in the wars between tribes, as in the family feuds of early times, a death must be balanced by a death, or else must be compounded for, as it once was in Germany and in England, by specified numbers of sheep and cattle, or by money.

Not only are the wars which societies carry on to effect the righting of alleged wrongs thus paralleled by family feuds in the respect that for retaliation in kind there may be substituted a penalty adjudged by usage or authority, but they are paralleled by feuds between individuals in the like respect. From the first stage in which each man avenges himself by force on a transgressing neighbor, as the whole community does on a transgressing community, the transition is to a stage in which he has the alternative of demanding justice at the hands of the ruler. We see this beginning in such places as the Hawaiian Islands, where an injured person who is too weak to retaliate appeals to the king or principal chief, and in quite advanced stages, option between the two methods of obtaining redress survives.

The feeling shown down to the 13th century by Italian nobles, who "regarded it as disgraceful to submit to laws rather than do themselves justice by force of arms" [Sismondi 1832, p. 90], is traceable throughout the history of Europe in the slow yielding of private rectification of wrongs to public arbitration. "A capitulary of Charles the Bald bids them [the freemen] go to court armed as for war, for they might have to fight for their jurisdiction" [Maine 1881, p. 614], and our own history furnishes an interesting example in the early form of an action for recovering land: the "grand assize" which tried the cause originally consisted of knights armed with swords [Reeves 1869, I, 153–4]. Again we have evidence in such facts as that in the 12th century in France legal decisions were so little regarded that trials often issued in duels. Further proof is yielded by such facts as that judicial duels (which were the authorized substitutes for private wars between families) continued in France down to the close of the 14th century; that in England, in 1768, a legislative proposal to abolish trial by battle was so strongly opposed that the measure was dropped, and that the option of such trial was not disallowed till 1819.

We may observe, also, that this self-protection gradually gives place to protection by the state only under stress of public needs — especially need for military efficiency. Edicts of Charlemagne and of Charles the Bald, seeking to stop the disorders consequent on private wars by insisting on appeals to the ordained authorities and threatening punishment of those who disobeyed, sufficiently imply the motive, and this motive was definitely shown in the feudal period in France by an ordinance of 1296, which "prohibits private wars and judicial duels so long as the king is engaged in war" [Guizot 1856, p. ref. lost].

Once more the militant nature of legal protection is seen in the fact that, as at first, so now, it is a replacing of individual armed force by the armed force of the state — always in reserve if not exercised. "The sword of justice" is a phrase sufficiently indicating the truth that action against the public enemy and action against the private enemy are in the last resort the same.

Thus recognizing the original identity of the functions, we shall be prepared for recognizing the original identity of the structures by which they are carried on. For that primitive gathering of armed men which, as we have seen, is at once the council of war and the political assembly, is at the same time the judicial body.

Of existing savages the Hottentots show this. The court of justice "consists of the captain and all the men of the kraal. . . . 'Tis held in the open fields, the men squatting in a circle. . . . All matters are determined by a majority." . . . If the prisoner is "convicted, and the court adjudges him worthy of death, sentence is executed upon the spot." The captain is chief executioner, striking the first blow, and is followed up by others [Kolb 1731, I, 294–6]. The records of various historic peoples yield evidence of kindred meaning. Taking first the Greeks in Homeric days, we read that "sometimes the king separately, sometimes the kings or chiefs or Gerontes, in the plural number, are named as deciding disputes and awarding satisfaction to complainants; always however in public, in the midst of the assembled agora," in which the popular sympathies were expressed, the meeting thus described being the same with that in which questions of war and peace were debated [Grote 1846–56, II, 99–100].

That in its early form the Roman gathering of "spearmen," asked by the king to say "yes" or "no" to a proposed military expedition or to some state measure, also expressed its opinion concerning criminal charges publicly judged, is implied by the fact that "the king could not grant a pardon, for that privilege was vested in the community alone" [Mommsen 1862, I, 159]. Describing the gatherings of the primitive Germans, Tacitus says:

> The multitude sits armed in such order as it thinks good . . . It is lawful also in the Assembly to bring matters for trial and to bring charges of capital crimes . . . In the same assembly chiefs are chosen to administer justice throughout the districts and villages. Each chief in so doing has a hundred companions of the commons assigned to him, to strengthen at once his judgment and his dignity [1823, Chs. 11, 12].

A kindred arrangement is ascribed by Lelevel to the Poles in early times, and to the Slavs at large. Among the Danes, too, "in all secular affairs, justice was administered by the popular tribunal of the Lands-Ting for each province, and by the Herreds-Ting for the smaller districts or subdivisions" [Crichton and Wheaton 1838, I, 263]. Concerning the Irish in past times, Prof. Leslie quotes Spenser to the effect that it was their usage "to make great assemblies together upon a rath or hill, there to parley about matters and wrongs between township and township, or one private person and another" [1875, p. 312]. And then there comes the illustration furnished by old English times. The local moots of various kinds had judicial functions, and the witenagemot sometimes acted as a high court of justice.

Interesting evidence that the original military assembly was at the same time the original judicial assembly is supplied by the early practice of punishing freemen for non-attendance. Discharge of military obligation being imperative, the fining of those who did not come to the armed gathering naturally followed, and fining for absence having become the usage, survived when, as for judicial purposes, the need for the presence of all was not imperative. Thence the interpretation of the fact that non-attendance at the hundred-court was thus punishable.

In this connection it may be added that in some cases where the primitive form continued there was manifested an incipient differentiation between the military assembly and the judicial assembly. In the Carolingian period judicial assemblies began to be held under cover, and freemen were forbidden to bring their arms. As was pointed out, . . . among the Scandinavians no one was allowed to come armed when the meeting was for judicial purposes. And since we also read that in Iceland it was disreputable (not punishable) for a freeman to be absent from the annual gathering, the implication is that the imperativeness of attendance diminished with the growing predominance of civil functions.

The judicial body being at first identical with the politico-military body, has necessarily the same triune structure, and we have now to observe the different forms it assumes according to the respective developments of its three components. We may expect to find kinship between these forms and the concomitant political forms.

Where, with development of militant organization, the power of the king has become greatly predominant over that of the chiefs and over that of the people, his supremacy is shown by his judicial absoluteness as well as by his absoluteness in political and military affairs. Such shares as the elders and the multitude originally had in trying causes almost or quite disappear. But though in these cases the authority of the king as judge is unqualified by that of his head men and his other subjects, there habitually survive traces of the primitive arrangement. For habitually his decisions are given in public and in the open air. Petitioners for justice bring their cases before him when he makes his appearance out of doors, surrounded by his attendants and by a crowd of spectators, as we have seen . . . that they do down to the present day in Kashmir. By the Hebrew rulers judicial sittings were held "in the gates" — the usual meeting-places of Eastern peoples [Cook 1871–81, Deut. XXI, 19]. Among the early Romans the king administered justice "in the place of public assembly, sitting on a 'chariot seat'" [Mommsen 1862, I, 158].

Mr. Gomme's *Primitive Folk-Moots* contains sundry illustrations showing that among the Germans in old times the Königs-stuhl, or king's judgment seat, was on the green sward, that in other cases the stone steps at the town gates constituted the seat before which causes were heard by him, and that again, in early French usage, trials often took place under trees. According to Joinville this practice long continued in France.

> Many a time did it happen that, in summer, he [Louis IX] would go and sit in the forest of Vincennes after mass, and would rest against an oak, and make us sit round him . . . he asked them with his own mouth, 'Is there any one who has a suit?' . . . I have seen him sometimes in summer come to hear his people's suits in the garden of Paris [1868, pp. 10–1].

And something similar occurred in Scotland under David I. All which customs among various peoples imply survival of the primitive judicial assembly, changed only by concentration in its head of power originally shared by the leading men and the undistinguished mass.

Where the second component of the triune political structure becomes supreme, this in its turn monopolizes judicial functions. Among the Spartans the oligarchic senate, and in a measure the smaller and chance-selected oligarchy constituted by the ephors, joined judicial functions with their political functions. Similarly in Athens under the aristocratic rule of the Eupatridae we find the Areopagus formed of its members discharging, either itself or through its nine chosen archons, the duties of deciding causes and executing decisions. In later days, again, we have the case of the Venetian council of ten. And then, certain incidents of the Middle Ages instructively show us one of the processes by which judicial power, as well as political power, passes from the hands of the freemen at large into the hands of a small and wealthier class. In the Carolingian period, besides the biannual meetings of the hundred-court, it was

> convoked at the *Graf's* will and pleasure, to try particular cases . . . in the one case, as in the other, non-attendance was punished . . . it was found that the *Grafs* used their right to summon these extraordinary Courts in excess, with a view, by repeated fines and amercements, to ruin the small freeholders, and thus to get their abodes into their own hands. Charlemagne introduced a radical law-reform . . . the great body of the freemen were released from attendance at the *Gebotene Dinge*, at which, from thenceforth, justice was to be administered under the presidency, *ex officio*, of the *Centenar*, by . . . permanent jurymen . . . chosen *de melioribus* — *i.e.*, from the more well-to-do freemen [Morier 1875, pp. 379–80; Sohm 1871, Sec. 6].

But in other cases, and especially where concentration in a town renders performance of judicial functions less burdensome, we see that along with retention or acquirement of predominant power by the third element in the triune political structure there goes exercise of judicial functions by it. The case of Athens after the replacing of oligarchic rule by democratic rule is, of course, the most familiar example of this. The Cleisthenian revolution made the annually appointed magistrates personally responsible to the people judicially assembled, and when, under Pericles, there were established the dicasteries or courts of paid jurors chosen by lot, the administration of justice was transferred almost wholly to the body of freemen, divided for convenience into committees.

Among the Frieslanders, who in early times were enabled by the nature of their habitat to maintain a free form of political organization, there continued the popular judicial assembly: "When the commons were summoned for any particular purpose, the assembly took the name of the Bodthing. The bodthing was called for the purpose of passing judgment in cases of urgent necessity" [ref. lost]. And M. de Laveleye, describing the Teutonic mark as still existing in Holland, "especially in Drenthe," a tract "surrounded on all sides by a marsh and bog" (again illustrating the physical conditions favorable to maintenance of primitive free institutions), goes on to say of the inhabitants as periodically assembled:

> They appeared in arms; and no one could absent himself, under pain of a fine. This assembly directed all the details as to the enjoyment of the common

property; appointed the works to be executed; imposed pecuniary penalties for the violation of rules, and nominated the officers charged with the executive power [1878, pp. 282–3]. . . .

A truth above implied and now to de definitely observed is that along with the consolidation of small societies into large ones effected by war there necessarily goes an increasing discharge of judicial functions by deputy.

As the primitive king is very generally himself both commander in chief and high priest, it is not unnatural that his delegated judicial functions should be fulfilled both by priests and soldiers. Moreover, since the consultative body, where it becomes established and separated from the multitude habitually includes members of both classes, such judicial powers as it exercises cannot at the outset be monopolized by members of either. And this participation is further seen to arise naturally on remembering how, as before shown, priests have in so many societies united military functions with clerical functions, and how, in other cases, becoming local rulers having the same tenures and obligations with purely military local rulers, they acquire in common with them, local powers of judgment and execution, as did medieval prelates. Whether the ecclesiastical class or the class of warrior-chiefs acquires judicial predominance probably depends mainly on the proportion between men's fealty to the successful soldier and their awe of the priest as a recipient of divine communications.

Among the Zulus, who, with an undeveloped mythology have no great deities and resulting organized priesthood, the king "shares his power with two soldiers of his choice. These two form the supreme judges of the country" [Arbousset and Daumas 1846, p. 140]. Similarly with the Eggarahs (Inland Negroes), whose fetish-men do not form an influential order, the first and second judges are "also commanders of the forces in times of war" [Allen and Thomson 1848, I, 326]. Passing to historic peoples, we have in Attica in Solon's time, the nine archons, who, while possessing a certain sacredness as belonging to the Eupatridae, united judicial with military functions — more especially the polemarch. In ancient Rome that kindred union of the two functions in the consuls, who called themselves indiscriminately, *praetores* or *judices*, naturally resulted from their inheritance of both functions from the king they replaced; but beyond this there is the fact that though the pontiffs had previously been judges in secular matters as well as in sacred matters, yet, after the establishment of the republic, the several orders of magistrates were selected from the non-clerical patricians, — the original soldier class.

And then throughout the Middle Ages in Europe we have the local military chiefs, whether holding positions like those of old English thanes or like those of feudal barons, acting as judges in their respective localities. Perhaps the clearest illustration is that furnished by Japan, where a long-continued and highly-developed military regime has been through-out associated with the monopoly of judicial functions by the military class, the apparent reason being that in presence of the god-descended Mikado, supreme in heaven as on earth, the indigenous Shinto religion never developed a divine ruler whose priests acquired, as his agents, an authority competing with terrestrial authority.

But mostly there is extensive delegation of judicial powers to the sacer-dotal class in early stages. We find it among existing uncivilized peoples, as the Kalmucks, whose priests, besides playing a predominant part in the greatest judicial council, exercise local jurisdiction: in the court of each subordinate chief, one of the high priests is head judge. Of extinct un-civilized or semi-civilized peoples may be named the Indians of Yucatan, by whom priests were appointed as judges in certain cases — judges who took part in the execution of their own sentences. Originally, if not after-wards, the giving of legal decisions was a priestly function in ancient Egypt, and that the priests were supreme judges among the Hebrews is a familiar fact, the Deuteronomic law condemning to death any one who disregarded their verdicts. In that general assembly of the ancient Germans which, as we have seen, exercised judicial powers, the priests were prominent, and, according to Tacitus, in war "none but the priests are permitted to judge offenders, to inflict bonds or stripes, so that chas-tisement appears not as an act of military discipline, but as the instiga-tion of the god whom they suppose present with warriors" [1823, Ch. VII].

In ancient Britain, too, according to Caesar, the Druids alone had authority to decide in both civil and criminal cases, and executed their own sentences, the penalty for disobedience to them being excommuni-cation. Grimm tells us that the like held among the Scandinavians. "In their judicial character the priests seemed to have exercised a good deal of control over the people. . . . In Iceland, even under Christianity, the judges retained the name and several of the functions of heathen goðar" [1880–83, I, 93]. And then we have the illustration furnished by that rise of ecclesiastics to the positions of judges throughout medieval Europe which accompanied belief in their divine authority. When, as during the Merovingian period and after, "the fear of hell, the desire of winning heaven," and other motives, prompted donations and bequests to the Church, till a large part of the landed property fell into its hands — when there came increasing numbers of clerical and semi-clerical dependents of the Church over whom bishops exercised judgment and discipline — when ecclesiastical influence so extended itself that, while priests became ex-empt from the control of laymen, lay authorities became subject to priests, there was established a judicial power of this divinely commissioned class to which even kings succumbed.

So was it in England too. Before the Conquest, bishops had become the assessors of ealdormen in the *scire-gemót*, and gave judgments on various civil matters. With that recrudescence of military organization which followed the Conquest came a limitation of their jurisdiction to spiritual offenses and causes concerning clerics. But in subsequent periods ecclesiastical tribunals, bringing under canon law numerous ordinary transgressions, usurped more and more the duties of secular judges, their excommunications being enforced by the temporal magistrates. Moreover, since prelates as feudal nobles were judges in their respective domains, and since many major and minor judicial offices in the central government were filled by prelates, it resulted that the administration of justice was largely, if not mainly, in the hands of priests.

This sharing of delegated judicial functions between the military class and the priestly class, with predominance here of the one and there of the other, naturally continued while there was no other class having wealth and influence. But with the increase of towns and the multiplication of traders, who accumulated riches and acquired education previously possessed only by ecclesiastics, judicial functions fell more and more into their hands. Sundry causes conspired to produce this transfer. One was lack of culture among the nobles, and their decreasing ability to administer laws, ever increasing in number and in complexity. Another was the political unfitness of ecclesiastics, who grew distasteful to rulers in proportion as they pushed further the powers and privileges which their supposed divine commission gave them. Details need not detain us. The only general fact needing to be emphasized is that this transfer ended in a differentiation of structures. For whereas in earlier stages judicial functions were discharged by men who were at the same time either soldiers or priests, they came now to be discharged by men exclusively devoted to them.

Simultaneously, the evolution of judicial systems is displayed in several other ways. One of them is the addition of judicial agents who are locomotive to the pre-existing stationary judicial agents.

During the early stages in which the ruler administers justice in person, he does this now in one place and now in another, according as affairs, military or judicial, carry him to this or that place in his kingdom. Societies of various types in various times yield evidence. Historians of ancient Peru tell us that "the Inca gave sentence according to the crime, for he alone was judge wheresoever he resided, and all persons wronged had recourse to him" [Herrera 1725–26, IV, 337]. Of the German emperor in the 12th century we read that "not only did he receive appeals, but his presence in any duchy or county suspended the functions of the local judges" [Dunham 1837, I, 120]. France in the 15th century supplies an instance. King Charles "spent two or three years in travelling up and down the kingdom . . . maintaining justice to the satisfaction of his subjects" [du Terrail 1848, pp. 70–1]. In Scotland something similar was done by David I, who "settled marches, forest rights, and rights of pasture," himself making the marks which recorded his decisions, or seeing them made [Innes 1872, p. 221]. In England, "Edgar and Canute had themselves made judicial circuits," and there is good evidence of such judicial travels in England up to the time of the Great Charter [Stubbs 1880, I, 443, 673]. Sir Henry Maine has quoted documents showing that King John, in common with earlier kings, moved about the country with great activity, and held his court wherever he might happen to be.

Of course with the progress of political integration and consequent growing power of the central ruler, there come more numerous cases in which appeal is made to him to rectify the wrongs committed by local rulers, and as state business at large augments and complicates, his inability to do this personally leads to doing it by deputy. In France, in Charlemagne's time, there were the "Missi Regii, who held assizes from place to place" [Hallam 1855, I, 239]. And then, not forgetting that during a subsequent period the chief heralds in royal state, as the king's representatives, made circuits to judge and punish transgressing nobles, we may pass to the fact that in the later feudal period, when the business of the king's court became too great, commissioners were sent into the provinces to judge particular cases in the king's name, a method which does not appear to have been there developed further. But in England, in Henry II's time, kindred causes prompted kindred steps which initiated a permanent system. Instead of listening to the increasing number of appeals made to his court personally or through his lieutenant the justiciar, the king commissioned his constable, chancellor, and co-justiciar to hear pleas in the different counties. Later, there came a larger number of these members of the central judicial court who made these judicial journeys, part of them being clerical and part military. And hence eventually arose the established circuits of judges who, like their prototypes, had to represent the king and exercise supreme authority.

It should be added that here again we meet with proofs that in the evolution of arrangements conducing to the maintenance of individual rights, the obligations are primary and the claims derived. For the business of these traveling judges, like the business of the king's court by which they were commissioned, was primarily fiscal and secondarily judicial. They were members of a central body that was at once Exchequer and *Curia Regis*, in which financial functions at first predominated, and they were sent into the provinces largely, if not primarily, for purposes of assessment, as instance the statement that in 1168 "the four Exchequer officers who assessed the aid *pur fille marier*, acted not only as taxers but as judges" [ref. lost]. In which facts we see harmony with those before given, showing that support of the ruling agency precedes obtainment of protection from it.

With that development of a central government which accompanies consolidation of small societies into a large one, and with the consequent increase of its business entailing delegation of functions, there goes, in the judicial organization as in the other organizations, a progressive differentiation. The evidence of this is extremely involved, both for the reason that in most cases indigenous judicial agencies have been subordinated but not destroyed by those which conquest has originated, and for the reason that kinds of power, as well as degrees of power, have become distinguished. A few leading traits only of the process can here be indicated.

The most marked differentiation, already partially implied, is that between the lay, the ecclesiastical, and the military tribunals. From those early stages in which the popular assembly, with its elders and chief, condemned military defaulters, decided on ecclesiastical questions, and gave judgments about offenses, there has gone on a divergence which, accompanied by disputes and struggles concerning jurisdiction, has parted ecclesiastical courts and courts martial from the courts administering justice in ordinary civil and criminal cases. Just recognizing these cardinal specializations, we may limit our attention to the further specializations which have taken place within the last of the three structures.

Originally the ruler, with or without the assent of the assembled people, not only decides, he executes his decisions, or sees them executed. For example, in Dahomey the king stands by, and if the deputed officer does not please him, takes the sword out of his hand and shows him how to cut off a head [ref. lost]. An account of death punishment among the Bedouins ends with the words — "the executioner being the sheikh himself" [Murray 1864, p. 9]. Our own early history affords traces of personal executive action by the king, for there came a time when he was interdicted from arresting anyone himself, and had thereafter to do it in all cases by deputy. And this interprets for us the familiar truth that, through his deputies the sheriffs, who are bound to act personally if they cannot themselves find deputies, the monarch continues to be theoretically the agent who carries the law into execution, a truth further implied by the fact that execution in criminal cases, nominally authorized by him though actually by his minister, is arrested if his assent is withheld by his minister. And these facts imply that a final power of judgment remains with the monarch, notwithstanding delegation of his judicial functions. How this happens we shall see on tracing the differentiation.

Naturally, when a ruler employs assistants to hear complaints and redress grievances, he does not give them absolute authority, but reserves the power of revising their decisions. We see this even in such rude

societies as that of the Hawaiian Islands, where one who is dissatisfied
with the decision of his chief may appeal to the governor, and from the
governor to the king, or as in ancient Mexico, where "none of the judges
were allowed to condemn to death without communicating with the
king, who had to pass the sentence" [Durán 1867–80, I, 216]. And the
principle holds where the political headship is compound instead of simple. "When the hegemony of Athens became, in fact, more and more a
dominion, the civic body of Attica claimed supreme judicial authority
over all the allies. The federal towns only retained their lower courts"
[Curtius 1868–73, II, 450]. Obviously by such changes are produced
unlikenesses of degree and differences of kind in the capacities of judicial
agencies. As political subordination spreads, the local assemblies which
originally judged and executed in cases of all kinds, lose part of their functions, now by restriction in range of jurisdiction, now by subjection of
their decisions to supervision, now by denial of executive power. To trace
up the process from early stages, as for instance from the stage in which
the old English tithing-moot discharged administrative, judicial, and executive functions, or from the stage in which the courts of feudal nobles
did the like, is here alike impracticable and unnecessary. Reference to
such remnants of power as vestries and manorial courts possess will sufficiently indicate the character of the change. But along with degradation
of the small and local judicial agencies goes development of the great and
central ones, and about this something must be said.

Returning to the time when the king with his servants and chief men,
surrounded by the people, administers justice in the open air, and passing to the time when his court, held more frequently under cover and
consequently with less of the popular element, still consists of king as
president and his household officers with other appointed magnates as
counsellors (who in fact constitute a small and permanent part of that
general consultative body occasionally summoned), we have to note two
causes which cooperate to produce a division of these remaining parts
of the original triune body — one cause being the needs of subjects, and
the other the desire of the king. So long as the king's court is held wherever
he happens to be, there is an extreme hindrance to the hearing of suits,
and much entailed loss of money and time to suitors. To remedy this
evil came, in our own case, the provision included in the Great Charter
that the common pleas should no longer follow the king's court, but be
held in some certain place. This place was fixed in the palace of Westminster. And then as Blackstone points out:

This precedent was soon after copied by King Philip the Fair in France, who
about the year 1302, fixed the parliament of Paris to abide constantly in that
metropolis; which before used to follow the person of the king wherever he
went . . . And thus also, in 1495, the Emperor Maximilian I. fixed the im-

perial chamber, which before always travelled with the court and household, to be constantly at Worms [1876, III, 41].

As a consequence of these changes it of course happens that suits of a certain kind come habitually to be decided without the king's presence; there results a permanent transfer of part of his judicial power.

Again, press of business or love of ease prompts the king himself to hand over such legal matters as are of little interest to him. Thus in France, while we read that Charles V, when regent, sat in his council to administer justice twice a week, and Charles VI once, we also read that in 1370 the king declared he would no longer try the smaller causes personally [Du Cange 1850, pp. 11–2]. Once initiated and growing into a usage, this judging by commission, becoming more frequent as affairs multiply, is presently otherwise furthered; there arises the doctrine that the king ought not, at any rate in certain cases, to join in judgment. Thus "at the trial of the duke of Brittany in 1378, the peers of France protested against the presence of the king" [Jourdan 1822–33, V, 346–7]. Again "at the trial of the Marquis of Saluces, under Francis I, that monarch was made to see that he could not sit" [Dareste de la Chavanne 1858, p. ref. lost]. When Louis XIII wished to be judge in the case of the Duke de la Valette, he was resisted by the judges, who said that it was without precedent. And in our own country there came a time when "James I was informed by the judges that he had the right to preside in the court, but not to express his opinion" [Fischel 1863, p. 238], a step towards that exclusion finally reached.

While the judicial business of the political head thus lapses into the hands of appointed agencies, these agencies themselves, severally parting with certain of their functions one to another, become specialized. Among ourselves, even before there took place the above-named separation of the permanently localized court of common pleas from the king's court which moved about with him, there had arisen within the king's court an incipient differentiation. Causes concerning revenue were dealt with in sittings distinguished from the general sittings of the king's court by being held in another room, and establishment of this custom produced a division. Adaptation of its parts to unlike ends led to divergence of them, until, out of the original *Curia Regis,* had come the court of exchequer and the court of common pleas, leaving behind the court of king's bench as a remnant of the original body. When the office of justiciar (who, representing the king in his absence, presided over these courts) was abolished, the parting of them became decided, and though, for a length of time, competition for fees led to trenching on one another's functions, yet, eventually, their functions became definitely marked off. . . .

In brief, then, we find proofs that, little trace as its structure now shows of such an origin, our complex judicial system, alike in its supreme central parts and in its various small local parts, has evolved by successive changes out of the primitive gathering of people, head men, and chief.

Were further details desirable, there might here be given an account of police systems, showing their evolution from the same primitive triune body whence originate the several organizations delineated in this and preceding chapters. As using force to subdue internal aggressors, police are like soldiers, who use force to subdue external aggressors, and the two functions, originally one, are not even now quite separated either in their natures or their agents. For besides being so armed that they are in some countries scarcely distinguishable from soldiers, and besides being subject to military discipline, the police are, in case of need, seconded by soldiers in the discharging of their duties. To indicate the primitive identity it will suffice to name two facts. During the Merovingian period in France, armed bands of serfs, attached to the king's household and to the households of dukes, were employed both as police and for garrison purposes, and in feudal England, the *posse comitatus*, consisting of all freemen between fifteen and sixty, under command of the sheriff, was the agent for preserving internal peace at the same time that it was available for repelling invasions, though not for foreign service — an incipient differentiation between the internal and external defenders which became in course of time more marked. Letting this brief indication suffice, it remains only to sum up the conclusions above reached.

Summary

Evidences of sundry kinds unite in showing that judicial action and military action, ordinarily having for their common end the rectification of real or alleged wrongs, are closely allied at the outset. The sword is the ultimate resort in either case, use of it being in the one case preceded by a war of words carried on before some authority whose aid is invoked, while in the other case it is not so preceded. As is said by Sir Henry Maine, "the fact seems to be that contention in Court takes the place of contention in arms, but only gradually takes its place" [1875, p. 289].

Thus near akin as the judicial and military actions originally are, they are naturally at first discharged by the same agency — the primitive triune body formed of chief, head men, and people. This which decides on affairs of war and settles questions of public policy also gives judgments concerning alleged wrongs of individuals and enforces its decisions.

According as the social activities develop one or other element of the primitive triune body, there results one or other form of agency for the administration of law. If continued militancy makes the ruling man all-powerful, he becomes absolute judicially as in other ways; the people lose all share in giving decisions, and the judgments of the chief men who surround him are overriden by his. If conditions favor the growth of the chief men into an oligarchy, the body they form becomes the agent for judging and punishing offenses as for other purposes, its acts being little or not at all qualified by the opinion of the mass. While if the surrounding circumstances and mode of life are such as to prevent supremacy of one man, or of the leading men, its primitive judicial power is preserved by the aggregate of freemen — or is regained by it where it re-acquires predominance. And where the powers of these three elements are mingled in the political organization, they are also mingled in the judicial organization.

In those cases, forming the great majority, in which habitual militancy entails subjection of the people, partial or complete, and in which, consequently, political power and judicial power come to be exercised exclusively by the several orders of chief men, the judicial organization which arises as the society enlarges and complicates is officered by the sacerdotal class, or the military class, or partly the one and partly the other, their respective shares being apparently dependent on the ratio between the degree of conscious subordination to the human ruler and the degree of conscious subordination to the divine ruler, whose will the priests are supposed to communicate. But with the progress of industrialism and the rise of a class which, acquiring property and knowledge, gains consequent influence, the judicial system comes to be largely, and at length chiefly, officered by men derived from this class, and these men become distinguished from their predecessors not only as being of other origin, but also as being exclusively devoted to judicial functions.

While there go on changes of this kind, there go on changes by which the originally simple and comparatively uniform judicial system is rendered increasingly complex. Where, as in ordinary cases, there has gone along with achievement of supremacy by the king a monopolizing of judicial authority by him, press of business presently obliges him to appoint others to try causes and give judgments, subject of course to his approval. Already his court, originally formed of himself, his chief men, and the surrounding people, has become supreme over courts constituted in analogous ways of local magnates and their inferiors — so initiating a differentiation. And now by delegating certain of his servants or assessors, at first with temporary commissions to hear appeals locally, and then as permanent itinerant judges, a further differentiation is produced. And to this are added yet further differentiations, kindred in nature, by which other assessors of his court are changed into the heads of specialized courts, which divide its business among them.

Though this particular course has been taken in but a single case, yet it serves to exemplify the general principle under which, in one way or other, there arises out of the primitive simple judicial body, a centralized and heterogeneous judicial organization.

CHAPTER 18

LAWS

. . . To recall vividly the truth set forth [earlier] . . . that the rudest men conform their lives to ancestral usages, I may name such further illustrations as that the Hawaiian Islanders had "a kind of traditionary code . . . followed by general consent" [Ellis 1826, p. 399], and that by the Bechuanas government is carried on according to "long-acknowledged customs" [ref. lost]. A more specific statement is that made by Mason concerning the Karens, among whom "the elders are the depositaries of the laws, both moral and political, both civil and criminal, and they give them as they receive them, and as they have been brought down from past generations" orally [1868, p. 131]. Here, however, we have chiefly to note that this government by custom persists through long stages of progress, and even still largely influences judicial administration. Instance the fact that as late as the 14th century in France an ordinance declared that "the whole kingdom is regulated by 'custom,' and it is as 'custom' that some of our subjects make use of the written law" [Koenigswarter 1851, p. 186]. Instance the fact that our own Common Law is mainly an embodiment of the "customs of the realm," which have gradually become established; its older part, nowhere existing in the shape of enactment, is to be learnt only from textbooks, and even parts, such as mercantile law, elaborated in modern times, are known only through reported judgments, given in conformity with usages proved to have been previously followed. Instance again the fact, no less significant, that at the present time custom perpetually reappears as a living supplementary factor, for it is only after judges' decisions have established precedents which pleaders afterwards quote, and subsequent judges follow, that the application of an act of parliament becomes settled. So that while in the course of civilization written law tends to replace traditional usage, the replacement never becomes complete.

And here we are again reminded that law, whether written or unwritten, formulates the rule of the dead over the living. In addition to that power which past generations exercise over present generations by transmitting their natures, bodily and mental, and in addition to the power they exercise over them by bequeathed private habits and modes of life, there is this power they exercise through these regulations for public conduct handed down orally or in writing. Among savages and in barbarous societies, the authority of laws thus derived is unqualified, and even in advanced stages of civilization, characterized by much modifying of old laws and making of new ones, conduct is controlled in a far greater degree by the body of inherited laws than by those laws which the living make. . . .

I wish to make it clear that when asking in any case — What is the Law? we are asking — What was the dictate of our forefathers? And my object in doing this is to prepare the way for showing that unconscious conformity to the dictates of the dead, thus shown, is, in early stages, joined with conscious conformity to their dictates. . . . There come methods by which the will of the ancestor, or the dead chief, or the derived deity, is sought; and the reply given, usually referring to a particular occasion, originates in some cases a precedent from which there results a law added to the body of laws the dead have transmitted.

The seeking of information and advice from ghosts takes here a supplicatory and there a coercive form. The Veddas, who ask the spirits of their ancestors for aid, believe that in dreams they tell them where to hunt; and then we read of the Scandinavian diviners that they "dragged the ghosts of the departed from their tombs and forced the dead to tell them what would happen" [Mallet 1847, p. 117]: cases which remind us that among the Hebrews, too, there were supernatural directions given in dreams as well as information derived from invoked spirits. . . .

Here, however, we are chiefly concerned with that more developed form of . . . guidance which results where the spirits of distinguished men, regarded with special fear and trust, become deities. Ancient Egyptian hieroglyphics reveal two stages of it. The "Instructions" recorded by King Rash'otephet are given by his father in a dream. "Son of the Sun Amenemhat — deceased: — He says in a dream — unto his son the Lord intact, — he says rising up like a god: — 'Listen to what I speak unto thee'" [Sayce, *et al.* 1873–81, II, 11]. And then another tablet narrates how Thothmes IV, travelling when a prince and taking his siesta in the shade of the Sphinx, was spoken to in a dream by that god, who said — "Look at me! . . . Answer me that you will do me what is in my heart" etc.; and when he ascended the throne Thothmes fulfilled the injunction [Sayce, *et al.* 1873–81, XII, 48]. Analogous stages were well exemplified among the ancient Peruvians. There is a tradition that Huayna Capac, wishing to marry his second sister, applied for assent to the dead body of his father, "but the dead body gave no answer, while fearful signs appeared in the heavens, portending blood" [Santa Cruz 1873, p. 107]. Moreover, . . . "the Inca gave them (the vassals) to understand that all he did with regard to them was by an order and revelation of his father, the Sun" [Garcilasso de la Vega 1869–71, Bk. I, ch. 23].

Turning to extant races, we see that in the Polynesian Islands, where the genesis of a pantheon by ancestor worship is variously exemplified,

divine direction is habitually sought through priests. Among the Tahitians, one "mode by which the god intimated his will" was to enter the
priest, who then "spoke as entirely under supernatural influence" [Ellis
1829, II, 235]. Mariner tells us that in Tonga, too, when the natives wished
to consult the gods, there was a ceremony of invocation, and the inspired
priest then uttered the divine command [1818, I, 105–8]. Similar beliefs
and usages are described by Turner as existing in Samoa. Passing to
another region, we find among the Todas of the Indian hills an appeal
for supernatural guidance in judicial matters.

> When any dispute arises respecting their wives or their buffaloes, it has to
> be decided by the priest, who affects to become possessed by the Bell-god, and
> . . . pronounces the deity's decision upon the point in dispute [Metz 1864,
> pp. 17–8].

These instances serve to introduce and interpret for us those which
the records of historic peoples yield. Taking first the Hebrews, we have
the familiar fact that the laws for general guidance were supposed to
be divinely communicated, and we have the further fact that special
directions were often sought. Through the priest who accompanied the
army, the commander "inquired of the Lord" about any military movement of importance and sometimes received very definite orders, as when,
before a battle with the Philistines, David is told to "fetch a compass
behind them, and come upon them over against the mulberry trees" [Cook
1871–81, 2 Sam. V, 22–25]. Sundry Aryan peoples furnish evidence. In
common with other Indian codes, the code of Manu, "according to Hindoo
mythology, is an emanation from the supreme God" [Maine 1861, p. 18].
So, too, was it with the Greeks. Not forgetting the tradition that by an
ancient Cretan king a body of laws was brought down from the mountain
where Jupiter was said to be buried, we may pass to the genesis of laws
from special divine commands, as implied in the Homeric poems. Speaking of these Grote says:

> The appropriate Greek word for human laws never occurs: amidst a very
> wavering phraseology, we can detect a gradual transition from the primitive
> idea of a personal goddess, Themis, attached to Zeus, first to his sentences or
> orders called Themistes, and next by a still farther remove to various estab-
> lished customs which those sentences were believed to satisfy — the authority
> of religion and that of custom coalescing into one indivisible obligation [1846–
> 56, II, 111–2].

Congruous in nature was the belief that "Lycurgus obtained not only
his own consecration to the office of legislator, but his laws themselves
from the mouth of the Delphic God" [Hermann 1836, p. 48]. To which
add that we have throughout later Greek times the obtainment of special
information and direction through oracles. Evidence that among the
Romans there had occurred a kindred process is supplied by the story

that the ancient laws were received by Numa from the goddess Egeria, and that Numa appointed augurs by whose interpretation of signs the will of the gods was to be ascertained. Even in the ninth century, under the Carolingians, there were brought before the nobles "articles of law named *capitula*, which the king himself had drawn up by the inspiration of God" [Hincmar 1884, pp. 7, 9].

Without following out the influence of like beliefs in later times, as seen in trial by ordeal and trial by judicial combat, in both of which God was supposed indirectly to give judgment, the above evidence makes it amply manifest that, in addition to those injunctions definitely expressed or embodied in usages tacitly accepted from seniors and through them from remote ancestors, there are further injunctions more consciously attributed to supernatural beings — either the ghosts of parents and chiefs who were personally known, or the ghosts of more ancient traditionally-known chiefs which have been magnified into gods. Whence it follows that originally, under both of its forms, law embodies the dictates of the dead to the living.

And here we are at once shown how it happens that throughout early stages of social evolution no distinction is made between sacred law and secular law. Obedience to established injunctions of whatever kind, originating in reverence for supposed supernatural beings of one or other order, it results that at first all these injunctions have the same species of authority.

The Egyptian wall sculptures, inscriptions, and papyri, everywhere expressing subordination of the present to the past, show us the universality of the religious sanction for rules of conduct. Of the Assyrians Layard says:

> The intimate connection between the public and private life of the Assyrians and their religion, is abundantly proved by the sculptures. . . . As among most ancient Eastern nations, not only all public and social duties, but even the commonest forms and customs, appear to have been more or less influenced by religion. . . . All his [the king's] acts, whether in war or peace, appear to have been connected with the national religion, and were believed to be under the special protection and superintendence of the deity [1849, II, 473–4].

That among the Hebrews there existed a like connection is conspicuously shown us in the Pentateuch, where, besides the commandments specially so-called, and besides religious ordinances regulating feasts and sacrifices, the doings of the priests, the purification by scapegoat, etc., there are numerous directions for daily conduct — directions concerning kinds of food and modes of cooking; directions for proper farming in respect of periodic fallows, not sowing mingled grain, etc.; directions for the management of those in bondage, male and female, and the payment of hired laborers; directions about trade transactions and the sales of lands and houses; along with sumptuary laws extending to the quality and fringes of garments and the shaping of beards — instances sufficiently showing that the rules of living, down even to small details, had a divine origin equally with the supreme laws of conduct. The like was true of the Aryans in early stages. The code of Manu was a kindred mixture of sacred and secular regulations — of moral dictates and rules for carrying on ordinary affairs. Says Tiele of the Greeks after the Doric migration: "No new political institutions, no fresh culture, no additional games, were established without the sanction of the Pythian oracle" [1877, p. 217]. . . .

Originating in this manner, law acquires stability. Possessing a supposed supernatural sanction, its rules have a rigidity enabling them to restrain men's actions in greater degrees than could any rules having an origin recognized as natural. They tend thus to produce settled social arrangements, both directly by their high authority, and indirectly by limiting the actions of the living ruler. As was pointed out [above] . . . , early governing agents, not daring to transgress inherited usages and regulations, are practically limited to interpreting and enforcing them, their legislative power being exercised only in respect of matters not already prescribed for. Thus of the ancient Egyptians we read: "It was not on his [the king's] own will that his occupations depended, but on those rules of duty and propriety which the wisdom of his ancestors had framed, with a just regard for the welfare of the king and of his people" [Wilkinson 1878, I, 164]. And how persistent is this authority of the sanctified past over the not-yet-sanctified present we see among ourselves in the fact that every legislator has to bind himself by oath to maintain certain political arrangements which our ancestors thought good for us.

While the unchangeableness of law, due to its supposed sacred origin, greatly conduces to social order during those early stages in which strong restraints are most needed, there of course results an unadaptiveness which impedes progress when there arise new conditions to be met. Hence come into use those "legal fictions" by the aid of which nominal obedience is reconciled with actual disobedience. Alike in Roman law and in English law, as pointed out by Sir Henry Maine, legal fictions have been the means of modifying statutes which were transmitted as immutable, and so fitting them to new requirements, thus uniting stability with that plasticity which allows of gradual transformation.

Such being the origin and nature of laws, it becomes manifest that the cardinal injunction must be obedience. Conformity to each particular direction presupposes allegiance to the authority giving it, and therefore the imperativeness of subordination to this authority is primary.

That direct acts of insubordination, shown in treason and rebellion, stand first in degree of criminality, evidently follows. This truth is seen at the present time in South Africa. "According to a horrible law of the Zulu despots, when a chief is put to death they exterminate also his subjects" [Arbousset and Daumas 1846, p. 161n.]. It was illustrated by the ancient Peruvians, among whom "a rebellious city or province was laid waste, and its inhabitants exterminated" [ref. lost], and again by the ancient Mexicans, by whom one guilty of treachery to the king "was put to death, with all his relations to the fourth degree" [Ternaux-Compans 1838, p. 78]. A like extension of punishment occurred in past times in Japan, where, when "the offence is committed against the state, punishment is inflicted upon the whole race of the offender" [ref. lost].

Of efforts thus wholly to extinguish families guilty of disloyalty, the Merovingians yielded an instance: king Guntchram swore that the children of a certain rebel should be destroyed up to the ninth generation [Gregory of Tours 1836–38, Bk. VII, ch. 21]. And these examples naturally recall those furnished by Hebrew traditions. When Abraham, treating Jahveh as a terrestrial superior (just as existing Bedouins regard as god the most powerful living ruler known to them), entered into a covenant under which, for territory given, he, Abraham, became a vassal, circumcision was the prescribed badge of subordination, and the sole capital offense named was neglect of circumcision, implying insubordination, Jahveh elsewhere announcing himself as "a jealous god," and threatening punishment "upon the children unto the third and fourth generation of them that hate me." And the truth thus variously illustrated, that during stages in which maintenance of authority is most imperative direct disloyalty is considered the blackest of crimes, we trace down through later stages in such facts as that, in feudal days, so long as the fealty of a vassal was duly manifested, crimes, often grave and numerous, were overlooked.

Less extreme in its flagitiousness than the direct disobedience implied by treason and rebellion is, of course, the indirect disobedience implied by breach of commands. This, however, where strong rule has been established, is regarded as a serious offense, quite apart from, and much exceeding, that which the forbidden act intrinsically involves. Its greater gravity was distinctly enunciated by the Peruvians, among whom, says Garcilasso, "the most common punishment was death, for they said that a culprit was not punished for the delinquencies he had committed, but for having broken the commandment of the Ynca, who was respected as God" [Garcilasso de la Vega 1869–71, Bk. II, ch. 12]. The like conception meets us in another country where the absolute ruler is regarded as divine. Sir R. Alcock quotes Thunberg to the effect that in Japan "most crimes are punished with death, a sentence which is inflicted with less regard to the magnitude of the crime than to the audacity of the attempt to transgress the hallowed laws of the empire" [1863, I, 63].

And then, beyond the criminality which disobeying the ruler involves, there is the criminality involved by damaging the ruler's property, where his subjects and their services belong wholly or partly to him. In the same way that maltreating a slave and thereby making him less valuable comes to be considered as an aggression on his owner, in the same way that even now among ourselves a father's ground for proceeding against a seducer is loss of his daughter's services, so, where the relation of people to monarch is servile, there arises the view that injury done by one person to another is injury done to the monarch's property. An extreme form of this view is alleged of Japan, where cutting and maiming of the king's dependents "becomes wounding the king, or regicide." And hence the general principle, traceable in European jurisprudence from early days, that a transgression of man against man is punishable mainly, or in large measure, as a transgression against the state. It was thus in ancient Rome: "every one convicted of having broken the public peace, expiated his offence with his life" [Mommsen 1862, I, 159]. An early embodiment of the principle occurs in the Salic law, under which "to the *wehrgeld* is added, in a great number of cases, . . . the *fred*, a sum paid to the king or magistrate, in reparation for the violation of public peace" [Guizot 1856, I, 464], and in later days the fine paid to the state absorbed the wergeld.

Our own history similarly shows us that, as authority extends and strengthens, the guilt of disregarding it takes precedence of intrinsic guilt. " 'The king's peace' was a privilege which attached to the sovereign's court and castle, but which he could confer on other places and persons, and which at once raised greatly the penalty of misdeeds committed in regard to them" [Innes 1860, p. 197]. Along with the growing check on the right of private revenge for wrongs — along with the increasing subordination of minor and local jurisdictions — along with that strengthening of a central authority which these changes imply, "offences against the law become offences against the king, and the crime of disobedience a crime of contempt to be expiated by a special sort of fine" [Stubbs 1880, I, 211]. And we may easily see how, where a ruler gains absolute power, and especially where he has the prestige of divine origin, the guilt of contempt comes to exceed the intrinsic guilt of the forbidden act.

A significant truth may be added. On remembering that Peru, and Japan till lately, above named as countries in which the crime of disobedience to the ruler was considered so great as practically to equalize the flagitiousness of all forbidden acts, had societies in which militant organization, carried to its extreme, assimilated the social government at large to the government of an army, we are reminded that even in societies like our own there is maintained in the army the doctrine that insubordination is the cardinal offense. Disobedience to orders is penal irrespective of the nature of the orders or the motive for the disobedience, and an act which, considered in itself, is quite innocent, may be visited with death if done in opposition to commands. . . .

What has been said in the foregoing sections brings out with clearness the truth that rules for the regulation of conduct have four sources. Even in early stages we see that beyond the inherited usages which have a quasi-religious sanction, and beyond the special injunctions of deceased leaders, which have a more distinct religious sanction, there is some, though a slight, amount of regulation derived from the will of the pre-dominant man, and there is also the effect, vague but influential, of the aggregate opinion. Not dwelling on the first of these, which is slowly modified by accretions derived from the others, it is observable that in the second we have the germ of the law afterwards distinguished as divine, that in the third we have the germ of the law which gets its sanction from allegiance to the living governor, and that in the fourth we have the germ of the law which eventually becomes recognized as expressing the public will.

Already I have sufficiently illustrated those kinds of laws which originate personally, as commands of a feared invisible ruler and a feared visible ruler. But before going further, it will be well to indicate more distinctly the kind of law which originates impersonally, from the prevailing sentiments and ideas, and which we find clearly shown in rude stages before the other two have become dominant. A few extracts will exhibit it. Schoolcraft says of the Chippewyans:

> Thus, though they have no regular government, as every man is lord in his own family, they are influenced more or less by certain principles which conduce to their general benefit [1853–56, V, 177].

Of the unorganized Shoshones Bancroft writes:

> Every man does as he likes. Private revenge, of course, occasionally overtakes the murderer, or, if the sympathies of the tribe be with the murdered man, he may possibly be publicly executed, but there are no fixed laws for such cases [1875–76, I, 435].

In like manner the same writer tells us of the Haidas that:

> Crimes have no punishment by law; murder is settled for with relatives of the victim, by death or by the payment of a large sum; and sometimes general or notorious offenders, especially medicine-men, are put to death by an agreement among leading men [Bancroft 1875–76, I, 168].

Even where government is considerably developed, public opinion continues to be an independent source of law. Ellis says that:

> In cases of theft in the Sandwich Islands, those who had been robbed retaliated upon the guilty party, by seizing whatever they could find; and this mode of obtaining redress was so supported by public opinion, and the latter, though it might be the stronger party, dare not offer resistance [1826, p. 400].

By which facts we are reminded that where central authority and administrative machinery are feeble, the laws thus informally established by aggregate feeling are enforced by making revenge for wrongs a socially imposed duty, while failure to revenge is made a disgrace, and a consequent danger. In ancient Scandinavia "a man's relations and friends who had not revenged his death, would instantly have lost that reputation which constituted their principal security" [ref. lost]. So that, obscured as this source of law becomes when the popular element in the triune political structure is entirely subordinated, yet it was originally conspicuous, and never ceases to exist. And now having noted the presence of this, along with the other mingled sources of law, let us observe how the several sources, along with their derived laws, gradually become distinguished.

Recalling the proofs above given that where there has been established a definite political authority, inherited from apotheosized chiefs and made strong by divine sanction, laws of all kinds have a religious character, we have first to note that a differentiation takes place between those regarded as sacred and those recognized as secular. An illustration of this advance is furnished us by the Greeks. Describing the state of things exhibited in the Homeric poems, Grote [1846–56, II, 107, 110] remarks that "there is no sense of obligation then existing, between man and man as such — and very little between each man and the entire community of which he is a member," while, at the same time, "the tie which binds a man to his father, his kinsman, his guest, or any special promisee towards whom he has taken the engagement of an oath, is conceived in conjunction with the idea of Zeus, as witness and guarantee:" allegiance to a divinity is the source of obligation. But in historical Athens "the great impersonal authority called 'The Laws' stood out separately, both as guide and sanction, distinct from religious duty or private sympathies." And at the same time there arose the distinction between breach of the sacred law and breach of the secular law: "the murderer came to be considered, first as having sinned against the gods, next as having deeply injured the society, and thus at once as requiring absolution and deserving punishment" [Grote 1846–56, II, 129].

A kindred differentiation early occurred in Rome. Though during the primitive period the head of the state, at once king and high priest, and in his latter capacity dressed as a god, was thus the mouthpiece of both sacred law and secular law, yet afterwards, with the separation of the ecclesiastical and political authorities, came a distinction between breaches of divine ordinances and breaches of human ordinances. In the words of Sir Henry Maine [1861, p. 372], there were

> laws punishing *sins*. There were also laws punishing *torts*. The conception of offence against God produced the first class of ordinances; the conception of offence against one's neighbour produced the second; but the idea of offence against the State or aggregate community did not at first produce a true criminal jurisprudence.

In explanation of the last statement it should, however, be added that since, during the regal period, according to Mommsen [1862, II, 130], "judicial procedure took the form of a public or a private process, according as the king interposed of his own motion, or only when appealed to by the injured party," and since "the former course was taken only in cases which involved a breach of the public peace," it must be inferred that when kingship ceased, there survived the distinction between transgression against the individual and transgression against the state, though the mode of dealing with this last had not, for a time, a definite form.

Again, even among the Hebrews, more persistently theocratic as their social system was, we see a considerable amount of this change at the same time that we are shown one of its causes. The Mishna contains many detailed civil laws, and these manifestly resulted from the growing complication of affairs. The instance is one showing us that primitive sacred commands, originating as they do in a compartively undeveloped state of society, fail to cover the cases which arise as institutions become involved. In respect of these there consequently grow up rules having a known human authority only. By accumulation of such rules is produced a body of human laws distinct from the divine laws, and the offense of disobeying the one becomes unlike the offenses of disobeying the other.

Though in Christianized Europe, throughout which the indigenous religions were superseded by an introduced religion, the differentiating process was interfered with, yet, on setting out from the stage at which this introduced religion had acquired that supreme authority proper to indigenous religions, we see that the subsequent changes were of like nature with those above described. Along with that mingling of structures shown in the ecclesiasticism of kings and the secularity of prelates, there went a mingling of political and religious legislation. Gaining supreme power, the Church interpreted sundry civil offenses as offenses against God, and even those which were left to be dealt with by the magistrate were considered as thus left by divine ordinance. But subsequent evolution brought about stages in which various transgressions, held to be committed against both sacred and secular law, were simultaneously expiated by religious penance and civil punishment, and there followed a separation which, leaving but a small remnant of ecclesiastical offenses, brought the rest into the category of offenses against the state and against individuals.

And this brings us to the differentiation of equal, if not greater, significance, between those laws which derive their obligation from the will of the governing agency, and those laws which derive their obligation from the consensus of individual interests — between those laws which, having as their direct end the maintenance of authority, only indirectly thereby conduce to social welfare, and those which, directly and irrespective of authority, conduce to social welfare, of which last, law, in its modern form, is substantially an elaboration. Already I have pointed out that the kind of law initiated by the consensus of individual interests precedes the kind of law initiated by political authority. Already I have said that though, as political authority develops, laws acquire the shape of commands, even to the extent that those original principles of social order tacitly recognized at the outset come to be regarded as obligatory only because personally enacted, yet that the obligation derived from the consensus of individual interests survives, if obscured. And here it remains to show that as the power of the political head declines — as industrialism fosters an increasingly free population — as the third element in the triune political structure, long subordinated, grows again predominant, there again grows predominant this primitive source of law — the consensus of individual interests.

We have further to note that in its redeveloped form, as in its original form, the kind of law hence arising has a character radically distinguishing it from the kinds of law thus far considered. Both the divine laws and the human laws which originate from personal authority have inequality as their common essential principle, while the laws which originate impersonally, in the consensus of individual interests, have equality as their essential principle. Evidence is furnished at the very outset. For what is this *lex talionis* which, in the rudest hordes of men, is not only recognized but enforced by general opinion? Obviously, as enjoining an equalization of injuries or losses, it tacitly assumes equality of claims among the individuals concerned. The principle of requiring "an eye for an eye and a tooth for a tooth" embodies the primitive idea of justice everywhere, the endeavor to effect an exact balance being sometimes quite curious. Thus we read in Arbousset and Daumas:

> A Basuto whose son had been wounded on the head with a staff, came to entreat me to deliver up the offender, — 'with the same staff and on the same spot where my son was beaten, will I give a blow on the head of the man who did it' [1846, p. 37].

A kindred effort to equalize in this literal way the offense and the expiation occurs in Abyssinia, where, when the murderer is given over to his victim's family, "the nearest of kin puts him to death with the same kind of weapon as that with which he had slain their relative" [Parkyns 1853, II, 204–5]. As the last case shows, this primitive procedure, when it does not assume the form of inflicting injury for injury between individuals, assumes the form of inflicting injury for injury between families or tribes, by taking life for life. With the instances given [above] . . . may be joined one from Sumatra.

> When in an affray [between families], there happen to be several persons killed on both sides, the business of justice is only to state the reciprocal losses, in the form of an account current, and order the balance to be discharged if the numbers be unequal [Marsden 1811, p. 249].

And then, from this rude justice which insists on a balancing of losses between families or tribes, it results that so long as their mutual injuries are equalized, it matters not whether the blamable persons are or are not those who suffer, and hence the system of vicarious punishment — hence the fact that vengeance is wreaked on any member of the transgressing family or tribe. Moreover, ramifying in these various ways, the principle applies where not life but property is concerned. Schoolcraft [1853–56, II, 185] tells us that among the Dakotas "injury to property is sometimes privately revenged by destroying other property in place thereof," and among the Araucanians families pillage one another for the purpose of making their losses alike.

The idea survives, though changed in form, when crimes come to be compounded for by gifts or payments. Very early we see arising the alternative between submitting to vengeance or making compensation. Kane says of certain North American races that "horses or other Indian valuables" were accepted in compensation for murder [1859, p. 115]. With the Iroquois "a present of white wampum," if accepted, condones the offense [Morgan 1851, p. 331]. Among the Araucanians, homicides "can screen themselves from punishment by a composition with the relations of the murdered" [Thompson, G. A. 1812, I, 405]. Recalling, as these few instances do, the kindred alternatives recognized throughout primitive Europe, they also make us aware of a significant difference. For with the rise of class distinctions in primitive Europe, the rates of compensation, equal among members of each class, had ceased to be equal between members of different classes. Along with the growth of personally derived law there had been a departure from the impersonally derived law as it originally existed.

But now the truth to be noted is that with the relative weakening of kingly or aristocratic authority and relative strengthening of popular authority there revives the partially suppressed kind of law derived from the consensus of individual interests, and the kind of law thus originating tends continually to replace all other law. For the chief business of courts of justice at present is to enforce, without respect of persons, the principle, recognized before governments arose, that all members of the community, however otherwise distinguished, shall be similarly dealt with when they aggress one upon another. Though the equalization of injuries by retaliation is no longer permitted, and though the government, reserving to itself the punishment of transgressors, does little to enforce restitution or compensation, yet, in pursuance of the doctrine that all men are equal before the law, it has the same punishment for transgressors of every class. And then in respect of unfulfilled contracts or disputed debts, from the important ones tried at assizes to the trivial ones settled in county courts, its aim is to maintain the rights and obligations of citizens without regard for wealth or rank.

Of course in our transition state the change is incomplete. But the sympathy with individual claims, and the consensus of individual interests accompanying it, lead to an increasing predominance of that kind of law which provides directly for social order, as distinguished from that kind of law which indirectly provides for social order by insisting on obedience to authority, divine or human. With decline of the regime of status and growth of the regime of contract, personally derived law more and more gives place to impersonally derived law, and this of necessity, since a formulated inequality is implied by the compulsory cooperation of the one, while, by the voluntary cooperation of the other, there is implied a formulated equality.

So that, having first differentiated from the laws of supposed divine origin, the laws of recognized human origin subsequently redifferentiate into those which ostensibly have the will of the ruling agency as their predominant sanction, and those which ostensibly have the aggregate of private interests as their predominant sanction, of which two the last tends, in the course of social evolution, more and more to absorb the first. Necessarily, however, while militancy continues, the absorption remains incomplete, since obedience to a ruling will continues to be in some cases necessary. . . .

Summary

Setting out with the truth, illustrated even in the very rudest tribes, that the ideas conveyed, sentiments inculcated, and usages taught to children by parents who themselves were similarly taught, eventuate in a rigid set of customs, we recognize the fact that at first, as to the last, law is mainly an embodiment of ancestral injunctions.

To the injunctions of the undistinguished dead, which, qualified by the public opinion of the living in cases not prescribed for, constitute the code of conduct before any political organization has arisen, there come to be added the injunctions of the distinguished dead, when there have arisen chiefs who, in some measure feared and obeyed during life, after death give origin to ghosts still more feared and obeyed. And when, during that compounding of societies effected by war, such chiefs develop into kings, their remembered commands and the commands supposed to be given by their ghosts become a sacred role of conduct, partly embodying and partly adding to the code pre-established by custom. The living ruler, able to legislate only in respect of matters unprovided for, is bound by these transmitted commands of the unknown and the known who have passed away, save only in cases where the living ruler is himself regarded as divine, in which cases his injunctions become laws having a like sacredness. Hence the trait common to societies in early stages, that the prescribed rules of conduct of whatever kind have a religious sanction. Sacrificial observances, public duties, moral injunctions, social ceremonies, habits of life, industrial regulations, and even modes of dressing, stand on the same footing.

Maintenance of the unchangeable rules of conduct thus originating, which is requisite for social stability during those stages in which the type of nature is yet but little fitted for harmonious social cooperation, presupposes implicit obedience, and hence disobedience becomes the blackest crime. Treason and rebellion, whether against the divine or the human ruler, bring penalties exceeding all others in severity. The breaking of a law is punished not because of the intrinsic criminality of the act committed, but because of the implied insubordination. And the disregard of governmental authority continues through subsequent stages to constitute, in legal theory, the primary element in a transgression.

In societies that become large and complex there arise forms of activity and intercourse not provided for in the sacred code, and in respect of these the ruler is free to make regulations. As such regulations accumulate there comes into existence a body of laws of known human origin, and though this acquires an authority due to reverence for the men who made it and the generations which approved it, yet it has not the sacredness of the god-descended body of laws: human law differentiates from divine law. But in societies which remain predominantly militant these two bodies of laws continue similar in the respect that they have a personally-derived authority. The avowed reason for obeying them is that they express the will of a divine ruler, or the will of a human ruler, or occasionally, the will of an irresponsible oligarchy.

But with the progress of industrialism and growth of a free population which gradually acquires political power the humanly derived law begins to subdivide, and that part which originates in the consensus of individual interests begins to dominate over the part which originates in the authority of the ruler. So long as the social type is one organized on the principle of compulsory cooperation, law, having to maintain this compulsory cooperation, must be primarily concerned in regulating status, maintaining inequality, enforcing authority, and can but secondarily consider the individual interests of those forming the mass. But in proportion as the principle of voluntary cooperation more and more characterizes the social type, fulfilment of contracts and implied assertion of equality in men's rights become the fundamental requirements, and the consensus of individual interests the chief source of law, such authority as law otherwise derived continues to have, being recognized as secondary, and insisted upon only because maintenance of law for its own sake indirectly furthers the general welfare. . . .

CHAPTER 19

PROPERTY

The fact referred to [earlier] . . . that even intelligent animals display a sense of proprietorship, negatives the belief propounded by some that individual property was not recognized by primitive men. When we see the claim to exclusive possession understood by a dog, so that he fights in defense of his master's clothes if left in charge of them, it becomes impossible to suppose that even in their lowest state men were devoid of those ideas and emotions which initiate private ownership. All that may be fairly assumed is that these ideas and sentiments were first less developed than they have since become.

It is true that in some extremely rude hordes rights of property are but little respected. Lichtenstein [1812–15, II, 194] tells us that among the Bushmen "the weaker, if he would preserve his own life, is obliged to resign to the stronger, his weapons, his wife, and even his children," and there are some degraded North American tribes in which there is no check on the more powerful who choose to take from the less powerful; their acts are held to be legitimized by success. But absence of the idea of property, and the accompanying sentiment, is no more implied by these forcible appropriations than it is implied by the forcible appropriation which a bigger schoolboy makes of the toy belonging to a less.

It is also true that even where force is not used, individual claims are in considerable degrees overridden or imperfectly maintained. We read of the Chippewyans that "Indian law requires the successful hunter to share the spoils of the chase with all present" [Bancroft 1875–76, I, 118], and Hillhouse says of the Arawaks that though individual property is "distinctly marked amongst them," "yet they are perpetually borrowing and lending, without the least care about payment" [1832, p. 231]. But such instances merely imply that private ownership is at first ill-defined, as we might expect a priori that it would be.

Evidently the thoughts and feelings which accompany the act of taking possession, as when an animal clutches its prey, and which at a higher stage of intelligence go along with the grasping of any article indirectly conducing to gratification, are the thoughts and feelings to which the theory of property does but give a precise shape. Evidently the use in legal documents of such expressions as "to have and to hold," and to be "seized" of a thing, as well as the survival up to comparatively late times of ceremonies in which a portion (rock or soil) of an estate bought, representing the whole, actually passed from hand to hand, point back to this primitive physical basis of ownership. Evidently the developed doctrine of property accompanying a social state in which men's acts have to be mutually restrained, is a doctrine which on the one hand asserts the freedom to take and to keep within specified limits, and denies it beyond those limits — gives positiveness to the claim while restricting it. And evidently the increasing definiteness thus given to rights of individual possession may be expected to show itself first where definition is relatively easy and afterwards where it is less easy. This we shall find that it does.

While in early stages it is difficult, not to say impossible, to establish and mark off individual claims to parts of the area wandered over in search of food, it is not difficult to mark off the claims to movable things and to habitations, and these claims we find habitually recognized. The following passage from Bancroft concerning certain North American savages well illustrates the distinction:

> Captain Cook found among the Ahts very 'strict notions of their having a right to the exclusive property of everything that their country produces,' so that they claimed pay for even wood, water, and grass. The limits of tribal property are very clearly defined, but individuals rarely claim any property in land. Houses belong to the men who combine to build them. Private wealth consists of boats and implements for obtaining food, domestic utensils, slaves, and blankets [1875–76, I, 191].

A like condition is shown us by the Comanches:

> They recognize no distinct right of *meum* and *tuum*, except to personal property; holding the territory they occupy, and the game that depastures upon it, as common to all the tribe: the latter is appropriated only by capture [Schoolcraft 1853–56, I, 232].

And the fact that among these Comanches, as among other peoples, "prisoners of war belong to the captors, and may be sold or released at their will," further shows that the right of property is asserted where it is easily defined. Of the Brazilian Indians, again, von Martius tells us that

> Huts and utensils are considered as private property; but even with regard to them certain ideas of common possession prevail. The same hut is often occupied by more families than one; and many utensils are the joint property of all the occupants. Scarcely anything is considered strictly as the property of an individual except his arms, accoutrements, pipe, and hammock [1832, pp. 195–6].

Dr. Rink's account of the Eskimos shows that among them, too, while there is joint ownership of houses made jointly by the families inhabiting them, there is separate ownership of weapons, fishing boats, tools, etc. [1877]. Thus it is made manifest that private right, completely recognized where recognition of it is easy, is partially recognized where partial recognition only is possible — where the private rights of companions are entangled with it. Instances of other kinds equally prove that among savages claims to possession are habitually marked off when practicable; if not fully, yet partially. Of the Chippewyans, "who have no regular government" to make laws or arbitrate, we yet read that

> In the former instance [when game is taken in inclosures by a hunting party], the game is divided among those who had been engaged in the pursuit of it. In the latter [when taken in private traps] it is considered as private property; nevertheless, any unsuccessful hunter passing by, may take a deer so caught, leaving the head, skin, and saddle, for the owner [Schoolcraft 1853–56, V, 177].

In cases still more unlike, but similar in the respect that there exists an obvious connection between labor expended and benefit achieved, rude peoples re-illustrate this same individualization of property. Burckhardt tells us of the Bedouins that wells "are exclusive property, either of a whole tribe, or of individuals whose ancestors dug the wells" [1830, p. 130].

Taken together such facts make it indisputable that in early stages private appropriation, carried to a considerable extent, is not carried further because circumstances render extension of it impracticable.

Recognition of this truth at once opens the way to explanation of primitive landownership, and elucidates the genesis of those communal and family tenures which have prevailed so widely.

While subsistence on wild food continues, the wandering horde inhabiting a given area must continue to make joint use of the area, both because no claim can be shown by any member to any portion, and because the marking out of small divisions, if sharing were agreed upon, would be impracticable. Where pastoral life has arisen, ability to drive herds hither and thither within the occupied region is necessary. In the absence of cultivation, cattle and their owners could not survive were each owner restricted to one spot: there is nothing feasible but united possession of a wide tract. And when there comes a transition to the agricultural stage, either directly from the hunting stage or indirectly through the pastoral stage, several causes conspire to prevent or to check the growth of private landownership.

There is first the traditional usage. Joint ownership continues after circumstances no longer render it imperative because departure from the sacred example of forefathers is resisted. Sometimes the resistance is insuperable, as with the Rechabites and the people of Petra, who by their vow "were not allowed to possess either vineyards or cornfields or houses" [Ewald 1878–86, IV, 79–80], but were bound "to continue the nomadic life" [Kuenen 1874–75, I, 181–2]. And obviously, where the transition to a settled state is effected, the survival of habits and sentiments established during the nomadic state must long prevent possession of land by individuals.

Moreover, apart from opposing ideas and customs, there are physical difficulties in the way. Even did any member of a pastoral horde which had become partially settled establish a claim to exclusive possession of one part of the occupied area, little advantage could be gained before there existed the means of keeping out the animals belonging to others. Common use of the greater part of the surface must long continue from mere inability to set up effectual divisions. Only small portions can at first be fenced off.

Yet a further reason why landowning by individuals and landowning by families establish themselves very slowly is that at first each particular plot has but a temporary value. The soil is soon exhausted, and, in the absence of advanced arts of culture, become useless. Such tribes as those of the Indian hills show us that primitive cultivators uniformly follow the practice of clearing a tract of ground, raising from it two or three crops, and then abandoning it, the implication being that whatever private claim had arisen, lapses, and the surface, again becoming wild, reverts to the community.

Thus throughout long stages of incipient civilization the impediments in the way of private landownership are great and the incentives to it small. Besides the fact that primitive men, respecting the connection between effort expended and benefit gained, and therefore respecting the right of property in things made by labor, recognize no claim thus established by an individual to a portion of land, and besides the fact that in the adhesion to inherited usage and the inability effectually to make bounds there are both moral and physical obstacles to the establishment of any such individual monopoly, there is the fact that throughout early stages of settled life no motive to maintain permanent private possession of land comes into play. Manifestly, therefore, it is not from conscious assertion of any theory, or in pursuance of any deliberate policy, that tribal and communal proprietorship of the areas occupied originate, but simply from the necessities of the case.

Hence the prevalence among unrelated peoples of this public ownership of land, here and there partially qualified by temporary private ownership. Some hunting tribes of North America show us a stage in which even the communal possession is still vague. Concerning the Dakotas Schoolcraft says:

> Each village has a certain district of country they hunt in, but do not object to families of other villages hunting with them. Among the Dacotas, I never knew an instance of blood being shed in any disputes or difficulties on the hunting grounds [1853–56, II, 185].

Similarly of the Comanches he remarks that "no dispute ever arises between tribes with regard to their hunting grounds, the whole being held in common" [1853–56, II, 131]. Of the semi-settled and more advanced Iroquois, Morgan tells us that

> No individual could obtain the absolute title to land, as that was vested by the laws of the Iroquois in all the people; but he could reduce unoccupied lands to cultivation to any extent he pleased; and so long as he continued to use them, his right to their enjoyment was protected and secured [1851, p. 326].

Sundry pastoral peoples of South Africa show us the survival of such arrangements under different conditions.

> The land which they [the Bechuanas] inhabit is the common property of the whole tribe, as a pasture for their herds [Burchell 1822–24, II, 531].

> Being entirely a pastoral people, the Damaras have no notion of permanent habitations. The whole country is considered public property. . . . There is an understanding that he who arrives first at any given locality, is the master of it as long as he chooses to remain there [Andersson 1856, pp. 114–5].

> Kaffir custom "does not recognize private property in the soil beyond that of actual possession" [Shooter, 1857, p. 16].

> No one possesses landed property [among the Xosa]; he sows his corn wherever he can find a convenient spot [Lichtenstein 1812–15, I, 271].

And various of the uncivilized, who are mainly or wholly agricultural, exhibit but slight modifications of this usage. Though by the New Zealanders some extra claim of the chief is recognized, yet "all free persons, male and female, constituting the nation, were proprietors of the soil:" there is a qualified proprietorship of land, obtained by cultivation, which does not destroy the proprietorship of the nation or tribe [Thomson 1859, I, 96]. In Sumatra, cultivation gives temporary ownership but nothing more. We read that the ground "on which a man plants or builds, with the consent of his neighbours, becomes a species of nominal property," but when the trees which he has planted disappear in the course of nature, "the land reverts to the public" [Marsden 1811, pp. 244–5]. From a distant region may be cited an instance where the usages, though different in form, involve the same principle. Among the modern Indians of Mexico

> Only a house-place and a garden are hereditary; the fields belong to the village, and are cultivated every year without anything being paid for rent. A portion of the land is cultivated in common, and the proceeds are devoted to the communal expenses [Sartorius 1858, p. 68].

This joint ownership of land, qualified by individual ownership only so far as circumstances and habits make it easy to mark off individual claims, leads to different modes of using the products of the soil, according as convenience dictates. . . . Among the Todas,

> Whilst the land is in each case the property of the village itself, . . . the
> cattle which graze on it are the private property of individuals, being males.
> . . . The milk of the entire herd is lodged in the pâlthchi, village dairy, from
> which each person, male and female, receives for his or her daily consump-
> tion; the unconsumed balance being divided, as personal and saleable prop-
> erty, amongst the male members of all ages, in proportion to the number of
> cattle which each possesses in the herd [Marshall 1873, p. 206].

And then in some cases joint cultivation leads to a kindred system of
division.

> When harvest is over, [the Congo people] put all the kidney-beans into one
> heap, the Indian wheat into another, and so of other grain: then giving the
> Macolonte [chief] enough for his maintenance, and laying aside what they
> design for sowing, the rest is divided at so much to every cottage, according
> to the number of people each contains. Then all the women together till and
> sow the land for a new harvest [Pinkerton 1808–14, XVI, 168].

In Europe an allied arrangement is exhibited by the southern Slavs.
"The fruits of agricultural labour are consumed in common, or divided
equally among the married couples; but the produce of each man's industrial labour belongs to him individually" [Laveleye 1878, p. 185]. Further,
some of the Swiss allmends show us a partial survival of this system, for
besides lands which have become in large measure private, there are "communal vineyards cultivated in common," and "there are also corn-lands
cultivated in the same manner," and "the fruit of their joint labour forms
the basis of the banquets, at which all the members of the commune take
part" [Laveleye 1878, p. 82].

Thus we see that communal ownership and family ownership at first
arose and long continued because, in respect of land, no other could well
be established. Records of the civilized show that with them in the far
past, as at present with the uncivilized, private possession, beginning
with movables, extends itself to immovables only under certain conditions. We have evidence of this in the fact named by Mayer, that "the
Hebrew language has no expression for 'landed property'" [1862–76, I,
362n.], and again in the fact alleged by Mommsen of the Romans that
"the idea of property was primarily associated not with immovable estate,
but with 'estate in slaves and cattle'" [1862, I, 160]. And if, recalling the
circumstances of pastoral life as carried on alike by Semites and Aryans,
we remember that as before shown, the patriarchal group is a result of
it, we may understand how, in passing into the settled state, there would
be produced such forms of land tenure by the clan and the family as,
with minor variations, characterized primitive European societies. It becomes comprehensible why among the Romans "in the earliest times, the
arable land was cultivated in common, probably by the several clans; each
of these tilled its own land, and hereafter distributed the produce among

the several households belonging to it" [Mommsen 1862, I, 193]. We are shown that there naturally arose such arrangements as those of the ancient Teutonic mark — a territory held "by a primitive settlement of a family or kindred," each free male member of which had "a right to the enjoyment of the woods, the pastures, the meadow, and the arable land of the mark," but whose right was "of the nature of usufruct or possession only," and whose allotted private division became each season common grazing land after the crop had been taken off while his more permanent holding was limited to his homestead and its immediate surroundings [Stubbs 1880, I, 56]. And we may perceive how the community's ownership might readily, as circumstances and sentiments determined, result here in an annual use of apportioned tracts, here in a periodic repartitioning, and here in tenures of more permanent kinds — still subject to the supreme right of the whole public.

Induction and deduction uniting to show as they do that at first land is common property, there presents itself the question — How did possession of it become individualized? There can be little doubt as to the general nature of the answer. Force, in one form or other, is the sole cause adequate to make the members of a society yield up their joint claim to the area they inhabit. Such force may be that of an external aggressor or that of an internal aggressor, but in either case it implies militant activity.

The first evidence of this which meets us is that the primitive system of landownership has lingered longest where circumstances have been such as either to exclude war or to minimize it. Already I have referred to a still-extant Teutonic mark existing in Drenthe, "surrounded on all sides by marsh and bog," forming "a kind of island of sand and heath" [Laveleye 1878, p. 282], and this example, before-named as showing the survival of free judicial institutions where free institutions at large survive, simultaneously shows the communal landownership which continues while men are unsubordinated. After this typical case may be named one not far distant and somewhat akin — that, namely, which occurs "in the sandy district of the Campine and beyond the Meuse, in the Ardennes region," where there is great "want of communication," the implied difficulty of access and the poverty of surface making relatively small the temptation to invade. So that while, says Laveleye, "except in the Ardennes, the lord had succeeded in usurping the eminent domain, without however destroying the inhabitants' rights of user" [1878, p. 301] in the Ardennes itself the primitive communal possession survived.

Other cases show that the mountainous character of a locality, rendering subjugation by external or internal force impracticable, furthers maintenance of this primitive institution, as of other primitive institutions. In Switzerland, and especially in its Alpine parts, the allmends above mentioned, which are of the same essential nature as the Teutonic marks, have continued down to the present day. Sundry kindred regions present kindred facts. Ownership of land by family communities is still to be found "in the hill-districts of Lombardy" [Laveleye 1878, p. 215]. In the poverty-stricken and mountainous portion of Auvergne, as also in the hilly and infertile department of Nièvre, there are still, or recently have been, these original joint ownerships of land. And the general remark concerning the physical circumstances in which they occur is that "it is to the wildest and most remote spots that we must go in search of them" — a truth again illustrated "in the small islands of Hoedic and Honat, situated not far from Belle Isle" on the French coast, and also in our own islands of Orkney and Shetland [Laveleye 1878, p. 212].

Contrariwise, we find that directly by invasion and indirectly by the chronic resistance to invasion which generates those class inequalities distinguishing the militant type, there is produced individualization of landownership, in one or other form. All the world over, conquest gives a possession that is unlimited because there is no power to dispute it. Along with other spoils of war the land becomes a spoil, and, according to the nature of the conquering society, is owned wholly by the despotic conqueror or, partially and in dependent ways, by his followers. Of the first result there are many instances. "The kings of Abyssinia are above all laws . . . the land and persons of their subjects are equally their property" [Bruce 1805, IV, 462]. "In Kongo the king hath the sole property of goods and lands, which he can grant away at pleasure" [Astley 1745–47, III, 258]. . . .

Of the second result, . . . ancient Mexico supplies . . . [an instance].

> Montezuma possessed in most of the villages . . . and especially in those he had conquered, fiefs which he distributed among those called 'the gallant fellows of Mexico.' These were men who had distinguished themselves in war [Ternaux-Compans 1838, pp. 253–4].

Under a more primitive form the like was done in Iceland by the invading Norsemen.

> When a chieftain had taken possession of a district, he allotted to each of the freemen who accompanied him a certain portion of land, erected a temple (hof), and became, as he had been in Norway, the chief, the pontiff, and the judge of the herad [Mallet 1847, p. 289].

But, as was shown when treating of political differentiation, it is not only by external aggressors that the joint possession by all freemen of the area they inhabit is overridden. It is overridden also by those internal aggressors whose power becomes great in proportion as the militancy of the society becomes chronic. With the personal subordination generated by warfare there goes such subordination of ownership that lands previously held absolutely by the community come to be held subject to the claims of the local magnate, until, in course of time, the greater part of the occupied area falls into his exclusive possession, and only a small part continues to be common property.

To complete the statement it must be added that occasionally, though rarely, the passing of land into private hands takes place neither by forcible appropriation, nor by the gradual encroachment of a superior, but by general agreement. Where there exists that form of communal ownership under which joint cultivation is replaced by separate cultivation of parts portioned out — where there results from this a system of periodic redistribution, as of old in certain Greek states, as among the ancient Suevi, and as even down to our own times in some of the Swiss allmends — ownership of land by individuals may and does arise from cessation of the redistribution. Says M. de Laveleye concerning the Swiss allmends: "in the work of M. Kowalewsky, we see how the communal lands became private property by the periodic partitioning becoming more and more rare, and finally falling into desuetude" [1878, p. 83]. When not otherwise destroyed, landowning by the commune tends naturally to end in this way. For besides the inconveniences attendant on relocalization of the members of the commune, positive losses must be entailed by it on many. Out of the whole number, the less skilful and less diligent will have reduced their plots to lower degrees of fertility, and the rest will have a motive for opposing a redistribution which, depriving them of the benefits of past labors, makes over these or parts of them to the relatively unworthy. Evidently this motive is likely, in course of time, to cause refusal to redivide, and permanent private possession will result. . . .

Spread of private ownership, which . . . goes along with decay of the system of status and growth of the system of contract, naturally passes on from movable property to fixed property. For when the multiplication of trading transactions has made it possible for each member of a family community to accumulate a *peculium*, and when the strengthening desire for individual domestic life has impelled the majority of the community to sell the land which they have jointly inherited, the several portions of it, whether sold to separate members of the body or to strangers, are thus reduced by definite agreement to the form of individual properties; private ownership of land thereby acquires a character apparently like that of other private ownership.

In other ways, too, this result is furthered by developing industrialism. If, omitting as not relevant the cases in which the absolute ruler allows no rights of property, landed or other, to his subjects, we pass to the cases in which a conqueror recognizes a partial ownership of land by those to whom he has parceled it out on condition of rendering services and paying dues, we see that the private landownership established by militancy is an incomplete one. It has various incompletenesses. The ownership by the suzerain is qualified by the rights he has made over to his vassals; the rights of the vassals are qualified by the conditions of their tenure; they are further qualified by the claims of serfs and other dependents, who, while bound to specified services, have specified shares of produce. But with the decline of militancy and concomitant disappearance of vassalage, the obligations of the tenure diminish and finally almost'lapse out of recognition, while, simultaneously, abolition of serfdom destroys or obscures the other claims which qualified private landownership.* As both changes are accompaniments of a developing industrialism, it follows that in these ways also the individualization of property in land is furthered by it. . . .

Summary

The rise and development of arrangements which fix and regulate private possession thus admit of tolerably clear delineation.

The desire to appropriate, and to keep that which has been appropriated, lies deep, not in human nature only, but in animal nature, being indeed a condition to survival. The consciousness that conflict and consequent injury may probably result from the endeavor to take that which is held by another, ever tends to establish and strengthen the custom of leaving each in possession of whatever he has obtained by labor, and this custom takes among primitive men the shape of an overtly admitted claim.

This claim to private ownership, fully recognized in respect of movables made by the possessor, and fully or partially recognized in respect of game killed on the territory over which members of the community wander, is not recognized in respect of this territory itself, or tracts of it. Property is individualized as far as circumstances allow individual claims to be marked off with some definiteness, but it is not individualized in respect of land because, under the conditions, no individual claims can be shown, or could be effectually marked off were they shown.

With the passage from a nomadic to a settled state, ownership of land by the community becomes qualified by individual ownership, but only to the extent that those who clear and cultivate portions of the surface have undisturbed enjoyment of its produce. Habitually the public claim survives, and either when, after a few crops, the cleared tract is aban-

---

* In our own case the definite ending of these tenures took place in 1660 when, for feudal obligations (a burden on landowners) was substituted a beer excise (a burden on the community).

doned, or when, after transmission to descendants, it has ceased to be used by them, it reverts to the community. And this system of temporary ownership, congruous with the sentiments and usages inherited from ancestral nomads, is associated also with an undeveloped agriculture, land becoming exhausted after a few years.

Where the patriarchal form of organization has been carried from the pastoral state into the settled state and, sanctified by tradition, is also maintained for purposes of mutual protection, possession of land partly by the clan and partly by the family long continues, at the same time that there is separate possession of things produced by separate labor. And while in some cases the communal landownership or family landowner-ship survives, it in other cases yields in various modes and degrees to qualified forms of private ownership, mostly temporary, and subject to supreme ownership by the public.

But war, both by producing class differentiations within each society and by effecting the subjugation of one society by another, undermines or destroys communal proprietorship of land, and partly or wholly substi-tutes for it either the unqualified proprietorship of an absolute conqueror or proprietorship by a conqueror qualified by the claims of vassals hold-ing it under certain conditions, while their claims are in turn qualified by those of dependents attached to the soil. That is to say, the system of status which militancy develops involves a graduated ownership of land as it does a graduated ownership of persons.

Complete individualization of ownership is an accompaniment of indus-trial progress. From the beginning, things identified as products of a man's own labor are recognized as his and throughout the course of civilization communal possession and joint household living have not excluded the recognition of a *peculium* obtained by individual effort. Ac-cumulation of movables privately possessed, arising in this way, increases as militancy is restrained by growing industrialism because this presup-poses greater facility for disposing of industrial products . . . and be-cause the more pacific relations implied render it safer for men to detach themselves from the groups in which they previously kept together for mutual protection. The individualization of ownership, extended and made more definite by trading transactions under contract, eventually affects the ownership of land. Bought and sold by measure and for money, land is assimilated in this respect to the personal property produced by labor, and thus becomes, in the general apprehension, confounded with it. . . .

CHAPTER 20

REVENUE

Broadly dividing the products of men's labors into the part which remains with them for private purposes and the part taken from them for public purposes, and recognizing the truism that the revenue constituted by this last part must increase with the development of the public organization supported by it, we may be prepared for the fact that in early stages of social evolution nothing answering to revenue exists.

The political head being at first distinguished from other members of the community merely by some personal superiority, his power, often recognized only during war, is, if recognized at other times, so slight as to bring him no material advantage. Habitually in rude tribes he provides for himself as a private man. Sometimes, indeed, instead of gaining by his distinction he loses by it. Among the Dakotas "the civil-chiefs and war-chiefs are distinguished from the rest by their poverty. They generally are poorer clad than any of the rest" [Schoolcraft 1853–56, IV, 69]. A statement concerning the Abipones shows us why this occasionally happens.

> The cacique has nothing, either in his arms or his clothes, to distinguish him from a common man, except the peculiar oldness and shabbiness of them; for if he appears in the streets with new and handsome apparel, . . . the first person he meets will boldly cry, Give me that dress . . . and unless he immediately parts with it, he becomes the scoff and the scorn of all, and hears himself called covetous [Dobrizhoffer 1822, II, 106].

Among the Patagonians the burdens entailed by relieving and protecting inferiors lead to abdication. Many "born Caciques refuse to have any vassals; as they cost them dear, and yield but little profit" [Falkner 1774, p. 123].

Generally, however, and always where war increases his predominance, the leading warrior begins to be distinguished by wealth accruing to him in sundry ways. The superiority which gains him supremacy, implying as it mostly does greater skill and energy, conduces to accumulation; not uncommonly, as we have seen, . . . the primitive chief is also the rich man. And this possession of much private property grows into a conspicuous attribute when, in the settled state, land held by the community begins to be appropriated by its more powerful members. Rulers habitually become large landowners. In ancient Egypt there were royal lands. Of the primitive Greek king we read that "an ample domain is assigned to him [? taken by him] as an appurtenance of his lofty position" [Grote

206

1846–56, II, 84]. And among other peoples in later times we find the monarch owning great estates. The income hence derived continues to the last to represent that revenue which the political head originally had when he began to be marked off from the rest only by some personal merit.

Such larger amount of private means as thus usually distinguishes the head man at the outset, augments as successful war, increasing his pre-dominance, brings him an increasing portion of the spoils of conquered peoples. In early stages it is the custom for each warrior to keep whatever he personally takes in battle, while that which is taken jointly is in some cases equally divided. But of course the chief is apt to get an extra share, either by actual capture or by the willing award of his comrades, or, it may be, by forcible appropriation. And as his power grows, this forcible appropriation is yielded to, sometimes tacitly, sometimes under protest, as we are shown by the central incident in the *Iliad*. Through later stages his portion of plunder, reserved before division of the remainder among followers, continues to be a source of revenue. And where he becomes absolute, the property taken from the vanquished, lessened only by such portions as he gives in reward for services, augments his means of sup-porting his dependents and maintaining his supremacy.

To these sources of income, which may be classed as incidental, is simultaneously added a source which is constant. When predominance of the chief has become so decided that he is feared, he begins to receive propitiatory presents, at first occasionally and afterwards periodically. . . . Describing the king among the Homeric Greeks, Grote writes: "Moreover he receives frequent presents, to avert his enmity, to conciliate his favour, or to buy off his exactions" [1846–56, II, 85]. So, too, of the primitive Germans we are told by Tacitus that "it is the custom of the states to bestow by voluntary and individual contribution on the chiefs, a present of cattle or of grain, which, while accepted as a compliment, supplies their wants" [1823, Ch. XV]. And gifts to the ruler voluntarily made to obtain good will, or prevent ill will, continue to be a source of revenue until quite late stages. Among ourselves "during the reign of Elizabeth, the custom of presenting New Year's gifts to the sovereign was carried to an extravagant height," and even "in the reign of James I the money gifts seem to have been continued for some time" [Thiselton-Dyer 1876, p. 3].

Along with offerings of money and goods there go offerings of labor. Not infrequently in primitive communities it is the custom for all to join in building a new house or clearing a plot of ground for one of their number, such benefits being reciprocated. Of course the growing predominance of a political head results in a more extensive yielding of gratuitous labor for his benefit, in these and other ways. The same motives which prompt gifts to the ruler prompt offers of help to him more than to other persons, and thus the custom of working for him grows into a usage. We read of the village chief among the Guaranís that "his subjects cultivated for him his plantation, and he enjoyed certain privileges on division of the spoils of the chase. Otherwise he possessed no marks of distinction" [Waitz, G. 1860–61, III, 422]. And the like practice was followed by some historic races during early stages. In ancient Rome it was "the privilege of the king to have his fields tilled by taskwork of the burgesses" [Mommsen 1862, I, 108].

Growth of the regular and definite out of the irregular and indefinite, variously exemplified in the foregoing chapters, is here again exemplified very clearly. For, as already said, it is from propitiatory presents and services, at first spontaneous and incidental, that there eventually come taxes specified in their amounts and times of payment.

It needs but to observe how such a custom as that of making wedding presents has acquired a partially coercive character to understand how, when once there begins the practice of seeking the good will of the head man by a gift, this practice is apt to be established. One having gained by it, another follows his example. The more generally the example is followed the greater becomes the disadvantage to those who do not follow it. Until at length all give because none dare stand conspicuous as exceptions. Of course if some repeat the presents upon such occasions as first prompted them, others have to do the like, and at length the periodic obligation becomes so peremptory that the gift is demanded when it is not offered.

In Loango, where presents are expected from all free subjects, "if the king thinks they do not give enough, he sends slaves to their places to take what they have" [Pinkerton 1808–14, XVI, 577]. Among the Tongans, who from time to time give their king or chief "yams, mats, gnatoo, dried fish, live birds, etc.," the quantity is determined "generally by the will of each individual, who will always take care to send as much as he can well afford, lest the superior chief should be offended with him, and deprive him of all that he has" [Mariner 1818, I, 231n.]. At the present time in Kashmir, at the spring festival,

> It is the custom . . . for the Maharajah's servants to bring him a nazar, a present. . . . This has now become so regulated that every one is on these days [festivals] obliged to give from a 10th to a 12th of his monthly pay. . . . The name of each is read from a list, and the amount of his nazar is marked down: those that are absent will have the sum deducted from their pay [Drew 1875, pp. 68–70].

Traces of a like transition are seen in the fact that in ancient times crowns of gold, beginning as gifts made by dependent states to Eastern rulers and by Roman provinces to generals or proconsuls, became sums of money demanded as of right, and again in the fact that in our own early history, we read of "exactions called benevolences."

Similarly with the labor which, at first voluntarily given to the chief, comes, as his power grows, to be compulsory. Here are some illustrations showing stages in the transition.

[A Kaffir chief] summons the people to cultivate his gardens, reap his crops, and make his fences; but in this, as in other respects, he has to consult the popular will, and hence the manual labour required by the chiefs has always been of very limited duration [Shooter 1857, p. 104].

[In the Hawaiian Islands,] when a chief wants a house, he requires the labour of all who hold lands under him. . . . Each division of the people has a part of the house allotted by the chief in proportion to its number [Ellis 1826, p. 292].

[In ancient Mexico] the personal and common service which furnished the water and wood required every day in the houses of the chiefs, was distributed from day to day among the villages and quarters [Zurita 1840, pp. 250–1].

[It was the same in Yucatan:] the whole community did the sowing for the lord, looked after the seed, and harvested what was required for him and his house [Landa 1864, Sec. XX].

So in the adjacent regions of Guatemala and El Salvador "the tribute was paid by means of the cultivation of estates" [Zurita 1840, p. 407]. And in Madagascar "the whole population is liable to be employed on government work, without remuneration, and for any length of time" [Ellis 1838, I, 316].

Occurring among peoples unallied in blood and unlike in their stages of civilization, these facts show the natural growing up of a forced labor system such as that which existed during feudal times throughout Europe, when labor was exacted from dependents by local rulers and became also a form of tribute to the central ruler, as instance the specified number of day's work which, before the Revolution, had to be given by French peasants to the state under the name of *corvée*.

After presents freely given have passed into presents expected and finally demanded, and volunteered help has passed into exacted service, the way is open for a further step. Change from the voluntary to the compulsory, accompanied as it necessarily is by specification of the amounts of commodities and work required, is apt to be followed eventually by substitution of money payments. During stages in which there has not arisen a circulating medium, the ruler, local or general, is paid his revenue in kind. In Fiji a chief's house is supplied with daily food by his dependents, and tribute is paid by the chiefs to the king "in yams, taro, pigs, fowls, native cloth, etc." [Seeman 1862, p. 232]. In Tahiti, where besides supplies derived from "the hereditary districts of the reigning family," there were "requisitions made upon the people," the food was generally brought cooked [Ellis 1829, II, 361]. In early European societies, too, the expected donations to the ruler continued to be made partly in goods, animals, clothes, and valuables of all kinds, long after money was in use. But the convenience both of giver and receiver prompts commutation when the values of the presents looked for have become settled. And from kindred causes there also comes, as we have seen in a previous chapter, commutation of military services and commutation of labor services. No matter what its nature, that which was at first spontaneously offered eventually becomes a definite sum taken, if need be, by force — a tax.

At the same time his growing power enables the political head to enforce demands of many other kinds. European histories furnish ample proofs.

Besides more settled sources of revenue, there had, in the early feudal period, been established such others as are typically illustrated by a statement concerning the Dukes of Normandy in the 12th century. They profited by escheats (lands reverting to the monarch in default of posterity of the first baron), by guardianships and reliefs, by seizure of the property of deceased prelates, usurers, excommunicated persons, suicides, and certain criminals, and by treasure-trove. They were paid for conceded privileges and for confirmations of previous concessions. They received bribes when desired to do justice, and were paid fines by those who wished to be maintained in possession of property or to get liberty to exercise certain rights. In England, under the Norman kings, there were such other sources of revenue as compositions paid by heirs before taking possession, sales of wardships, sales to male heirs of rights to choose their wives, sales of charters to towns and subsequent resales of such charters, sales of permissions to trade, and there was also what was called "money-age" — a shilling paid every three years by each hearth to induce the king not to debase the coinage. Advantage was taken of every favorable opportunity for making and enforcing a demand, as we see in such facts as that it was customary to mulct a discharged official, and that Richard I "compelled his father's servants to re-purchase their offices" [Stubbs 1880, II, 612–3].

Showing us, as such illustrations do, that these arbitrary seizures and exactions are numerous and heavy in proportion as the power of the ruler is little restrained, the implication is that they reach their extreme where the social organization is typically militant. . . .

While in the ways named in the foregoing sections there arise direct taxes, there simultaneously arise, and insensibly diverge, the taxes eventually distinguished as indirect. These begin as demands made on those who have got considerable quantities of commodities exposed in transit or on sale, and of which parts, originally offered as presents, are subsequently seized as dues.

Under other heads I have referred to the familiar fact that travelers among rude peoples make propitiatory gifts, and by frequent recurrence the reception of these generates a claim. Narratives of recent African explorers confirm the statements of Livingstone, who describes the Portuguese traders among the Quanga people as giving largely, because "if they did not secure the friendship of these petty chiefs, many slaves might be stolen with their loads while passing through the forests," and who says of a Balonda chief that "he seemed to regard these presents as his proper dues, and as a cargo of goods had come by Senhor Pascoal, he entered the house for the purpose of receiving his share" [1861, pp. 296, 307]. Various cases show that instead of attempting to take all at the risk of a fight, the head man enters into a compromise under which part is given without a fight, as instance the habitual arrangement with Bedouin tribes, which compound for robbery of travelers by amounts agreed upon, or as instance the mountain Bhils of India, whose chiefs have "seldom much revenue except plunder," who have officers "to obtain information of unprotected villagers and travellers," and who claim "a duty on goods passing their hills," apparently a composition accepted when those who carry the goods are too strong to be robbed without danger [Malcolm 1832, I, 551–2, 185].

Where the protection of individuals depends mainly on family organizations and clan organizations, the subject as well as the stranger, undefended when away from his home, similarly becomes liable to this qualified blackmail. Now to the local ruler, now to the central ruler, according to their respective powers, he yields up part of his goods that possession of the rest may be guaranteed him and his claims on buyers enforced. This state of things was illustrated in ancient Mexico, where:

Of all the goods which were brought into the market, a certain portion was paid in tribute to the king, who was on his part obliged to do justice to the merchants, and to protect their property and their persons [Clavigero 1787, Bk. VII, ch. 37].

We trace the like in the records of early European peoples. Part of the revenue of the primitive Greek king consisted of "the presents paid for licenses to trade" [Gladstone 1858, III, 62] — presents which in all probability were at first portions of the commodities to be sold. At a later period in Greece there obtained a practice that had doubtless descended from this. "To these men [magistrates of markets] a certain toll or tribute was paid by all those who brought anything to sell in the market" [Potter 1837, p. 90]. In western Europe indirect taxation had a kindred origin. The trader, at the mercy of the ruler whose territory he entered, had to surrender part of his merchandise in consideration of being allowed to pass. As feudal lords, swooping down from their castles on merchants passing along neighboring roads or navigable rivers, took by force portions of what they had, when they did not take all, so their suzerains laid hands on what they pleased of cargoes entering their ports or passing their frontiers, their shares gradually becoming defined by precedent.

In England, though there is no clear proof that the two tuns which the king took from wineladen ships (wine being then the chief import) was originally an unqualified seizure, yet, since this quantity was called "the king's prisage" we have good reason for suspecting that it was so, and that though, afterwards, the king's officer gave something in return, this, being at his option, was but nominal. The very name "customs," eventually applied to commuted payments on imports, points back to a preceding time when this yielding up of portions of cargoes had become established by usage. Confirmation of this inference is furnished by the fact that internal traders were thus dealt with. So late as 1309 it was complained "that the officers appointed to take articles for the king's use in fairs and markets, took more than they ought, and made a profit of the surplus" [Lingard 1849, III, 7].

Speaking generally of indirect taxes we may say that arising when the power becomes sufficient to change gifts into exactions, they at first differ from other exactions simply in this, that they are enforced on occasions when the subject is more than usually at the ruler's mercy, either because he is exposing commodities for sale where they can be easily found and a share taken, or because he is transferring them from one part of the territory to another and can be readily stopped and a portion demanded, or because he is bringing commodities into the territory and can have them laid hands on at one of the few places of convenient entrance. The shares appropriated by the ruler, originally in kind, are early commuted into money where the commodities are such as, by reason of quantity or distance, he cannot consume: instance the load-penny payable at the pit's mouth on each wagon-load to the old English kings. And the claim comes to be similarly commuted in other cases as fast as increasing trade brings a more abundant circulating medium and a greater quantity of produced and imported commodities, the demanded portions of which it becomes more difficult to transport and to utilize. . . .

Summary

From the outset the growth of revenue has, like that growth of the political headship which it accompanies, been directly or indirectly a result of war. The property of conquered enemies, at first goods, cattle, prisoners, and at a later stage, land, coming in larger share to the leading warrior, increases his predominance. To secure his good will, which it is now important to do, propitiatory presents and help in labor are given, and these, as his power further grows, become periodic and compulsory. Making him more despotic at the same time that it augments his kingdom, continuance of this process increases his ability to enforce contributions, alike from his original subjects and from tributaries, while the necessity for supplies, now to defend his kingdom, now to invade adjacent kingdoms, is ever made the plea for increasing his demands of established kinds and for making new ones. Under stress of the alleged needs, portions of their goods are taken from subjects whenever they are exposed to view for purposes of exchange. And as the primitive presents of property and labor, once voluntary and variable, but becoming compulsory and periodic, are eventually commuted into direct taxes, so these portions of the trader's goods which were originally given for permission to trade and then seized as of right come eventually to be transformed into percentages of value paid as tolls and duties.

But to the last as at first, and under free governments as under despotic ones, war continues to be the usual reason for imposing new taxes or increasing old ones, at the same time that the coercive organization in past times developed by war, continues to be the means of exacting them.

CHAPTER 21

SUMMARY

. . . We [have seen] . . . that societies are aggregates which grow; that in the various types of them there are great varieties in the growths reached; that types of successively larger sizes result from the aggregation and reaggregation of those of smaller sizes; and that this increase by coalescence, joined with interstitial increase, is the process through which have been formed the vast civilized nations.

Along with increase of size in societies goes increase of structure. Primitive hordes are without established distinctions of parts. With growth of them into tribes habitually come some unlikenesses, both in the powers and occupations of their members. Unions of tribes are followed by more unlikenesses, governmental and industrial — social grades running through the whole mass, and contrasts between the differently occupied parts in different localities. Such differentiations multiply as the compounding progresses. They proceed from the general to the special. First the broad division between ruling and ruled; then within the ruling part divisions into political, religious, military, and within the ruled part divisions into food-producing classes and handicraftsmen; then within each of these divisions minor ones, and so on.

Passing from the structural aspect to the functional aspect, we note that so long as all parts of a society have like natures and activities, there is hardly any mutual dependence, and the aggregate scarcely forms a vital whole. As its parts assume different functions they become dependent on one another, so that injury to one hurts others, until, in highly evolved societies, general perturbation is caused by derangement of any portion. This contrast between undeveloped and developed societies arises from the fact that with increasing specialization of functions comes increasing inability in each part to perform the functions of other parts.

The organization of every society begins with a contrast between the division which carries on relations habitually hostile with environing societies and the division which is devoted to procuring necessaries of life, and during the earlier stages of development these two divisions constitute the whole. Eventually there arises an intermediate division serving to transfer products and influences from part to part. And in all subsequent stages, evolution of the two earlier systems of structures depends on evolution of this additional system.

While the society as a whole has the character of its sustaining system determined by the character of its environment, inorganic and organic, the respective parts of this system differentiate in adaptation to local circumstances, and, after primary industries have been thus localized and specialized, secondary industries dependent on them arise in conformity with the same principle. Further, as fast as societies become compounded and recompounded and the distributing system develops, the parts devoted to each kind of industry, originally scattered, aggregate in the most favorable localities, and the localized industrial structures, unlike the governmental structures, grow regardless of the original lines of division.

Increase of size, resulting from the massing of groups, necessitates means of communication, both for achieving combined offensive and defensive actions, and for exchange of products. Faint tracks, then paths, rude roads, finished roads, successively arise, and as fast as intercourse is thus facilitated, there is a transition from direct barter to trading carried on by a separate class, out of which evolves a complex mercantile agency of wholesale and retail distributors. The movement of commodities effected by this agency, beginning as a slow flux to and reflux from certain places at long intervals, passes into rhythmical, regular, rapid currents, and materials for sustentation distributed hither and thither, from being few and crude become numerous and elaborated. Growing efficiency of transfer with greater variety of transferred products, increases the mutual dependence of parts at the same time that it enables each part to fulfil its function better.

Unlike the sustaining system, evolved by converse with the organic and inorganic environments, the regulating system is evolved by converse, offensive and defensive, with environing societies. In primitive headless groups temporary chieftainship results from temporary war; chronic hostilities generate permanent chieftainship; and gradually from the military control results the civil control. Habitual war, requiring prompt combination in the actions of parts, necessitates subordination. Societies in which there is little subordination disappear, and leave outstanding those in which subordination is great, and so there are produced societies in which the habit fostered by war and surviving in peace brings about permanent submission to a government. The centralized regulating system thus evolved, is in early stages the sole regulating system. But in large societies which have become predominantly industrial there is added a decentralized regulating system for the industrial structures, and this, at first subject in every way to the original system, acquires at length substantial independence. Finally there arises for the distributing structures also an independent controlling agency.

Societies fall firstly into the classes of simple, compound, doubly compound, trebly compound, and from the lowest the transition to the highest is through these stages. Otherwise, though less definitely, societies may be grouped as militant and industrial, of which the one type in its developed form is organized on the principle of compulsory cooperation, while the other in its developed form is organized on the principle of voluntary cooperation. The one is characterized not only by a despotic central power, but also by unlimited political control of personal conduct, while the other is characterized not only by a democratic or representative central power, but also by limitation of political control over personal conduct.

Lastly we noted the corollary that change in the predominant social activities brings metamorphosis. If, where the militant type has not elaborated into so rigid a form as to prevent change, a considerable industrial system arises, there come mitigations of the coercive restraints characterizing the militant type, and weakening of its structure. Conversely, where an industrial system largely developed has established freer social forms, resumption of offensive and defensive activities causes reversion towards the militant type. . . .

The many facts contemplated unite in proving that social evolution forms a part of evolution at large. Like evolving aggregates in general, societies show *integration*, both by simple increase of mass and by coalescence and recoalescence of masses. The change from *homogeneity* to *heterogeneity* is multitudinously exemplified, up from the simple tribe, alike in all its parts, to the civilized nation, full of structural and functional unlikenesses. With progressing integration and heterogeneity goes increasing *coherence*. We see the wandering group dispersing, dividing, held together by no bonds; the tribe with parts made more coherent by subordination to a dominant man; the cluster of tribes united into a political plexus under a chief with subchiefs; and so on up to the civilized nation, consolidated enough to hold together for a thousand years or more. Simultaneously comes increasing *definiteness*. Social organization is at first vague; advance brings settled arrangements which grow slowly more precise; customs pass into laws which, while gaining fixity, also become more specific in their applications to varieties of actions; and all institutions, at first confusedly intermingled, slowly separate, at the same time that each within itself marks off more distinctly its component structures. Thus in all respects is fulfilled the formula of evolution. There is progress towards greater size, coherence, multiformity, and definiteness.

Besides these general truths, a number of special truths have been disclosed by our survey. Comparisons of societies in their ascending grades have made manifest certain cardinal facts respecting their growths, structures, and functions — facts respecting the systems of structures, sustaining, distributing, regulating, of which they are composed; respecting the relations of these structures to the surrounding conditions and the dominant forms of social activities entailed; and respecting the metamorphoses of types caused by changes in activities. The inductions arrived at, thus constituting in rude outline an empirical sociology, show that in social phenomena there is a general order of co-existence and sequence, and that therefore social phenomena form the subject matter of a science. . . .

REFERENCES CITED

Acosta, Joaquín
    1848   *Compendio histórico del descubrimiento y colonización de la Nueva Granada.* Paris.

Adams, Sir Francis O.
    1874–75   *The history of Japan.* 2 Vols. London.

Alcock, Sir Rutherford
    1863   *The capital of the Tycoon.* 2 Vols. London.

Allen, William, and T. R. H. Thomson
    1848   *A narrative of the expedition sent by Her Majesty's government to the River Niger, in 1841.* 2 Vols. London.

Andersson, Charles John
    1856   *Lake Ngami; or, explorations and discoveries during four years' wanderings in the wilds of Southwestern Africa.* New York.

Angas, George F.
    1847   *Savage life and scenes in Australia and New Zealand.* 2 Vols. London.

Arbousset, Thomas, and F. Daumas
    1846   *Narrative of an exploratory tour to the north-east of the colony of the Cape of Good Hope.* Translated from the French. Cape Town.

Astley, Thomas (ed.)
    1745–47   *New general collection of voyages and travels.* 4 Vols. London.

Backhouse, James
    1844   *A narrative of a visit to the Mauritius and South Africa.* London.

Baker, Sir Samuel W.
    1866   *The Albert N'Yanza.* 2 Vols. London.
    1867   The races of the Nile basin. *Transactions of the Ethnological Society of London,* New Series 5:228–38.

Bancroft, Hubert H.
    1875–76   *The native races of the Pacific States of North America.* 5 Vols. London.

Barth, Heinrich
    1857–58   *Travels and discoveries in North and Central Africa.* 5 Vols. London.

Bastian, Adolf
    1859   *Africanische Reisen.* Bremen.
    1860   *Der Mensch in der Geschichte.* 3 Vols. Leipzig.

Bates, Henry Walter
    1873   *The naturalist on the river Amazons.* 3rd ed. London.

Beecham, John
    1841   *Ashanti and the Gold Coast.* London.

Blackstone, Sir William
    1876   *The commentaries on the laws of England.* 4th ed. 4 Vols. London.

Bollaert, William
    1850   Observations of the Indian tribes in Texas. *Journal of the Ethnological Society of London*, Old Series 2:262–83.

Bonwick, James
    1870   *Daily life and origin of the Tasmanians*. London.

Bossuet, Jacques B.
    1865   *Œuvres choisies*. 4 Vols. Paris.

Boué, Ami
    1840   *La Turquie d'Europe*. 4 Vols. Paris.

Bourquelot, Félix
    1865   *Études sur les foires de la Champagne*. Mémoires Présentés par divers Savants a l'Académie des Inscriptions et Belles-Lettres de l'Institut Impérial de France, 2nd Series, Vol. 5.

Bowring, Sir John
    1857   *The kingdom and people of Siam*. 2 Vols. London.

Boyle, Frederick
    1865   *Adventures among the Dyaks of Borneo*. London.

Brentano, Lujo
    1870   *Preliminary essay on gilds: English gilds*. London.

Brooke, Charles
    1866   *Ten years in Saráwak*. 2 Vols. London.

Bruce, James
    1805   *Travels to discover the source of the Nile*. 7 Vols. Edinburgh.

Brugsch, Heinrich K.
    1879   *History of Egypt under the Pharaohs*. Translated from the German. 2 Vols. London.

Burchell, William J.
    1822–24 *Travels in southern Africa*. 2 Vols. London.

Burckhardt, John L.
    1830   *Notes on the Bedouins and Wahábys*. London.

Burton, John Hill
    1873   *History of Scotland*. 2nd ed. 9 Vols. Edinburgh.

Burton, Capt. Richard F.
    1855–56 *Pilgrimage to El Medinah and Mecca*. 3 Vols. London.
    1860   *The Lake regions of Central Africa*. London.
    1861   *The city of the saints, and across the Rocky Mountains to California*. London.
    1864   *A mission to Gelele, King of Dahome*. 2nd ed. 2 Vols. London.

Butler, Maj. John
    1855   *Travels and adventures in Assam*. London.

Caesar, Gaius Julius
    1863   *Commentarii de bello gallico*. Edited by Franciscus Oehler. Leipzig.

Callaway, Canon Henry
    1868–70 *The religious system of the Amazulu*. 3 Parts. Natal.

Cassels, Walter R.
    1874   *Supernatural religion*. 3 Vols. London.

Catlin, George
    1876   *Illustrations of the North American Indians, with letters and notes*. 2 Vols. London.

Chéruel, Pierre Adolphe
1855   *Histoire de l'administration monarchique en France.* 2 Vols. Paris.
Cieza de León, Pedro de
1864   *Travels.* Translated from the Spanish. Hakluyt Society, Vol. 33. London.
Clavigero, Francisco J.
1787   *The History of Mexico.* Translated from the Spanish. 2 Vols. London.
Cook, Canon Frederick C. (ed.)
1871–81   The Holy Bible. 11 Vols. London.
Cranz, David
1820   *History of Greenland.* Translated from the German. 2 Vols. London.
Crichton, Andrew, and Henry Wheaton
1838   *History of Scandinavia.* 2 Vols. Edinburgh.
Cruickshank, Brodie
1853   *Eighteen years on the Gold Coast of Africa.* 2 Vols. London.
Curtius, Ernst
1868–73   *History of Greece.* Translated from the German. 5 Vols. London.
Dalzel, Archibald
1793   *History of Dahomy.* London.
Dareste de la Chavanne, C.
1858   *Histoire des classes agricoles en France.* Paris.
Darwin, Charles
1839   Journal and remarks. Vol. 3 of Capt. Robert Fitzroy, *Narrative of the surveying voyages of His Majesty's ships Adventure and Beagle between the years 1826 and 1836.* London.
Denham, Maj. Dixon, Capt. H. Clapperton, and Dr. Oudney
1828   *Travels in northern and central Africa.* 3rd ed. 2 Vols. London.
Dickson, Walter G.
1869   *Japan; being a sketch of the history, government and officers of the empire.* London.
Dobrizhoffer, Martin
1822   *Account of the Abipones.* Translated from the Latin. 3 Vols. London.
Domenech, Emmanuel
1860   *Seven years' residence in the great deserts of North America.* 2 Vols. London.
Dove, Rev. T.
1842   Moral and social characteristics of the aborigines of Tasmania as gathered from intercourse with the surviving remnant of them now on Flinder's Island. *The Tasmanian Journal of Natural Science* 1:247–54.
Drew, Fredric
1875   *The Jummoo and Kashmere Territories.* London.
Du Cange, Charles Du Fresne
1850   Dissertations sur l'histoire de Saint Louys. Appendix to his *Glossarium mediae et infimae latinitatis, conditum a Carolo Dufresne,* Vol. 7. Paris.

Dunham, S. Astley
1837   *History of the Germanic Empire.* 3 Vols. Lardner's Cabinet Cyclopaedia Series, Nos. 29–31. London.
Durán, Fr. Diego
1867–80 *Historia de las Indias de Nueva España.* 2 Vols. Mexico City.
Duruy, Victor
1870–79 *Histoire des Romains.* 6 Vols. Paris.
du Terrail, Pierre (Seigneur de Bayard)
1848   *History of the feats of the good knight . . . the gentle lord de Bayard.* Translated from the French. London.
Edwards, Bryan
1801–19 *History of the British colonies in the West Indies.* 5 Vols. London.
Eginhardus, Abbot of Seligenstadt
1877   *Life of the Emperor Karl the Great.* Translated from the Latin. London.
Ellis, Rev. William
1826   *Tour through Hawaii.* London.
1829   *Polynesian researches.* 2 Vols. London.
1838   *History of Madagascar.* 2 Vols. London.
Erskine, Capt. John E.
1853   *Journal of a cruise among the islands of the western Pacific.* London.
Ewald, Heinrich
1878–86 *The history of Israel.* Translated from the German. 8 Vols. London.
Falkner, Thomas
1774   *A description of Patagonia.* Hereford.
Felińska, Ewa
1853   *Revelations of Siberia.* By a Banished Lady. Edited by Col. Lach Szyrma. 2nd ed. 2 Vols. London.
Fernández de Piedrahita, Lucas
1688   *Historia del Nuevo Reyno de Granada.* 8 Books. Antwerp.
Fischel, Edward
1863   *The English constitution.* Translated from the German. 2nd ed. London.
Fitzroy, Capt. Robert
1839   *Narrative of the surveying voyages of His Majesty's ships Adventure and Beagle between the years 1826 and 1836.* 3 Vols. London.
Forster, Johann R.
1778   *Observations made during a voyage round the world.* London.
Franklin, Sir John
1823   *Narrative of a journey to the shores of the Polar Sea, in the Years 1819, 20, 21, and 22.* London.
Freeman, Edward A.
1867–79 *History of the Norman conquest of England.* 6 Vols. Oxford.
1876   *The growth of the English constitution.* London.
Froissart, Sir Jean
1839   *Chronicles of England, France, Spain, etc.* Translated from the French. 2 Vols. London.

Fustel de Coulanges, Numa D.
1864   *La cité antique*. Paris.
1872   L'Invasion Germanique au Ve siècle, son caractère et ses effets. *Revue des deux Mondes* 99:241–69.
Galton, Francis
1852   Recent expedition into the interior of south-western Africa. *The Journal of the Royal Geographical Society of London* 22:140–63.
Garcilasso de la Vega
1869–71 *First part of the royal commentaries of the Yncas*. Translated from the Spanish. Hakluyt Society, Vols. 41 and 45. London.
Gardiner, Capt. Allen F.
1836   *Narrative of a journey to the Zoolu Country*. London.
Gladstone, William E.
1858   *Studies on Homer and the Homeric age*. 3 Vols. Oxford.
Gomme, George Laurence
1880   *Primitive folk-moots*. London.
Grant, James A.
1864   *A walk across Africa*. Edinburgh.
Grattan, Thomas C.
1830   *History of the Netherlands*. Lardner's Cabinet Cyclopaedia Series, No. 53. London.
Gregory of Tours
1836–38 *Historiae Ecclesiasticae Francorum*. 2 Vols. Paris.
Grey, Sir George
1841   *Journals of two expeditions of discovery in Australia*. 2 Vols. London.
Griffith, Dr. William
1837   Journal of a visit to the Mishmee hills of Assam. *Journal of the Asiatic Society of Bengal* 6:325–41.
Grimm, Jakob
1880–83 *Teutonic mythology*. Translated from the German. 4th ed. 4 Vols. London.
Grote, George
1846–56 *A history of Greece*. 12 Vols. London.
Guizot, François P. G.
1856   *The history of civilization, from the fall of the Roman Empire to the French Revolution*. Translated from the French. 3 Vols. London.
Gützlaff, Rev. Karl F.
1838   *China opened*. 2 Vols. London.
Hallam, Henry
1854   *The constitutional history of England*. 7th ed. 3 Vols. Boston.
1855   *View of the state of Europe during the Middle Ages*. 11th ed. 3 Vols. London.
1867   *The constitutional history of England*. 5th ed. 3 Vols. London.
Harris, Sir William Cornwallis
1844   *Highlands of Aethiopia*. 2nd ed. 3 Vols. London.
Hawkesworth, John
1773   *Account of voyages in the southern hemisphere*. 3 Vols. London.
Hearne, Samuel
1795   *Journey to the northern ocean*. London.

Hermann, Karl F.
1836   *Manual of the political antiquities of Greece.* Translated from the
        German. Oxford.
Herodotus
1858   *History.* Translated from the Greek by G. Rawlinson. 4 Vols. Lon-
        don.
Herrera, Antonio de
1725–26 *General history of the continent and islands of America.* Trans-
        lated from the Spanish. 6 Vols. London.
Heuglin, Theodor von
1869   *Reise in das Gebiet des weissen Nil.* Leipzig.
Hillhouse, William
1832   Notices of the Indians settled in the interior of British Guiana.
        The Journal of the Royal Geographical Society of London, 2:227–
        49.
Hincmar
1884   De Ordine Palatii. *Bibliothéque de l'École des Hautes Études;
        Sciences Philologiques et Historiques,* Fascicule 58.
Hodgson, Brian H.
1847   *Kocch, Bódo and Dhimál tribes.* Calcutta.
1849   On the origin, location, numbers, creed, customs, character and
        condition of the Kocch, Bódo and Dhimál tribes. *Journal of the
        Asiatic Society of Bengal* 18:702–47.
Homer
1883   *The Iliad of Homer.* Translated from the Greek. Edited by A.
        Lang, W. Leaf, and E. Myers. London.
Humboldt, Alexander von
1852–53 *Travels to the equinoctial regions of America, during the years
        1799–1804.* Translated from the French. 3 Vols. London.
Hunter, William W.
1868   *Annals of rural Bengal.* London.
Hutchinson, Thomas J.
1865   *Buenos Ayres and Argentine gleanings.* London.
Innes, Cosmo N.
1860   *Scotland in the Middle Ages.* Edinburgh.
1872   *Lectures on Scotch legal antiquities.* Edinburgh.
Joinville, Sir Jean de
1868   *Saint Louis.* Translated from the French. London.
Jourdan, Athanase J. L. (ed.)
1822–33 *Recueil général des anciennes lois françaises.* 29 Vols. Paris.
Kane, Paul
1859   *Wanderings of an artist among Indians of North America.* London.
Kelly, William
1851   *Excursion to California.* 2 Vols. London.
Kemble, John M.
1849   *The Saxons in England.* 2 Vols. London.
1876   *The Saxons in England.* Rev. ed. 2 Vols. London.
Kenrick, Rev. John
1850   *Ancient Egypt under the Pharaohs.* 2 Vols. London.
Kitchin, George W.
1873–77 *A history of France.* 3 Vols. Oxford.

Koenigswarter, Louis J.
    1851   *Histoire de l'organisation de la famille en France.* Paris.
Kolb, Peter
    1731   *Present state of the Cape of Good-Hope.* Translated from the
              German. 2 Vols. London.
Kolff, Dirk H.
    1840   *Voyage of the Dutch brig of war "Dourga."* Translated from the
              Dutch. London.
Kotzebue, Otto von
    1830   *A new voyage round the world, in the years 1823, 24, 25 and 26.*
              Translated from the German. 2 Vols. London.
Krapf, Ludwig
    1860   *Travels in eastern Africa.* London.
Krasheninnikov, Stepan P.
    1764   *The history of Kamtschatka, and the Kurilski Islands, with the
              countries adjacent.* Translated from the Russian. London.
Kuenen, Abraham
    1874–75   *The religion of Israel.* Translated from the Dutch. 3 Vols. London.
Kutorga, Mikhail S.
    1839   *Essai sur l'organisation de la tribu dans l'antiquité.* Translated
              from the Russian. Paris.
Laird, Macgregor, and R. A. K. Oldfield
    1837   *Narrative of an expedition into the interior of Africa, by the River
              Niger.* 2 Vols. London.
La Loubère, Simon de
    1691   *Du royaume de Siam en 1687–8.* 2 Vols. Amsterdam.
Landa, Diego de
    1864   *Relation des choses de Yucatan.* Translated from the Spanish.
              Paris.
Lander, Richard
    1830   *Records of Capt. Clapperton's last expedition.* 2 Vols. London.
Lappenberg, Johann M.
    1845   *History of England under the Anglo-Saxon kings.* Translated
              from the German. 2 Vols. London.
Laveleye, Émile de
    1878   *Primitive property.* Translated from the French. London.
Layard, Sir Austin H.
    1849   *Nineveh and its remains.* 2 Vols. New York.
Leslie, Prof. Thomas E.
    1875   Maine's early history of institutions. *The Fortnightly Review,*
              New Series 17:305–20.
Levasseur, Émile
    1859   *Histoire des classes ouvrières.* 2 Vols. Paris.
Lewis, Meriwether, and Capt. William Clarke
    1814   *Travels to the source of the Missouri.* London.
Lichtenstein, Heinrich
    1812–15   *Travels in southern Africa.* Translated from the German. 2 Vols.
              London.
Lingard, Rev. Dr. John
    1849   *History of England.* 5th ed. 10 Vols. London.

Livingstone, David
1861   *A popular account of missionary travels and researches in South Africa.* London.
Lloyd, George T.
1862   *Thirty-three years in Tasmania and Victoria.* London.
Low, Hugh
1848   *Sarawak, its inhabitants and productions.* London.
Lubbock, Sir John
1882   *The origin of civilization and the primitive condition of man.* 4th ed. London.
Macaulay, Lord Thomas B.
1849–61 *History of England.* 5 Vols. London.
Machiavelli, Niccolò
1775   *The works of Nicholas Machiavel.* Translated from the Italian by Ellis Farneworth. 2nd ed. 4 Vols. London.
Macpherson, Samuel C.
1842   *Report upon the Khonds of Ganjani and Cuttack.* Calcutta.
McCulloch, John Ramsay
1857   *Selections from the Records of the Government of India.* Published by the Foreign Department. No. 27. Calcutta.
Maine, Sir Henry
1861   *Ancient law.* London.
1875   *Early history of institutions.* New York.
1876   *Village-communities in the east and west.* New York.
1881   The king in his relation to early civil justice. *The Fortnightly Review,* New Series 30:603–17.
Malcolm, Sir John
1832   *Memoir of central India.* 3rd ed. 2 Vols. London.
Mallet, Paul H.
1847   *Northern antiquities.* Translated from the French. New ed. London.
Mann, Dr. Robert J.
1866   The Kaffir race of Natal. *Transactions of the Ethnological Society of London,* New Series 5:277–97.
Marcy, Col. Randolph B.
1866   *Thirty years of army life on the border.* New York.
Mariner, William
1818   *Account of the natives of the Tonga Islands.* 2nd ed. 2 Vols. London.
Markham, Clements R. (ed.)
1873   *Narrative of the rites and laws of the Yncas.* Translated from the Spanish. *Hakluyt Society,* Vol. 47. London.
Marsden, William
1811   *History of Sumatra.* 3rd ed. London.
Marshall, Lieut.-Col. William E.
1873   *A phrenologist among the Todas.* London.
Martin, Martin
1716   *Description of the western islands of Scotland.* London.
von Martius, Dr. K. F. P.
1832   On the state of civil and natural rights among the aboriginal in-

habitants of Brazil. *The Journal of the Royal Geographical Society of London* 2:191–227.

Mason, Rev. Francis
1868   On dwellings, works of art, laws, etc., of the Karens. *Journal of the Asiatic Society of Bengal* 37:125–69.

Maspero, Sir Gaston C. C.
1878   *Histoire ancienne des peuples de l'Orient.* Paris.

Maury, Alfred
1873   L'administration française avant la Révolution de 1789. *Revue des deux Mondes* 107:580–608.

May, Sir Thomas E.
1877   *Democracy in Europe.* 2 Vols. London.

Mayer, Samuel
1862–76 *Die Rechter der Israeliten, Athener und Römer.* 3 Vols. Leipzig.

Méray, Antony
1873   *La vie au temps des trouvères.* Paris.

Metz, Rev. J. Franz
1864   *Tribes inhabiting the Neilgherry Hills.* Mangalore.

Michie, Alexander
1864   *Siberian overland route.* London.

Mommsen, Theodor
1862   *History of Rome.* Translated from the German. 4 Vols. London.

Morgan, Lewis H.
1851   *League of the Ho-dé-no-sau-nee, or Iroquois.* Rochester.

Morier, Sir Robert B. D.
1875   Local government considered in its historical development in Germany and England. In *Local government and taxation*, Cobden Club Essays, ed. by J. W. Probyn, pp. 357–454. London.

Motley, John L.
1855   *Rise of the Dutch Republic.* 3 Vols. New York.

Mouat, Fredrick J.
1863   *Adventures and researches among the Andaman Islanders.* London.

Movers, Franz K.
1841–56 *Die Phoenizier.* 2 Vols. Bonn.

Murray, John
1864   *Rambles in the deserts of Syria and among the Turkomans and Bedaweens.* London.

Oldfield, Augustus
1864   The aborigines of Australia. *Transactions of the Ethnological Society of London*, New Series 3:215–98.

Palacio, Diego García de
1860   *Carta dirijida al rey de España.* Combined Spanish and English edition, ed. by E. G. Squier. New York.

Palgrave, Sir Francis
1832   *The rise and progress of the English commonwealth: Anglo-Saxon Period.* 2 Vols. London.

Palgrave, William G.
1875   Arabia. *Encyclopaedia Britannica.* 9th ed. Vol. 2, pp. 235–65.

Pallas, Peter S.
1788–93 *Voyages en différentes provinces de l'Empire de Russie et dans l'Asie septentrionale.* Translated from the German. 5 Vols. Paris.

Parkyns, Mansfield
1853 *Life in Abyssinia.* 2 Vols. London.

Pearson, Charles H.
1867 *History of England during the Early and Middle Ages.* 2 Vols. London.

Pinkerton, John
1808–14 *General collection of voyages and travels.* 17 Vols. London.

Polo de Ondegardo, Juan
1873 Report. In *Narrative of the rites and laws of the Yncas,* pp. 149–71. Translated from the Spanish and edited by C. R. Markham. Hakluyt Society, Vol. 47. London.

Postans, Capt. Thomas
1848 On the Biluchi tribes inhabiting Sindh in the lower valley of the Indus and the Cutchi. *Journal of the Ethnological Society of London,* Old Series 1:103–27.

Potter, Bishop John
1837 *Archaeologia Graeca; or, the antiquities of Greece.* Ed. by J. Boyd. London.

Prescott, William H.
1847 *History of the conquest of Peru.* 2 Vols. London.

Raffles, Sir Thomas S.
1817 *History of Java.* 2 Vols. London.

Ranke, Leopold von
1852 *The civil wars and monarchy in France.* Translated from the German. 2 Vols. London.

Rawlinson, George
1862–67 *Five great monarchies.* 4 Vols. London.

Reeves, John
1869 *History of the English law.* New ed. 5 Vols. London.

Rennie, Dr. David F.
1866 *Bhotan and the story of the Dooar War.* London.

Rink, Dr. H.
1877 *Danish Greenland, its people and its products.* London.

Ross, Alexander
1849 *Adventures of the first settlers on the Oregon.* 2 Vols. London.

Rowlatt, Lieut. E. A.
1845 Report of an expedition into the Mishmee hills to the northeast of Sudyah. *Journal of the Asiatic Society of Bengal* 14:477–94.

Sahagún, Bernardino de
1829–30 *Historia general de las cosas de Nueva España.* 3 Vols. Mexico City.

St. John, Sir Spenser
1862 *Life in the forests of the Far East.* 2 Vols. London.
1863 *Life in the forests of the Far East.* 2nd rev. ed. 2 Vols. London.

Saint-Simon, Louis, Duc de
1857 *Memoirs.* Abridged from the Original French edition. 4 Vols. London.

Sangermano, Fr. Vicentius
1833   *Description of the Burmese Empire.* Rome.
Santa Cruz, Juan de
1873   An account of the antiquities in Peru. In *Narrative of the rites and laws of the Yncas*, pp. 65–120. Translated from the Spanish and edited by C. R. Markham. Hakluyt Society, Vol. 47. London.
Sartorius, Christian
1858   *Mexico.* Ed. by Dr. Gaspey. New York.
Sayce, Archibald, *et al.*
1873–81   *Records of the past, being English translations of the Assyrian and Egyptian monuments.* Edited by Samuel Birch. 12 Vols. London.
Schoolcraft, Henry R.
1853–56   *Information respecting the Indian tribes of the United States.* 5 Vols. London.
Schweinfurth, George A.
1873   *The heart of Africa.* 2 Vols. London.
Seeman, Berthold C.
1862   *Viti: an account of a mission to the Vitian or Fijian Islands.* Cambridge.
Sharpe, Samuel
1876   *The history of Egypt.* 6th ed. 2 Vols. London.
Shooter, Rev. Joseph
1857   *The Kaffirs of Natal and the Zulu country.* London.
Shortt, Dr. John
1868   An account of the hill tribes of the Neilgherries. *Transactions of the Ethnological Society of London,* New Series 7:230–90.
Simón, Pedro
1830   "Noticias historiales de las conquistas de Tierra Firme en el Reyno de Granada." In Lord Kingsborough's *Antiquities of Mexico*, Vol. 8, pp. 219–271. London.
Sismondi, Jean C. Simonde de
1826   *Histoire des républiques Italiennes.* New ed. 16 Vols. Paris.
1832   *History of the Italian republics.* Lardner's Cabinet Cyclopaedia Series, No. 14. London.
Skene, William F.
1876–80   *Celtic Scotland.* 3 Vols. Edinburgh.
Smiles, Samuel
1861–62   *Lives of the engineers.* 3 Vols. London.
Smith, Edmond Reuel
1855   *The Araucanians.* New York.
Smyth, Robert Brough
1878   *Aborigines of Victoria.* 2 Vols. Melbourne.
Sohm, Rudolph
1871   *Die altdeutsche Reichs- und Gerichtsverfassung.* Vol. 1. Weimar.
Southey, Robert
1810–19   *History of Brazil.* 3 Vols. London.
Spix, Johann B. von, and K. F. P. von Martius
1824   *Travels in Brazil.* Translated from the German. 2 Vols. London.

Squier, Ephraim G.
    1852   *Nicaragua.* 2 Vols. New York.
    1870   *Observations on the geology and archaeology of Peru.* London.
Stewart, Lieut. R.
    1855   Notes on northern Cachar. *Journal of the Asiatic Society of Bengal* 24:582–702.
Stubbs, Bishop William
    1870   *Select charters.* London.
    1880   *The constitutional history of England.* 3 Vols. Oxford.
Sturt, Capt. Charles
    1833   *Two expeditions into the interior of southern Australia.* 2 Vols. London.
Tacitus, Cornelius
    1823   *A treatise on the situation, manners, and inhabitants of Germany.* Translated from the Latin by R. G. Latham. London.
Taylor, Dr. William Cooke
    1849   *Student's manual of ancient history.* London.
Tennent, Sir James E.
    1859   *Ceylon: an account of the island.* 2 Vols. London.
Ternaux-Compans, Henri (ed.)
    1838   "Recueil de pièces relatives à la conquète du Mexique." *Voyages, Relations et Mémoires Originaux pour Servir à l'Histoire de la Découverte de l'Amerique,* Vol. 10. Paris.
Thierry, Augustin
    1859   *Formation and progress of the Tiers État.* Translated from the French. 2 Vols. London.
Thiselton-Dyer, Thomas K.
    1876   *British popular customs.* London.
Thompson, George
    1827   *Travels and adventures in southern Africa.* 2nd ed. 2 Vols. London.
Thompson, George Alexander (transl.)
    1812   *Alçedo's geographical and historical dictionary of America.* Translated from the Spanish. 5 Vols. London.
Thomson, Arthur S.
    1859   *The story of New Zealand: past and present — savage and civilized* 2 Vols. London.
Thorpe, Benjamin (ed.)
    1865   *Diplomarium Anglicum Oevi Saxonici, a collection of English charters, etc.* Translated from the Anglo-Saxon. London.
Tiele, Cornelius Petrus
    1877   *Outlines of the history of religion to the spread of the universal religions.* Translated from the Dutch. London.
Titsingh, Isaac (transl.)
    1834   *Annales des empereurs de Japan.* Translated from the Japanese and Chinese. Paris.
Tozer, Rev. Henry F.
    1873   *Lectures on the geography of Greece.* London.
Turner, Rev. George
    1861   *Nineteen years in Polynesia.* London.

Valikhanov, Chokan C.
1865   *The Russians in Central Asia; by Russian travelers.* Translated from the Russian. London.
Vieusseux, André
1840   *History of Switzerland.* London.
Waitz, Georg
1860–61 *Deutsche Verfassungsgeschichte.* Vols. 3 and 4. Kiel.
1865–70 *Deutsche Verfassungsgeschichte.* 2nd ed. Vols. 1 and 2. Kiel.
Waitz, Dr. Theodor
1859–72 *Anthropologie der Naturvölker.* 6 Vols. Leipzig.
Wallace, Alfred Russel
1869   *The Malay Archipelago.* 2 Vols. London.
Warnkoenig, Leopold A., and L. Stein
1846–48 *Französische Staats- und Rechtsgeschichte.* 3 Vols. Basel.
Wilkes, Comm. Charles
1845   *Narrative of the United States exploring expedition during the years 1838, 1839, 1840, 1841, 1842.* 5 Vols. Philadelphia.
Wilkinson, Sir John G.
1878   *Manners and customs of the ancient Egyptians.* New ed. 3 Vols. London.
Williams, Thomas, and J. Calvert
1858   *Fiji and the Fijians.* 2 Vols. London.
Winterbottom, Thomas M.
1803   *Account of the native Africans in the neighbourhood of Sierra Leone.* 2 Vols. London.
Wood, Lieut. John
1841   *Journey to the source of the river Oxus.* London.
Ximénez, Francisco
1857   *Las historias del origen de los Indios de Guatemala.* Vienna.
Young, Ernest
1876   Anglo-Saxon family law. In *Essays in Anglo-Saxon law,* pp. 121–182. Boston.
Zurita, Alonzo de
1840   Rapports sur les différentes classes de chefs de la Nouvelle-Espagne. Translated from the Spanish. In H. Ternaux-Compans, *Voyages, Relations et Mémoires Originaux pour Servir à l'Histoire de la Découverte de l'Amerique,* Vol. 11. Paris.

INDEX

Abipones, 79, 110, 113, 206
Abraham, 87, 185
Abyssinia, 91, 122, 191, 202
Accadians, 125
Achilles, 73
Acropolis, 127
Actinozoa, 41
Adat, 105
Administration: impediments to, 121; by deputy, 121–22, 123–24
Africa, 10, 16, 20, 29, 66, 75, 84, 146
Agora, 98, 168
Agriculture: and size of society, 10; and social differentiation, 29; and disputes over land, 73
Agyd, 112, 158
Ahts, 196
Alba, 130
Albanians, 94, 148
Aleuts, 118
Alexander the Great, 98
Alfred the Great, 156
Alliances: between villages, 76–77; against common enemy, 117
Allmends, 200, 202, 203
Al-thing, 99
Amazulus. *See* Zulus
Amenemhat, 181
Amenhotep IV, 107
Ammonites, 34
Amoebae, 5, 10
Amphictyonic council, 67
Ancestors, as a source of social rules, 103–5
Andamanese, 9, 10, 82
Angamis, 109
Animal organisms, increased density in, 12
Animals, as concrete wholes, 7
Annulosa, 9, 36, 37
Antrustions, 163
Apprentices, 21
Arabs, 119, 147, 166. *See also* Bedouins
Arafuras, 33, 59, 105
Araucanians, 36, 104, 118, 162, 191
Arawaks, 195
Archons, 170, 171

Areopagus, 170
Army: standing, 5, 163; command of, 137; coextensive with society, 153; composed of freemen, 154; ratio to the rest of society, 156, 157; differentiated units of, 161
Artisans, 139, 140
Aryans, 99, 127, 147, 148, 182, 184, 200
Ashanti, 11, 35, 36, 54, 55, 91, 105, 154, 163
Assemblies: public, 98–99; of burgesses, 131; judicial, 167–68
Assizes, 167, 174
Assyria, 35, 52, 56, 113, 161, 183
Astrologers, 18
Athens, 34, 40, 60, 76, 77, 138, 146, 163, 170, 176, 188
Attica, 139, 150, 162, 171, 176. *See also* Greece
Attitudes, as affected by office, 69–70
Australia, 23
Australian aborigines, 9, 14, 16, 82, 97–98, 102, 110, 112
Aztecs, 17, 20, 26, 41, 45, 52, 54, 55, 56, 80, 105, 113, 115, 124, 143, 146, 149, 158, 162, 176, 185, 202, 209

Babylonia, 56
Bacchiadae, 129
Bachapin, 39
Baganda, 162
Bakwains, 150
Balonda, 79, 211
Bands: forerunners of largest societies, 9; in barren environments, 10; weakening of chieftainship among, 14; ease of fissioning among, 24; nomadic, 109–10; land held jointly by, 197
Banishment, as punishment, 102
Barter, 16, 26, 30, 215
Basutos, 190
Batak. *See* Sumatra
Battle, single combat in, 160
Bechuanas, 38–39, 73, 94, 180, 199
Bedouins, 66, 110, 111, 112, 147, 158, 175, 185, 197, 211
Beetjuans, 38